Trial of the Offic

of the Privateer Savannah

On the Charge of Piracy, in the United States Circuit Court for the Southern District of New York

A. F. Warburton

Alpha Editions

This edition published in 2024

ISBN : 9789362095664

Design and Setting By
Alpha Editions
www.alphaedis.com
Email - info@alphaedis.com

PRELIMINARY PROCEEDINGS

During the month of May, 1861, the schooner Savannah, of Charleston, of about fifty-three tons burden, and mounting one pivot gun, was fitted out as a privateer, in the City of Charleston; and on the second of June, under the authority of "a paper, purporting to be a letter of marque, signed by Jefferson Davis," she sailed from that port for the purpose of making captures among the commercial marine of the United States.

On the following day (Monday, June 3), after having captured the brig Joseph, laden with sugar, she was, in turn, herself taken by the United States brig-of-war Perry, Captain Parrott, and carried to the blockading squadron, off Charleston, to the commander of which (Commodore Stringham) she was surrendered by her captors.

On the fifth of June the officers and crew of the Savannah were transferred from the Perry to the United States steam-frigate Minnesota, while the prize was taken in charge by a prize crew from the Perry and sent to New York.

The Minnesota, with the prisoners on board, proceeded, on her way to New York, to Hampton Roads, where the prisoners were transferred to the steam-cutter Harriet Lane; and thence, on board that vessel, they were conveyed to New York, at which port they arrived in the course of the month of June.

On the arrival of the Harriet Lane at New York, the prisoners were given in charge to the United States Marshal; and, on application of the District Attorney of the United States, a warrant was issued, under which the prisoners were committed for trial.

On the 16th of July following, the Grand Jury of the Federal Court, then sitting in this city, came into court and presented a true bill against the prisoners, a copy of which Indictment is as follows:—

CIRCUIT COURT OF THE UNITED STATES OF AMERICA FOR THE SOUTHERN DISTRICT OF NEW YORK, IN THE SECOND CIRCUIT. [1]

At a stated Term of the Circuit Court of the United States of America for the Southern District of New York, in the Second Circuit, begun and held at the City of New York, within and for the District and Circuit aforesaid, on the first Monday of April, in the year of our Lord 1861, and continued by adjournments to the 26th day of June in the year last aforesaid:

Southern District of New York, ss.:—The Jurors of the United States of America, within and for the District and Circuit aforesaid, on their oath, present:

That Thomas Harrison Baker, late of the City and County of New York, in the District and Circuit aforesaid, mariner; and John Harleston, late of the same place, mariner; Charles Sidney Passalaigue, late of the same place, mariner; Henry Cashman Howard, late of the same place, mariner; Joseph Cruz del Carno, late of the same place, mariner; Henry Oman, late of the same place, mariner; Patrick Daly, late of the same place, mariner; William Charles Clark, late of the same place, mariner; Albert Gallatin Ferris, late of the same place, mariner; Richard Palmer, late of the same place, mariner; John Murphy, late of the same place, mariner; Alexander Carter Coid, late of the same place, mariner; and Martin Galvin, late of the same place, mariner, on the 3d day of June, A.D. 1861, upon the high seas, out of the jurisdiction of any particular State, and within the admiralty and maritime jurisdiction of the said United States of America, and within the jurisdiction of this Court, did, with force and arms, piratically, feloniously, and violently set upon, board, break, and enter a certain vessel, to wit, a brig called the Joseph, the same being then and there owned in whole or in part, by a citizen or citizens of the United States of America, whose name or names are to the Jurors aforesaid unknown, and did then and there in and on board of the said brig, the Joseph, in and upon one Thies N. Meyer, then and there being a mariner, and then and there one of the ship's company of the said brig, the Joseph, and then and there master and commander thereof, and in and upon Horace W. Bridges, Albert Nash, William H. Clanning, John J. Merritt, John Quin, and Joseph H. Golden, each then and there being a mariner and one of the ship's company of the said brig, the Joseph, piratically, feloniously, and violently make an assault, and them did then and there piratically, feloniously, and violently, put in personal fear and danger of their lives, and did then and there, the brig, the said Joseph, of the value of $3,000, and the tackle, apparel, and furniture thereof, of the value of $500, and 250 hogsheads of sugar, of the value of $100 each hogshead, of the goods, chattels, and personal property of certain persons whose names are to the jurors aforesaid unknown, the said 250 hogsheads of sugar being then and there in and on board of the said brig, and being then and there the lading thereof, and the said brig, the tackle, apparel, and furniture thereof, and the said 250 hogsheads of sugar, being then and there in the care, custody, and possession of the said Thies N. Meyer, Horace W. Bridges, Albert Nash, William H. Clanning, John J. Merritt, John Quin, and Joseph H. Golden, from the said Thies N. Meyer, Horace W. Bridges, Albert Nash, William H. Clanning, John J. Merritt, John Quin, and Joseph H. Golden, and from their said possession, care, and custody, and in their presence and against their will, violently, piratically, and feloniously seize, rob, steal, take, and carry away against the form of the statute of the said United States of America in such case made and provided, and against the peace of the said United States and their dignity.

Second Count: And the jurors aforesaid, upon their oath aforesaid, do further present: That Thomas Harrison Baker, late of the City and County of New York, in the District and Circuit aforesaid, mariner; and John Harleston, late of the same place, mariner; Charles Sidney Passalaigue, late of the same place, mariner; Henry Cashman Howard, late of the same place, mariner; Joseph Cruz del Carno, late of the same place, mariner; Henry Oman, late of the same place, mariner; Patrick Daly, late of the same place, mariner; William Charles Clark, late of the same place, mariner; Albert Gallatin Ferris, late of the same place, mariner; Richard Palmer, late of the same place, mariner; John Murphy, late of the same place, mariner; Alexander Carter Coid, late of the same place, mariner; and Martin Galvin, late of the same place, mariner, on the third day of June, in the year of our Lord 1861, upon the high seas, out of the jurisdiction of any particular State, and within the admiralty and maritime jurisdiction of the said United States of America, and within the jurisdiction of this Court, did, with force and arms, piratically, feloniously, and violently set upon, board, break, and enter a certain American vessel, to wit, a brig called the Joseph, the same then and there being owned, in part, by George H. Cables, John Cables, and Stephen Hatch, then citizens of the United State of America, and did then and there, in and on board of the said brig, the Joseph, in and upon one Thies N. Meyer, then and there being a mariner and one of the ship's company of the said brig, the Joseph, and master and commander thereof, and in and upon divers other persons, each then and there being a mariner and one of the ship's company of the said brig, the Joseph, whose names are to the jurors aforesaid unknown, piratically, feloniously, and violently make an assault, and them did then and there piratically, feloniously, and violently put in bodily fear and danger of their lives, and did then and there, the said brig, the said Joseph, of the value of three thousand dollars, and the tackle, apparel, and furniture of the same, of the value of five hundred dollars, of the goods, chattels, and personal property of George H. Cables, John Cables, and Stephen Hatch, citizens of the United States of America, and two hundred and fifty hogsheads of sugar, of the value of one hundred dollars each hogshead, of the goods, chattels, and personal property of one Morales, whose Christian name is to the jurors aforesaid unknown, the said sugar being then and there in and on board of the said brig, the Joseph, and being then and there the lading thereof, and the said brig and the tackle, apparel, and furniture thereof, and the said two hundred and fifty hogsheads of sugar then and there being in the care, custody, and possession of the said Thies N. Meyer, and the said divers other persons, mariners, as aforesaid, and of the ship's company of the said brig, the Joseph, and whose names are to the jurors aforesaid unknown, from the said Thies N. Meyer and the said divers other persons, mariners, aforesaid, and of the ship's company of the said brig, the Joseph, whose names are, as aforesaid, to the jurors aforesaid, unknown, and from their care, custody, and possession, and in their presence and against their will, piratically, feloniously, and violently, rob, seize, steal, take and carry away, against the form of the statute of the said United States of America in such case made and provided, and against the peace of the said United States and their dignity.

Third Count: And the jurors aforesaid, upon their oath aforesaid, do further present: That Thomas Harrison Baker, late of the City and County of New York, in the District and Circuit aforesaid, mariner; and John Harleston, late of the same place, mariner; Charles Sidney Passalaigue, late of the same place, mariner; Henry Cashman Howard, late of the same place, mariner; Joseph Cruz del Carno, late of the same place, mariner; Henry Oman, late of the same place, mariner; Patrick Daly, late of the same place, mariner; William Charles Clark, late of the same place, mariner; Albert Gallatin Ferris, late of the same place, mariner; Richard Palmer, late of the same place, mariner; John Murphy, late of the same place, mariner; Alexander Carter Coid, late of the same place, mariner; and Martin Galvin, late of the same place, mariner, on the 3d day of June, A.D. 1861, upon the high seas, out of the jurisdiction of any particular State, and within the admiralty and maritime jurisdiction of the said United States of America, and within the jurisdiction of this Court, did, with force and arms, piratically, feloniously, and violently set upon, board, break, and enter a certain vessel, to wit: a brig called the Joseph, then and there being owned by certain persons, citizens of the United States of America, to wit: George H. Cables, John Cables, and Stephen Hatch, of Rockland, in the State of Maine, and in and upon certain divers persons whose names are to the jurors aforesaid unknown, the said last-mentioned persons each being then and there a mariner, and of the ship's company of the said brig called the Joseph, and then and there being in and on board of the said brig the Joseph, did then and there, piratically, feloniously, and violently make an assault, and them did then and there piratically, feloniously, and violently put in bodily fear, and the said brig, the Joseph, of the value of $3,000; the apparel, tackle, and furniture thereof, of the value of $500; of the goods, chattels, and personal property of the said George H. Cables, John Cables, and Stephen Hatch, and 250 hogsheads of sugar of the value of $100 each hogshead, of the goods, chattels, and personal property of one Thies N. Meyer, from the said divers persons, mariners, as aforesaid, whose names are to the jurors aforesaid unknown, in their presence, then and there, and against their will, did then and there piratically, feloniously, and violently seize, rob, steal, take, and carry away, against the form of the statute of the said United States of America in such case made and provided, and against the peace of the said United States and their dignity.

Fourth Count: And the jurors aforesaid, upon their oath aforesaid, do further present: That Thomas Harrison Baker, late of the City and County of New

York, in the District and Circuit aforesaid, mariner; and John Harleston, late of the same place, mariner; Charles Sidney Passalaigue, late of the same place, mariner; Henry Cashman Howard, late of the same place, mariner; Joseph Cruz del Carno, late of the same place, mariner; Henry Oman, late of the same place, mariner; Patrick Daly, late of the same place, mariner; William Charles Clark, late of the same place, mariner; Albert Gallatin Ferris, late of the same place, mariner; Richard Palmer, late of the same place, mariner; John Murphy, late of the same place, mariner; Alexander Carter Coid, late of the same place, mariner; and Martin Galvin, late of the same place, mariner, on the third day of June, in the year of our Lord one thousand eight hundred and sixty one, upon the high seas, out of the jurisdiction of any particular State, and within the admiralty and maritime jurisdiction of the said United States of America, and within the jurisdiction of this Court, did, with force and arms, piratically, feloniously, and violently set upon, board, break, and enter a certain vessel then and there being, to wit, a brig called the Joseph, and in and upon one Thies N. Meyer, then and there being in and on board of the said brig, and being a mariner and master and commander of the said brig, and the said Thies N. Meyer then and there being a citizen of the United States of America, did then and there piratically, feloniously, and violently make an assault, and him, the said Thies N. Meyer, did then and there piratically, feloniously, and violently put in great bodily fear, and the said brig, the Joseph, of the value of $3,000, and the tackle, apparel, and furniture thereof, of the value of $500, and 250 hogsheads of sugar, of the value of $100 each hogshead, the same then and there being of the lading of the said brig, of the goods, chattels, and personal property of the said Thies N. Meyer, in his presence and against his will, did violently, feloniously, and piratically rob, steal, seize, take, and carry away, against the form of the statute of the said United States of America in such case made and provided, and against the peace of the said United States and their dignity.

Fifth Count: And the jurors aforesaid, upon their oath aforesaid, do further present: That Thomas Harrison Baker, late of the City and County of Nev York, in the District and Circuit aforesaid, mariner; and John Harleston, late of the same place, mariner; Charles Sidney Passalaigue, late of the same place, mariner; Henry Cashman Howard, late of the same place, mariner; Joseph Cruz del Carno, late of the same place, mariner; Henry Oman, late of the same place, mariner; Patrick Daly, late of the same place, mariner; William Charles Clark, late of the same place, mariner; Albert Gallatin Ferris, late of the same place, mariner; Richard Palmer, late of the same place, mariner; John Murphy, late of the same place, mariner; Alexander Carter Coid, late of the same place, mariner; and Martin Galvin, late of the same place, mariner, each being a citizen of the United States of America, on the 3d day of June, in the year of our Lord 1861, upon the high seas, out of the jurisdiction of any particular State, and within the admiralty and maritime jurisdiction of the

United States of America, and within the jurisdiction of this Court, in and upon one Thies N. Meyer, then and there being, the said Thies N. Meyer then and there being a citizen of the said United States, and he, the said Thies N. Meyer, then and there being in and on board of a certain American vessel of the United States of America, to wit, a brig called the Joseph, and the said brig then and there being on the high seas as aforesaid, did, piratically, feloniously and violently, make an assault, and him, the said Thies N. Meyer, did, piratically, feloniously and violently, then and there put in bodily fear, and the said brig, the Joseph, of the value of $3,000, the tackle, apparel and furniture of the same, of the value of $500, and 250 hogsheads of sugar, of the value of $100 each hogshead, of the goods, chattels and personal property of the said Thies N. Meyer, from the said Thies N. Meyer, and in his presence, and against his will, did, piratically, feloniously and violently, seize, rob, steal, take and carry away, against the form of the statute of the said United States of America in such case made and provided, and against the peace of the said United States and their dignity.

Sixth Count: And the Jurors aforesaid, upon their oath aforesaid, do further present: That Thomas Harrison Baker, late of the City and County of New York, in the District and Circuit aforesaid, mariner; and John Harleston, late of the same place, mariner; Charles Sidney Passalaigue, late of the same place, mariner; Henry Cashman Howard, late of the same place, mariner; Joseph Cruz del Carno, late of the same place, mariner; Henry Oman, late-of the same place, mariner; Patrick Daly, late of the same place, mariner; William Charles Clark, late of the same place, mariner; Albert Gallatin Ferris, late of the same place, mariner; Richard Palmer, late of the same place, mariner; John Murphy, late of the same place, mariner; Alexander Carter Coid, late of the same place, mariner; and Martin Galvin, late of the same place, mariner, on the 3d day of June, in the year of our Lord 1861, upon the high seas, out of the jurisdiction of any particular State, and within the admiralty and maritime jurisdiction of the said United States of America, and within the jurisdiction of this Court, each then and there being a citizen of the said United States of America, did, on pretense of authority from a person, to wit, one Jefferson Davis, with force and arms, piratically, feloniously and violently set upon, board, break and enter, a certain vessel, to wit, a brig called the Joseph, the same being then and there owned, in whole or in part, by a citizen or citizens of the United States of America, whose name or names are to the Jurors aforesaid unknown, and did, on pretense of authority from a person, to wit, one Jefferson Davis, then and there in and on board of the said brig, the Joseph, in and upon one Thies N. Meyer, then and there being a mariner, and then and there one of the ship's company of the said brig, the Joseph, and then and there master and commander thereof, and in and upon Horace W. Bridges, Albert Nash, William H. Clanning, John J. Merritt, John Quin, and Joseph H. Golden, each then and there being a mariner and one of the ship's company of the said brig, the Joseph, piratically, feloniously and violently make an assault, and them did, on pretense of authority from a person, to wit, one Jefferson Davis, then and there piratically, feloniously and violently, put in personal fear and danger of their lives, and did, on pretense of authority from a person, to wit, one Jefferson Davis, then and there, the brig, the said Joseph, of the value of $3,000, and the tackle, apparel and furniture thereof, of the value of $500, and two hundred and fifty hogsheads of sugar, of the value of $100 each hogshead, of the goods, chattels and personal property of certain persons whose names are to the Jurors aforesaid unknown, the said two hundred and fifty hogsheads of sugar being then and there in and on board of the said brig, and being then and there the lading thereof, and the said brig, the tackle, apparel and furniture thereof and the said two hundred and fifty hogsheads of sugar, being then and there in the care, custody and possession of the said Thies N. Meyer, Horace W. Bridges, Albert Nash, William H. Clanning, John J. Merritt, John Quin and Joseph H. Golden, from the said Thies N. Meyer, Horace W. Bridges, Albert Nash, William H. Clanning, John J. Merritt, John Quin and Joseph H. Golden, and from their said possession, care and custody, and in their presence and against their will, violently, piratically and feloniously, seize, rob, steal, take and carry away, against the form of the statute of the said United States of America in such case made and provided, and against the peace of the said United States and their dignity.

Seventh Count: And the Jurors aforesaid upon their oath aforesaid, do further present: That Thomas Harrison Baker, late of the City and County of New York, in the District and Circuit aforesaid, mariner; and John Harleston, late of the same place, mariner; Charles Sidney Passalaigue, late of the same place, mariner; Henry Cashman Howard, late of the same place, mariner; Joseph Cruz del Carno, late of the same place, mariner; Henry Oman, late of the same place, mariner; Patrick Daly, late of the same place, mariner; William Charles Clark, late of the same place, mariner; Albert Gallatin Ferris, late of the same place, mariner; Richard Palmer, late of the same place, mariner; John Murphy, late of the same place, mariner; Alexander Carter Coid, late of the same place, mariner; and Martin Galvin, late of the same place, mariner, on the third day of June, in the year of our Lord one thousand eight hundred and sixty-one, upon the high seas, out of the jurisdiction of any particular State, and within the admiralty and maritime jurisdiction of the said United States of America, and within the jurisdiction of this Court, each then and there being a citizen of the said United States of America, did, on pretense of authority from a person, to wit, one Jefferson Davis, with force and arms, piratically, feloniously and violently set upon, board, break and enter a certain American vessel, to wit, a brig called the Joseph, the same then and there being owned in part by George H. Cables, John Cables and Stephen Hatch, then citizens of the United States of America, and did, on pretense of authority from a person, to wit, one Jefferson Davis, then and there in and on board of the said brig, the Joseph, in and upon one Thies N. Meyer, then and there being a mariner and one of the ship's company of the said brig, the Joseph, and master and commander thereof, and in and upon divers other persons, each then and there being a mariner, and one of the ship's company of the said brig, the Joseph, whose names are to the Jurors aforesaid unknown, piratically, feloniously and violently make an assault, and them did, on pretense of authority from a person, to wit, one Jefferson Davis, then and there, piratically, feloniously and violently, put in bodily fear and danger of their lives, and did, on pretense of authority from a person, to wit, one Jefferson Davis, then and there, the said brig, the said Joseph, of the value of $3,000, and the tackle, apparel and furniture of the same, of the value of $500, of the goods, chattels and personal property of George H. Cables, John Cables and Stephen Hatch, citizens of the United States of America, and two hundred and fifty hogsheads of sugar, of the value of $100 each hogshead, of the goods, chattels and personal property of one Morales, whose Christian name is to the Jurors aforesaid unknown, the said sugar being then and there in and on board the said brig, the Joseph, and being then and there the lading thereof, and the said brig, and the tackle, apparel and furniture thereof, and the said two hundred and fifty hogsheads of sugar, then and there being in the care, custody and possession of the said Thies N. Meyer and the said divers other persons, mariners as aforesaid, and of the ship's company of the said brig, the Joseph, and whose names are to the Jurors aforesaid unknown, from the said Thies N. Meyer and the said divers other persons, mariners as aforesaid, and of the ship's company of the said brig, the Joseph, whose names are as aforesaid to the Jurors aforesaid unknown, and from their care, custody and possession, and in their presence and against their will, piratically, feloniously, and violently, rob, seize, steal, take and carry away, against the form of the statute of the said United States of America in such case made and provided, and against the peace of the said United States and their dignity.

Eighth Count: And the Jurors aforesaid, upon their oath aforesaid, do further present: That Thomas Harrison Baker, late of the City and County of New York, in the District and Circuit aforesaid, mariner; and John Harleston, late of the same place, mariner; Charles Sidney Passalaigue, late of the same place, mariner; Henry Cashman Howard, late of the same place, mariner; Joseph Cruz del Carno, late of the same place, mariner; Henry Oman, late of the same place, mariner; Patrick Daly, late of the same place, mariner; William Charles Clark, late of the same place, mariner; Albert Gallatin Ferris, late of the same place, mariner; Richard Palmer, late of the same place, mariner; John Murphy, late of the same place, mariner; Alexander Carter Coid, late of the same place, mariner; and Martin Galvin, late of the same place, mariner, on the 3d day of June, in the year of our Lord, 1861, upon the high seas, out of the jurisdiction of any particular State and within the admiralty and maritime jurisdiction of the said United States of America and within the jurisdiction of this Court, each then and there being a citizen of the said United States of America, did, on pretense of authority from a person, to wit, one Jefferson Davis, with force and arms, piratically, feloniously, and violently, set upon, board, break, and enter a certain vessel, to wit, a brig, called the Joseph, then and there being owned by certain persons, citizens of the United States of America, to wit, George H. Cables, John Cables, and Stephen Hatch, of Rockland, in the State of Maine, and in and upon certain divers persons whose names are to the Jurors aforesaid unknown, the said last-mentioned persons each being then and there a mariner, and of the ship's company of the said brig called the Joseph, and then and there being in and on board of the said brig, the Joseph, did, on pretense of authority from a person, to wit, one Jefferson Davis, then and there, piratically, feloniously, and violently, make an assault, and them did, on pretense of authority from a person, to wit, one Jefferson Davis, then and there, piratically, feloniously, and violently, put in bodily fear, and the said brig, the Joseph, of the value of $3,000, and the apparel, tackle, and furniture thereof, of the value of $500, of the goods, chattels, and personal property of the said George H. Cables, John Cables, and Stephen Hatch, and 250 hogsheads of sugar, of the value of $100 each hogshead, of the goods, chattels, and personal property of one Thies N. Meyer, from the said divers persons, mariners as aforesaid, whose names are to the Jurors aforesaid unknown, in their presence, then and there, and against their will, did, on pretense of authority from a person, to wit, one Jefferson Davis, then and there, piratically, feloniously, and violently, seize, rob, steal, take and carry away, against the form of the statute of the said United States of America in such case made and provided, and against the peace of the said United States and their dignity.

Ninth Count: And the Jurors aforesaid, upon their oath aforesaid, do further present: That Thomas Harrison Baker, late of the City and County of New York, in the District and Circuit aforesaid, mariner; and John Harleston, late of the same place, mariner; Charles Sidney Passalaigue, late of the same place, mariner; Henry Cashman Howard, late of the same place, mariner; Joseph Cruz del Carno, late of the same place, mariner; Henry Oman, late of the same place, mariner; Patrick Daly, late of the same place, mariner; William Charles Clark, late of the same place, mariner; Albert Gallatin Ferris, late of the same place, mariner; Richard Palmer, late of the same place, mariner; John Murphy, late of the same place, mariner; Alexander Carter Coid, late of the same place, mariner; and Martin Galvin, late of the same place, mariner, on the 3d day of June, in the year of our Lord 1861, upon the high seas, out of the jurisdiction of any particular State, and within the admiralty and maritime jurisdiction of the said United States of America, and within the jurisdiction of this Court, each then and there being a citizen of the said

United States of America, did, on pretense of authority from a person, to wit, one Jefferson Davis, with force and arms, piratically, feloniously, and violently set upon, board, break, and enter a certain vessel then and there being, to wit, a brig called the Joseph, and in and upon one Thies N. Meyer, then and there being in and on board of the said brig, and being a mariner and master and commander of the said brig, and the said Thies N. Meyer then and there being a citizen of the United States of America, did, on pretense of authority from a person, to wit, one Jefferson Davis, then and there, piratically, feloniously, and violently, make an assault, and him, the said Thies N. Meyer, did, on pretense of authority from a person, to wit, one Jefferson Davis, then and there, piratically, feloniously, and violently, put in great bodily fear, and the said brig, the Joseph, of the value of $3,000, and the tackle, apparel, and furniture thereof, of the value of $500, and 250 hogsheads of sugar, of the value of $100 each hogshead, the same then and there being of the lading of the said brig, of the goods, chattels, and personal property of the said Thies N. Meyer, in his presence and against his will, did, on pretense of authority from a person, to wit, one Jefferson Davis, violently, feloniously, and piratically, rob, steal, seize, take, and carry away, against the form of the statute of the said United States of America in such case made and provided, and against the peace of the said United States and their dignity.

Tenth Count: And the Jurors aforesaid, upon their oath aforesaid, do further present: That Thomas Harrison Baker, late of the City and County of New York, in the District and Circuit aforesaid, mariner; and John Harleston, late of the same place, mariner; Charles Sidney Passalaigue, late of the same place, mariner; Henry Cashman Howard, late of the same place, mariner; Joseph Cruz del Carno, late of the same place, mariner; Henry Oman, late of the same place, mariner; Patrick Daly, late of the same place, mariner; William Charles Clark, late of the same place, mariner; Albert Gallatin Ferris, late of the same place, mariner; Richard Palmer, late of the same place, mariner; John Murphy, late of the same place, mariner; Alexander Carter Coid, late of the same place, mariner; and Martin Galvin, late of the same place, mariner, each being a citizen of the United States of America, on the 3d day of June, in the year of our Lord 1861, upon the high seas, out of the jurisdiction of any particular State, and within the admiralty and maritime jurisdiction of the United States of America, and within the jurisdiction of this Court, in and upon one Thies N. Meyer, then and there being, the said Thies N. Meyer, then and there being a citizen of the said United States, and he, the said Thies N. Meyer, then and there being in and on board of a certain American vessel, of the United States of America, to wit, a brig called the Joseph, and the said brig then and there being on the high seas as aforesaid, did, on pretense of authority from a person, to wit, one Jefferson Davis, piratically, feloniously and violently, make an assault, and him, the said Thies N. Meyer, did, on pretense of authority from a person, to wit, one Jefferson Davis, piratically, feloniously and violently, then and there put in bodily fear, and the said brig, the Joseph, of the value of $3,000, the tackle, apparel and furniture of the same, of the value of $500, and 250 hogsheads of sugar, of the value of $100 each hogshead, of the goods, chattels and personal property of the said Thies N. Meyer, from the said Thies N. Meyer, and in his presence, and against his will, did, on pretense of authority from a person, to wit, one Jefferson Davis, piratically, feloniously and violently seize, rob, steal, take and carry away, against the form of the statute of the said United States of America in such case made and provided, and against the peace of the said United States and their dignity.

And the Jurors aforesaid, on their oath aforesaid, do further present: That the Southern District of New York, in the Second Circuit, is the district and circuit in which the said Thomas Harrison Baker, John Harleston, Charles Sidney Passalaigue, Henry Cashman Howard, Joseph Cruz del Carno, Henry Oman, Patrick Daly, William Charles Clark, Albert Gallatin Ferris, Richard Palmer, John Murphy, Alexander Carter Coid, and Martin Galvin, were brought and in which they were found, and is the district and circuit where they were apprehended, and into which they were first brought, for the said offense.

E. DELAFIELD SMITH,

Attorney of the United States for the Southern District of New York.

On Wednesday, the seventeenth of July, the prisoners were brought into Court to plead to the Indictment, when MR. E. DELAFIELD SMITH, United States District Attorney, said:

If the Court please,—In the case of Baker and others, the prisoners now at the bar, indicted for robbery on the high seas, I move that they be arraigned. I may here remark, that I have caused the service of a notice of this motion upon all the counsel known to me as engaged in the case; and if any gentleman has not received a notification, the omission proceeds from the fact that his name has not been given to the District Attorney. I understand that Mr. Larocque is counsel for one or two of the prisoners, and that he is in the building.

Mr. Larocque here entered the Court.

The District Attorney: I would now renew my motion that the prisoners at the bar be arraigned under the indictment presented yesterday.

Mr. Larocque: If your honor please, I represent but one of the prisoners. There are other counsel, I believe, who represent them generally. I appear for Mr. Harleston (the mate), and I will now state what I have to say with respect to the motion made by the District Attorney. Mr. Daniel Lord is associated with me, and I believe he is now engaged in the adjoining Court, but will soon be here. The Court will perceive that the learned District Attorney has very properly taken a considerable period of time for the framing of this indictment. It is some weeks now since the warrant of arrest was issued, and the course which he has taken certainly deserves great commendation; for the indictment in this case, more than any other that has ever been found in this Court, required greater care in its preparation, and it is one which will certainly present more important questions than probably any that has ever been tried in this Court. The indictment was only presented yesterday, and, as far as I am concerned, I was only informed of its presentation late yesterday afternoon. Of course, I had no opportunity to examine it. I believe it is quite a voluminous document, and contains a great many counts; and before the prisoners at the bar would be prepared to plead to the indictment, it will certainly be necessary that their counsel should examine it with care, and determine what course to take with regard to it; and then, probably, there may be some application that it will be necessary to make to the Court before the prisoners will be prepared to plead. I therefore desire a postponement for that purpose, until we can have time to examine this indictment.

The District Attorney: I doubt not it is proper that time should be given to examine this indictment, and to adopt such course with respect to it as gentlemen standing in the sacred relation of counsel may deem it their duty to take. I should be very glad, however, if that time could be, with due regard to the convenience of counsel, so near as that the pleas may be recorded and the trial set down for some day before the Court adjourns. I shall be ready, if your honor please, on behalf of the Government, to try the prisoners on any day. I shall be prepared to try them within two or three days; but, certainly, it is right that counsel should have time to examine the indictment, as suggested. I hope only that such examination may be made speedily, as I understand your honor will adjourn the Court at an early day.

Mr. Larocque: It would be utterly impossible for this case to be tried this term. In conversation with the counsel for the Government, a few days ago, the gentleman himself declared that the case could not be tried this term of the Court, and it would be impossible, your honor, for us to be ready for trial during this term. It will be necessary for us to obtain testimony from abroad, out of the limits of this State, and that cannot be procured in time to try the case this term. Certainly, no interest of public justice can suffer by a delay of the trial of this case; and I think it is eminently proper, and I am sure the Court will agree with me, that a proceeding of this importance should be conducted with deliberation, and that ample time should be given to the prisoners to prepare their defence. I had understood, moreover, that some intimation had been made by your honor's associate on the bench (Judge Nelson) that he would attend upon the trial of this case. I am told that Judge Nelson met with an accident shortly after his return home from his attendance upon his judicial duties, by being run away with by a horse, and that he is so lame that he is unable to move at present; and I am very credibly assured that Judge Nelson has expressed his conviction that it was his duty to attend and to sit on the trial of this case. Very important questions of law will be presented, and your honor is aware that in a criminal case in this Court there is no writ of error. The prisoner has the right to a review of any decision that might be made in this Court, in case a difference of opinion should arise between the Judges who preside. And certainly, in a case of such great importance as this is, where the lives of so many prisoners are at stake, it is of the utmost consequence that there should be a full Court present when the prisoners are tried. So far with respect to the trial of the case. Now, your honor is also aware that, by the statutes of the United States, the prisoners have a right to a certain period of time before any movement can be made with a view to trial. We certainly cannot be ready to plead to this indictment in less than a week.

The District Attorney: The Court will permit a single remark concerning the conversation to which my learned friend has alluded. I never intended to say decidedly that the trial could not take place during the present term. I did, however, at one time, express an opinion that, as the term was nearly ended, and as the summer was upon us, probably I should not succeed in bringing the case on for trial until the autumn. As, however, the indictment has been promptly found, delay till fall is, I trust, unnecessary. Events continually taking place upon the ocean seem to render it important that the trial should take place at an early day. With these suggestions, I leave the matter entirely with the Court, where, of course, it ultimately belongs.

Mr. Sullivan: May it please the Court, I appear for Captain Baker, the first prisoner named in the indictment.

Judge Shipman asked who appeared for the other prisoners. He wished to know if all the prisoners were supplied with counsel; if not, he would assign them counsel.

Mr. Sullivan said he did not desire a week's postponement, as he understood his honor had intimated that the Court would adjourn on Wednesday. As to the time of trial, he was authorized and instructed specially to say for Captain Baker that he would ask for no delay other than what was absolutely necessary for his counsel to prepare. He (Mr. Sullivan) hoped that the Court would continue its session specially to hear the case, or at least to try some portion of the defendants. He made that remark on the presumption that the defendants would ask to be tried separately.

Mr. Mayer said he appeared for one of the seamen, Wm. C. Clark; and he concurred in Mr. Larocque's remarks.

Judge Shipman: It is hardly necessary now to discuss when the case will be set down for trial. The motion now before the Court is for the arraignment of the prisoners, and counsel asks for time to plead. I should like to know the names of the counsel who appear for the prisoners.

Mr. Larocque said he appeared, in conjunction with Mr. Lord, for Mr. Harleston.

Mr. Ridgway appeared for the sailors Carno, Oman, Daly, Palmer, Murphy, Galvin, and Coid; and he, also, concurred in the motion for time to plead.

Mr. Sandford appeared for Albert G. Ferris, and desired that the trial should be brought on as speedily as possible.

The District Attorney: I have a suggestion to make as to the time of pleading. With regard to the indictment, when counsel come to examine it, I think they will find, that although the counts are numerous, yet, after all, the indictment is simple. I would suggest that counsel should examine the record between this and to-morrow morning, and then the prisoners could undoubtedly be arraigned without objection.

Mr. Daniel Lord: I perceive that the prisoners are brought here to plead in chains. If that is to be repeated each time they are brought here, I would wish to have the time named when they are to plead.

Mr. James T. Brady said that he believed the engagement under which he acted, in connection with some other gentlemen, covered the cases of all the accused who had not already been represented before his honor by distinct counsel.

Judge Shipman: There is no necessity, then, for the Court to assign counsel?

Mr. Brady: In response to your honor, allow me to say that I represent Captain Baker more particularly. From the very necessity of this case a number of counsel have been employed, and more, probably, than will take part, as your honor is well aware, in the trial. I have had the pleasure of conferring with Mr. Lord only once since this case arose; and as he is in every respect the senior of the gentlemen who are employed in the case, we should like an opportunity for conference. It is highly important to determine what species of plea should be put into the indictment; and while, as I remarked, all the counsel may not take a prominent part in the argument or the trial, yet their judgments ought to be considered by each other, and some decisive course concluded upon. There certainly can be no great occasion for hurry, as these men are closely confined, and certainly are under the closest kind of restraint, from what I see around me (glancing at the prisoners, handcuffed). I don't suppose there is any apprehension, even if the prison doors were opened, that they would be likely to escape, from the state of feeling which at present exists in this city and this section of the country. We only wish for time that is necessary to determine what kind of an answer to make to this indictment; and after that we will proceed, I venture to say, with the utmost diligence, to have this case prepared for trial, or it may probably turn out that there will be no necessity for any trial. That may occur to a legal mind, or it may not.

Judge Shipman: Well, let the prisoners be remanded until Tuesday morning next.

The Court then adjourned.

On Tuesday, the twenty-third of July, the prisoners were again brought into Court, and were placed within the bar, at the south end of the room.

E. Delafield Smith, Esq., District Attorney, moved that the prisoners be arraigned.

Algernon S. Sullivan, Esq., of counsel for the prisoners, stated that all the prisoners were represented by counsel, and that they were acquainted with the charges contained in the indictment.

The prisoners were ordered to stand up; and the Clerk of the Court called T. Harrison Baker, saying: "You have been indicted for robbery on the high seas; how do you plead—guilty, or not guilty?" To which Mr. Baker replied, "Not guilty."

The District Attorney suggested that the indictment be read to the prisoners, unless each one of them expressly waived the reading. He would prefer to have it read, however.

The prisoners' counsel respectively submitted that it was of no consequence. The accused knew the contents of it.

Judge Shipman remarked that the reading of the indictment would consume some time; but the District Attorney said that questions had been raised on this point, and, to insure regularity, he desired to have the indictment read; whereupon the Court ordered the Clerk to read the instrument.

At the conclusion of the reading, the prisoners severally pleaded, each for himself, "not guilty."

District Attorney Smith: If the Court please, the facts in this case are exceedingly simple. The evidence in reference to them—as well such as is required by the prosecution, as that which we may suppose to be desired by the defendants—is within a narrow range and easily attainable. I have examined the testimony with care. There can be no doubt, upon the evidence in the case, that the prisoners are guilty, and that as a matter of law, as well as a matter of fact, they ought to be convicted. It is impossible to close our eyes to the facts relating to this case, as they bear upon what is daily taking place upon the high seas. The merchant marine of the country is subjected to piratical seizure from day to day. Murder is the natural child of robbery, and we may daily expect to hear of bloodshed on the ocean, in attempting the execution of the purpose conceived by so many of our countrymen, to deal a death-blow to American commerce.

It seems to me, that the ends of public justice require that I should urge upon your Honor the propriety and necessity of an early trial of this issue. If, peradventure, the prisoners are innocent, it can work no injury to them; if guilty, they ought to be convicted, and in my judgment, the law ought to take its course to the end, in order that an example may be set to those who are pursuing the species of marauding, of which I think the testimony will show the prisoners to have been guilty.

I respectfully urge, that the trial be set down for Wednesday, July 31st, a week from to-morrow. I may add that I shall be happy to render to the counsel for the prisoners every facility within my power for the presentation of all the facts. The plea of authority, which we can anticipate, is set forth in the indictment, and a copy of the letter of marque has been furnished to counsel for the defence. I can see no valid reason for postponing the trial; none, certainly, in the present state of the country.

Mr. Larocque said, it seemed to him the idea might have occurred to the District Attorney, that these men had not yet been convicted. The law presumed every man to be innocent until he was proved guilty. The counsel should not presume these men to be guilty until they were tried. There were questions of international law involved in this case which would be entitled to consideration. The counsel for the United States would learn that he had misunderstood the meaning of the statute under which these men were indicted. The prisoners' counsel were not ready. They required documentary evidence and witnesses to be procured from a distance. They could not be ready to go on at this term of the Court. He submitted that a cause of this magnitude should not be disposed of so hurriedly. What had the prisoners to do with others on the ocean? Did the counsel for the Government desire to hurry them to trial unprepared for the purpose of striking terror to those on the ocean? He could not believe it to be so.

Mr. Sullivan said the prisoners would not ask any further delay after procuring their testimony. Some of the evidence could not be obtained this side of Charleston, and it would be impossible to procure it under three or four weeks. The case involved the legal status between the United States and the seceded States. He opposed setting down the case for trial on next Wednesday.

Mr. Davega, of counsel for the prisoners, also opposed the motion, reiterating the statements in relation to the testimony to be procured.

Mr. Mayer called the attention of the District Attorney to the fifth count of the indictment, describing the prisoners as citizens of the United States. His client was a citizen of Hamburg, and he would not be ready to try the case in several weeks.

Mr. Daniel Lord, in behalf of Mr. Harleston, said this case involved the lives of thirteen men. If the District Attorney supposed the law of the case was simple, he took a very different view of it from what that gentleman did.

The District Attorney, in reply, said that in respect to the intimation of a necessity to refer to Charleston, it was a matter of notoriety that the prisoners were in constant communication with that city. Counsel were bound to disclose the nature of testimony required, that the Court might judge of the sufficiency of the reasons for a postponement. Much of it might be to facts which the prosecution would admit; as, in reference to the question of citizenship, there would be no difficulty in conceding the fact that certain of the prisoners were not citizens of the United States. He was not tenacious as to the very day named. Without throwing the case over to the fall term, the trial could be so fixed as to afford counsel ample opportunity to collect their proofs and examine the questions of law involved. All the difficulties suggested to impede the trial were obstructions created by these defendants themselves and their confederates, and it was in the nature of taking advantage of their own wrong to seek a postponement because of the existence of a state of things for which they were responsible. It had been said, thirteen lives are at issue. He would say that many more lives were at stake—lives, in his judgment, of far greater value—the lives of innocent officers and sailors in the merchant marine. The facts are simple. The law appears to be certain. There can be no defence here, the nature of which is not visible. The only justification for the piracy would seem to be the treason. If the prisoners ought justly to be convicted, such conviction should be speedy, in order to deter their confederates from expeditions partaking of the character of both treason and piracy.

Judge Shipman said, that he had no doubt in relation to the disposition to be made of this motion. The Court could not have several sets of rules to apply at will to the same class of cases; and even if the Court had power to adopt a different rule in some criminal cases from that fixed in others of the same grade, it would be very questionable whether such power ought to be exercised. The law had made no distinction in regard to this class of criminal offences. Upon the statute book of the United States are various acts of Congress defining atrocious crimes punishable capitally; and among these, is the crime of piracy, or robbery upon the high seas, for which the defendants are indicted. In all cases where parties are charged with criminal offences, and especially with capital crimes, it is customary to give the defendants a reasonable time for the preparation of their defence; and the Court must always assume and act, so far as the technical proceedings are concerned, upon the presumption of innocence which the law always interposes. The Court cannot take into consideration many of the suggestions made by counsel for the Government or for the defence; and in disposing of this motion, I wish it to be distinctly understood that I do so just as I should in any other case of alleged robbery or piracy upon the high seas, where, if the defendants be convicted, they must suffer, according to the statute, the penalty of death. I cannot look at other considerations. I cannot anticipate other defences. In the administration of the criminal law, although the principles are usually very simple, and although, for aught I know, they may be as simple when applied to this case as to any other, yet in the application of those principles, there is often ground for difference of opinion. Courts that have been long regarded as entitled to very great respect for learning, discrimination, and experience, frequently differ as to the application of principles of law to particular cases. In view of this fact, in capital cases, it has been a rule usually adhered to in the United States Circuit Courts (which are so constituted by the Act of Congress that two Judges are authorized to sit) to have, if applied for, a full Court, so that the defendant might have the benefit, if I may so speak, of the chance of a division of opinion. For such division of opinion constitutes the only ground upon which the case can be removed to a higher Court for revision. In this view of the case, and upon the strenuous application of the defendants for the presence of a full Court, I certainly cannot deny the application consistently with my judgment of what is right and proper; and I say this with a full recognition of the importance of this trial. I might add, it may be desirable for the Government, in the event of a certain determination of this case, that in the preliminary proceedings—the time fixed for trial and the constitution of the Court—there should be nothing to weaken the full and appropriate effect of such determination.

After some observations in regard to two exceptional cases—that of Gordon, on his first trial for engaging in the slave trade, [2] and the case of the parties convicted of murder on board the ship "Gen. Parkhill," both cases having been tried before a District Judge sitting alone, the counsel for the defendant in each case making no request to have a full Court—Judge

Shipman went on to say, that in consequence of Judge Nelson's engagements in another District, in September, and in view of his confinement with the effects of a fall from his carriage, which would prevent his sitting in August, he (Judge Nelson) could not probably hear this case until the October term. He therefore ordered the trial to be set down for the third Monday of October, at eleven o'clock.

The prisoners were remanded to the custody of the Marshal, and their manacles, which had been removed while they were in Court, being replaced, they were taken to the Tombs.

TRIAL OF THE

OFFICERS AND CREW OF THE SCHOONER SAVANNAH, ON THE CHARGE OF PIRACY.

UNITED STATES CIRCUIT COURT,

SOUTHERN DISTRICT OF NEW YORK.

Wednesday, Oct. 23, 1861.

THE UNITED STATES

against

- THOMAS HARRISON BAKER,
- CHARLES SYDNEY PASSALAIGUE,
- JOHN HARLESTON,
- JOSEPH CRUSE DEL CARNO,
- PATRICK DALY,
- JOHN MURPHY,
- MARTIN GALVIN,
- HENRY CASHMAN HOWARD,
- HENRY OMAN,
- WILLIAM CHARLES CLARKE,
- RICHARD PALMER,
- ALEXANDER CARTER COID,
- ALBERT G. FERRIS.

HON. JUDGES NELSON AND SHIPMAN PRESIDING.

Counsel for the United States:

E. DELAFIELD SMITH, WM. M. EVARTS, SAML. BLATCHFORD, ETHAN ALLEN.

Counsel for the Defendants:

BOWDOIN, LAROCQUES & BARLOW, DANIEL LORD, JAMES T. BRADY, ALGERNON S. SULLIVAN, JOSEPH H. DUKES, ISAAC DAVEGA, MAURICE MAYER.

E. Delafield Smith, Esq., United States District Attorney, stated that he desired to use Albert Gallatin Ferris, one of the prisoners indicted, as a witness, and would therefore enter a *nolle prosequi* in regard to him.

The Court: Are the prisoners to be tried jointly?

Mr. Lord: I believe so, sir.

The Clerk called over the names of the prisoners, directing them to challenge the Jurors as called.

Judge Nelson: Those of the prisoners who desire to do so may take seats by the side of their counsel.

The Clerk proceeded to call the panel.

Edward Werner called, and challenged for principal cause by Mr. Smith:

Q. Have you any conscientious scruples that would prevent your finding a verdict of guilty, in a capital case, where the evidence was sufficient to convince you that the prisoner was guilty?

A. No, sir.

By Mr. Larocque, for the prisoners:

Q. Have you read the account in the newspapers of the capture of the Savannah privateers?

A. Yes, sir.

Q. Have you ever formed or expressed any opinion as to the guilt or innocence of these prisoners?

A. No, sir.

Q. Have you ever formed or expressed any opinion as to whether they were guilty of piracy, if the facts were as alleged?

A. No, sir.

Challenge withdrawn. *Juror sworn.*

William H. Marshall called, and challenged for principal cause:

Q. Have you any conscientious scruples that would prevent your finding a verdict of guilty in a capital case, where the evidence was sufficient to convince you that the prisoner was guilty?

A. No, sir.

By Mr. Larocque, for the prisoners:

Q. You read the account of the privateer Savannah?

A. I believe I have.

Q. Have you formed or expressed any opinion as to the guilt or innocence of the prisoners?

A. No, sir.

Q. Have you ever formed or expressed any opinion as to whether they were guilty of piracy, if the facts were as alleged?

A. I have not formed any opinion as to these men.

Q. As to the general question, whether cruising under a commission from the Confederate States is piracy?

A. I do not think I have formed any opinion, or expressed one.

Challenge withdrawn. *Juror sworn.*

William Powell called, and challenged for principal cause by Mr. Smith:

Q. Have you any conscientious scruples that would prevent your finding a verdict of guilty, in a capital case, where the evidence was sufficient to convince you that the prisoner was guilty?

A. No, sir.

By Mr. Larocque, for the prisoners:

Q. Have you formed or expressed any opinion as to the guilt or innocence of these prisoners?

A. I have not formed any opinion that would prevent me from giving a verdict according to the facts of the case. I have read the account, and I presume have formed such an opinion as most men do from reading an account, if the facts be so and so.

Q. Have you formed any opinion as to whether cruising, under a commission from the Confederate States, is piracy?

A. Yes, sir, I have.

Mr. Evarts objected that this was purely a question of law, and one jurors should not be inquired of.

The Court sustained the objection.

Q. Did you believe the accounts which you read of this transaction?

A. Well, it is difficult to say. There is so much published in the papers now-a-days that is not correct, that I am hardly prepared to say I believe anything I see, without palpable evidence. I believe the fact of the capture of the Savannah.

Q. Did you read what had been done by the Savannah before she was captured?

A. Well, I formed no opinion with regard to that.

Q. Did you form an opinion of the character of the act with which the defendants were charged?

A. No, sir.

Q. Do you entertain the settled opinion that acting under a commission from President Davis, or the Confederate Government, constitutes piracy?

Mr. Evarts objected that this was a question of law.

The Court: I doubt whether that is a question that would be proper.

Mr. Larocque: This is a very peculiar case, as your honor is well aware. It is a case of first impression in the courts of the United States. It is a case in which, probably, there will be very little difference between the prosecution and the defendants as to the mere facts which are charged in this indictment, and it is a case in which jurors who present themselves to be sworn, if they have any bias or prejudice whatever, have it rather in reference to the character of the acts than as to the acts themselves having been committed or not having been committed. Now, we all know, if your honor please, that in all criminal trials a great deal of discussion has always taken place with reference to the jurisdiction of the jury over questions of law. The Courts have held that they are bound to receive their instructions on the law from the Court; but, at the same time, if they do not act in pursuance of the instructions which they receive, it is a matter between them and their own consciences, and it is a matter which no form of review in these Courts will reach. Now, one of my associates has handed to me an authority upon this subject from 1st Baldwin's Reports—that on the trial of Handy, in 1832, for treason, Judge Grier held that a juror who had formed an opinion that the riots in question did not amount to treason, was incompetent; and, in the case of the United States *v.* Wilson, it was held that a juror was incompetent who stated, on being challenged, that he had read the newspaper account of the facts at the time, and had come to his own conclusion, and had made up his mind that the offence was treason, although he had not expressed that opinion, nor formed or expressed an opinion that the defendant was or was not engaged in the offence. It seems to me that these authorities cover precisely the case before the Court, the only difference being that this is a charge of piracy, and the other a charge of treason.

Judge Nelson: The only difference is that there the question was put to the juror as to the crime, after it appeared he had read the account of the transaction, which involved both the law and the facts—involved the whole case; but as we understand your question, you put a pure question of law, which we do not think belongs to the juror.

Mr. Larocque: I understand your honor to rule the question is not admissible.

Judge Nelson: Yes.

Defendants' Counsel took exception.

Mr. Larocque: Permit me to put the question in two forms.

Q. Have you formed or expressed the opinion that the acts charged, if proved, constitute the offence of piracy?

The Court: That question is admissible.

A. I have not expressed the opinion, and I can hardly say I have formed an opinion, because I am not sufficiently informed on the law to do so.

Challenge withdrawn. *Juror sworn.*

The Court: Then the other form of the question is withdrawn?

Mr. Larocque: Yes, sir; we are satisfied with the form of the question the Court allows us to put.

James Cassidy called. Challenged for principal cause, by Mr. Larocque, for the defendants.

Q. Did you read the account of the capture of the Savannah privateer?

A. I believe I did.

Q. Have you formed or expressed any opinion upon the guilt or innocence of these prisoners?

A. I believe not, sir. I may have made some mention of it at the time of reading the transaction, but not to express any opinion.

Q. Have you formed or expressed an opinion whether the facts, if proved, constitute the offence of piracy?

A. No, sir.

By Mr. Smith:

Q. Have you any conscientious scruples on the subject of capital punishment that would interfere with your rendering a verdict of guilty, if the evidence proved the prisoners to be guilty?

A. No, sir.

Challenge withdrawn. *Juror sworn.*

Joel W. Poor called. Challenged for principal cause by Mr. Smith:

Q. Have you any opinion on the subject of capital punishment which would prevent your rendering a verdict of guilty, if the evidence was such as to satisfy you?

A. No, sir.

By Mr. Larocque, for the prisoners:

Q. Have you read the account of the capture of the Savannah privateers?

A. I have.

Q. Have you formed or expressed any opinion as to the guilt or innocence of the prisoners?

A. I think not, sir.

Q. Have you formed or expressed any opinion whether the facts charged, if proved, constitute the offence of piracy?

A. I have not.

Q. Have you never conversed on this subject?

A. I do not think I have.

Q. Have you no recollection of having conversed upon it at all?

A. I may have talked about it something at the time, but I do not recollect.

Q. Are you a stockholder, or connected with any marine insurance company?

A. No, sir.

Q. Have you been engaged in Northern trade?

A. No, sir.

Challenged peremptorily, by prisoners.

Thomas Dugan called. Challenged for principal cause, by Mr. Smith:

Q. Have you any conscientious scruples that would interfere with your rendering a verdict of guilty, if you deemed the prisoners guilty upon the evidence?

A. I have strong conscientious scruples.

Mr. Smith asked that the juror stand aside.

Defendants' Counsel objected to the question, as not proper in form. Objection sustained.

Q. In a capital case, where the evidence is sufficient to satisfy your mind of the prisoner's guilt, have you any conscientious scruples that would prevent your finding a verdict of guilty?

A. If I may explain, I would endeavor to find a verdict; but I believe my sympathy would control my judgment to that extent that I would not be able to do my duty between the people and the prisoner. I have been on a jury before, and I doubt that my judgment would be controlled by my sympathy.

Mr. Larocque. The witness has not said his sympathies would be of that strength that would prevent his finding a verdict of guilty, if the evidence was satisfactory. A juror that has doubts of himself is the most honest and reliable, according to all experience in criminal trials.

The Court. Examine him on that point.

By Mr. Larocque.

Q. Suppose that upon this trial the facts charged in this indictment were proved by clear and satisfactory evidence, and the Court should instruct you, upon that evidence, that those facts constitute the offence of piracy, would your conscientious scruples be so strong as to prevent your finding a verdict of guilty in such a case as that?

A. There must be not a shadow of doubt. It must be strong and conclusive in my mind before a verdict is rendered.

Q. But where there was strong, conclusive evidence, you would render a verdict of guilty?

A. Yes, sir.

Mr. Evarts. It is pretty apparent that the juror does not regard himself as in a position to deal impartially with this question, which involves human life. The intention of this cause of challenge is, that the juror should be in a position to yield to the evidence that just assent which its character is entitled to call for, unimpeded by his repugnance to the result when fatal to human life. Still, if your honor should not think that upon this ground he ought to be excluded absolutely, certainly it would be consistent with the course of practice, and with the just feeling of the juror, that he should stand aside until the panel be made up.

Mr. Brady: That practice I understand not to prevail any longer, since it has been provided that the empanneling of jurors in the United States Courts shall be the same as in the State Courts, and we do not consent to any such principle as the gentleman proposes. Your honor has decided that a juror, to disqualify him from serving in a capital case, must say that his conscientious scruples are of such a character that, though the evidence be clear and conclusive under the law, as stated by the Court, they would prevent his doing his duty and giving a verdict of guilty. To my mind, nothing can be more clear and satisfactory than the statement of the juror himself, which exhibits a state of mind that should be possessed by every juror; that is, that he must be satisfied beyond all reasonable doubt of the guilt of the accused before rendering a verdict of guilty; and when be speaks of his sympathy on behalf of human life, it is only that sympathy which the law recognizes where it gives the prisoner the benefit of every doubt. It is true he does use the expression that there must not be the shadow of a doubt; but when the Court comes to expound the law, he will be instructed that it must be a reasonable doubt. I do not see anything against the juror on the ground of conscientious scruples. Your honor knows that the prosecution have no peremptory challenge in cases of piracy or treason, and the old practice of setting aside jurors until the panel is exhausted, and then, if not able to make up twelve without the rejected jurors, requiring their acceptance, has passed. That is decided in the case of Shackleford, in 18 Howard's Reports.

The Court (to the Juror): We do not exactly comprehend the views you entertain upon this question; therefore we desire, for our own satisfaction, to put some questions to you, to ascertain, if we can, the state of your mind and opinions upon these questions, and see whether you are a competent juryman or not in a capital case. It is a very high duty, and a common duty, devolving upon every respectable citizen. The question is this—and we desire that there may be no delusion or misapprehension on your mind in respect to it—in a capital case, if the proof on behalf of the Government should be such as to satisfy your mind that the prisoner was guilty of the capital offence, whether or not you have any conscientious scruples as respects capital punishment, that would prevent your rendering a verdict of guilty?

A. In answer to that I would say that this is what troubles me: I want to do my duty; I want to render a verdict fairly and squarely as between the prisoner and the people; but I have this to contend with—I have read that people have been convicted upon the clearest testimony, and afterwards found to be innocent; and before I would have such feelings I would as soon go to the scaffold as send a person there who was not guilty. Therefore my sympathy is so strong that I am afraid to trust myself. I did serve on a former occasion, and I do not know that even then I did my duty.

Q. What do you mean by being afraid to trust yourself? Is it a conscientious feeling and opinion against the penalty of capital punishment?

A. Yes, sir, it is. I have a great abhorrence of it, if I may so express myself. Yet I should like to render a verdict, and do what is right; but I believe my feelings are too great to trust myself.

The Court: We think we are bound to set the juror aside.

Mr. Larocque: Permit me to put one question.

Q. It strikes me that you are a little at fault as to what the purport of this question is. It is not whether you have an abhorrence of convicting a prisoner of a capital offence. The question is, whether you have such conscientious scruples against capital punishment as would prevent your finding the prisoner guilty, if the facts were proved, and the Court instructed you that those facts constituted the offence?

A. I answered before. It places me in rather a peculiar position. As I said, I want it understood distinctly, I desire to do my duty; but there is a struggle between that and my sympathy, and I am afraid to trust myself.

Q. But you can draw a distinction between your sympathy and any conscientious scruples against the punishment of death, can you not?

A. Well, sir, where it comes to the point——

Q. Allow me to put the question in another way: If you are entirely satisfied, upon the evidence and instructions of the Court, that the prisoner was guilty, your conscience would not trouble you in finding him guilty?

A. Well, sir, there would be this: I would feel that persons, under the strongest kind of testimony, have been found guilty, wrongfully, and it would operate on me—the fear that I had judged wrong on the facts, and committed murder. That feeling is very strong.

Q. If the evidence satisfied you that the prisoner was guilty, would your conscience prevent your saying so?

A. It would not now. It might in the jury-room. When it comes to the point, and I feel that I hold the life of a human being, it is pretty hard to know what I would do then.

Q. Your conscience would only trouble you if you doubted that your judgment was right?

A. Yes, sir.

Mr. Larocque: I submit that the juror is competent.

Juror: You must take your chances if you take me. I still think I am not fit to sit on a jury to represent the people.

The Court: I think we must take the opinion of the juror as against himself.

Set aside. [Defendants took exception.]

John Fife called, and challenged for principal cause:

Q. In a capital case, where the evidence is sufficient to convince you of the guilt of the prisoner, have you any conscientious scruples that would prevent your finding a verdict of guilty?

A. No, sir.

By Mr. Larocque, for the prisoners:

Q. Did you read the account of the capture of the privateer Savannah?

A. I did.

Q. Have you formed or expressed an opinion as to the guilt or innocence of the prisoners?

A. I believe not, sir.

Q. Have you formed or expressed an opinion whether the facts charged, if proved, constitute the offence of piracy?

A. I have not, sir.

Q. You think you have no bias or prejudice in this case?

A. No, sir.

Challenge withdrawn. *Juror sworn.*

Thomas Costello called. Challenged for principal cause.

By Mr. Smith:

Q. In a capital case, where the evidence is sufficient to convince you of the guilt of the prisoner, have you any conscientious scruples that would prevent your finding a verdict of guilty?

A. No, sir.

By Mr. Larocque, for the prisoners:

Q. You know that this case is an indictment for piracy against the prisoners. Have you formed or expressed any opinion upon their guilt or innocence?

A. No, sir.

Q. Have you formed or expressed any opinion whether the facts charged against them, if proved, constitute the offence of piracy?

A. I have not, sir.

Challenge withdrawn. *Juror sworn.*

Tuganhold Kron called. Challenged for principal cause.

By Mr. Smith:

Q. In a capital case, where the evidence was sufficient to convince you of the guilt of the prisoner, have you any conscientious scruples that would prevent your finding a verdict of guilty?

A. Yes, sir. (Question repeated.)

A. No, sir.

Q. Do you readily understand English?

A. Pretty well.

Q. You did not understand me when I asked the question the first time?

A. No, sir.

Q. Do you understand English well?

A. Yes, pretty well. There may be some words I do not understand.

Q. Did you ever sit as a juror on a trial?

A. Yes, sir.

Q. Did you understand all the witnesses said?

A. No, because I did not hear, sometimes.

Q. Do you think you understand English well enough, so that you can hear a trial intelligently?

A. I cannot say, sir.

Q. You are not sure?

A. No, sir.

By Mr. Larocque:

Q. What is your occupation?

A. A bookbinder.

Q. Have you an establishment of your own?

A. Yes, sir.

Q. The men you employ—do they speak English or German?

A. Some English—the most of them German.

Q. And you transact your business with gentlemen who speak English?

A. Yes, sir.

Q. How long have you done so?

A. Eight years.

By the Court:

Q. How long have you been in this country?

A. Seventeen years.

Q. Have you been in business all that time?

A. I worked as journeyman ten years, and have been seven years in business of my own.

By Mr. Smith:

Q. Do you think you can understand English well enough so that you can, from the evidence, form an opinion of your own?

A. I think I will.

By Mr. Larocque:

Q. You read the account of the capture of the privateer Savannah in the newspapers?

A. Yes, sir; in some German paper.

Q. Did you form or express any opinion as to the guilt or innocence of these prisoners?

A. No, sir.

Q. Did you form or express an opinion whether the facts charged against them, if proved, constitute the offence of piracy?

A. No, sir.

Mr. Evarts. We think the juror's knowledge of the language is shown, by his own examination, to be such as should at least entitle the Government to ask that he should stand aside until it is seen if the panel shall be filled from other jurors—if that right exists. Your honor held, in the case of the United States *v.* Douglass—a piracy case tried some ten years ago—that that right did exist.

The Court. I think we have since qualified that in the case of Shackleford. It was intended to settle that debatable question, and it was held that the Act of Congress, requiring the empanneling of jurors to be according to the practice in State Courts, did not necessarily draw after it this right of setting aside. We think the objection taken is not sustained.

Juror sworn.

Matthew P. Bogart called. Challenged for principal cause by Mr. Smith:

Q. In a capital case, where the evidence is sufficient to convince you of the guilt of the prisoner, have you any conscientious scruples that would prevent your rendering a verdict of guilty?

A. No, sir.

By Mr. Larocque, for the prisoners:

Q. Have you read the account of the capture of the privateer Savannah in the newspapers?

A. I recollect reading it at the time—not since.

Q. Have you ever formed or expressed an opinion upon the guilt or innocence of these prisoners?

A. Not to my recollection.

Q. Have you ever formed or expressed an opinion whether the facts charged against them, if proved, constitute the offence of piracy?

A. I have not.

Challenge withdrawn. *Juror sworn.*

George Moeller called. Challenged for principal cause by Mr. Smith:

Q. In a capital case, where the evidence is sufficient to convince you of the guilt of the prisoner, have you any conscientious scruples that would prevent your finding a verdict of guilty?

A. No, sir.

By Mr. Larocque, for the prisoners:

Q. Have you read the account of the capture of the Savannah? *A*. Yes, sir.

Q. Have you formed or expressed any opinion as to the guilt or innocence of these prisoners?

A. No, sir.

Q. Have you formed or expressed any opinion as to whether, if the facts were proved, as alleged, it was piracy?

A. I do not know what the facts are, sir. I have only read an account of the capture.

Challenge withdrawn. *Juror sworn.*

Robert Taylor called. Challenged for principal cause, by Mr. Smith:

Q. In a capital case, where the evidence is sufficient to convince you of the guilt of the prisoner, have you any conscientious scruples that would prevent your finding a verdict of guilty?

A. No, sir.

By Mr. Larocque, for the prisoners:

Q. You read of the capture of the privateer Savannah?

A. I think I have.

Q. Did you form or express any opinion as to the guilt or innocence of the prisoners?

A. Not that I know of, sir.

Q. Have you formed or expressed any opinion whether the facts, if proved, constitute the offence of piracy?

A. No, sir, not any.

Challenge withdrawn. *Juror sworn.*

Daniel Bixby called. Challenged for principal cause, by Mr. Smith:

Q. In a capital case, where the evidence is sufficient to convince you of the guilt of the prisoner, have you any conscientious scruples that would prevent your finding a verdict of guilty?

A. I have not.

By Mr. Larocque:

Q. Have you ever formed or expressed any opinion as to the guilt or innocence of the prisoners?

A. I have not.

Q. Or whether the facts, if proved, constitute the offence of piracy?

A. No, sir.

Challenge withdrawn. *Juror sworn.*

Ira L. Cady called. Challenged for principal cause, by Mr. Smith:

Q. In a capital case, where the evidence is sufficient to convince you of the guilt of the prisoner, have you any conscientious scruples that would prevent your finding a verdict of guilty?

A. No, sir.

By Mr. Larocque:

Q. You know what this case is for?

A. I believe I understand it.

Q. An indictment of piracy against the privateersmen captured on the Savannah?

A. Yes, sir.

Q. Have you formed or expressed any opinion upon the guilt or innocence of the prisoners?

A. I do not recollect that I have.

Q. Have you formed or expressed any opinion whether the facts, if proved, constitute piracy?

A. I do not think I have.

Q. Have you any opinion now upon either of these subjects?

A. I cannot say that I am entirely indifferent of opinion on the subject, but still I have not formed any definite opinion.

Q. Your mind, however, is not entirely unbiased upon the question?

A. Well, no, sir—not if I understand the question; that is, the question whether the facts, if proved, constitute the offence of piracy?

Mr. Larocque submitted that the juror was not indifferent.

Mr. Evarts: All that has been said by the juror is that, on the question of whether the facts charged constitute the offence of piracy, he has no fixed opinion; but he cannot say he has no opinion on the subject. He is ready to receive instruction from the Court.

Mr. Larocque contended that, as the question of whether the facts alleged constituted piracy, or not, was a most important one to be discussed, they were entitled to have the mind of the juror entirely blank and unbiased on that subject.

The Court: Let us see what the state of mind of the juror is.

Q. You mentioned, in response to a question put to you, that you had read an account in the newspapers of the capture of this vessel.

A. I was not asked that question. I have no mind made up in respect to the subject that would prevent my finding a verdict in accordance with the evidence; but I said I was not entirely devoid of an opinion in regard to the case—that is, the offence.

Q. Have you read an account of the capture of this vessel?

A. Yes, sir; I read it at the time.

Q. Is it from the account, thus read, of the transaction of the capture, that you found this opinion upon?

A. No, sir; it is not that. It is upon the general subject that I mean to be understood—not in reference to this case particularly.

Q. Do you say, upon the general question, that you have an opinion?

A. Well, not fully made up. I have the shadow of an opinion about it.

Q. Not a fixed opinion?

A. No, sir; I would be governed by the law and instructions of the Court.

Q. You are open to the control of your opinion upon the facts and law as developed in the course of the trial?

A. Certainly, sir.

The Court: We do not think the objection sustained.

Challenged peremptorily by the prisoners.

Samuel Mudget called. Challenged for principal cause.

By Mr. Smith:

Q. In a capital case, where the evidence is sufficient, in your opinion, to convict the prisoner, have you any conscientious scruples that would prevent your finding a verdict of guilty?

A. I have not.

By Mr. Larocque:

Q. You have read the account of the capture of the privateer Savannah?

A. Yes, sir; at the time.

Q. Have you formed or expressed any opinion upon the guilt or innocence of these privateersmen?

A. I have not.

Q. Have you formed or expressed an opinion whether the acts charged upon them, if proved, constitute piracy?

A. No, sir; I have not formed any opinion with regard to the question whether it was piracy or not.

Challenged peremptorily by the prisoners.

George H. Hansell challenged for principal cause.

Q. In a capital case, where the evidence is sufficient to convince you that the prisoner was guilty, have you any conscientious scruples that would prevent your finding a verdict of guilty?

A. No, sir.

By Mr. Larocque:

Q. Have you read the account of the capture of the Savannah privateer?

A. I believe I read the account at the time. I have a very indistinct recollection of it.

Q. Have you formed or expressed an opinion as to the guilt or innocence of the prisoners?

A. I do not remember that I have, sir. I certainly do not have any opinion now; and certainly would not have until I have heard the evidence.

Q. Do you say you do not recollect whether you have formed or expressed any opinion?

A. I do not remember that I have, sir. I may, on reading the article, have expressed an opinion on it; but I am not positive of that.

Q. Have you formed or expressed an opinion whether the facts charged, if proved, amount to piracy?

A. I should not consider myself competent to form an opinion upon that until I have heard the law on the subject.

Challenge withdrawn. *Juror sworn.*

Panel completed.

DISTRICT ATTORNEY'S OPENING.

MR. E. DELAFIELD SMITH opened the case for the prosecution. He said:

May it please the Court, and you, Gentlemen of the Jury:

The Constitution of the United States, in the eighth section of the first article, authorized the Congress, among other things, to define and punish piracies and felonies committed on the high seas, and offences against the law of nations.

In pursuance of that authority, the Congress, on the 30th of April, 1790, made provisions contained in an act entitled "An Act for the punishment of certain crimes against the United States." I refer to the 8th and 9th sections of that act, which is to be found in the first volume of the U.S. Statutes at Large, page 112.

In the State Courts, gentlemen, it is common to say that the jury is judge both of the law and the fact; but such is not the case in the United States Courts. The Court will state to you the law, which you are morally bound to follow. But in opening this case, I refer to the statutes for the purpose of showing you precisely what the law is supposed to be under which this indictment is found, and under which we shall ask you for a verdict.

The 8th section of the act of 1790, commonly called "The Crimes Act," and to which I have just referred, declares, that if any person or persons shall commit, upon the high seas, or in any river, haven, basin, or bay, out of the jurisdiction of any particular State, murder or robbery, or any other offence which, if committed within the body of a county, would, by the laws of the United States, be punishable with death; or if any captain or mariner of any ship or other vessel shall piratically and feloniously run away with such ship or vessel, or any goods or merchandize to the value of fifty dollars, or yield up such ship or vessel voluntarily to any pirate; or if any seaman shall lay violent hands upon his commander, thereby to hinder and prevent his fighting in defence of his ship or goods committed to his trust, or shall make a revolt in the ship; every such offender shall be deemed, taken, and adjudged to be a pirate and felon, and, being thereof convicted, shall suffer death; and the trial of crimes committed on the high seas, or in any place out of the jurisdiction of any particular State, shall be in the district where the offender is apprehended, or into which he may first be brought.

The 9th section of the same act provides, that if any citizen shall commit any piracy or robbery aforesaid, or any act of hostility against the United States, or any citizen thereof, upon the high sea, under color of any commission from any foreign prince or state, or on pretence of authority from any person, such offender shall, notwithstanding the pretence of any such authority, be deemed, adjudged, and taken to be a pirate, felon, and robber, and, on being thereof convicted, shall suffer death.

A statute, on this subject, enacted in 1819, expired by its own limitation; but on the 15th of May, 1820, an act was passed making further provisions for punishing the crime of piracy. This law is printed in the third volume of the U.S. Statutes at Large, page 600. The 3d section provides, that if any person shall, upon the high seas, or in any open roadstead, or in any haven, basin, or bay, or in any river where the sea ebbs and flows, commit the crime of robbery in or upon any ship or vessel, or upon any of the ship's company of any ship or vessel, or the lading thereof, such person shall be adjudged to be a pirate; and, being thereof convicted before the Circuit Court of the United States for the district into which he shall be brought, or in which he shall be found, shall suffer death.

I now refer to the act of March 3d, 1825, to be found in the 4th volume of the Statutes at Large, page 115. It is entitled, "An act more effectually to provide for the punishment of certain crimes against the United States, and for other purposes." I cite it simply on the question of jurisdiction. The 14th section provides, that the trial of all offences which shall be committed upon the high seas or elsewhere, out of the limits of any State or district, shall be in the district where the offender is apprehended, or into which he may be first brought. The twenty-fifth section of this act repeals all acts, or parts of acts, inconsistent therewith.

Under the act of 1790 a question of construction arose, in the Supreme Court of the United States, as to whether robbery on the high seas was punishable with death. It was settled (3 Wheaton, 610) that the statute did punish robbery with death if committed on the high seas, even though robbery on land might not incur that extreme penalty. I refer to the United States *v.* Palmer, 3 Wheaton, 610; the United States *v.* Jones, 3 Washington's Circuit Court Reports, 209; United States *v.* Howard, Id., 340; 2 Whar. Crim. Law, fifth ed., p. 543.

I have been thus particular in referring to the laws under which this indictment is framed, in order that you may perceive precisely the inquiry which we now have to make. It is, whether the statutory law of the United States has or has not been violated? You have all, undoubtedly, heard more or less of the crime of piracy as generally and popularly understood. A pirate is deemed by the law of nations, and has always been regarded as the enemy of the human race,—as a man who depredates generally and indiscriminately on the commerce of all nations. Whether or not the crime alleged here is piracy under the law of nations, is not material to the issue. It might well be a question whether, in regard to depredations committed on the high seas, by persons in a foreign vessel, under the acknowledged authority of a foreign country, Congress could effectively declare that to be piracy which is not piracy under the law of nations; but it is not material in this case. Congress is unquestionably empowered to pass laws for the protection of our national commerce and for the punishment of those who prey upon it. Congress has done so in the statutes to which I have referred. If the words "pirate and felon" were stricken out from the act of 1790, and if the statutes simply read that any person committing robbery on the high seas should suffer death, the law would be complete, and could be administered without reference to what constitutes piracy by the law of nations.

Having thus referred to the statutory law under which this indictment was found, I will state as succinctly as possible, with due regard to fullness, fairness, and completeness, the facts in this case. In the middle or latter part of May, 1861, a number of persons in the city of Charleston, South Carolina, conceived the purpose of purchasing or employing a vessel to cruise on the Atlantic with the object of depredating on the commerce of the United States. They proceeded to the fulfillment of that design by procuring persons willing to act as captain, officers, and crew of such piratical vessel. This there was at first considerable difficulty in effecting, and it was not until many men were thrown out of employment in Charleston, by the acts of South Carolina and of what is called the Confederate Government, and by the action of the United States Government in blockading the port of Charleston and other Southern ports, that a crew could be found to man this vessel. There were no shipping articles or agreement as to wages; but it was understood that all were to share in the plunder or proceeds arising from the capture of American vessels on the high seas. We shall show to you that the prisoners at the bar were finally induced to embark on this enterprise; that Captain Baker was one of the first to engage in it; that he used exertions to obtain a crew, and succeeded, after considerable difficulty. On Saturday, the first of June, 1861, the crew were embarked on a small pilot boat and proceeded down to opposite Fort Sumter, where they were transferred, in small boats, to the schooner Savannah. We shall show, by the declarations of the parties who stand charged here to-day, and also by the facts and circumstances of the equipment of the vessel, the intent and purpose of this voyage. The Savannah, a schooner of fifty-three or fifty-four tons, was armed with cannon and small arms. Pistols and cutlasses were provided for her men. On Sunday afternoon, the 2d of June, she sailed from opposite Fort Sumter, her crew numbering about twenty men, all of whom are here with the exception of six, who were detached to form a prize crew of the brig Joseph. On the morning of Monday, the 3d of June, a sail was descried; it was remarked among the crew that the vessel, from her appearance, was undoubtedly a Yankee vessel, as they termed it—a vessel owned in one of the Northern States of the Union. She proved to be the brig Joseph, laden with sugar, and bound from Cardenas, in Cuba, to Philadelphia. The Savannah, displaying the American flag, gave chase. When within hailing distance, Captain Baker spoke the Joseph, ordered her captain on board his schooner, and ran up the rebel standard. Captain Meyer, of the Joseph, perceiving that the Savannah was armed, and that her men were ready for assault, fearing for his safety and that of his crew, obeyed the summons. A prize crew was placed on board the Joseph—the captain of the Savannah declaring that he "was sailing under the flag of the Confederate Government." The Savannah proceeded on her cruise. In a few hours afterward, she descried the United States brig-of-war Perry. Supposing her to be a merchant vessel, she started in pursuit, fired a gun, and finally fired several guns. On discovering, however, that the brig was a United States vessel-of-war, she attempted resistance, Captain Baker saying to his men, "Now, boys, prepare for action!" When within speaking distance, the commander of the Perry asked Captain Baker whether he surrendered, and he replied that he did. The prisoners were transferred from the Savannah to the Perry; thence to the United States steam ship-of-war, Minnesota. The Savannah was then taken in charge by a prize crew from on board the Perry and brought to New York. The Minnesota, with the prisoners on board, proceeded—on her way to New York—to Hampton Roads, where, after two days, she transferred the prisoners to the Harriet Lane, which delivered them at New York. Here they were given in charge to the United States Marshal. On my official application, a warrant was issued by a United States Commissioner, and under it the Marshal, as directed, took formal possession of and held the prisoners. They were committed for trial and were, within a few weeks afterwards, indicted by the United States Grand Jury. Although the guilt and mischief of both piracy and treason may be embraced in the crime and its consequences, the charge is not one of treason, nor necessarily of piracy, as commonly understood, but the simple one of violating the statutes to which I have referred.

The learned District Attorney here stated the evidence which he was prepared to submit, with the decisions upon which he would rest the case, and he proceeded to cite and comment upon the following, among other authorities:—U.S. *v.* Furlong, 5 Wheaton, 184; U.S. *v.* Klintock, 5 *Id.*, 144; Nueva Anna and Liebre, 6 *Id.*, 193; U.S. *v.* Holmes, 5 *Id.*, 412; U.S. *v.* Palmer, 3 *Id.*, 610; U.S. *v.* Tully, 1 Gallison, first ed., 247; U.S. *v.* Jones, 3 Wash. Circuit Court Rep., 209; U.S. *v.* Howard, 3 *Id.*, 340; U.S. *v.* Gibert, 2 Sumner, 19; U.S. *v.* Smith, 5 Wheaton, 153; 3 Chitty's Criminal Law, 1128; 1 Kent's Com., 25, note *c*, and cases cited; 1 *Id.*, 99, 100, and cases cited; 1 *Id.*, 184, 185, 186, 187, 188, 191, and cases cited. Decisions as to jurisdiction: U.S. *v.* Hicks, MS. Judge Nelson; Irvine *v.* Lowry, 14 Peters, 293, 299; Sheppard *v.* Graves, 14 Howard, 505; D'Wolf *v.* Rabaud, 1 Peters, 476, 498. Mr. SMITH then continued as follows:

The atrocity of the authors and leaders of this rebellion against a government whose authority has never been felt, with the weight of a feather, upon the humblest citizen, except for crime, has been portrayed so much more eloquently than I could present it, that I should not indulge in extended remarks on that subject, even if relevant to the case. Ignominy and death will be their just portion. The crime of those who have acted as the agents and servants of these leaders is also a grave one—a very grave one—mitigated, no doubt, by ignorance, softened by a credulous belief of misrepresentations, and modified by the very air and atmosphere of the place from which these prisoners embarked. It is, undoubtedly, a case where the sympathies of the jury and of counsel—whether for the prosecution or the defence—may be well excited in reference to many, if not all, of the prisoners at the bar, misguided and misdirected as they have been. But it will be your duty, gentlemen, while allowing these considerations to induce caution in rendering your verdict, to disregard them so far as to give an honest and truthful return on the evidence, and on the law as it will be stated to you by the Court. This is all the prosecution asks. As to the policy of ultimately allowing the law to take its course in this case, it is not necessary for us to express any opinion whatever. That is a question which the President of the United States must determine if this trial should result in a conviction. It is for him, not for us. You must leave it wholly to those who are charged with high duties, after you shall have performed yours.

The case is of magnitude; but the issue for you to determine is simple. Leaving out of view the alleged authority under which the prisoners claim to have acted, you will inquire, in the first instance, whether the seizure of the Joseph and her lading was robbery. You will be unable to discover that any element of the crime was wanting. If no actual force was employed in compelling the surrender, it is enough that the captain and crew were put in bodily fear. So the traveler delivers his purse in obedience to a request, and the crime is complete, although violence proves unnecessary. That the humble owners of the brig were despoiled of their property—how hardly earned we know not—will not be disputed. Nor is it material that the proceeds were to be shared between the prisoners and absent confederates. As to the question of intent, it cannot be denied that the prisoners designed to do, and to profit by, what they did. They are without excuse, unless possessed of a valid commission. This brings us to the plea of authority.

A paper, purporting to be a letter of marque, signed by Jefferson Davis, was found on the Savannah. Such a commission is of no effect, in our courts of law, unless emanating from some government recognized by the Government of the United States. The political authority of the nation, at Washington, has never recognized the so-called Confederate States as one of the family of nations. On the contrary, it resists their pretensions, and proclaims them in rebellion. In this position of affairs, a court of justice will not, nor can you as its officers, regard the letter as any answer to the case which the prosecution will establish. Such is the law. It is so determined in decisions of the Supreme Court of the United States, which I have just cited.

I will now proceed with the examination of the witnesses.

Albert G. Ferris called and sworn. Examined by District Attorney Smith:

Q. Where were you born?

A. In Barnstable, Massachusetts.

Q. How old are you?

A. Fifty on the 10th of September last.

Q. Have you a family?

A. Yes, sir.

Q. Does your family reside at Charleston?

A. Yes, sir, at Charleston, South Carolina.

Q. How long have you resided at Charleston?

A. Since 1837.

Q. What has been your business there?

A. Sea-faring man.

Q. In what capacity have you acted as a sea-faring man?

A. As master and mate.

Q. In what crafts?

A. In various crafts, small and large, and steamers.

Q. Sailing out of the port of Charleston?

A. Yes, and from ports of New York, and Virginia, and other places.

Q. In what capacity were you acting just prior to the time you embarked on board the Savannah?

A. I was acting as master of a vessel sailing from Charleston on the Southern rivers, in the rice and cotton trade.

Q. What was the name of the vessel?

A. The James H. Ladson, a schooner of about seventy-five tons.

Q. Was the business in which you were engaged stopped?

A. Yes, sir.

Q. At what time?

A. In December, 1860.

Q. What was your employment after that?

A. I had no employment after that. The blockade prevented vessels from going out, although some did get out after the blockade was established.

Q. State the facts and circumstances which preceded your connection with the Savannah?

A. I joined the Savannah as a privateer, through the influence of acquaintances of mine, with whom I had sailed, and from the necessity of having something to do, and under the idea of legal rights from the Confederate Government.

Q. What did you first do in reference to shipping on the Savannah?

A. I was on the bay with an acquaintance of mine, named James Evans, who is now, I believe, at Charleston, and who spoke to me about it.

Q. Was Evans one of the crew of the Savannah?

A. Yes, he was one of the prize crew that went off with the Joseph. He solicited me to join him, and said that he knew Captain Baker, and that he and others were going in the Savannah.

Q. Where did you see him?

A. I saw him on the bay at Charleston.

Q. Did you go anywhere with him in reference to enlisting?

A. Yes, we went to the house of Bancroft & Son, and I was there introduced to Captain Baker.

Q. Did you recognize Captain Baker on the cruise?

A. Yes, I recognized him then and since.

Q. State the conversation?

A. Mr. Evans recommended me to Captain Baker as a man who was acquainted with the coast, and who was likely to be just the man to answer his purpose. I partly made arrangements with Captain Baker to—that is, he was to send for me when he wanted me. He further proposed, as nothing was doing, that he would give me a job to go to work on board the Savannah and fit her out; but I had some little business to attend to at the time and declined.

Q. State the conversation at Bancroft & Son's when you and Evans and Captain Baker were there?

A. These were the items, as near as my memory serves me: that we were going on a cruise of privateering. I considered it was no secret. It was well known, and posted through the city. Previous to that I had met some of the party, who talked about going, and who asked me whether I had an idea of going, and I said I had talked about it. They said that Captain Baker was the officer. I then declined to go, and did not mean to go in her until Saturday morning.

Q. Did you have a further interview with Captain Baker, or any others of these men?

A. I had no other interview with Captain Baker at that time. I had no acquaintance with Captain Baker, or any on board, except these men who came from shore with me.

Q. Did you see any one else in reference to shipping on this vessel, except those you mentioned?

A. I believe there was a man by the name of Mills who talked of it. He did not proceed in the vessel. I believe he fitted her out, but did not go in her.

Q. Did you talk to any one else in regard to going?

A. No; he only told me he was going to get a crew.

Q. What articles did you see drawn up?

A. There were no articles whatever drawn up, and I do not know what arrangements were made. I understood since I have been here that arrangements were made, but they were not proposed to me. It was a mere short cruise to be undertaken.

Q. Was the purpose or object of the cruise stated?

A. It was the object of going out on a cruise of privateering.

Q. When did you embark on the vessel?

A. On Saturday night, the 1st of June, 1861.

Q. Do you recollect who embarked with you that night?

A. Some five or six of us.

Q. Give their names?

A. Alexander Coid was one (witness identified him in Court), Charles Clarke was another, and Livingston or Knickerbocker was another. I do not recollect any more names. There was a soldier, whose name I do not know, who went on the prize vessel.

Q. How did you get from the dock at Charleston?

A. In a small boat to a pilot-boat, and in the pilot-boat to the Savannah in the stream. She was lying about three miles from the city, and about three-quarters of a mile from Fort Sumter.

Q. How did you get from the pilot-boat to the Savannah?

A. In a small boat.

Q. And from the dock at Charleston to the pilot-boat?

A. In a small boat.

Q. Did any one have any direction in the embarkation?

A. No one, particular. There were some agents employed to carry us down. There was no authority used whatever.

Q. When did you sail from Charleston in the Savannah?

A. On Sunday afternoon from the outer roads.

Q. When did you weigh anchor and sail from Fort Sumter?

A. On Sunday morning, about 9 or 10 o'clock.

Q. Do you know the men you saw on board?

A. Yes, sir.

Q. Do you know the names of all the prisoners?

A. I believe I do, pretty nearly. I do not know that I could pronounce the name of the steward or cook, but I know that they were with us.

(The prisoner, Passalaigue, was asked to stand up, and the witness identified him.)

Q. What was his position on board?

A. I do not know what his position was. I never learned that. He was on board as if superintending the provisions, or something of that kind.

(The prisoner, John Harleston, was asked to stand up, and witness identified him.)

Q. What position had he on board?

A. I do not know what he did on board, anything more than that he arranged the big gun, and asked assistance to lend him a hand in managing the gun.

Q. Was he an officer, or seaman?

A. I believe he is no seaman.

Q. In what capacity did he act on board?

A. Nothing further than that, so far as I learned.

Q. Did you hear him give any directions?

A. No, sir; I was at the helm most of the time, when anything was done at the gun.

(The prisoner, Henry Howard, was asked to stand up, and witness identified him.)

Q. In what capacity was he?

A. That was more than I learned. They were all on board when I joined her.

Q. Was he a seaman or officer?

A. He stood aft with the rest of us, and assisted in working the vessel.

(The prisoner, Del Carno, was directed to stand up, and witness identified him as being the steward. He also identified Henry Oman as attending to the cooking department. The prisoner was directed to stand up, and was identified by the witness.)

Q. In what capacity was he?

A. The same as the rest—a seaman.

(Witness also identified William Charles Clarke, Richard Palmer, and John Murphy, as seamen, and Alexander C. Coid, as seaman. Martin Galvin, the prisoner, was directed to stand up, and was identified by the witness.)

Q. Was he a seaman?

A. I do not think he was either seaman or officer.

Q. What did he do on board?

A. Little of anything. There was very little done any way.

Q. Did he take part in working the vessel?

A. Very little, if anything at all. I believe he took part in weighing anchor.

Q. You identify Captain Baker as captain of the vessel?

A. Yes, I could not well avoid that.

Q. How many more were there besides those you have identified?

A. Some six. I think about eighteen all told, not including Knickerbocker and myself.

Q. How many went off on the Joseph?

A. There were six of them.

Q. Did any of those that are now here go off on the Joseph?

A. No, I believe not. I know all here. We have been long enough in shackles together to know one another.

Q. Do you remember the names of those that went on the Joseph?

A. I know two of them—one named Hayes, and Evans, the Charleston pilot.

Q. The same Evans who went on board with you?

A. Yes, sir; he was a Charleston pilot.

Q. What did Hayes and Evans do on board?

A. They did the same as the rest—all that was to be done.

Q. Were either of them officers?

A. Mr. Evans was the Charleston pilot. He gave the orders when to raise anchor and go out. He acted as mate and pilot when he was there. I presume he had as much authority, and a little more, than any one else; he was pilot.

Q. What did Hayes do?

A. He was an old, experienced man—did the same as the rest—lived aft with the rest. He was a seaman.

Q. The other four, whose names you do not recollect, did they act as seamen?

A. Exactly, sir.

Q. Any of them as officers?

A. No, sir; if they were, they were not inaugurated in any position while I was there.

Q. What did you do?

A. I did as I was told by the captain's orders—steered and made sail.

Q. What time did you get off from the bar in Charleston?

A. We got off Sunday afternoon and made sail east, outside of the bar, and proceeded to sea.

Q. Do you remember any conversation on board when any of the prisoners were present?

A. Yes; we talked as a party of men would talk on an expedition of that kind.

Q. What was said about the expedition?

A. That we were going out privateering. The object was to follow some vessels, and that was the talk among ourselves.

Q. Did anything happen that night, particularly?

A. No, sir; nothing happened, except losing a little main-top mast.

Q. What course did you take?

A. We steered off to the eastward.

Q. Did you steer to any port?

A. No, sir; we were not bound to any port, exactly.

Q. What directions were given in respect to steering the vessel?

A. To steer off to the eastward, or east by south, just as the wind was; that was near the course that was ordered.

Q. When did you fall in with the Joseph?

A. On Monday morning, the 3d.

Q. Do you remember who discovered the Joseph?

A. I think it was Evans, at the masthead.

Q. What did he cry out?

A. He sung out there was a sail on the starboard bow, running down, which proved afterwards to be the brig Joseph.

Q. State all that was said by or in the presence of the prisoners when and after the vessel was descried?

A. We continued on that course for two or three hours. We saw her early in the morning, and did not get up to her until 9 or 10 o'clock.

Q. How early did you see her?

A. About 6 o'clock. There were other vessels in sight. We stood off on the same course, when we saw this brig,—I think steering northeast by east. We made an angle to cut her off, and proceeded on that course until we fell in with her.

Q. What was said while running her down?

A. When near enough to be seen visibly to the eye, our men, Mr. Hayes, and the others, said she was a Yankee vessel; she was from the West Indies, laden with sugar and molasses. The general language was very little among the men; in fact, sailor-like, being on a flare-up before we left port, not much was said.

Q. State what was said?

A. Well, first the proposition was made that it was a Yankee prize; to run her down and take her. That was repeated several times. Nothing further, so far as I know of.

Q. During the conversation were all hands on deck?

A. Yes, sir, all hands on deck. In fact, they had been on deck. It was very warm; our place was very small for men below. In fact, we slept on deck. No one slept below, while there, much. It was a very short time we were on board of her—from Saturday to Monday night—when we were taken off.

Q. What was said was said loud, so as to be heard?

A. Yes; it was heard all about deck. That was the principal of our concern in going out; it was our object and our conversation.

Q. When you ran along down towards the Joseph, state what was said.

A. That was about the whole of what occurred—the men talking among themselves.

Q. When you got to the Joseph what occurred?

A. She was hailed by Captain Baker, and requested to send a boat on board.

Q. Who answered the hail?

A. I believe Captain Meyer, of the brig.

Q. Would you recognize Captain Meyer now?

A. Yes, sir.

Q. State what Captain Baker said?

A. Captain Baker, as near as I can bear in mind, hailed him, and told him to come on board and fetch his papers.

Q. Did Captain Meyer come on board?

A. He lowered his boat, and came on board with his own boat and crew. Captain Baker said to him that he was under the Confederate flag, and he considered him a prisoner, and his vessel a prize to the Confederate Government.

Q. Repeat that?

A. If I bear in mind, Captain Meyer asked what authority he had to hail his vessel, or to that effect. The reply of Captain Baker, I think, was that he was under a letter of marque of the Confederate Government, and he would take him as a prisoner, and his vessel as a prize to the Southern Confederacy. I do not know the very words, but that was the purport of the statement, as near as I understood.

Q. When Captain Baker hailed the Joseph, do you remember the language in which he hailed her?

A. I think, "Brig, ahoy! Where are you from?" He answered him where from—I think, from Cardenas; I think, bound to Philadelphia or New York.

Q. Did he inquire about the cargo?

A. No, sir, I think not, until Captain Meyer came on board. We were but a short distance from the brig. The brig was hove to.

Q. Do you remember anything further said by Captain Baker, or any of the prisoners?

A. He had some further conversation with Captain Meyer, on the deck, with respect to the vessel, where from, the cargo, and the like of that. She had in sugars, as near as my memory serves me.

Q. What flag had the Savannah, or how many?

A. She had the Confederate flag.

Q. What other flags, if any?

A. She had the United States flag.

Q. Any other?

A. No, sir, I do not know that she had any other.

Q. Did you notice what flag the Joseph had?

A. I did not see her flag, or did not notice it. I saw her name, and where she hailed from. I knew where she belonged.

Q. What was on her stern?

A. I think "The Joseph, of Rockland." I knew where it was. I had been there several times.

Q. When the sail was first descried was there any flag flying on the Savannah?

A. No, sir.

Q. When you ran down towards the Joseph was there any flying?

A. Yes, sir, we had the Confederate flag flying, and, I believe, the American flag.

Q. Which was it?

A. I believe both flying—first one, and then the other.

Q. Which first?

A. I think the Stars and Stripes first. I am pretty certain that Mr. Evans then hauled that down.

Q. When running down toward the Joseph you had the American flag flying?

A. Yes, sir; I think so; and Mr. Evans hauled down that, and put up the Confederate flag, when we got close to her.

Q. She ran with the American flag until close to her, and then ran up the Confederate flag?

A. Yes, when some mile or so of her—in that neighborhood.

Q. Do you remember who gave the order to the prize crew to leave the Savannah and go on board the Joseph?

A. Issued the orders? Well, Captain Baker, I believe, told the pilot, Mr. Evans, to select his men, and go with the boat.

Q. And they went on board?

A. Yes, they went on board.

Q. Do you remember anything said among the men, after the prize crew went off, in respect to the Joseph, or her cargo, or her capture?

A. Captain Meyer was there, and stated what he had in her, and where he was from, and so forth. We were merely talking about that from one to the other.

Q. Do you remember any directions given to the prize crew, as to the Joseph—where to go to?

A. I do not recollect Captain Baker directing where to get her in, or where to proceed with her. Evans was better authority, I presume, than Captain Baker, where to get her in.

Q. Any directions as to where the vessel was to be taken?

A. No, sir; either to Charleston or Georgetown—the nearest place where they could get in, and evade the blockade. That was the reason of having the pilot there.

Q. Did Captain Meyer remain on board the Savannah?

A. Yes, sir, until we were captured, and then he was transferred to the brig Perry, with the rest of us.

Q. What direction did the Joseph take after she parted from you?

A. Stood in northward and westward. Made her course about northwest, or in that neighborhood.

Q. In what direction from Charleston and how far from Charleston was the Joseph?

A. I think Charleston Bar was west of us about 50 or 55 miles.

Q. Out in the open ocean?

A. Yes, sir. I calculated that Georgetown light bore up about 35 miles in the west; but whether that is correct or not I cannot say.

Q. Where was the nearest land, as nearly as you can state?

A. I think the nearest land was Ball's Island, somewhere in the neighborhood of north and west, 35 or 40 miles.

Q. What sail did you next fall in with?

A. We fell in with a British bark called the Berkshire.

Q. What did you do when you fell in with her?

A. We passed closely across her stern. She was steering to the northward and eastward—I suppose bound to some Northern port.

Q. That was a British brig?

A. Yes, sir.

Q. What was the next sail you fell in with?

A. The next sail we fell in with was the brig-of-war Perry.

Q. At what time did you descry her?

A. I suppose about 3 o'clock in the afternoon of the same day.

Q. Where were you when you fell in with her?

A. We were somewhere in the same parallel. We saw the brig Perry from the masthead, and stood towards her.

Q. What was said when she was seen?

A. We took her to be a merchant vessel. That was our idea, and we stood to the westward.

Q. Did you make chase?

A. Yes, sir, we stood to the westward when we saw her; and the brig Joseph, that we took, saw her. The Perry, I presume, saw us before we saw her, and was steering for us at the time we were in company with the Joseph.

Q. How far off was the Joseph at the time?

A. Not more than three or four miles. When we made her out to be the brig-of-war Perry, we then tacked ship and proceeded to sea, to clear her.

Q. How near was the brig Perry when you first discovered she was a man-of-war?

A. I should think she was all of 10 or 11 miles off.

Q. The brig Perry made chase for you?

A. Yes, sir.

Mr. Larocque: If the Court please, from the opening of counsel I suppose he is now proceeding to that part of the case that he laid before the jury in his opening, that consists in an exchange of shots between the brig Perry and the Savannah. We object to that. There is no charge in the indictment of resisting a United States cruiser, or of any assault whatever.

Mr. Smith: What the vessel did on the same day, before and after the main charge, goes to show the purpose of the voyage—the general object of the Savannah and her crew. It may be relevant in that respect.

Mr. Larocque: We are not going to dispute the facts testified to by this witness. There will be no dispute on this trial that this was a privateer—that her object was privateering under the flag of the Confederate Government, and by authority of that Government, and, under these circumstances, the gentleman has no need to trouble himself to characterize these acts by showing anything that occurred between the Savannah and the Perry. Your honor perceives at once that this indictment might have been framed in a different way, under the 8th section of the Act of 1790, with a view of proving acts of treason, if you please, which are made piracy, as a capital offence, by that act. The counsel has elected his charge, and he has strictly confined the charge in the indictment to the allegation of what occurred between the Savannah and the Joseph. There is not one word in the indictment of any hostilities between the Perry and the Savannah, and therefore it must be utterly irrelevant and immaterial under this indictment. Evidence on that subject would go to introduce a new and substantial charge that we have not been warned to appear here and defend against, and have not come prepared to defend against, for that reason. So far as characterizing the acts we are charged with in the indictment, there can be no difficulty whatever.

The Court: I take it there is no necessity for this inquiry after the admission made.

Mr. Evarts: We propose to show the arrest and bringing of the vessel in, with her crew.

The Court: Of course.

Mr. Evarts: That cannot very well be done without showing the way in which it was done.

The Court: But it is not worth while to take up much time with it.

Mr. Brady: The witness has stated that this vessel was captured, and he has stated the place of her capture; and of course it is not only proper, but, in our view, absolutely necessary, that the prosecution should show that, being captured, she was taken into some place out of which arose jurisdiction to take cognizance of the alleged crime. But the cannonading is no part of that.

Q. By Mr. Smith: State the facts in regard to the capture of the Savannah by the Perry.

A. Well, the brig Perry ran down after dark and overtook us; came within hail.

Q. At what time?

A. Near 8 o'clock at night. Without any firing at all, she hailed the captain to heave to, and he said yes; she told him to send his boat on board. He said that he had no boat sufficient to go with. They then resolved to send a boat for us, and did so, and took us off. That was the result.

Q. The Perry sent her boat to the Savannah?

A. Yes, sir; we had no boat sufficient to take our crew aboard of her. We had a small boat, considerably warped, and it would not float.

Q. Where at sea was the capture made of the Savannah by the Perry?

A. It was in the Atlantic Ocean.

Q. About how far from Charleston?

A. Well, about 50 miles from Charleston light-house, in about 45 fathoms of water.

Q. How far from land?

A. I suppose the nearest land was Georgetown light, about 35 or 40 miles; I should judge that from my experience and the course we were running.

Q. Were you all transferred to the Perry?

A. Yes, sir.

Q. When was that?

A. Monday night; it was later than 8 o'clock.

Q. Transferred by boats?

A. Yes, sir; the Perry's boats. She sent her boat, with arms and men, and took us on board. There we were all arrested and put in irons that night, except the captain and Mr. Harleston, I believe. I do not know whether they were, or not.

Q. Was Mr. Knickerbocker put on board the Perry, with the rest?

A. Yes, sir, and on board the Minnesota, with us.

Q. Who were put in charge of the Savannah? Were there any men of the Perry?

A. Yes, sir; I believe they sent a naval officer on board to take charge of her, and a crew; and I think they took Mr. Knickerbocker and Capt. Meyer, too, on board the Savannah.

Q. Did you hear the direction as to the port the Savannah should sail to after the prize crew were put on board?

A. To New York I understood it was ordered. I was told that she was ordered to New York.

(Objected to as incompetent.)

Q. In respect to the Perry, what course did she take after you were taken on board?

A. As informed by the captain, next day, she was bound to Florida, to Fernandina, to blockade.

Q. When did she fall in with the Minnesota?

A. About the third day after our capture, I think; lying 8 or 10 miles off Charleston.

Q. In the open ocean?

A. Yes, sir.

Q. You were all transferred to the Minnesota?

A. Yes, sir.

Q. What did the Minnesota do?

A. We were confined on board the Minnesota.

Q. When was it you went on board the Minnesota?

A. I think on Wednesday or Thursday; I forget which.

Q. You were captured on Monday night?

A. Yes, sir, the 3d of June, and I think it was on Wednesday or Thursday (I do not know which) we went on board the Minnesota.

Q. How long did you lie off Charleston?

A. Several days.

Q. At anchor?

A. The ship was under way sometimes, steering off and on the coast.

Q. How far from Charleston?

A. I think in 8 or 9 fathoms of water, 8 or 10 miles from the land.

Q. Where did the Minnesota proceed from there?

A. To Hampton Roads.

Q. Were all the persons you have identified here on board the Minnesota?

A. Yes, sir.

Q. State the facts as to transfer from ship to ship?

A. We were transferred from the Savannah to the Perry; from the Perry to the Minnesota; from the Minnesota to the Harriet Lane.

Q. All of you?

A. Yes, sir; all.

Q. State, as near as you can, where, at Hampton Roads, the Minnesota came?

A. She came a little to the westward of the Rip Raps; I suppose Sewall's Point was bearing a little to the west of us, 3/4 or 1/2 a mile to the west of us; I should judge west by south. I am well acquainted there. We call it 24 miles from Old Point Comfort.

Q. What was the nearest port of entry to where you were anchored?

A. Norfolk, Va.

Q. How far from Fortress Monroe?

A. A mile, or 1-1/8 or 1-1/4—not a great distance.

Q. How long did you lie there before you were transferred to the Harriet Lane?

A. Several days. I did not keep any account. Some two or three days.

Q. And you were brought to this port in the Harriet Lane?

A. Yes, sir.

Q. And all the prisoners you identified to-day were brought here?

A. Yes, sir, to the Navy Yard, Brooklyn; there transferred to a ferry-boat and brought to the Marshal's office here.

Mr. Evarts. If the Court please, we deem it a regular and necessary part of our proof to show the manner of the seizure of this vessel by the U.S. ship Perry; to show that it was a forcible seizure, by main force, and against armed forcible resistance of this vessel. Besides being almost a necessary part of the circumstances of the seizure, it is material as characterizing the purpose of this cruise, and the depth and force of the sentiment which led to it, and the concurrence and cohesion of the whole ship's crew in it.

The Court. What necessity for that after what has been conceded on the other side?

Mr. Evarts. They concede that she was seized; but do they concede that, as against all those accused, the crime of piracy is proved—the concurrence of the whole—and that the only question is, whether the protection claimed from what is called the privateering character of the vessel shields them?

The Court. I understand the admission to be broad.

Mr. Evarts. If as broad as that, that there is no distinction taken between the concurrence of these men, it is sufficient.

Mr. Brady. We have said nothing about that?

The Court. So far as the capture is concerned, that does not enter into any part of the crime, and has no materiality to the elements of this case at all. The force that may enter into the crime is in the capture by the privateer of the Joseph. I do not want to confound this case by getting off on collateral issues; and so far as concerns the animus, or intent, I understand it to be admitted.

Mr. Evarts: My learned friends say that on this point they have not said anything as to the jointness or complicity of the parties in this crime. Now I think your honor would understand that a concurrence in resistance, by force, of an armed vessel of the United States, bearing the flag of the United States, and undertaking to exercise authority over it, would show their design.

The Court: Have you any question as to the facts?

Mr. Evarts: The Government have all the facts. Stripped of all the circumstances that attended the actual transaction, it would appear as if, when the brig Perry came along, these people at once surrendered, gave up, and submitted quietly and peacefully. As against that, we submit the Government should protect itself by proving the actual transaction.

Mr. Brady: One thing is certain, that if these men committed any offence whatever, it was committed before they saw the Perry; it was an act consummated and perfect, whatever may have been its legal character, and whatever may have been the consequences which the law would attach to it. The proof of the capture of the Savannah by the Perry is in no way relevant, except in proving jurisdiction, for which purpose alone is it of any importance that it should be mentioned here. And whether the capture was effected after a chase, or without one, against resistance, or by the consent of the persons to that from which they could not escape, is of no possible consequence in any aspect of the case. Whether there was firing or armed resistance can make no difference. It cannot bear on the question whether all the defendants are responsible for the acts of each other, like conspirators. It may be, as the counsel for the prosecution holds, that when you show they did set out on a common venture each became the agent of the other. That may be, and they must take the responsibility of trying the case on such a theory of the law as they think proper. We would not feel any hesitation in saying they all acted with a common design, only that there are some of the prisoners that we have had no communication with, and it may be that some of them went on board without knowing what the true character of the enterprise was. It is sufficient now to object that the question, whether there was resistance or not, after the Perry came up, is of no consequence in deciding the question of whether the men are responsible.

Mr. Evarts: My learned friend is certainly right in saying that the crime was completed when the Joseph was seized; but it does not follow that the proof of what the crime was, and what the nature of the act was, is completed by the termination of that particular transaction. You might as well say that the fact of a robbery or theft has been completed by a pickpocket or highwayman when his victim has been despoiled of his property; and that proof of the crime prohibits the Government from showing the conduct of the alleged culprit after the transaction—such as evading the officer, running away from or resisting the officer.

The Court: You do not take into account the admission of the counsel. I believe the subsequent conduct of the privateers, if the intent with which they seized and captured the Joseph was in question, would be admissible; but when this is admitted broadly by the counsel for the defendants, I do not see why it is necessary to go into proof with a view to make out that fact, except to occupy the time of the Court.

Mr. Evarts: I am sure your honor will not impute to us any such motive. The point of difficulty is: my learned friends do not admit the completeness of the crime by all the prisoners, subject only to the answer whether the privateering character of the enterprise protects them. The moment that is admitted, I have no occasion to dwell upon the facts.

The Court: I understand the admission as covering all the prisoners, as to the intent.

Mr. Brady: That she was fitted out as a privateer—the enterprise, and capture of the Joseph.

Mr. Smith: Is the admission that all were engaged in a common enterprise, and all participators in the fact?

The Court: So I understand the admission, without any qualification.

Mr. Smith: Do we understand the counsel as assenting to the Court's interpretation as to the breadth of the admission?

Mr. Brady: There is no misunderstanding between the Court and the counsel; but the learned gentlemen seem not to be satisfied with the admission we made. The intent is, of course, an element in the crime of piracy. There must be an *animus furandi* established, in making out the crime; and that is, of course, a question about which we have a great deal to say, both as to the law and the fact, at a subsequent stage of the case. When the counsel proposed to prove the firing of cannon, and armed resistance, we said—what we say now—that we do not intend to dispute the facts proved by the witness on the stand: that the Savannah was, at the port of Charleston, openly and publicly, without any secresy (to use the witness's language, it was "posted"), fitted out as a privateer, in the service of the Confederate States, under their flag, and by their authority; that it was so announced, and that these men were shipped on board of her as a privateer. All that, there is no intention to dispute at all; and, of course, that all the men who shipped for that purpose were equally responsible for the consequences, we admit.

Mr. Evarts: Do you admit that all shipped for the purpose? If we can prove their conduct, concurring in this armed resistance, then I show that they were not there under any deception about its being a peaceable mercantile transaction. I may be met by the suggestion that, so far as the transaction disclosed about the Joseph is concerned, there was not any such depth of purpose in this enterprise as would have opposed force and military power in case of overhauling the vessel. It would seem to me, with great respect to the learned Court, that when the facts of the transaction can be brought within very narrow compass, as regards time, it is safer that we should disclose the facts than that admissions should be accepted by the Court and counsel when there is so much room for difference of opinion as to the breadth of the admission. We may run into some misunderstanding or difference of view as to how far the actual complicity of these men, or the strength of their purpose and concurrence in this piratical (as we call it) enterprise, was carried.

Mr. Lord: If your honor will permit, it appears to me that this is exceedingly plain. The notoriety and equipment of the vessel—all the character of the equipment—the sailing together—all that is covered by the admission of my friend, Mr. Brady. So far as to there being a joint enterprise up to the time of the capture of the Joseph, it seems to me there is nothing left. Now, what do they wish? They wish to show, what is in reality another, additional, and greater crime, after this capture of the Joseph, for which we alone are indicted, as they say, for the purpose of showing that we assented to this, which we went out to do.

Your honor knows that, if we have any fact to go to the jury, they are getting into this case a crime of a very different character and of a deeper dye, for which they have made no charge, and which does not bear upon that which, if a crime at all, was consummated in the capture of the Joseph—the only crime alleged in the indictment. I submit that they cannot, with a view of showing complicity in a crime completed, show that the next day the men committed another crime of a deeper character. I think it is not only irrelevant, but highly objectionable.

The Court: We are of opinion that this testimony is superfluous, and superseded by the admission of the counsel. I understand the admission of the counsel to be, that the vessel was fitted out and manned by common understanding on the part of all the persons on board, as a privateer; and that in pursuance of that design and intent, and the completion of it, the Joseph was captured. That is all the counsel can ask. That shows the intent—all that can be proved by this subsequent testimony; and unless there is some legitimate purpose for introducing this testimony, which might, of itself, go to show another crime, we are bound to exclude it.

Mr. Evarts: We consider the decision of your honor rests upon that view of the admission, and we shall proceed upon that as being the admission.

The Court: Certainly; if anything should occur hereafter that makes it necessary, or makes it a serious point, the Court will look into it.

Examination resumed by District Attorney Smith.

Q. You stated, I believe, that it was after 8 o'clock in the evening when the boat of the Perry came to the Savannah?

A. Yes, sir.

Q. Who was in that boat?

A. There was a gentleman from the Perry; I do not know that I ever saw him before; an officer and boat's crew,—I suppose 15 or 20 men.

Q. One of the United States officers?

A. Yes, sir; some officer from the brig Perry boarded us, and demanded us to go on board the Perry.

Q. Where were the crew of the Savannah at the time the boat came from the Perry?

A. All on deck, sir.

Q. At the time the Savannah was running down the Joseph, what time was it?

A. We got up to the Joseph somewhere late in the forenoon, as near as my memory serves me.

Q. I want to know whether all the officers and crew of the Savannah were on duty, or not, at the time you were running down?

A. Yes, sir; there were some walking the deck, and some lying down, right out of port; the men, after taking a drink, did not feel much like moving about; they were all on deck.

Q. Was there any refusal to perform duty on the part of any one?

A. No, sir; all did just as they were told.

Q. How was the Savannah armed, if armed at all?

A. I never saw all her arms, sir.

Q. What was there on deck?

A. A big gun on deck.

Q. What sort of a gun?

A. They said an eighteen-pounder; I am no judge; I never saw one loaded before.

Q. A pivot gun?

A. No, sir, not much of a pivot. They had to take two or three handspikes to round it about.

Q. It was mounted on a carriage, the same as other guns?

A. Yes, sir.

Q. With wheels?

A. I believe so; I took no notice of the gun.

Q. Reflect, and tell us how the gun was mounted?

A. It was mounted so that it could be altered in its position by the aid of handspikes; it could be swung by the use of handspikes.

Q. The gun could be swung on the carriage without moving the carriage?

A. I do not know that part of it; I know the men complained that moving the gun was hard work.

Q. What other arms had you on board?

A. I saw other arms on board,—pistols, I believe, and cutlasses.

Q. How many pistols did you see?

A. I saw several; I do not know how many.

Q. About how many cutlasses?

A. I cannot say how many; I saw several, such as they were—cutlasses or knives, such as they were.

Q. Where were the cutlasses?

A. Those were in the lockers that I saw; I never saw them until Monday noon, when we ran down the Joseph; I saw them then.

Q. Where were they then?

A. I saw them in the lockers that lay in the cabin.

Q. When the Perry's boat came to you where were they?

A. Some out on the table, and some in the lockers.

Q. When you captured the Joseph where were they?

A. I think there were some out on the table, and about the cabin; the pistols, too; but there were none used.

Q. Were any of the men armed?

A. No, sir; I saw none of our men armed, except in their belt they might have a sheath knife.

Q. Where were all hands when you captured the Joseph, in the forenoon of Monday?

A. All on deck, sir; there might be one or two in the forecastle, but most on deck, some lying down, and some asleep.

Q. What size is the Savannah?

A. I think in the neighborhood of 50 to 60 tons.

Q. What is the usual crew for sailing such a vessel, for mercantile purposes?

A. I have been out in such a boat with four men and a boy, besides myself; that was all-sufficient.

Q. Where did you run to?

A. I ran to Havana, and to Key West, with the mails, and returned again in a pilot boat of that size, with four men and a boy, some years ago.

Q. Was the Savannah in use as a pilot boat before that expedition?

A. Yes; that is what she was used for.

Q. Do you know where the Savannah was owned?

A. I believe she was owned in Charleston.

Q. How long have you known her?

A. Two or three years, as a pilot boat.

Q. Do you know her owners?

A. I know one of them.

Q. What was his name?

A. Mr. Lawson.

Q. Is he a citizen of the United States?

A. Yes, I believe so.

Cross-examined by Mr. Larocque.

Q. In speaking of your meeting with the Joseph, you spoke of a conversation that took place between Captain Baker and Captain Meyer, after Captain Meyer came on board the Savannah. Do you not recollect that before that, when Captain Meyer was still on the deck of the Joseph, Captain Baker having called him to come on board the Savannah, and bring his papers, he asked Captain Baker by what authority he called on him to do that?

A. I think this conversation occurred on board the Savannah.

Q. The way you stated was this: that Captain Baker, on board the Savannah, stated to Captain Meyer that he must consider himself and crew prisoners, and his vessel a prize to the Confederate States?

A. Yes, sir.

Q. That was on board the Savannah?

A. It was.

Q. But do you not recollect that before that, when Captain Baker called on the Captain of the Joseph to come on board the Savannah, and bring his papers, Captain Meyer asked by what authority Captain Baker called on him to do that?

A. I do not bear that in mind. I cannot vouch for that. I do not exactly recollect those words, I think the proposition was only made when he was on board the Savannah, but probably it might have been made before.

Q. Did Captain Meyer bring his papers with him?

A. I do not know. I did not see them.

Q. You spoke of having met another vessel after that, and before you fell in with the Perry—I mean the Berkshire—you spoke of her as a British vessel?

A. Yes. We did not speak her.

Q. How did you ascertain the fact that she was a British vessel?

A. We could tell a British vessel by the cut of her sails.

Q. Was the Berkshire, so far as you observed, an armed or an unarmed vessel?

A. I think she was an unarmed vessel. I considered she had been at some of the Southern ports, and had been ordered off.

Q. She was a merchant vessel?

A. Yes.

Q. Which you, from your seamanlike knowledge, thought to be a British vessel?

A. Yes; and I think that the words, "Berkshire, of Liverpool," were on her stern.

Q. Did you read the name on the stern?

A. I think I did.

Q. You had fallen in with the Joseph, one unarmed vessel, and had made her a prize, and her crew prisoners?

A. Yes.

Q. You fell in with the Berkshire, another unarmed vessel, and passed under her stern and did not interfere with her. What was the reason of that difference?

A. We had no right to interfere with her.

Q. Why not?

A. She was not an enemy of the Confederate Government. The policy we were going on, as I understood it, was to take Northern vessels.

Q. Then you were not to seize all the vessels you met with?

A. No; we were not to trouble any others but those that were enemies to the Confederate Government. That was the orders from headquarters. The Captain showed no disposition to trouble any other vessels.

Q. When you were taken on board the Perry were you put in irons?

A. Yes.

Q. Where were those irons put on. Was it on board the Savannah, or after you were put on board the Perry?

A. When we got on board the Perry.

Q. How soon after you went on board the Perry were those irons put on?

A. As soon as our baggage was searched. We were put in the between-decks on board the Perry and irons put on us immediately after we were searched.

Q. Were you in irons when you were transferred from the Perry to the Minnesota?

A. No, sir.

Q. When were the irons taken off?

A. On board the Perry, when we were going into the boat to go on board the Minnesota.

Q. When you were on board the Minnesota were your irons put on again?

A. They were, at night.

Q. Was that the practice—taking them off in the day, and putting them on at night?

A. Yes; we were not ironed at all on that day on board the Minnesota.

Q. When you arrived in Hampton Roads,—you have described the place where the Minnesota lay, about half a mile from the Rip Raps?

A. Yes. (A chart was here handed to witness, and he marked on it the position of the Minnesota off Fortress Monroe.)

Q. As I understand it, you have marked the position of the anchorage of the Minnesota a little further up into the land than on a direct line between the Rip Raps and Fortress Monroe? *A.* Yes, sir.

Q. You were then taken on board the Harriet Lane, from the Minnesota?

A. Yes.

Q. Where did the Harriet Lane lie when you were taken on board of her?

A. She was further up into the Roads, about half a mile from the Minnesota, westward. (Witness marked the position of the Harriet Lane on the chart.)

Q. You are familiar with these Roads?

A. Yes, sir; for years.

Q. You know the town of Hampton?

A. Yes.

Q. And the college there?

A. Yes.

Q. How, with reference to the college at Hampton, did the Harriet Lane lie?

A. The college at Hampton appeared N.N.W., and at a distance of a mile and a quarter, or a mile and a half.

Q. How were you taken from the Minnesota on board the Harriet Lane?

A. The ship's crew took us in a boat.

Q. In one trip, or more trips?

A. We all went in one of the ship's boats.

Q. On what day was that?

A. I do not bear in mind exactly.

Q. Was the Harriet Lane ready to sail when you were taken on board of her?

A. Yes; she sailed in a few hours afterwards.

Q. She had already had steam up?

A. Yes; they were waiting for the commander, who was on shore.

Q. How long were you lying on board the Minnesota after your arrival there?

A. I think we were transferred from the Minnesota on Saturday, the 20th of June.

Q. How long had you been lying on board the Minnesota, in Hampton Roads?

A. Two or three days; I do not recollect exactly.

Q. You have been a seafaring man a good many years?

A. I have been about 34 years at it.

Q. In the capacity of master and mate?

A. Yes, sir.

Q. As pilot, also?

A. I have run pilot on all the coasts of America.

Q. How often had you been in Hampton Roads?

A. Many a time. I sailed a vessel in and out in the West India trade.

Q. How familiar are you with the localities about there?

A. I am so familiar that I could go in, either night or day, or into Norfolk.

Q. Do you know the ranges, bearings, distances, depth of water, and all about it?

A. Yes; and could always find my way along there.

Q. (*By a Juror.*) I understood you to say that the Savannah carried both the American flag and the Confederate flag?

A. Yes.

Q. And that the American flag was flying when you were bearing on the Joseph?

A. Yes.

Q. What was the object of sailing under that flag?

A. I presume our object was to let her know that we were coming; and, no doubt, the vessel heaved to for us. Suddenly enough we raised the Confederate flag.

Q. Then it was deception?

A. Of course; that was our business—that was as near as I understood it.

William Habeson called, and sworn. Examined by District Attorney Smith.

Q. You are the Deputy Collector of the port of Philadelphia? *A.* Yes, sir.

Q. Have you charge of the register of vessels there?

A. Yes.

Q. Did you take this certified copy of the register of the Joseph from the original book?

A. It is copied from the original book.

Mr. Evarts: It is a temporary register, dated 26th January, 1861, showing the building of the vessel, and the fact of her owners being citizens of the United States.

Q. Who was the master of the vessel then?

A. George H. Cables.

Q. Do you know who was the master afterwards?

A. Yes; I saw him afterwards. That man (pointing to Captain Meyer) is the man. He was endorsed as master after the issuing of this register.

Q. And you recollect this person being master of the vessel mentioned in that register?

A. I do, sir.

George Thomas called, and sworn. Examined by District Attorney Smith.

Q. Where do you reside?

A. Quincy, Massachusetts.

Q. What is your business?

A. Shipbuilder.

Q. Do you know the brig Joseph?

A. I have known her; I built her.

Q. Where did you build her?

A. At Rockland, Maine.

Q. Who did you build her for?

A. For Messrs. Crocket, Shaller, Ingraham, and Stephen N. Hatch—all of Rockland.

Q. Were they American citizens?

A. They were all American citizens.

Q. What was the tonnage of the vessel?

A. About 177 tons. She was a hermaphrodite brig.

Q. Look at this description in the register and say whether it was the vessel you built.

A. I have no doubt that this is the vessel.

George H. Cables called, and sworn. Examined by District Attorney Smith.

Q. Where do you reside?

A. Rockland, Maine.

Q. Look at the description of the brig Joseph, in this register, and see if you know her?

A. Yes, sir.

Q. You were formerly master of the vessel?

A. Yes, sir.

Q. Who was the master that succeeded you?

A. I put Captain Meyer in charge of her.

Q. You recognize Mr. Meyer here?

A. Yes, sir.

Q. Did you own any part of that vessel?

A. I bought a part of it, and gave it to my wife.

Q. Is your wife an American-born woman?

A. She is.

Q. Where does she reside?

A. In Rockland.

Q. Do you know any others of the part-owners of her?

A. Yes; my brother and myself bought a three-eighth interest.

Q. Where does your brother reside?

A. In Rockland.

Q. Is he an American-born citizen?

A. Yes.

Q. Are you an American citizen?

A. Yes.

Q. You spoke of some other owner?

A. Yes; Messrs. Hatch and Shaler.

Q. Are they American citizens?

A. Yes.

Q. Did you know all the owners?

A. Yes.

Q. Were they all American citizens?

A. Yes.

Q. When did you put Meyer in charge of the vessel?

A. On the 26th or 27th of April last.

Q. Where?

A. In Philadelphia.

Q. Where did you sail from?

A. From Cardenas, in Cuba, on a round charter which I made at Cardenas myself with J. L. Morales & Co., consigned to S. H. Walsh & Co.

Q. The ownership remained the same?

A. Just the same.

Q. Was there any change up to the time of her capture?

A. No, sir.

Thies N. Meyer, examined by District Attorney Smith.

Q. You were Captain of the brig Joseph at the time of her capture?

A. I was.

Q. What American port had you sailed from?

A. Philadelphia.

Q. Where did you go to?

A. Cardenas, in Cuba.

Q. What port did you sail for from Cardenas?

A. Back to Philadelphia.

Q. What cargo had you?

A. Sugar.

Q. By whom was it owned?

A. By J. M. Morales & Co., of Cardenas.

Q. When did you leave the port of Cardenas?

A. 28th May, 1861.

Q. And you were captured by the Savannah on the 3d June?

A. Yes.

Q. State the particulars of the capture by the Savannah of the brig Joseph from the time she first hove in sight?

A. Mr. Bridges, my mate, called me some time between 6 and 7 o'clock in the morning, and told me there was a suspicious looking vessel in sight, and he wished me to look at her. I went on deck and asked him how long he had seen her, he told me he had seen her ever since day-light. When I took the spy-glass and looked at her I found that she was a style of vessel that we do not generally see so far off as that. I hauled my vessel to E.N.E., and when I found that she was gaining on me I hauled her E. by N. and so until she ran E. About 8 o'clock she came near enough for me to see a rather nasty looking thing amid-ships, so that I mistrusted something; but when I saw the American flag hanging on her main rigging, on her port side, I felt a little easier—still, I rather mistrusted something, and kept on till I found I could not get away at all. When she got within half a gun shot of me I heaved my vessel to, hoping the other might be an American vessel.

Q. Had she any gun on board?

A. I saw a big gun amid-ships, on a pivot.

Q. How far on was she when you saw the gun?

A. About a mile and a half or two miles; I could see it with the spy-glass very plainly.

Q. Can you give us the size of the gun?

A. Not exactly; I believe it was an old eighteen pound cannonade.

Q. How was it mounted?

A. On a kind of sliding gutter, which goes on an iron pivot: it was on a round platform on deck, so that it could be hauled round and round.

Q. So that it could be pointed in any direction?

A. Yes, in any direction. After she came up alongside of me, Captain Baker asked me where I was from, and where bound, and ordered me with my boat and papers on board his vessel. I asked him by what authority he ordered me on board, and he said, by authority of the Confederate States. I lowered my boat and went on board with two of my men. When I got alongside, Captain Baker helped me over the bulwarks, or fence, and said he was sorry to take my vessel, but he had to retaliate, because the North had been making war upon them. I told him that that was all right, but that he ought to do it under his own flag. He then hoisted his own flag, and ordered a boat's crew to go on board the brig. Some of them afterwards returned, leaving six on board the brig.

Q. Did Captain Baker take your papers?

A. Yes.

Q. Do you recognize Captain Baker in court?

A. Yes. As soon as they secured my crew they hauled the brig on the other tack, and stood into the westward, with the privateer in company. Captain Baker desired me to ask my mate to take the sun, as he had a chronometer on board, and the privateer had not. At 3 o'clock the privateer stood back to find out the longitude; while so doing she got astern of the brig, and about that time the brig Perry hove in sight, steering southward and eastward. When they saw the brig Perry they hauled the privateer more on the wind, because she would go a point or two nearer to the wind than the brig Joseph, so as to cut off the Perry if they could. They went aloft a good deal with opera glasses, to find out what she was, and they made her out to be a merchant vessel, as they thought. Then they saw the Perry's quarter boats, and rather mistrusted her. They backed ship and stood the same as the Perry. The Perry then set gallant stern-sail, and kept her more free, because she got the weather-gauge of the privateer.

Q. At the time of the capture of the Joseph by the Savannah did you observe all the crew, and in what attitude they were on deck?

A. I saw them working around the gun and hauling at it. Whether it was loaded or not, I could not say.

Q. Were any of the men armed?

A. None at that time that I know of; but after I went on board I saw them armed with a kind of cutlass, and old-fashioned boarding-pistols; and they had muskets with bayonets on.

Q. At the time you left your vessel for the Savannah, in what attitude were the men on board the Savannah?

A. They were all around on deck. Perhaps half of them were armed.

Q. How was the gun pointed?

A. The gun was pointing toward the brig.

Q. Who were about the gun?

A. Before I went on board I saw that a man was stationed beside the gun; I could not say which of them it was.

Q. What crew had you?

A. I had four men, a cook, and mate.

Q. Were they armed?

A. No, sir.

Q. Were you armed?

A. I had one old musket that would go off at half-cock.

Q. Was there any gun on board your vessel?

A. None except that.

Q. How many men did you see on the deck of the Savannah? *A.* Some 16, or 18, or 20.

Q. Were you transferred to the Perry from the Savannah?

A. Yes.

Q. And from the Perry to the Minnesota?

A. Yes.

Q. And from the Minnesota to the Harriet Lane?

A. No; to the Savannah. I came to New York in the Savannah.

Q. Then the Savannah sailed to New York before the Harriet Lane did?

A. Yes, sir.

Q. Where were you born?

A. In the Duchy of Holstein, under the flag of Denmark.

Q. You have been naturalized?

A. Yes.

Q. In what Court?

A. In the Court of Common Pleas, New York.

Q. When did you come to this country?

A. In the winter of '47.

Q. Did you hail from here ever since?

A. I hailed from almost all over the States. I never had a home until lately. I have hailed from here about a year. Before that, wherever my chest was was my home.

Q. You have resided in the United States ever since you were naturalized?

A. Yes, sir; I have never been out of it except on voyages.

Q. You have continued to be a citizen of the United States since you were naturalized?

A. Yes.

Q. And to reside in the United States?

A. Yes.

Q. Do you recollect the names of your crew?

A. No, sir; none except the mate; his name was Bridges.

Q. Is he here?

A. Yes.

Q. When the Joseph was seized by the Savannah, what was done with the Joseph?

A. She was taken a prize, a crew of six was put on board of her, and they started with her to westward.

Q. What became of the rest of the men of the Joseph besides yourself?

A. They were carried on with the Joseph; I continued on the Savannah.

Q. When did you first observe, on board the Savannah, that the American flag was flying?

A. When she was within about a mile and a half off.

Q. At what time, in reference to her distance from you, did she run up the Confederate flag?

A. The Confederate flag was not run up until after I had asked Captain Baker by what authority he ordered me to go on board; then the Confederate flag was run up; that was just before I went on board.

Cross-examined by Mr. Larocque.

Q. Be good enough to spell your name.

A. Thies N. Meyer.

Q. Was there any flag hoisted on board the Savannah at the time she was captured by the Perry, or immediately preceding that?

A. They were trying to hoist the Stars and Stripes up, but it got foul and they could not get it up, and they had to haul it down again.

Q. Then she had no flag flying at the time?

A. No, sir.

The District Attorney here put in evidence the certified copy of the record of naturalization of Thies N. Meyer, captain of the Joseph, dated 28th January, 1856.

Horace W. Bridges, examined by District Attorney Smith.

Q. You were mate of the Joseph when she was captured by the Savannah?

A. Yes.

Q. Do you know the names of the others of the crew beside yourself and the captain?

A. I do not know all of them.

Q. State those you know?

A. The cook's name is Nash, and there was another man named Harry Quincy; that is all I know.

Q. Were they citizens of the United States?

A. I think they were both.

Q. Are you a citizen of the United States?

A. Yes; I was born in the State of Maine.

Q. You have heard the statement of Captain Meyer as to the seizure of the vessel?

A. Yes.

Q. You were on board the Joseph after she parted company with the Savannah and sailed for South Carolina?

A. Yes, sir.

Q. Under whose direction did she sail?

A. By the direction of the prize-master.

Q. With a prize crew from the Savannah?

A. Yes.

Q. Do you recollect the name of the prize-master?

A. Evans.

Q. How many men did the crew consist of?

A. Six, with the prize-master.

Q. What did they do with the vessel?

A. Took her into Georgetown.

Q. What was done with you and the others of the crew?

A. We were taken to jail at Georgetown.

Q. What was done with the vessel?

A. I believe she was sold, from what I saw in the papers and what I was told.

Q. Where were you taken from Georgetown?

A. To Charleston.

Q. What was done with you there?

A. We were put in jail again.

Q. How long were you kept in jail in Georgetown?

A. About 2 months and 20 days.

Q. How long were you kept in jail in Charleston?

A. Three days.

Cross-examined by Mr. Larocque.

Q. You said that, while you were held as a prisoner at Georgetown, you saw something in reference to the sale of the Joseph in the papers?

A. Yes.

Q. What was the purport of it?

A. She was advertised for sale.

Q. Under legal process?

A. I do not know about that. I was also told of it by one of the prize crew that took us in.

Q. You saw in the newspapers an advertisement of the sale?

A. Yes.

Q. Was that of a sale by order of a Court?

A. It was a sale by order of the Sheriff or Marshal.

Q. As a prize?

Objected to by District Attorney Smith, for two reasons:

First—That it was a mere newspaper account; and,

Secondly—That the newspaper was not produced.

After argument, the Court decided that there was no foundation laid for this hearsay evidence.

Q. Did the advertisement state by whose authority the sale was to take place?

A. I do not recollect anything about that.

Q. Do you recollect the name of a judge as connected with it?

A. No, sir. There was no judge connected with the sale.

Q. Do you recollect the name of Judge Magrath in connection with it?

A. No, sir; I recollect his name in connection with some prize cases, but not in connection with the sale of the Joseph.

Q. Since your arrival at New York, you have been examined partially by the District Attorney, and have made a statement to him?

A. Yes.

Q. Did you not state on that examination that while you were in confinement the vessel was confiscated by Judge Magrath, and sold at Georgetown?

A. No, sir; I do not think I did.

Q. You were released at Charleston, after a confinement of three days?

A. Yes.

Q. How did you get out?

A. The Marshal let us out.

Q. While you were in confinement at Georgetown or Charleston was your examination taken in any proceeding against the bark Joseph, or in relation to her?

A. Yes, sir. In Georgetown.

Q. By whom was that examination taken?

Mr. Evarts suggested that there was a certain method of proving a judicial inquiry.

Judge Nelson: They may prove the fact of the examination.

Q. Before whom were you examined?

A. Before a man who came from Charleston.

Q. Did he take your examination in writing?

A. Yes, sir.

Q. Did you learn what his name was?

A. I think his name was Gilchrist.

Q. Were you sworn, as a witness?

A. Yes.

Q. What proceeding was that, as you were given to understand, and what was the object of the examination?

A. The object of it was to find out what vessel she was, what was her nationality, and who owned the cargo belonging to her.

Q. And you gave your testimony on these subjects.

A. Yes.

Q. Was it in written questions put to you?

A. I think so.

Q. And you signed your examination?

A. Yes.

Q. And what came of it afterwards?

A. I do not know.

Q. Was it taken away by Mr. Gilchrist?

A. I expect so.

Q. Was there any other of the crew besides yourself examined? *A.* Yes; all of them.

Q. On the same subject?

A. I expect so.

Q. Were you present during the examination of them all?

A. No; only at my own.

Q. What newspaper was it that you saw that advertisement in?

A. I think in the Charleston Courier.

Q. Do you recollect its date?

A. No, sir.

Q. What had become of the vessel when you went to Charleston?

A. She was lying in Georgetown.

Q. Do you know in whose possession, or under whose charge, she was?

A. I do not.

Q. Was she in Georgetown, in the hands of the Marshal, to your knowledge?

A. No, sir; not to my knowledge. I was in prison at the time.

Commodore Silas H. Stringham, examined by District Attorney Smith.

Q. You are in the United States Navy?

A. I am.

Q. The Minnesota was the flag ship of the Atlantic Blockading Squadron, off Charleston?

A. Yes, sir. I was the commanding officer.

Q. The Minnesota took the prisoners off the Perry?

A. Yes; on the 5th of June, in the afternoon.

Q. State precisely where the transfer from the Perry to the Minnesota was made?

A. I discovered, about mid-day, a vessel close in to Charleston. I stood off to make out what she was. A short time afterwards we discovered it was the Perry, and were surprised to find her there, as she had been ordered, some time previously, to Fernandina, Fla. She hailed us, and informed us she had captured a piratical vessel. The vessel was half a mile astern. Captain Parrott, of the Perry, came and made to me a report of what had taken place. I ordered him to send the prisoners on board, and sent a few men on board the Savannah to take charge of her during the night. The vessels were then anchored. The next morning I made arrangements to put a prize crew on board the Savannah, and send her to New York, and I directed the Captain of the Joseph to take passage in her. I took the prisoners from the Perry, and directed the Perry to proceed on her cruise, according to her previous orders. I then got the Minnesota under weigh, and took the privateer in tow, and brought her close in to Charleston harbor, within 3 miles, so as to let them see that their vessel was captured. Some slaves in a boat told me next day that they had seen and recognized the vessel.

Mr. Brady: The question you were called upon to answer is, as to the place where the prisoners were transferred from the Perry to the Minnesota.

A. The transfer was made about 10 miles from Charleston Harbor, out at sea. It was fully 10 miles off.

Q. State the design of transferring the prisoners to the Minnesota?

Objected to by Mr. Larocque.

ARGUMENT ON THE JURISDICTION.

The District Attorney, Mr. Smith, stated that he would prove that every thing done from that time onward was done in pursuance of a design then conceived of sending the prisoners, to the port of New York.

Mr. Larocque contended that the naked question of jurisdiction, or want of jurisdiction, could not be affected by showing that the prisoners were taken on board a particular vessel, with or without a particular design. All that affected that question was, the place where the prisoners were first taken to after they were captured. The only question their honors could consider was, whether, after their apprehension, the prisoners were or were not brought within the District of Virginia, so as to give the Court of Virginia jurisdiction, before they were brought to New York. The fact that Commodore Stringham did, or did not, entertain in his own mind a design to bring the prisoners to New York, was of no relevancy whatever. Their objection was based on the broad ground, that the statute had fixed the only District that was to have jurisdiction of these criminals, namely, the District within which they are first brought. If they were first brought within the District of Virginia, the design which the Commodore might have entertained made no manner of difference, and the fact could not be got rid of by any evidence to show that the design was not to put themselves in that dilemma.

Mr. James T. Brady submitted an argument on the same side. He said that the true test of the correctness of the objection could be ascertained thus: If a man were arrested anywhere on the high seas, supposed to be amenable to the Act of 1790, and was brought into a port of the United States, within a Judicial District of the United States, could he not demand, under the Act of Congress, to be tried in that District? Could the commander of the vessel supersede that Act of Congress, and say he would take the prisoner into the port of New York, or any other port? What answer would that be to a writ of *habeas corpus* sued out by either of these men confined on that ship, within that Judicial District? If any such rule as that could prevail, the Act of Congress would become perfectly nugatory and subservient to the will of the individual who apprehended prisoners on the high seas. If he had started on a cruise round the world, he could carry them with him, and, after returning to the United States, could take them into every District till he came to the one that suited him. Mr. Brady, therefore, claimed that it was wholly immaterial what might have been the design of Commodore Stringham; and that the question of jurisdiction was determined by the physical fact, as to what was the first Judicial District into which these men were brought after being apprehended on the high seas.

Mr. Evarts considered that this was a question rather of regularity of discussion, than a question to be now absolutely determined by the Court. He supposed that they were entitled to lay before the Court all the attendant facts governing the question of, whether the introduction of these criminals from the point of seizure on the high seas was, within the legal sense, made into the District of New York, or into that of Virginia—whether the physical introduction of prisoners, in the course of a voyage toward the port of New York, into the roads at Hampton, is, within the meaning of the law, a bringing them into the District of Virginia. If the substantial qualification of the course of the voyage from the point of seizure to the place of actual debarcation was to affect the act, this was the time for the prosecution to produce that piece of evidence; and he supposed that that important inquiry should be reserved till the termination of the case, when the proof would be all before the Court. He suggested that no large ship could enter the port of New York without physically passing through what might be called the District of New Jersey; and argued that, in no sense of the act, and in no just sense, should these prisoners be tried in New Jersey, because the ship carrying them had passed through her waters.

Mr. Larocque, for the defendants, contended that the arrest of the parties as criminals was at the moment when they were taken from on board the Savannah, placed on board the Perry, and put in irons. The learned gentleman (Mr. Evarts) had said that it would be impossible to bring them within the District of New York without first bringing them within the District of New Jersey; but that objection was met by the fact that, over the waters of the bay of New York, the States of New Jersey and New York exercised concurrent jurisdiction, and therefore they came within the District of New York, to all intents and purposes. He proposed to refer to the authorities on which the point rested.

In this case, the place where the arrest was made was the Perry, a United States cruiser, which, in one sense, was equivalent to a part of the national soil; and he held that the idea under this statute was, that their apprehension and confinement from the moment they were arrested as criminals was complete, without being required to be under legal process, it being sufficient that they were arrested by the constituted authorities of the United States. The moment they were brought within a Judicial District of the United States, that moment the jurisdiction attached; and no jurisdiction could attach anywhere else. This was an offence committed on the high seas. All the Districts of the country could not have concurrent jurisdiction over it; and this very case was an exemplification of the injustice that would result from permitting an officer, in times of high political excitement, to have the privilege, at his mere pleasure or caprice, of selecting the place of jurisdiction, and the place of trial. Suppose these prisoners, instead of being landed at the first place where the vessel touched, could have been taken up the Mississippi river in a boat, and up the Ohio river in another boat, and landed within the District of Ohio, for the purpose of being tried there,—would not their honors' sense of justice and propriety revolt at that? The same injustice would result in a different degree, and under different circumstances, if, after taking these prisoners to Virginia and ascertaining the difficulties in the way of their being tried there, the officer could change their course and bring them into the port of New York. The prisoners were entitled to the benefit of being tried in the District where they were first taken, in preference to any other District; and justice would be more surely done by holding a strict rule on that subject, by requiring that the facts should control, and that no mere intention on the part of the captors should be allowed to govern.

One of the cases on this subject which had produced a misapprehension of the question was that of the United States *vs.* Thompson, 1st Sumner's Reports, which was an indictment for endeavoring to create a revolt, under the Act of 1790. It was in the Massachusetts District. The facts in the case were these:—"The vessel arrived at Stonington, Connecticut, and from thence sailed to New Bedford, Massachusetts, where the defendant was arrested, and committed for trial. It did not appear that he had been in confinement before. Judge Story ruled on the question of jurisdiction. He said: 'The language of the Crimes Act of 1790 (Cap. 36, sec. 8) is, that the trial of crimes committed on the high seas, or in any place out of the jurisdiction of any particular State, shall be in the District in which the offender is apprehended, or into which he shall first be brought. The provision is in the alternative, and therefore the crime is cognizable in either District. And there is wisdom in the provision; for otherwise, if a ship should, by stress of weather, be driven to take shelter temporarily in any port of the Union, however distant from her home port, the master and all the crew, as well as the ship, might be detained, and the trial had far from the port to which she belonged, or to which she was destined. And if the offender should escape into another District, or voluntarily depart from that into which he was first brought, he would, upon an arrest, be necessarily required to be sent back for trial to the latter. And now there is no particular propriety, as to crimes committed on the high seas, in assigning one District rather than another for the place of trial, except what arises from general convenience; and the present alternative provision is well adapted to this purpose.'"

This was noticed, in the first place, in the case of the United States *vs*. Edward C. Townsend, of which he (Mr. Larocque) held in his hand a copy of the exemplification of the record. Townsend was charged, in the District Court of Massachusetts, with piracy, in having been engaged in the slave trade, in 1858. He was captured on board the brig Echo, by a United States cruiser. That vessel first made the port of Key West, putting in there for water; and thence proceeded to Massachusetts, where the prisoner was landed, taken into custody under a warrant of the Commissioner, and the matter brought before the Grand Jury, for the purpose of having an indictment found against him. In that case Judge Sprague charged the Grand Jury that, under the law, the prisoner could only be tried in Key West, because that was the first port which the vessel had made after he had been captured and confined as a prisoner. Under that instruction the Grand Jury refused to find a bill of indictment; and thereupon the District Attorney (Mr. Woodbury) applied to the court for a warrant of removal, to remove him to Key West, for trial; and also to have the witnesses recognized to appear at Key West, to testify on the trial. The counsel read a note from Mr. Woodbury on the subject, showing that Mr. Justice Clifford, of the Supreme Court of the United States, sat and concurred with Judge Sprague in granting the warrant of removal. He referred also to another case, decided by Judge Sprague—the United States *vs*. Bird—volume of Judge Sprague's Decisions, page 299: "This indictment alleged an offence to have been committed on the high seas, and that the prisoner was first brought into the District of Massachusetts. Questions of jurisdiction arose upon the evidence. The counsel for the prisoner contended that the offence, if any, was committed on the Mississippi river, and within the State of Louisiana; and, further, that if committed beyond the limits of that State, the prisoner was not first brought into this District. Sprague, J., said that, if an offence be committed within the United States, it must be tried in the State and District within which it was committed. Constitution Amendment 6, If the offence be committed without the limits of the United States, on the high seas, or in a foreign port, the trial must be had in the District 'where the offender is apprehended, or into which he may be first brought.'—Stat. 1790, cap. 9, sec. 8; Stat. 1825, cap. 65, sec. 14. By being brought within a District, is not meant merely being conveyed thither by the ship on which the offender may first arrive; but the statute contemplates two classes of cases: one, in which the offender shall have been apprehended without the limits of the United States, and brought in custody into some Judicial District; the other, in which he shall not have been so apprehended and brought, but shall have been first taken into legal custody, after his arrival within some District of the United States, and provides in what District each of these classes shall be tried. It does not contemplate that the Government shall have the election in which of two Districts to proceed to trial. It is true that, in United States *vs*. Thompson, 1 Sumner, 168, Judge Story seems to think that a prisoner might be tried either in the District where he is apprehended, or in the District into which he is first brought. But the objection in that case did not call for any careful consideration of the meaning of the word 'brought,' as used in the statute; nor does he discuss the question, whether the accused, having come in his own ship, satisfies that requisition. In that case the party had not been apprehended abroad; and the decision was clearly right, as the first arrest was in the District of Massachusetts. The statute of 1819, cap. 101, sec. 1 (3 U.S. Statutes at Large, 532), for the suppression of the slave trade, is an example of a case in which an offender may be apprehended without the limits of the United States, and sent to the United States for trial. Ex parte Bollman *vs*. Swartwout, 4 Cranch, 136."

Their honors would observe that in both the cases cited, correcting the manifest misapprehension of Judge Story, the point was distinctly held that the question of jurisdiction was controlled exclusively by the fact as to what District the prisoner was first brought into after his arrest on the high seas, out of the United States, for a crime committed on the high seas.

Judge Nelson stated that, as it was now late (half-past 5 P. M.), the question might go over till morning.

The counsel on each side assenting, the Jury were allowed to separate, with a caution from the Court against conversing in respect to the case.

Adjourned to Thursday, at 11 A.M.

SECOND DAY.

Thursday, Oct. 24, 1861.

The Court met at 11 o'clock A.M.

Judge Nelson, in deciding the question raised yesterday, said:

So far as regards the question heretofore under consideration of Judge Sprague, we do not think that at present involved in the case. We will confine ourselves to the decision of the admissibility of the question as it was put by the District Attorney and objected to, as respects the purpose with which the Minnesota, with the prisoners, was sent to Hampton Roads. We think that the fact of their being sent by the commanding officer of that place, with the prisoners, to Hampton Roads, is material and necessary; and, in order to appreciate fully the fact itself, the purpose is a part of the *res gestæ* that characterizes the fact. What effect it may have upon the more general question, involving the jurisdiction of the Court, is not material or necessary now to consider. We think the question is proper.

Counsel for defendants took exception to the ruling of the Court.

Commodore Stringham recalled. Direct examination resumed by Mr. Smith.

Q. What was your object in transferring the prisoners from the Perry to the Minnesota?

A. Sending them to a Northern port. The port of New York was the port I had in my mind. To send them by the first ship from the station, as soon as possible, to a Northern port, for trial. I could not send them to a Southern port for trial. The only way I could do so would be by guns. I could get no landing in those places otherwise; and I could get no judge or jury to give them a trial.

Mr. Larocque asked if, conceding the propriety of the inquiry, the statement of the witness was competent, viz.: that he had a port in his mind.

The Court: No; the question was not put in the shape I supposed. The question should have been—for what purpose or object did he send the prisoners in the Minnesota to Hampton Roads? That is the point in the case—the intent with which the vessel was sent to Hampton Roads?

A. I sent them there with the intention of sending them to a Northern port, for trial. The Harriet Lane being the first vessel that left, after my arrival there, they were sent in the Harriet Lane to the Northern port of New York.

Q. Why did you not take them in the Minnesota directly to New York, instead of taking them to Hampton Roads?

- 85 -

A. My station was at Hampton Roads, and I went there to arrange the squadron that might be there, and to get a supply of fuel for the ship. I do not think we had enough to go to New York, if we wished to go there. I had supplied vessels on the coast below, and had exhausted pretty nearly all the coal from the Minnesota when we arrived at Hampton Roads.

Q. What directions did you give to the officers of the Harriet Lane?

A. I gave no directions to the officers of the Harriet Lane. I gave directions to the commander of the Minnesota. I left on the day previous, I think, to their being transferred to the Harriet Lane,—giving directions that, as soon as she came down from Newport News, to send her to New York, with the prisoners. I had been called to Washington, by the Secretary of the Navy, the day before she sailed.

Q. Are you aware of any facts which rendered it impossible to land the prisoners in the Virginia District, or on the Virginia shore?

A. It was impossible to land without force of arms, and taking possession of any port. We *could* land them there, but not for trial, certainly. The Harriet Lane had been fired into but a short time previous; and that was one cause of sending her to New York.

Q. Fired into from the Virginia shore?

A. Yes, sir; from Field Point; I should judge, about 8 miles from Norfolk port, on the southern shore, nearly opposite Newport News. I was not there, but it was reported to me. She was fired into, and she was ordered to New York to change her armament.

Q. Was that fort in the way, proceeding to Norfolk?

A. Not on the direct way to Hampton Roads, but a little point on the left.

Q. Would a vessel, going the usual way to Norfolk, be in range of the guns that were fired at the Harriet Lane?

A. Not of these; but she would be in the range of four or five forts that it would be necessary to pass in order to land the prisoners at Norfolk.

Q. What was the nearest port to where the Minnesota went with the prisoners?

A. The nearest port of entry was Norfolk. Hampton Roads was a little higher up. We were not anchored exactly at the Roads, but off Old Point, which is not considered Hampton Roads.

[*Map produced.*] I have marked the position of the Minnesota on this map, in blue ink. [Exhibits the position to the Court.]

Q. State the position of the Minnesota?

A. That is as near as I can put it—between the Rip Raps and Fortress Monroe—a little outside of the Rip Raps.

Q. In what jurisdiction is the Fort?

A. In the United States.

(Objected to, as matter of law.)

Q. At what distance were you from Fortress Monroe?

A. About three-quarters of a mile, and nearly the same from the Rip Raps.

Q. What distance from Norfolk?

A. I think 14 miles, as near as I can judge; 12 or 14.

Q. Had you any instructions from the Government, in respect to any prisoners that might be arrested on the high seas, as to the place they were to be taken to?

A. Not previous to my arriving at Hampton Roads. After that, I had. Those instructions were in writing.

Q. You had no particular or general instructions previous to that?

A. No, sir; it was discretionary with me, previous to that, where to send the prisoners I had.

Q. When vessels are sent from one place to another, state whether it is not frequently the case that they take shelter in roadsteads?

(Objected to. Excluded.)

Q. Where did your duties, as flag-officer of the squadron, require you to be with your ship, the Minnesota?

(Objected to. Excluded.)

Q. Where do Hampton Roads commence on this map, and where end?

A. In my experience, I have always considered it higher up than where we were anchored. This is anchoring off Fortress Monroe, when anchoring there. When they go a little higher up, they go to Hampton Roads; and, before the war, small vessels anchored up in Newport News, in a gale of wind.

Q. Where did the Minnesota anchor, in respect to Hampton Roads?

A. We anchored outside, sir. I can only say this from the pilot. When commanding the Ohio, he asked me whether I wished to anchor inside the

Roads. Baltimore pilots have permission to go into Hampton Roads, and no farther. That is considered as neutral ground for all vessels.

By the Court:

Q. What is the width of the entrance to the Hampton Roads?

A. I should judge about 3-1/2 miles, or 3-1/4, from Old Point over to Sewall's Point. I have not measured it accurately. It is from 3 to 4 miles.

By Mr. Smith:

Q. Was the Minnesota brought inside or outside of a line drawn from Old Point to the Rip Raps?

A. A little outside of the line, sir.

By a Juror:

Q. Would a person be subject to any port-charges where the Minnesota lay?

A. No, sir.

Defendants' counsel objected to the question and answer.

The Court:

Q. What do you mean by port dues?

A. I mean they do not have to enter into the custom-house to pay port-charges. It is not a port of entry, that compels them to carry their papers. The only port-charges I know of are the pilot-charges, in and out.

(The Court ruled it out as immaterial.)

Cross-examined by Mr. Brady.

Q. I want, for the purpose of preventing any misapprehension, to ask if there is any line that you know of, which you could draw upon that map, distinguishing the place at which Hampton Roads begins?

A. Nothing only among sea-faring men;—just as the lower bay of New York, which is considered to be down below the Southwest Spit. When anchored between this and that, it is called off a particular place, as Coney Island, &c. So, there, after you pass up from Fortress Monroe, it is called Hampton Roads.

Q. Is there any specific point you can draw a line from on the map that distinctly indicates where Hampton Roads begin? *A.* I cannot, sir.

Q. Designate where the Harriet Lane was?

A. I cannot say, sir. She was at Newport News when I left, and came down the next day, I believe, and took the prisoners on board and proceeded to New York.

Q. The Minnesota was anchored?

A. Yes, sir, but not moored; with a single anchor.

Q. How much cable was out?

A. From 65 to 70 fathoms, I think. I generally order 65 fathoms; but the captain gave her 5 fathoms more.

Q. Would she swing far enough to affect the question whether she was in or outside of Hampton Roads, as you understood it?

A. No, sir.

Q. Had you often been there before?

A. I had, sir, often. I was there 51 years ago. I started there.

Q. Did you ever have occasion, for any practical purposes, to locate where Hampton Roads began?

A. Yes, sir; several times I have anchored there with ships under my command, and the pilots have said, "Will you go up into the Roads?" and I said, "Yes;" and we never anchored within two or three miles of where we lay with the Minnesota.

Q. But it was not your object to get at any particular line which separated Hampton Roads?

A. No; we considered it a better anchorage. The only importance was a better anchorage.

Q. You had no instructions of any kind in regard to the prisoners before you left for Washington?

A. I would say I had not, before I arrived at Hampton Roads, or at Old Point.

Q. Did you receive any between the time of your arrival and your departure for Washington?

A. I cannot say, but I think not.

Q. The only instructions you gave were that, when the Harriet Lane came up, the prisoners should be removed, and sent to New York?

A. I gave orders that they should be sent to New York and delivered to the Marshal.

Q. There would be no difficulty to transfer prisoners to Fortress Monroe?

A. No, sir, no difficulty.

Q. Could they not have been taken to Hampton?

A. I think not. Our troops had abandoned Hampton and moved in, I think. There was nothing there to land at Hampton. We may have had possession at that time.

Q. Do you know of any obstacle whatever to these men having been taken ashore at Old Point Comfort and carried to Hampton?

A. I went up twice to Washington, with Colonel Baker, when he abandoned Hampton; but I think at the time the prisoners were on board we had the occupation of Hampton by our troops. My impression is, we occupied it partly with our troops at that time. I went to Washington at another time, when the troops had abandoned Hampton, and Colonel Baker took his soldiers up in the same boat.

Q. A college has been described on shore, and the locality described. Was it not occupied as an hospital?

A. Yes, sir, at the time the Minnesota arrived. It is not in Hampton.

Q. When the Minnesota arrived with the prisoners was not that building in possession of our Government?

A. It was, sir, I believe. I was not in it.

By Mr. Evarts: Is not the hospital at Old Point?

A. Near Old Point.

By Mr. Brady: Designate on the chart where it is?

A. I have done so,—the square mark, on the shore, in the rear of the fort, on the Virginia shore.

By the Court: How much of a town is Hampton?

A. There is none of it left now. I suppose it was a town of 4,000 or 5,000 inhabitants.

Q. Was it not formerly a port of entry?

A. No, sir, I believe not; not that I know of. That was 4 or 5 miles off from the vessel.

By Mr. Brady: How far was Hampton from Fortress Monroe?

A. I should judge 3 miles.

Q. I ask again, before you left the Minnesota, after the arrival of the prisoners, had you any instructions from Washington in regard to these prisoners?

A. I cannot bring to my mind whether I had any or not. I had instructions, subsequent to my arrival, about all prisoners, and that was the reason why I came here. There was some question as to why I came with 700 prisoners; but I had instructions to bring all prisoners taken, and turn them over to Colonel Burke, of New York.

Q. After you arrived at Washington did you receive any instructions in regard to these prisoners?

A. I do not know that I did. I had some discussion in Washington.

Q. Did you communicate from Washington, in any way, to Fortress Monroe, or the Minnesota, in regard to the prisoners? *A.* No, sir.

Q. They went forward under the directions you gave before leaving to go to Washington?

A. They did, sir; I gave the instructions. I did not know whether the Harriet Lane would be ready. She was waiting until the vessel arrived to relieve her from the station.

Q. Was General Butler at Fortress Monroe at the time of the arrival of the prisoners?

A. He was, sir.

Q. Did you confer with him about it?

A. No, sir.

Q. Neither then nor at Washington?

A. No, sir.

Q. Was there any conversation between you and him in regard to that?

A. I do not think there was until after my return and the prisoners had gone to New York.

Re-direct.

Q. How large a space is occupied by the hospital to which you have referred?

A. I cannot give the number of feet, but I think about 150 feet square. I never was in it but once, when I passed in for a moment, and right out of the hall.

David C. Constable called by the prosecution and sworn.

Examined by Mr. Smith.

Q. You are a Lieutenant in the United States Navy?

A. Not now; I am First Lieutenant of the *Harriet Lane*. We were then serving under the Navy; I am now in a revenue cutter.

Q. Were you on board the Harriet Lane when she received the prisoners from the Minnesota?

A. I was, sir.

Q. Who did you receive your orders from on the subject?

A. Captain Van Brunt, of the Minnesota.

Q. Was that a verbal order?

A. No; a written one, sir.

Q. Was it an order to bring the prisoners to New York?

A. To proceed with the prisoners to New York, and deliver them to the civil authorities, I think.

Q. Where was the Harriet Lane, in respect to the Rip Raps and fort at Old Point Comfort, when the prisoners were taken on board from the Minnesota?

A. We were about half a mile, I should judge, from the Minnesota; a little nearer in shore.

Q. Where had the Harriet Lane come from?

A. From Newport News.

Q. Did she, or not, come from Newport News in pursuance of the object to go to New York?

A. Yes, sir; although at the time we had received no orders in regard to any prisoners. We were coming on for a change of armament and for repairs.

Q. The Harriet Lane had been fired into?

A. She had, sir.

Q. Where was she when fired into?

(Objected to. Offered to show the impossibility of landing. Ruled out as immaterial.)

Q. How was the transfer made from the Minnesota to the Harriet Lane?

A. By boats.

Q. Show on this map where the Harriet Lane was when the transfer was made of the prisoners from the Minnesota, and also where the Minnesota lay?

[Witness marked the place on map.]

Q. State the relative position of the vessels as you have marked it?

A. I should judge we were about a mile from Old Point, in about eleven fathoms of water, and probably about a mile from the Rip Raps. I do not remember exactly.

Q. The Harriet Lane was about half a mile further up?

A. Yes, a little west of the Minnesota, but farther in shore.

Q. What is your understanding in respect to where Hampton Roads commence, in reference to the position of these vessels?

A. I had always supposed it was inside of Old Point and the Rip Raps, after passing through them,—taking Old Point as the Northern extremity, and out to Sewall's Point.

Q. How in respect to where the Harriet Lane lay?

A. I consider she was off Old Point, and not, properly speaking, in Hampton Roads.

Q. The Minnesota was still further out?

A. Yes, sir, a very little.

Q. You brought the prisoners to New York in the Harriet Lane and delivered them to the United States Marshal at New York?

A. Yes, sir.

Q. You delivered them from your vessel to the United States Marshal?

A. Yes, sir; the United States Marshal came alongside our ship, while in the Navy Yard, in a tug, and they were delivered to him.

Q. Do you remember the day they arrived at New York?

A. On the 25th of June, in the afternoon.

Q. In what service was the Harriet Lane?

A. In the naval service of the United States.

Cross-examined by Mr. Brady.

Q. As has already been stated, there was no difficulty about landing the prisoners from the Minnesota at Fortress Monroe, or at the College Hospital, or at Hampton. Was there any difficulty in taking them to Newport News?

A. No, sir; I suppose they might have been taken to Newport News.

Q. Who was in possession of Newport News at that time?

A. The United States troops, sir. Our vessel had been stationed there for six weeks preceding.

Re-direct.

Q. What occupation had the United States of Fortress Monroe, and of this hospital building, and of Newport News? Was it other than a military possession?

(Objected to by defendants' counsel.)

The Court: It is not relevant.

Mr. Evarts: We know there was no physical difficulty in landing them; we want to know whether there was any other.

The Court: We need not go into any other. Practically, they could have been landed there. That is all about it. As to being a military fort, and under military authority, that is not of consequence.

Mr. Evarts: As to military forts receiving prisoners at all times?

The Court: We do not care about that. It is not important to go into that. We know it is a military fort, altogether under military officers. Civil justice is not administered there, I take it.

Daniel T. Tompkins called by the Government; sworn.

Examined by Mr. Smith.

Q. You were Second Lieutenant on the Harriet Lane?

A. I was, sir.

Q. You were present at the transfer of these prisoners from the Minnesota to the Harriet Lane?

A. Yes, sir.

Q. You were with them to New York?

A. Yes; but I was ashore when they were delivered here.

Q. You accompanied the prisoners on the voyage?

A. Yes, sir.

Q. Where did the Harriet Lane lie at Hampton Roads, in relation to the Fort and Rip Raps?

A. I should think we were about a mile from the Rip Raps, and probably three-fourths of a mile from the Fort.

Q. At the time of the transhipment?

A. Yes, sir.

Q. The transhipment was made in boats?

A. Yes, sir,—in a boat from the Minnesota. I believe all came in one boat.

Q. Where do Hampton Roads commence, as you understand, in respect to where the Harriet Lane was?

A. I think they commence astern of where we lay; a little to the westward, as we were lying off of Old Point.

Q. Look upon that map and indicate, by a pencil, where the vessels lay, without any reference to the marks already made there—in the first place the Minnesota and then the Harriet Lane—when the transhipment was made, taken in relation to the Fort and the Rip Raps?

Witness marks the positions, and adds: We were about half a mile from the Minnesota, I should say.

J. Buchanan Henry called by the prosecution; sworn. Examined by Mr. Smith.

Q. In June and July last you were United States Commissioner? *A.* From the 15th of June.

Q. [Producing warrant.] Is that your signature?

A. It is.

Counsel for prosecution reads warrant, issued by J. Buchanan Henry, in the name of the President, addressed to the Marshal, dated June 26, 1861.

(Objected to as irrelevant. Objection overruled.)

Q. This warrant was issued by you?

A. It was, sir.

Q. On an affidavit filed with you?

A. Yes, sir.

Cross-examined.

Q. Against all these prisoners?

A. Yes, sir.

Defendants take exception to the admission of the testimony.

The U.S. District Attorney was about to call the Marshal, to prove that he arrested the prisoners.

Defendants' counsel admitted the prisoners were arrested, under this warrant, by the Marshal, in this district.

Mr. Brady: Perhaps you can state, Mr. Smith, where they were when arrested under that warrant?

Mr. Smith: They had been brought to the Marshal's office, I think.

Mr. Brady: They were in the Marshal's office when arrested?

Mr. Smith: They were brought to the Marshal's office before the writ was served.

Ethan Allen called by the prosecution; sworn. Examined by Mr. Smith.

Q. You are Assistant District Attorney?

A. I am, sir.

Q. And were in June last?

A. Yes, sir.

Q. Do you remember, at my request, calling upon the prisoners now in Court?

A. I do, sir.

Q. Did you call upon every one?

A. I called upon all the prisoners at the Tombs.

Q. Upon each one separately?

A. I called upon them in the different cells. They were confined two by two.

Q. Had you previously attended, as Assistant District Attorney, upon the examination of these prisoners?

A. I had, upon one or two occasions.

Q. Were the prisoners all present on those occasions?

A. They were present once, I distinctly recollect.

Q. Did you then talk with them?

A. No, sir; I addressed myself to the Commissioner in adjourning the case.

Q. Was there any examination proceeded with?

A. There was no examination.

Q. State what you said to the prisoners, the object of your calling, and what their reply was. I ask, first, did you make a memorandum at the time?

A. I did, sir.

Q. Was it made at the very time you asked the questions?

A. I took paper and pencil in hand, and asked the questions which you requested, and took a note of it.

Q. What was the object of your calling upon them?

A. To ask them where they were born; and, if born elsewhere, were they naturalized.

Q. Did you state for what purpose you made this inquiry?

A. I do not recollect that I made any statement to the prisoners for what purpose I wanted the information. I told them I wanted it. They seemed to recognize me as Assistant District Attorney; and as to those that did not recognize me, I told them I was Assistant District Attorney. The memorandum produced is the one I made at the time.

Q. Referring to that, give the statements that were made by each of the prisoners in reply to your questions?

A. Henry Cashman Howard said he was born in Beaufort, North Carolina.

Charles Sydney Passalaigue said he was born in Charleston, South Carolina.

Joseph Cruse del Carno said he was born in Manilla, in the Chinese Seas, and was never naturalized.

Thomas Harrison Baker said he was born in Philadelphia.

John Harleston said he was born in Anderson District, or County, in South Carolina.

Patrick Daly was born in Belfast, Ireland. Has never been naturalized.

William C. Clarke born in Hamburg, Germany. Never naturalized.

Henry Oman born in Canton. Never was naturalized.

Martin Galvin born in the County Clare, Ireland. Not naturalized.

Richard Palmer born in Edinburgh. Never naturalized.

Alexander C. Coid was born in Galloway, Scotland. Was naturalized in Charleston,—about 1854 or 1855, he thinks.

John Murphy born in Ireland. Never naturalized.

Mr. Brady: We will insist, hereafter, that this admission of naturalization cannot be used at all.

Mr. Evarts: We will concede that.

By Mr. Smith: Do you remember asking the prisoners for their full names?

A. I asked them particularly for their full names.

Q. Are they correctly stated in the indictment?

A. They are stated from the memorandum which I then took; that is my only means of recollection.

Mr. Smith: The Assistant District Attorney desires me to state that he did not know that he was to be called as a witness in the case; that if he had had any idea that he would be called as a witness, he would not have made the visit. Yesterday, for the first time, he ascertained that he would be called. I would also state that I did not send him there for the purpose of making him a witness, but with the object of obtaining particulars which might render the allegations in the indictment entirely accurate in respect to every detail.

Mr. Smith added: I now close the case for the prosecution.

OPENING FOR THE DEFENCE.

Mr. LAROCQUE opened the case for the defence. He said:

May it please the Court, and you, Gentlemen of the Jury:

We have now reached that stage in this interesting trial where the duty has been assigned to me, by my associates in this defence, of presenting to you the state of facts and the rules of law on which we expect to ask from you an acquittal of these prisoners. I could wish that it had been assigned to some one more able to present it to you than myself, for I feel the weight of this case pressing upon me, from various considerations connected with it, in a manner almost overpowering. I think that we have proceeded far enough in this case for you to have perceived that it is one of the most interesting trials that ever took place on the continent of America, if not in the civilized world.

For the first time, certainly in this controversy, twelve men are put on trial for their lives, before twelve other men, as pirates and—as has been well expressed to you by the learned District Attorney who opened this case on behalf of the prosecution—as enemies of the human race. If you have had time, in the exciting progress of this trial, to reflect in your own minds as to what the import of these words was, it must certainly, ere this, have occurred to you that, in regard to these prisoners, whatever may be the legal consequences of the acts charged upon them, it was a misapplication of the term. Look for a moment, gentlemen, first, at the position of things in our country under which this trial takes place. All these prisoners come before you from a far distant section of the country. Some of them were not born there—some of them were. At the time when these events occurred all of the prisoners lived there, and were identified with that country, with its welfare, with its Government, whatever it was. They had there their homes, their families, everything which attaches a man to the spot in which he lives. Those of them who had not been born in America had sought it as an asylum. They had come from distant regions of the earth—some from the Chinese Sea and the remote East—because they had been taught there that America was the freest land on the globe. They had lived there for years. Suddenly they had seen the country convulsed from one end to the other. They had seen hostile armies arrayed against each other, the combatants being for the most part divided by geographical lines as to the place where they were born or as to the State in which they lived. This very morning a newspaper in the city of New York estimates the numbers thus arrayed in hostility against each other at no less than seven hundred thousand souls. These prisoners have the misfortune, as I say, of being placed on their trial far from their homes. They have been now in confinement and under arrest on this charge for some four or five months. During that whole period they have had no opportunity whatever of communicating with their friends or relatives. Intercourse has been cut off. They have had no opportunity of procuring means to meet their necessary expenses, or even to fee counsel in their defence. Without the solace of the company of their families, immured in a prison among those who, unfortunately, from friends and fellow-countrymen have become enemies, they are now placed in this Court on trial for their lives. You will certainly reflect, gentlemen, that it was not for a case of this kind that any statute punishing the crime of piracy was ever intended to be enacted. You will reflect, when you come to consider this case, after the evidence shall have been laid before you, and after you have received instructions from the Court, that however by technical construction our ingenious friends on the other side may endeavor to force on your minds the conviction that this was a case intended to be provided for by statutes passed in the year 1790, and by statutes passed in the year 1820,—it is a monstrous stretch of the provisions of those statutes to ask for a conviction in a case of this kind. And I may be permitted, with very great respect for the constitutional authorities of our Government, to which we all owe our allegiance and respect, to wonder that this case has been brought for trial before you. I cannot help, under the circumstances surrounding these trials—for while you are sitting here, another jury is passing on a similar case in the neighboring City of Philadelphia—attributing the determination of the Government to submit these cases to the judicial tribunals at this time to a desire to satisfy the mind of the community itself, which has been naturally excited on this subject, that these men are not pirates within the meaning of the law. And I do most sincerely hope, for the credit of our Government, that that is the object which it has in view, and that the heart of every officer of the Government, at Washington or elsewhere, will be most rejoiced at the verdict of acquittal, which, I trust, on every consideration, you will pronounce. We all know that in a time of civil commotion and civil war like this, the minds of the people, particularly at the incipient stages of the controversy, become terribly excited and aroused. We could not listen, at the outbreak of these commotions, to any other name but that of pirate or traitor, as connected with those arrayed against our Government and countrymen. One of the misfortunes of a time of popular excitement like this is, that it pervades not only the minds of the community, but reaches the public halls of legislation, and the executive and administrative departments of the Government. And it is no disrespect, even to the Chief Magistrate of the country to say, that he might, in a time like this, put forward proclamations and announce a determination to do what his more sober judgment would tell him it was imprudent to announce his intention of doing. You will all probably recollect that when this outbreak occurred the Government at Washington announced the determination of treating those who might be captured on board of privateers fitted out in the Confederate States as pirates. Such an announcement once made, it is difficult to depart from. And therefore I do most sincerely hope that the administration in Washington, as my heart tells me must be the case, are looking at these trials in progress here and in Philadelphia, with an earnest desire that the voice of the Juries shall be the voice of acquittal,—thus disembarrassing the Government of the trammels of a proclamation which it were better, perhaps, had never been issued. This civil war had at that time reached no such proportions as those which it has since acquired. It was then a mere beginning of a revolution. The cry was, that Washington was in danger. There were no hostile forces arrayed on the opposite sides of the Potomac. There was a fear that they would soon make their appearance; and there was also an earnest hope—which I lament most deeply has not been realized—that that outbreak would be stopped in its commencement, and that no armies approaching to the proportions of those which have since been in hostile conflict would be arrayed on the field of battle. Look at the state of things now. Scarcely a day elapses on which battles are not taking place, from one end to the other of this broad continent—in Virginia, Kentucky, Missouri, and other States—and where the opposing forces are not larger than those that met in any battle of the Revolution which gave this country its independence. Does humanity, which rules war as well as peace, permit that while whole States, forming almost one half of the Confederacy; have arrayed themselves as one man—for aught we know to the contrary—while they think, no matter how mistakenly, that they have grievances to be redressed, and that they have a right to exercise that privilege of electing their own Government, which we claimed for ourselves in the day of our own Revolution—does humanity, I say, permit, in such a state of things, one side or the other to treat its opponents as pirates and robbers, as enemies of the human race? Gentlemen, our brave men who are fighting our battles on land and sea have a deep interest in this question; and if the votes of our whole army could be taken on the question of whether, as a matter of State policy, these men should be treated as pirates and robbers, I believe, in my heart, that an almost unanimous vote would go up from its ranks not to permit such a state of things to take place.

I wish to say a word here, gentlemen, preliminarily, on another subject, and that is, what the duty and right of counsel is on a trial of this kind. I hold the doctrine that counsel, when he appears in Court to defend the life of one man, much less the lives of twelve men, is the *alter ego* of his clients—that he has no trammels on his lips, and that his conscience, and his duty to God, and to his profession, must direct him in his best efforts to save the lives of his clients,—and that it becomes his duty; regardless of all other considerations, except adherence to truth and the laws of rectitude, to present every argument for his clients which influenced their minds when they embarked in the enterprise for which they are placed before the Jury on trial for their lives. It is not the fault of counsel, in a case of this kind, if he is obliged to call the attention of the Jury to the past history of his own country, to the cotemporaneous expositions of its Constitution, to the decisions of its Courts of Judicature, and of the highest Court of the Union, which have laid down doctrines with reference to the Constitution of the Government, which are accepted at the present day, entirely incompatible with the success of this prosecution. In doing so, you will certainly perceive that, however much these men on trial for their lives may have been deceived and deluded, as I sincerely think they have been to a very great extent, and, as was frankly admitted by the learned counsel who opened the case for the prosecution, that at least, there was the strongest excuse for that deception and delusion among those of them who had read the Constitution of their Government, who had read its Declaration of Independence, who had read the cotemporaneous exposition of its Constitution, put forward by the wisest of the men who framed it, and on the honeyed accents of whose lips the plain citizens of the States reposed when they adopted the Constitution. If it had been their good fortune to be familiar with the decisions of its Courts, they had learned what the Supreme Court had said with reference to the sovereign rights of the States, and with reference to the strict limit and measure of power which they had conceded to the General Government, and there was, at least, a very strong excuse for their following those doctrines, however unpopular they may have become in a later day of the Republic.

One of the reasons why I most regret that the Government has thought fit to force these cases to trial at the present time is, that it forces the counsel for the prisoners, in the solemn discharge of their duty to their clients, whose lives hang in the balance, to call the attention of the Jury and the attention of the public to those doctrines, doing which, under other circumstances, might be considered as a needless interference with the efforts of the Government to restore peace to the country. But, as I say, I hold that our clients in this case have a right to all the resources of intelligence with which it has pleased God to bless their counsel. They have a right to every pulsation of their hearts, and I do not know that I can sum up the whole subject in more appropriate language than that used by the Marquis of Beccaria, which was quoted by John Adams on the trial of some British soldiers in Boston, who, in a time of great public excitement, had shot some citizens, and were placed on trial for their lives before a Jury in Boston. He quoted and adopted on that occasion, as his own, these memorable words of that great philanthropist: "If I can be but the instrument of saving one human life, his blessing and tears of gratitude will be a sufficient consolation to me for the contempt of all mankind." I hold, with John Adams, that counsel on a trial like this has no right to let any earthly consideration interfere with the full and free discharge of his duty to his client; and in what I have to say, and in my course on this trial, I will be actuated by that feeling, and by none other. And, gentlemen, I love my country when I say that; I feel as deep a stake in her prosperity as does any man within the hearing of my voice, and as deep a stake as any man who lives under the protection of her flag.

The Jury have a great and solemn duty to discharge on this occasion. They have the great and solemn duty to discharge of forgetting, if possible, that they are Americans, and of thinking, for the moment, that they have been transformed into subjects of other lands; of forgetting that there is a North or a South, an East or a West, and of remembering only that these twelve men are in peril of their lives, and that this Jury is to judge whether they have feloniously and piratically, with a criminal intent, done the act for which it is claimed their lives are forfeited to their country. I wish to dispel from the minds of the Jury, at the outset of this case, an illusion which has been attempted to be produced on them, with no improper motive, I am sure, by the counsel who opened the case on the part of the Government—that this trial is a mere matter of form. I tell you, gentlemen, that it is a trial involving the lives of twelve men, and this Jury are bound to assume, from the beginning to the end of the case, that if their verdict shall pronounce these men guilty of the crime of piracy, with which they are charged, every one of them will as surely terminate his life on the scaffold, as the sun will rise on the morrow of the day on which the verdict shall be pronounced. We have nothing to do with what the Government in its justice and clemency may see fit to do after that verdict has been pronounced. We are bound to believe that the Government does not put these men upon their trial with an intention to make the verdict, if it shall be one of guilty, a mere idle mockery. I, for one, while I love my country, and wish its Government to enjoy the respect of the whole world, would not be willing to believe that it would perform a solemn farce of that kind; and, gentlemen, as you value the peace and repose of your own consciences, you will, in the progress of this trial, from its beginning to its end, look on it in this light, and in none other.

Now, gentlemen, what is the crime of piracy, as we have all been taught to understand it from our cradle? My learned friend has given one definition of what a pirate is, by saying that he is the enemy of the human race. And how does his crime commence? Is it blazoned, before he starts on his wicked career, in the full light of the sun, or is it hatched in secret? Does it commence openly and frankly, with the eyes of his fellow-citizens looking on from the time that the design is conceived, or does it originate in the dark forecastle of some vessel on the seas, manned by wicked men, to whom murder and robbery have been familiar from their earliest days, and who usually commence by murdering the crew of the vessel, the safety of which has been partly entrusted to them? And when the first deed of wickedness has been done which makes pirates and outcasts of the men who perpetrated it, what is their career from that moment to the time when they end their lives, probably on the scaffold? Is it not one of utter disregard to the laws of God and man, and to those of humanity? Is it not a succession of deeds of cruelty, of rapine, of pillage, of wanton destruction? Who ever heard of pirates who, in the first place, commenced the execution of their design by public placards posted in the streets of a populous city like Charleston, approved of by their fellow-citizens of a great and populous city, and not only by them, but by the people of ten great and populous States? And who ever heard of pirates who, coming upon a vessel that was within the limits of the commission under which they were acting, took her as a prize, with an apology to her Captain for the necessity of depriving him of his property, and claiming to act under the authority of ten great and populous States, and under that authority alone? And who ever heard of pirates doing what has been testified to in this case by the witnesses for the Government,—taking one ship because she belonged to the enemies of the Confederate States, to which they sincerely believed they owed the duty of allegiance, and passing immediately under the stern of another vessel, because they knew by her build and appearance that she was a British vessel, and not an enemy of their country, as they believed?

But, gentlemen, the difficulties with which the prosecution had to contend, in making out this case, are too great to be lost sight of; and the Jury must certainly have seen how utterly preposterous it is to characterize as piracy acts of this kind. Who ever heard of a pirate who, having seized a prize, put a prize-crew on board of her, sent her home to his native port—a great and civilized city, in a great and populous country—to be submitted to the adjudication of the Courts in that city, and to be disposed of as the authorities of his home should direct? I beg to call your attention to the facts that have been brought out on the testimony for the prosecution itself—that, in regard to this vessel, instead of her crew having been murdered—instead of helpless women and children having been sent to a watery grave, after having suffered, perhaps, still greater indignities—that not a hair of the head of any one was touched,—that not a man suffered a wound or an indignity of any kind—that they were sent, as prisoners of war, into the neighboring port of Georgetown, where, in due time, by decree of a court, the vessel was condemned and sold—and the prisoners, having been kept in confinement some time as prisoners of war, were released, and have been enabled to come into Court and testify before you.

Comparing this case, gentlemen, with the cases which are constantly occurring in the land, what earthly motive can you conceive, on the part of the Government, for having made the distinction between these poor prisoners, taken on board of this paltry little vessel of 40 or 50 tons, and the great bands in arms in all parts of the country? Look what occurred a little while ago in Western Virginia, where a large force of men, in open arms against the Government, who had been carrying ravage and destruction through that populous country, and over all parts of it, were captured as prisoners. Were any of those men sent before a court, to be tried for their lives? Did not the commanding officer of the forces there, acting under the authorization, and with the approval, of the Government, release every one of those men, on his parole of honor not to bear arms any more against the country? And what earthly motive can be conceived for making the distinction which is attempted to be made between these men and those? Shall it be said, to the disgrace of our country—for it would be a disgrace if it could be justly said—that we had not courage and confidence enough in our own resources to believe that we would be able to cope with these adversaries in the field in fair and equal warfare? Gentlemen, I think it would be a cowardly act, which would redound to the lasting disgrace of the country, to have it said, one century or two centuries hence, that, in this great time of our country's troubles and trials, eighteen States of this Confederacy, infinitely the most populous, infinitely the most wealthy, abounding in resources, with a powerful army and navy, were obliged to resort to the halter or the ax for the purpose of intimidating those who were in arms against them. I do not think that any one of this Jury would be willing to have such a thing said.

Now, gentlemen, with regard to the conduct of these men, an impression has been attempted to be created on your minds by one circumstance, and that is, that at the time of the capture of the Joseph by the Savannah the American flag was hoisted on board the Savannah, and that the Joseph came down to her, and permitted her to approach from the false security and confidence occasioned by that circumstance. The time has now arrived to dispel the illusion from your mind that there was anything reprehensible in that, or anything in it not warranted by the strictest rules of honor and of naval warfare. Why, gentlemen, I could not give you a more complete parallel on that subject than one which occurred at the time of the chase of the Constitution by a British fleet of men-of-war, and the escape of the Constitution from which fleet at that time reflected such lasting honor on our country and her naval history. You will all recollect that the Constitution, near the coast of our country, fell in with and was chased for several days by a large British fleet. Let me read to you one short sentence, showing what occurred at that time. I read from Cooper's Naval History:

"The scene, on the morning of this day, was very beautiful, and of great interest to the lovers of nautical exhibitions. The weather was mild and lovely, the sea smooth as a pond, and there was quite wind enough to remove the necessity of any of the extraordinary means of getting ahead that had been so freely used during the previous eight and forty hours. All the English vessels had got on the same tack with the Constitution again, and the five frigates were clouds of canvas, from their trucks to the water. Including the American ship, eleven sail were in sight; and shortly after a twelfth appeared to windward; that was soon ascertained to be an American merchantman. But the enemy were too intent on the Constitution to regard anything else, and though it would have been easy to capture the ships to leeward, no attention appears to have been paid to them. *With a view, however, to deceive the ship to windward, they hoisted American colors, when the Constitution set an English ensign, by way of warning the stranger to keep aloof.*"

After that, I hope we will hear no more about the Savannah having hoisted the American flag for the purpose of inducing the Joseph to approach her.

It now becomes my duty, gentlemen, to call your attention, very briefly, to the grounds on which the prosecution rests this case. There are two grounds, and I will notice them in their order. The first is, that this was robbery. Well,

I have had occasion, already, in what I have said to you, to call your attention to some of the points that distinguish this case from robbery. I say it was not robbery, because, in the first place, one of the requisites of robbery on the sea, which is called piracy, is, that it shall be done with a piratical and felonious intent. The intent is what gives character to the crime; and the point that we shall make on that part of the case is this, that if these men, in the capture of the Joseph (leaving out of view for the present the circumstance of their having acted under a commission from the Confederate States), acted under the belief that they had a right to take her, there was not the piratical and felonious intent, and the crime of robbery was not committed. I will very briefly call your attention to a few authorities on that subject. One of the most standard English works, and the most universally referred to on this subject of robberies, is *Hale's Pleas of the Crown*. Hale says:

"As it is *cepit* and *asportavit* so it must be *felonice* or *animo furandi*, otherwise it is not felony, for it is the mind that makes the taking of another's goods to be a felony, or a bare trespass only; but because the intention and mind are secret, they must be judged by the circumstances of the fact, and though these circumstances are various and may sometimes deceive, yet regularly and ordinarily these circumstances following direct in this case.

"If *A*, thinking he hath a title to the horse of *B*, seizeth it as his own, or supposing that *B* holds of him, distrains the horse of *B* without cause, this regularly makes it no felony, but a trespass, because there is a pretence of title; but yet this may be but a trick to color a felony, and the ordinary discovery of a felonious intent is, if the party does it secretly, or being charged with the goods, denies it. * * * * *

"But in cases of larceny, the variety of circumstances is so great, and the complications thereof so weighty, that it is impossible to prescribe all the circumstances evidencing a felonious intent; on the contrary, the same must be left to the due and attentive consideration of the Judge and Jury, wherein the best rule is, *in dubiis*, rather to incline to acquittal than conviction."

The next authority on that subject to which I will refer you is *2d East's Pleas of the Crown, p.* 649. The passage is:

"And here it may be proper to remark, that in any case, if there be *any fair pretence* of property or *right* in the prisoner, *or if it be brought into doubt at all, the court will direct an acquittal; for it is not fit that such disputes should be settled in a manner to bring men's lives into jeopardy.*

"The owner of ground takes a horse *damage feasant*, or a lord seizes it as an estray, though perhaps without title; yet these circumstances explain the intent, and show that it was not felonious, unless some act be done which manifests the contrary: as giving the horse new marks to disguise him, or altering the old ones; for these are presumptive circumstances of a thievish intent."

I call attention also to the case of *Rex* vs. *Hall, 3d Carrington & Payne*, 409, which was a case before one of the Barons of the Exchequer in England. It was an indictment for robbing John Green, a gamekeeper of Lord Ducie, of three hare-wires and a pheasant. It appeared that the prisoner had set three hare-wires in a field belonging to Lord Ducie, in one of which this pheasant was caught; and that Green, the gamekeeper, seeing this, took up the wires and pheasant, and put them into his pocket; and it further appeared that the prisoner, soon after this, came up and said, "Have you got my wires?" The gamekeeper replied that he had, and a pheasant that was caught in one of them. The prisoner asked the gamekeeper to give the pheasant and wires up to him, which the gamekeeper refused; whereupon the prisoner lifted up a large stick, and threatened to beat the gamekeeper's brains out if he did not give them up. The gamekeeper, fearing violence, did so.

Maclean, for the prosecution, contended—

"That, by law, the prisoner could have no property in either the wires or the pheasant; and as the gamekeeper had seized them for the use of the Lord of the Manor, under the statute 5 Ann, c. 14, s. 4, it was a robbery to take them from him by violence."

Vaughan, B., said:

"I shall leave it to the Jury to say whether the prisoner acted on an impression that the wires and pheasant were his property, for, however he might be liable to penalties for having them in his possession, yet, if the Jury think that he took them under a *bona fide* impression that he was only getting back the possession of his own property, there is no *animus furandi*, and I am of opinion that the prosecution must fail.

"Verdict—Not guilty."

Without detaining the Court and Jury to read other cases, I will simply give your honors a reference to them. I refer to the *King* vs. *Knight*, cited in 2d

East's Pleas of the Crown, p. 510, decided by Justices *Gould* and *Buller*, the case of the *Queen* vs. *Boden*, 1*st Carrington and Kirwan*, p. 395; and for the purpose of showing that this is the same rule which has been applied by the Courts of the United States, in these very cases of piracy, I need do nothing more than read a few lines from a case cited by the counsel for the prosecution in opening the case of the *United States* vs. *Tully*, 1*st Gallison's Circuit Court Reports*, 247, where Justices Story and Davis say, that to constitute the offence of piracy, within the Act of 30th April, 1790, by "piratically and feloniously" running away with a vessel, "the act must have been done with the wrongful and fraudulent intent thereby to convert the same to the taker's own use, and to make the same his own property, against the will of the owner. The intent must be *animo furandi*."

Now, gentlemen, I think that when you come to consider this case in your jury-box, whatever other difficulties you may have, you will very speedily come to the conclusion that the taking of the Joseph was with no intent of stealing on the part of these prisoners.

But, gentlemen, there is another requisite to the crime of robbery, which, I contend, and shall respectfully attempt to show to you, is absent from this case. I mean, it must be by violence, or putting him in fear that the property is taken from the owner, and that the crime of robbery is committed. I beg to refer the Court to the definition of robbery in *1st Blackstone's Commentaries*, p. 242, and *1st Hawkins' Pleas of the Crown*, p. 233, where robbery at common law is defined to be "open and violent *larceny*, the rapina of the civil law, the *felonious* and *forcible* taking from the person of another of goods or money to any value by violence, or putting him in fear."

Now, gentlemen, I say there was nothing of that kind in this case. What are the circumstances as testified to by the witnesses for the prosecution? The circumstances are, that the Joseph and the Savannah, having approached within hailing distance, the Captain of the Savannah hailed the Captain of the Joseph, standing on the deck of his own vessel, and requested him to come on board and bring his papers. The answer of the Captain of the Joseph was an inquiry by what authority that direction was given; and the Captain of the Savannah replied, "by the authority of the Confederate States." Whereupon the Captain of the Joseph, in his own boat, with two of his crew, went alongside the Savannah, was helped over the side by the Captain of the Savannah, and was informed by him that he was under the disagreeable necessity of taking his vessel and taking them prisoners; and without the slightest force or violence being used by the Captain, or by a single member of the crew of the Savannah—without a gun being fired, or even loaded, so far as anything appears—the Captain of the Joseph voluntarily submitted, yielded up his vessel, and there was not the slightest violence or putting any body in fear.

Therefore, gentlemen, I say, that so far as the crime charged here is the crime of robbery, there is no evidence in the case under which, on either of these grounds, by reason of the secrecy of the act, or the violence or putting in fear, or the showing a felonious intent, by the evidence for the prosecution, these prisoners can be convicted under the indictment before you. To show that the definition of robbery at common law is the one that applies to these statutes of the United States, I beg to refer your honors to cases in the Supreme Court of the United States. I refer to the case of the *United States* vs. *Palmer, 3 Wheaton, 610*; the *United States* vs. *Wood, 3d Washington, 440*; and the *United States* vs. *Wilson, 1 Baldwin,* p. 78.

But, gentlemen, there is another set of counts in this indictment on which, probably, as to those who are citizens, a conviction will be pressed for by counsel on the part of the Government. That is a set of counts to which I am about to call your attention in reference to the acts under which they were framed. You will recollect this, gentlemen, that under the counts charging the offence of robbery, the majority of these prisoners must be convicted, or none of them can be convicted at all, for reasons which I will immediately give you. The only statute under which it is claimed on the part of the prosecution that a conviction can be had, if not for robbery on the high seas, imperatively requires that the prisoners to be convicted must be citizens of the United States. There are twelve prisoners here, and by the statement of the last witness produced on the part of the prosecution, only four of them appear to be citizens of the United States, or ever to have been citizens of the United States. The others were all born in different countries in Europe and Asia, and had never been naturalized; and the Court, whenever this case comes before you, so far as that point is concerned, will give you the evidence on the subject, by which you will see exactly which of these prisoners had ever been citizens of the United States, and which of them had not been. I therefore proceed to examine as to what the statute is, and what the requisites are for a conviction of those who were citizens of the United States at any time. I will read to you the section of the statute to which I have reference. It is the 9th section of the Act of 1790. It reads, "That if any *citizen* shall commit any piracy or robbery aforesaid, or any act of hostility against the United States, or any citizen thereof, upon the high seas, under color of any commission from any *foreign Prince* or *State*, or on pretence of authority from any person, such offender shall, notwithstanding the pretence of any such authority, be deemed, adjudged, and taken to be a pirate, felon, and robber, and, on being thereof convicted, shall suffer death."

Now, it will be interesting and necessary to understand the circumstances under which that statute was passed, and the application which it was intended to have. I will briefly read to you the explanation of that subject, which your honors will find in *Hawkins' Pleas of the Crown, 1st Vol., p.* 268. Hawkins says:

"It being also doubted by many eminent civilians whether, during the Revolution, the persons who had captured English vessels by virtue of commissions granted by James 2nd, at his court at St. Germain, after his abdication of the throne of England, could be deemed pirates, the grantor still having, as it was contended, the right of war in him; it is enacted by 11 and 12 Will. III., chap. 7, sec. 8, 'That if any of his Majesty's natural born subjects or denizens of this Kingdom shall commit any piracy or robbery, or any act of hostility against others of his Majesty's subjects upon the sea, under color of any commission from any foreign Prince or State, or pretence of authority from any person whatsoever, such offender or offenders, and every of them, shall be deemed, adjudged, and taken to be pirates, felons, and robbers; and they and every of them, being duly convicted thereof according to this Act or the aforesaid statute of King Henry the Eighth, shall have and suffer such pains of death, loss of land and chattels, as pirates, felons, and robbers upon the sea ought to have and suffer.'"

Your honors will find that further referred to in the case of the *United States* vs. *Jones, 3d Wash. Cir. Court Reps. p.* 219, in these terms:

"The 9th sec. of this law (the Act of 1790) is in fact copied from the statute of the 11th and 12th Wm. 3d, ch. 7, the history of which statute is explained by Hawkins. It was aimed at Commissions granted to Cruisers by James II., after his abdication, which, by many, were considered as conferring a legal authority to cruise, so as to protect those acting under them against a charge of piracy. Still, we admit that unless some other reason can be assigned for the introduction of a similar provision in our law, the argument which has been founded on it would deserve serious consideration. We do not think it difficult to assign a very satisfactory reason for the adoption of this section without viewing it in the light of a legislative construction of the 8th sec, or of the general law.

"If a citizen of the United States should commit acts of depredation against any of the citizens of the United States, it might at least have been a question whether he could be guilty of piracy if he acted under a foreign commission and within the scope of his authority. He might say that he acted under a commission; and not having transgressed the authority derived under it, he could not be charged criminally. But the 9th sec. declares that this shall be no plea, because the authority under which he acted is not allowed to be legitimate. It declares to the person contemplated by this section, that in cases where a commission from his own Government would protect him from the charge of piracy, that is, where he acted within the scope of it or even where he acted fairly but under a mistake in transgressing it, yet that a *foreign* commission should afford him no protection, even although he had not exceeded the authority which it professed to give him. But it by no means follows from this that a citizen committing depredations upon foreigners or citizens, not authorized by the commission granted by his own Government, *and with a felonious intention*, should be protected by that commission against a charge of piracy. Another object of this section appears to have been to declare that acts of hostility committed by a citizen against the United States upon the high seas, *under pretence of a commission issued by a foreign Government, though they might amount to treason, were nevertheless piracy and to be tried as such.*"

Your honors will find another very interesting history in reference to this statute in *Phillimore's International Law, 1st vol., sec. 398*. Phillimore says:

"Soon after the abdication of James II., an international question of very great importance arose, namely, what character should be ascribed to privateers commissioned by the monarch, who had abdicated, to make war against the adherents of William III., or rather against the English, while under his rule. The question, in fact, involved a discussion of the general principle, whether a deposed sovereign, claiming to be sovereign *de jure*, might lawfully commission privateers against the subjects and adherents of the sovereign *de facto* on the throne; or whether such privateers were not to be considered as pirates, inasmuch as they were sailing *animo furandi et depraedundi*, without any *national* character. The question, it should be observed, did not arise in its full breadth and importance *until James II. had been expelled from Ireland as well as England, until, in fact, he was a sovereign, claiming to be such de jure*, BUT CONFESSEDLY WITHOUT TERRITORY. It appears that James, after he was in this condition, continued to issue letters of marque to his followers. The Privy Council of William III. desired to hear civilians upon the point of the piratical character of such privateers. The arguments on both sides are contained in a curious and rather rare pamphlet, published by one of the counsel (Dr. Tindal) for King William, in the years 1693-4. The principal arguments for the piratical character of the privateers appear to have been—

"That they who acted under such commission may be dealt with as if they had acted under their own authority or the authority of any private person, and therefore might be treated as pirates. That if such a titular Prince might grant commissions to seize the ships and goods of all or most trading nations, he might derive a considerable revenue as a chief of such freebooters, and that it would be madness in nations not to use the utmost rigor of the law against such vessels.

"That the reason of the thing which pronounced that robbers and pirates, when they formed themselves into a civil society, became just enemies, pronounced also that A KING WITHOUT TERRITORY, without power of protecting the innocent or punishing the guilty, or in any way of administering justice, dwindled into a pirate if he issued commissions to seize the goods and ships of nations; and that they who took commissions from him must be held by legal inference to have associated *sceleris causâ*, and could not be considered as members of a civil society."

I will not occupy the time of the Court and Jury by recapitulating the rest of the arguments which were urged with very great ability by the learned and distinguished civilians arrayed against each other in that interesting debate. But the points which arise, and which the Court will have, in due time, to instruct you upon, we respectfully claim and insist are these: That this English statute, after which our own statute was precisely copied, was intended only to apply to the case of pirates cruising under a commission pretended to have been given, in the first place, by a Prince deposed, abdicated, not having a foot of territory yielding him obedience in any corner of the world; and, in the next place, that it was intended to be aimed against those cruising under a commission issued under the pretence of authority from a foreigner, and not from the authorities over them *de jure* or *de facto*, or from any authorities of the land in which they lived, and where the real object was depredation; because, where it was issued by a monarch without territory—by a foreigner, having no rule, and no country in subjection to him—there could be no prize-court, and none of the ordinary machinery for disposing of prizes captured, according to the rules of international law; and, lastly, it was intended to apply to the case of a citizen, taking a privateer's commission from a foreign Government as a pretence to enable him to cruise against the commerce of his own countrymen. But it was never intended to apply to a case of this kind, where the commission was issued by the authorities of the land in which the parties receiving it live, exercising sway and dominion over them, whether *de jure* or *de facto*.

Now, gentlemen, so far I have thought it necessary to go in explanation of what the statutes were, of the circumstances bearing on them, and of the requisites which the prosecution had to make out, in order to ask a conviction at your hands. I come now, for the purpose of this opening, to lay before you what we shall rely upon in our defence. The first defence, as has already appeared to you from the course of the examination of the prosecution's witnesses, has reference to the question of the jurisdiction of this Court to hear and determine this controversy. The statute has been already read to you, on which that question of jurisdiction rests; but, for fear that you do not recollect it, I will beg once more to call your attention to it. The concluding paragraph of sec. 14 of the Act of 1825, 4th vol. of the Statutes at Large, p. 118, is as follows:

"And the trial of all offences which shall be committed on the high seas or elsewhere out of the limits of any State or District, shall be in the District where the offender is apprehended, or into which he may first be brought."

Now, you observe that the language of the statute is imperative—the reasons which led to its adoption were also imperative and controlling. It is necessary that the law shall make provision for the place where a man shall be put on trial under an indictment against him; and the law wisely provides that in cases of offences committed on the land, the trial shall only take place where the offence was committed. It was thought even necessary to provide for that by an amendment to the Constitution of the United States, in order that there might be no misunderstanding of, and no departure from, the rule.

The Constitution, by one of its amendments, in the same paragraph which provides for the right of every accused to a speedy and impartial trial, provides also that that trial shall take place in the District, which District shall first have been ascertained by law; and as I said to you, in cases of crimes committed on the land, that District must be the District where the offence was committed, and no other.

Now look at the state of things here, gentlemen. These men are all citizens or residents of the State of South Carolina, and have been so for years. This vessel was fitted out in South Carolina. The authority under which she professed to act was given there. The evidence for the defence, if it could be got, must come from there. All the circumstances bearing on the transaction occurred in that section of the country, and not elsewhere,—occurred in a country which is now under the same Government and domination as Virginia, because Virginia is included at present under the domination and Government of the Confederate States.

Well, with reference to offences committed at sea, the officers capturing a prize have a right to bring it into any port, it is true, and the port where the prisoners are brought is, as we claim under the construction of the statute, the port where the trial is to take place; the port where the prisoners are first brought, whether they are landed or not. On that question of jurisdiction the rule is this: The jurisdiction of the State extends to the distance of a marine league from shore; and if these prisoners were brought on this vessel within the distance of three miles from the shores of Virginia, where the vessel anchored, as in port, having communication with the land, the jurisdiction of the Circuit Court of the Eastern District of Virginia attached, and they could not, after that, be put on trial for that offence elsewhere. It is not necessary for me now to trouble the Jury with re-reading authorities which were read upon this subject yesterday. In a case which occurred some years ago, before Judge Story, the learned Judge had fallen into a misapprehension on a question which did not necessarily arise, because the facts to give rise to it did not occur in the case. An offence had been committed—an attempt to create a revolt on board of a vessel at sea. Those who had made the attempt had either repented of the design, or had not succeeded in it; at all events, they had afterwards gone on to do their duty on the vessel, and had not been incarcerated on board the vessel at all. The vessel first got into a port in Connecticut, and finally got into a port in Massachusetts, and there, for the first time, those prisoners were arrested and put into confinement. Undoubtedly the Court in Massachusetts had jurisdiction in that case; but Judge Story, speaking on a question which did not arise, appeared to treat the language of the statute as being alternative, giving the Government the right to select one of two places for the trial. That was corrected in a late case which came before the Court in Massachusetts, in the same District where Judge Story had decided the previous case. Both Judge Sprague, of the District Court, and Judge Clifford, of the Circuit Court, held that in a case where prisoners had been captured as malefactors on the high seas, and had been confined on board a United States vessel, where the vessel had gone into Key West for a temporary purpose, to get water, without the prisoners ever having been landed, and where they went from thence to Massachusetts, where the prisoners were arrested by the civil authorities and imprisoned, that the Court of Massachusetts had no jurisdiction whatever. Under the instructions of the Court, the Grand Jury refused to find an indictment, and a warrant of removal was granted to remove the prisoners for trial in the Court at Key West,—the Court of Massachusetts holding that that was the only place where they could be tried for the offence, because the vessel having them in custody as prisoners had touched there to get water on her voyage. We have not even the information in that case as to whether the vessel went within three miles of the shore; it was enough that she had communicated with Key West, and that the prisoners might have been landed there; but it was held that the Government had not a right to elect the place of trial of the prisoners; and it is important, particularly in cases of this kind, that no one shall have the right to elect a place of trial. I say that, not with the slightest intention of imputing any unfair motives to the Government, to the officers of the Navy, or any one else. It is a great deal better that where men are to be put on trial for their lives, they should have the benefit of the chapter of accidents.

If it would have been any better for these prisoners to have had a Jury to try them in Virginia, they were entitled to the benefit of that. In saying so, I mean no reflection on any Jury in New York. I have no doubt you will try this case as honestly, as fairly, and as impartially as any Jury in Virginia could try it. But at the same time we all know that if this right of election can be resorted to on the part of the United States, men might suffer, not from any wrong intention, but from the natural and inevitable and often unconscious tendency of those who are to prosecute, to select the place of prosecution most convenient for themselves.

We shall therefore claim before you, gentlemen, following the rule laid down in Massachusetts by Judge Clifford and Judge Sprague, that this vessel, having been within a marine league of the shore of Virginia, was within the jurisdiction of the District Court of Virginia, and that that was the only place where they could be tried. Suppose, as was well suggested to me by one of my associates, that on the Minnesota, lying where she did, or on the Harriet Lane, lying where she did in Hampton Roads, a murder had been committed: could it be contended by any one that the United States Court in Virginia would not have had jurisdiction, and the only jurisdiction over the case?

Now, gentlemen, that is all which, on the opening of this case, I am going to say on the subject of jurisdiction.

Our next defence will be, that the commission in this case affords adequate protection to these prisoners; and we will put that before you in several points of view. It will undoubtedly be read to you in evidence. It was one of the documents found on board this vessel.

Mr. Evarts: It is not in evidence; and how can counsel open to the Jury upon a commission which is not in evidence?

Judge Nelson: Counsel can refer to it as part of his opening.

Mr. Larocque: Now, gentlemen, you will recollect that the counsel for the prosecution, in framing this indictment, has treated this in the way in which we claim he was bound to treat it; that is to say, that the 9th section of the Act of 1790 was intended to refer exclusively to offences claimed to have been committed under a commission; throwing on the prosecution the necessity of setting forth the commission or the pretence of authority. Having set it forth, the prosecution is bound by the manner in which it is described in the indictment; and if it is described as something which it is not, the prisoners must have the benefit of that mis-description.

Now, in framing this indictment, the counsel for the prosecution has set forth that the prisoners claimed to act under a commission issued by one Jefferson Davis. That is to say, he has attempted to ground his claim to a conviction on that section of the statute. You will recollect that the statute reads, "under pretence of any commission granted by any foreign Prince or State" (which the Courts of the United States have held, to mean a foreign

State), "or under pretence of authority from any person." And it was necessary, in order to ground an indictment on that section of the statute, to bring this case within the exact letter or words of one or the other clause of that section of this statute. It would not do for them to claim that this commission was issued by a foreign Prince or foreign State, because, if by a foreign Prince or foreign State, there would be no doubt or question that all of these parties were citizens of that foreign State or residents there, and were not citizens of the United States. Of course, if this were a foreign State, they were foreign citizens, and not citizens of the United States.

What is this commission? As we shall lay it before you, it reads in this way:

"JEFFERSON DAVIS,

"President of the Confederate States of America,

"To all who shall see these Presents, Greeting:

"Know ye, That by virtue of the power vested in me by law, I have commissioned, and do hereby commission, have authorized, and do hereby authorize, the schooner or vessel called the 'Savannah' (more particularly described in the schedule hereunto annexed), whereof T. Harrison Baker is commander, to act as a private armed vessel in the service of the Confederate States, on the high seas, against the United States of America, their ships, vessels, goods, and effects, and those of their citizens, during the pendency of the war now existing between the said Confederate States and the said United States.

"This commission to continue in force until revoked by the President of the Confederate States for the time being.

	"Given under my hand and the seal of the Confederate States,
[c.s.]	at Montgomery, this eighteenth day of May, A.D. 1861.

"(Signed) JEFFERSON DAVIS.

"By the President.

"R. TOOMBS,
"*Secretary of State.*

"SCHEDULE OF DESCRIPTION OF THE VESSEL.

- "Name—Schooner 'Savannah.'

- "Tonnage—Fifty-three 41/95 tons.

- "Armament—One large pivot gun and small arms.

- "No. of Crew—Thirty."

That is the document, bearing the seal of ten States, signed by Jefferson Davis as President—signed by the Secretary of State for those ten States, which the learned counsel who framed the indictment has undertaken to call "a pretence of authority from one Jefferson Davis." The counsel was forced to frame his indictment in that way; for if he had alleged in the indictment that it was by pretence of authority from the Confederate States—to wit, South Carolina, Georgia, &c., naming States which this Government, for the purpose of bringing this prosecution at all, must claim to be in the Union— it would be clearly outside of the provision of the statute, and could never get before a Jury, because it would have been dismissed on application to the Court beforehand. But the learned counsel has sought, by stating an argumentative conclusion of law in his indictment, according to his understanding of it, to bring within the statute a case which the statute was not meant to meet—an entirely different and distinct case. I submit to you, that that cannot be done,—that the commission on its face does not purport to be a commission granted by any person. It purports to be, and, if anything, it is, a commission granted by authority of the States that are joined together under the name of Confederate States; and, gentlemen, as I said, we shall claim before you that this commission is a protection to these parties, against the charge of piracy, upon various distinct grounds.

In the first place, we shall claim before you that the Government, called the Government of the Confederate States (whether you call it a Government *de jure* or a Government *de facto*, or whatever name under the nomenclature of nations you choose to give it), is the present existing Government of those States, exercising dominion over them, without any other Government having an officer or court, or any insignia of Government within them.

This is a point which, at a future stage of the case, my learned associate, who is much better able to do so than I am, will have occasion to dwell upon. I wish, however, to call your attention to the rules as they have been laid down; and first, I would desire to refer you, and also to call the attention of the Court, to what is said by Vattel,—who, as you all probably know, is one of the most celebrated authors upon international rights, and international law, and who is received as authority upon that subject in every Court in Europe and America. I refer to Vattel, book 1, chap. 17, secs. 201 and 202, where he says:

"*Sec. 201.* When a city or province is threatened, or actually attacked, it must not, for the sake of escaping a danger, separate itself, or abandon its natural Prince, even when the State or the Prince is unable to give it immediate and effectual assistance. Its duty, its political engagements, oblige it to make the greatest efforts in order to maintain itself in its present state. If it is overcome by force, necessity, that irresistible law, frees it from its former engagements, and gives it a right to treat with the conqueror, in order to obtain the best terms possible. If it must either submit to him or perish, who can doubt but it may, and even ought to prefer the former alternative? Modern usage is conformable to this decision,—a city submits to the enemy, when it cannot expect safety from vigorous resistance. It takes an oath of fidelity to him, and its sovereign lays the blame on fortune alone."

"*Sec. 202.* The State is obliged to protect and defend all its members; and the Prince owes the same assistance to his subjects. If, therefore, the State or the Prince refuses or neglects to succor a body of people who are exposed to imminent danger, the latter, being thus abandoned, become perfectly free to provide for their own safety and preservation in whatever manner they find most convenient, without paying the least regard to those who, by abandoning them, have been the first to fail in their duty. The Canton of Zug, being attacked by the Swiss in 1352, sent for succor to the Duke of Austria, its sovereign; but that Prince, being engaged in discourse concerning his hawks at the time when the deputies appeared before him, would scarcely condescend to hear them. Thus abandoned, the people of Zug entered into the Helvetic Confederacy. The city of Zurich had been in the same situation the year before. Being attacked by a band of rebellious citizens, who were supported by the neighboring nobility, and the House of Austria, it made application to the head of the Empire; but Charles IV., who was then Emperor, declared to its deputies that he could not defend it, upon which Zurich secured its safety by an alliance with the Swiss. The same reason has authorized the Swiss in general to separate themselves entirely from the Empire which never protected them in any emergency. They had not denied its authority for a long time before their independence was acknowledged by the Emperor, and the whole Germanic Body, at the treaty of Westphalia."

I also refer to the case of the United States *v.* Hayward, 2 Gallison, 485, which was a writ of error to the District Court of Massachusetts, in a case of alleged breach of the revenue laws. It appears that Castine (in Maine) was taken possession of by the British troops on the 1st of September, 1814, and was held in their possession until after the Treaty of Peace.

Judge Story says:

"The second objection is, that the Court directed the Jury that Castine was, under the circumstance, a foreign port. By 'foreign port,' as the terms are here used, may be understood a port within the dominions of a foreign sovereign, and without the dominions of the United States. The port of Castine is the port of entry for the District of Penobscot, and is within the acknowledged territory of the United States. But, at the time referred to in the bill of exceptions, it had been captured, and was in the open and exclusive possession of the enemy. *By the conquest and occupation of Castine, that territory passed under the allegiance and sovereignty of the enemy. The sovereignty of the United States over the territory was, of course, suspended, and the laws of the United States could no longer be rightfully enforced, or be obligatory upon the inhabitants, who remained and submitted to the conquerors.*"

Now, gentlemen, I must trouble you, very briefly, with a reference to one or two other authorities on that subject. At page 188 of Foster's Crown Law that learned author says:

"*Sec 8.* Protection and allegiance are reciprocal obligations, and consequently the allegiance due to the Crown must, as I said before, be paid to him who is in the full and actual exercise of the regal powers, and to none other. I have no occasion to meddle with the distinction between Kings *de facto* and Kings *de jure*, because the warmest advocates for that distinction, and for the principles upon which it hath been founded, admit that even a King *de facto*, in the full and sole possession of the Crown, is a King within the Statute of Treasons; it is admitted, too, that the throne being full, any other person out of possession, but claiming title, is no King within the act, be his pretensions what they may.

"These principles, I think, no lawyer hath ever yet denied. They are founded in reason, equity, and good policy."

And again, at page 398, he continues:

"His Lordship [Hale] admitted that a temporary allegiance was due to Henry VI. as being King *de facto*. If this be true, as it undoubtedly is, with what color of law could those who paid him that allegiance before the accession of Edward IV. be considered as traitors? For call it a temporary allegiance, or by what other epithet of diminution you please, still it was due to him, while in full possession of the Crown, and consequently those who paid him that due allegiance could not, with any sort of propriety, be considered as traitors for doing so.

"The 11th of Henry VII., though subsequent to these transactions, is full in point. For let it be remembered, that though the enacting part of this excellent law can respect only future cases, the preamble, which his Lordship doth not cite at large, is declaratory of the common law: and consequently will enable us to judge of the legality of past transactions. It reciteth to this effect, 'That the subjects of England are bound by the duty of their allegiance to serve their Prince and Sovereign Lord for the time being, in defence of him and his realm, against every rebellion, power, and might raised against him; and that whatsoever may happen in the fortune of war against the mind and will of the Prince, as in this land, some time past it hath been seen, it is not reasonable, but against all laws, reason, and good conscience, that such subjects attending upon such service should suffer for doing their true duty and service of allegiance.' It then enacteth, that no person attending upon the King for the time being in his wars, shall for such service be convict or attaint of treason or other offence by Act of Parliament, or otherwise by any process of law."

The author says then:

"Here is a clear and full parliamentary declaration, that by the antient law and Constitution of England, founded on principles of reason, equity, and good conscience, the allegiance of the subject is due to the King for the time being, and to him alone. This putteth the duty of the subject upon a rational, safe bottom. He knoweth that protection and allegiance are reciprocal duties. He hopeth for protection from the Crown, and he payeth his allegiance to it in the person of him whom he seeth in full and peaceable possession of it. He entereth not into the question of title; he hath neither leisure or abilities, nor is he at liberty to enter into that question. But he seeth the fountain, from whence the blessings of Government, liberty, peace, and plenty flow to him; and there he payeth his allegiance. And this excellent law hath secured him against all after reckonings on that account."

And another author on that subject [Hawkins], in his Pleas of the Crown, Book I., chap. 17, sec. 11, says:

"As to the third point, who is a King within this act? [26 Edw. 3, ch. 2.] It seems agreed that every King for the time being, in actual possession of the crown, is a King within the meaning of this statute. For there is a necessity that the realm should have a King by whom and in whose name the laws shall be administered; and the King in possession being the only person who either doth or can administer those laws, must be the only person who has a right to that obedience which is due to him who administers those laws; and since by virtue thereof he secures to us the safety of our lives, liberties, and properties, and all other advantages of Government, he may justly claim returns of duty, allegiance, and subjection."

"*Sec. 12.* And this plainly appears by the prevailing opinions in the reign of King Edward IV., in whose reign the distinction between a King *de jure* and *de facto* seems first to have begun; and yet it was then laid down as a principle, and taken for granted in the arguments of Bagot's case, that a treason against Henry VI. while he was King, in compassing his death, was punishable after Edward IV. came to the Crown; from which it follows that allegiance was held to be due to Henry VI. while he was King, because every indictment of treason must lay the offence *contra ligeantiæ debitum.*"

"*Sec. 13.* It was also settled that all judicial acts done by Henry VI. while he was King, and also all pardons of felony and charters of denization granted by him, were valid; but that a pardon made by Edward IV., before he was actually King, was void, even after he came to the Crown."

"And by the 11th Henry VII., ch. 1, it is declared 'that all subjects are bound by their allegiance to serve their Prince and Sovereign Lord for the time being in his wars for the defence of him and his land against every rebellion, power, and might reared against him, &c., and that it is against all laws, reason, and good conscience that he should lose or forfeit any thing for so doing;' and it is enacted 'that from thenceforth no person or persons that attend on the King for the time being, and do him true and faithful allegiance in his wars, within the realm or without, shall for the said deed and true duty of allegiance *be convict of any offence.*'"

"*Sec. 15.* From hence it clearly follows: *First,* that every King for the time being has a right to the people's allegiance, because they are bound thereby to defend him in his wars, against every power whatsoever.

"*Sec. 16. Secondly,* that one out of possession is so far from having any right to allegiance, by virtue of any other title which he may set up against the King in being, that we are bound by the duty of our allegiance to resist him."

And these doctrines, if the Court please, have been recently acted upon and enforced by a learned Judge in the case of the United States *vs.* The General Parkhill, tried in Philadelphia, and published in the newspapers, although not yet issued in the regular volumes of Reports.

I need not tell you, gentlemen, that what is said there of the King, applies to any other form of Government equally well, whether it be a republican form of Government, or whatever it may be. These doctrines belong to this country as well as they belong to England. They belong to every country which has adopted the common law; and what would be due to a King in the actual possession of the Government in England, under our statutes and decisions, and under the rules adopted here, would be equally due to a President of the United States in any part of the country in which we live.

I have only to call your attention, in that connection, in opening the defence, to what the condition of things was in the South at the time the acts charged in the indictment occurred. You will bear in mind there is no pretence in this case that any one of these prisoners had anything whatever to do with the initiation of this controversy,—with the overthrow or disappearance of the United States authority in those Confederate States, or with any act occurring anterior to the 2d of June, when this vessel, the Savannah, started upon her career. Nothing, so far, appears, and, in reality, nothing can be made to appear, to show any event, before that time, with which they were connected.

The question, then, is, What was the state of things existing in Charleston, and in the Confederate States, at that time? In the course of the evidence, we will lay that before you, in the completest form it can be laid. We will show you, by the official documents, by the messages of the President, by proclamations, and by the Acts of Congress themselves, that there was not an officer of the United States exercising jurisdiction in one of these Confederate States—not a Judge, or Marshal, or District Attorney, or any other officer by whom the Government had been previously administered on the part of the United States. Every one of them had resigned his office. This new Government had been formed. It was the existing Government, which had replaced the United States in all these States, long anterior to the time that this vessel was fitted out and sailed from the port of Charleston; and upon these questions, whether that was a *de jure* or *de facto* Government, we say it was the existing Government that was in authority over these men—that exercised the power of life and death over them, for it had Courts administering its decrees, as well as every other form and all the other insignia of power; and they were justified by overruling necessity, and by every other title, in yielding obedience to that Government, and in yielding their allegiance to it, as the cases I have read decide; and that duty enjoined upon their consciences to aid and support it by all means in their power from that time forward, until there was another Government over them.

I say, therefore, gentlemen, that this was not a commission issued by a "person, to wit, one Jefferson Davis." I say it was a commission issued by several of the States of the Union, represented, if you please, by Jefferson Davis, and by authority, in fact, from those States, and from the Government in force over them. And more than that, gentlemen, to bring the case still more clearly within the authorities I have read to you, and which you, no doubt, carry in your minds, we will show by the declarations of the Presidents of the United States—by the declaration of Mr. Buchanan, in December,

1860, and by the declaration of Mr. Lincoln, on the 4th of March, 1861—
that neither of them, at either of those dates, intended to interfere, or to
attempt to interfere, by force, with this existing Government. They both,
publicly and solemnly, in the presence of the United States, declared that they
would not attempt, by any forcible invasion of those States, to overthrow the
Government established over them;—that there would be no "invasion," is
the expression;—that they would leave it to the sober second thought of the
people of those States, by process of time, by maturer thought and better
reflection, to return, probably, to their former position under the
Government of the United States. And what were men to do, in that
condition of things, in the State of South Carolina, in the State of Georgia,
or in any one of those States, with not an officer of the United States to
protect them—with not a Court of Justice to protect them—with Courts of
Justice, on the contrary, organized by the new Government, and exercising
dominion of life and death, and every other dominion that Government
could exercise—but to yield their allegiance to it, and from thenceforth to
support it, as honest men should do, who yield their allegiance to the
Government?

As I said before, in respect to this question, even if this were a voluntary act
on the part of the prisoners—if they were not controlled by necessity—if
they had a state of things before them which authorized them to believe that
their conduct was right—that the States did nothing more than they had a
right to do—they were justified in giving allegiance to the Government in
existence. We have nothing to say as to the correctness of the political views
or opinions of the prisoners whatever. The question is, What did these men
believe—what were they taught to believe, by your own expounders of the
Constitution—what did they conscientiously and sincerely believe? When
they acted under this commission, did they believe that it was a legitimate
authority, and had they full color for the belief which they held?

And now, gentlemen, another point that we shall maintain before you is, that
under the Constitution of the United States, those States had color of
authority to grant this commission; and that the executive government of the
State had the jurisdiction to decide, for all the citizens of the State, whether
the emergency for taking hostile proceedings against the General
Government had arrived, or not. And I know that, in saying that, I am
speaking to this Jury an unpalatable doctrine, at the present day; but it is a
doctrine which is amply borne out by the cotemporaneous expositions of the
Constitution, penned by its own framers, by the decisions of the Courts, and
by authorities on which we are accustomed to rely for questions of that
character.

Now, the Constitution of the country is a complex one. There are two
sovereigns in every State, exercising allegiance over the inhabitants of the

State. The one sovereign is the United States of America, and the other sovereign is the State in which the citizen lives. And when I say that, I am speaking in the language of the Supreme Court of the United States itself, over and over repeated, as late as the 21st of Howard's Reports (but a few removes, I believe, from the last volume issued from that Court), without a dissenting voice. The theory of our Government is, that the States are sovereign and independent, and that, in coming into the Union, they have retained that sovereignty and independence for every purpose, and in every case, except those in which an express grant of power has been made to the Government of the United States, either in express words, or by necessary implication; and the Courts have held, over and over again, that any act of the General Government of the United States, which transcends the express grant of power made by the Constitution, is absolutely void, to all intents and purposes whatever.

And more than that, gentlemen, the citizen of a State cannot only commit treason against the United States, or other kindred political offences; but he can, in like manner, commit treason against the State in which he lives, or other kindred political offences against its government.

The Constitution of the United States defines treason to be, "levying war against the United States, or adhering to their enemies, giving them aid and comfort." The Constitution of the State of New York defines treason against the State of New York to be, "levying war against the State, or adhering to its enemies, giving them aid and comfort." The Constitution of South Carolina defines and punishes treason against the State, in the language of the old English statute, bringing it to precisely the same thing.

As I said, therefore, the citizen of New York or the citizen of South Carolina (because, whether in one or the other locality, it is the same thing) is under two sovereigns, owing allegiance to each of them—the sovereign State in which he is, owning the whole mass of residuary power (as it has been happily expressed in the decisions of the Court) beyond the express, limited power granted to the Federal Government by the Constitution of the United States.

I want to call your attention to another thing, as I go along with this line of the argument. I contend that, among the powers which have been delegated to the State governments by the Constitutions of the States, is the power in the executive government of the State, co-ordinately with the General Government, to decide whether itself or the General Government has transcended the line which bounds their respective jurisdictions, upon any case in which a collision may arise between them, which affects the public domain of the State, or the whole State, or its citizens, considered as a body politic. And you will see, in a moment, the reason why I state my proposition in that way.

You have all heard of what, in the history of the country, has been called *nullification*, and you probably all understand very nearly what that is. By *nullification*, as it has been spoken of in the history of our country, was meant the claim on the part of a State, by a convention of its people, or otherwise, to decide that the laws of the United States should not operate within its limits upon its citizens, in cases where the law could legitimately operate upon individual citizens. Because you will all recollect that the laws of the United States, in their operation throughout the Union—their criminal laws, laws for the collection of duties, and similar laws—operate upon individual citizens, without reference to whether they are citizens of one State or another. The law operates upon them as people of the United States. And therefore, if you are carrying on business in the port of New York, and a consignment comes to you, it is a question between you as a citizen of the United States and the Government whether the tariff, under which duties are attempted to be collected is valid, as between you and the Government, or not—whether it was legitimate for Congress to pass that tariff; and, in all cases arising on these subjects, the Constitution has provided a tribunal, an arbiter, which is supreme and final, without any appeal. For instance, if you deny the validity of the law under which duties are attempted to be collected upon the goods imported by you, and the Collector attempts to collect them, you refuse to pay, or pay under protest,—and the case must come into the District Court of the United States; and if the Court decides that the law was unconstitutional, you get immediate redress; if it decides that it was constitutional, the question can be carried to the Supreme Court of the United States, and there finally settled. And, therefore, I say that in all cases that come within the purview of the judicial department of the Government, the laws of the United States, as administered by the Courts, and their decisions, bind the citizens of the States in every part of the land.

But, gentlemen, there are an immense class of cases constantly arising where no opportunity can ever be presented to a Court to pass upon them, which were never intended to be passed upon by a Court, which are cases of collision between the executive department of the General Government and the State government in matters, as I expressed it to you before, affecting the public domain, or the State or its citizens as a body politic. As laid down by the expounders of the Constitution of the United States, that instrument is one to which the States are parties, as well as the people of the United States and people of each State.

Suppose a case of this kind. It is not a case likely to arise; but every case may arise, as we have been sadly admonished by the events of the last few months. Suppose we had a President in the executive chair at Washington who was a citizen of the State of Massachusetts, and greatly interested in the prosperity of the commerce of the City of Boston; and suppose that, being a wicked man (for wicked men have been sometimes elected to offices in this and every country), he had conceived the iniquitous design of ruining the commerce of New York, for the purpose of benefiting the commerce of the City of Boston; and suppose, in the prosecution of that wicked design, without the pretense of authority to do so under the Constitution of the United States, without a pretense that Congress had passed any law authorizing him to do anything of the kind, he should station a fleet of vessels, by orders to the commander of his squadron, off the harbor of New York, and should say, from this day forward the commerce of the port of New York is hermetically closed, and the commerce which has formerly gone to New York must go to Boston. Is the State of New York, under a condition of things of that kind, to submit to the closing of her commerce, to her ruin and destruction? Can she get before the Courts for redress against such an infringement of the Constitution by the President? How is she to get there? She cannot go to the Supreme Court of the United States, for in the Courts of the United States there is no form of jurisdiction by which the question can be brought before the Courts by any possibility whatever; and New York is a sovereign and independent State, and, so far as she has not conceded jurisdiction to the United States by the Constitution, has a right to exercise every sovereign and independent power that she has. *There* is a case, therefore, in which the Courts of law can afford no redress,—in which the Constitution has erected no common arbiter between the General Government and the government of the State.

Who, then, is the arbiter in such a case? Why, gentlemen, the books have expressed it. It is the last argument of Kings—it is the law of might; and in case of a collision of that kind, I maintain before you, upon this trial, that the State has a right to redress herself by force against the General Government; that she has a right, if necessary, to commission cruisers, to drive the squadron away from the port of New York; and she has a right, if more effectual, to commission private armed vessels to aid in driving them away, or to capture or subdue them. There being no common arbiter between her and the General Government in a case of that kind, she has a right to use force in redressing herself, and to take the power into her own hands.

And the authorities are uniform upon that subject. I have been obliged to detain you so long that I shall not read them to you; but I have them collected before me, and in the future discussions which may take place before the Court I shall be able to show that that right was maintained by Hamilton, one of the most distinguished members of the Convention who helped to frame the Constitution, and the strongest advocate of placing large powers in the hands of the Federal Government; by Madison, Jefferson, and all the Fathers of the Constitution, and by all who have written upon the subject; that it is a doctrine which has been asserted by the Legislature of the State of

New Jersey, and, indeed, by the State Legislatures of all the States, pretty much, in which the question has arisen—that the Supreme Court of the United States have themselves over and over again declared that the only safeguard that existed, under the Constitution, against the right of the State to come into collision with the General Government, in all cases whatever, was the existence of the judiciary power, in cases where that was applicable between them, and that in all cases where that judiciary power failed, they were left to the law of nature and the might of Kings to redress themselves.

Now, gentlemen, if I am right in that step in my argument,—if that right would exist at any time or under any circumstances,—there must be some authority, in the State that has the jurisdiction, to decide for the citizens of the State when that occasion has arisen; and there must be some authority in the United States which has a right to decide for the Government of the United States when that occasion has arisen; whose decision (that is, in the General Government) is binding for the people of all the States, except the State in collision with the Federal Government and which makes a contrary decision; and whose decision, in that State, is an authority and protection for all the citizens of that State.

I say to you, moreover, gentlemen, that that right, under the law of nature, to resist the attempted usurpation of a power which has not been granted by the Constitution, resides, in a State, in the executive government, and necessarily in the Governor of the State; because you will recollect one of the premises upon which we started was, that all the residuary power in the government, beyond what had been expressly ceded to the Government of the United States by the Federal Constitution, is, by the Constitution, reserved to the State; and the Governor of the State is the sentinel upon the watch-tower for the protection of the rights of the State. He is placed in that position to watch the danger from afar. He communicates with the General Government. Any steps taken having reference to the State, pass under his inspection; and he alone has the materials within his reach for knowing the circumstances and deciding upon the facts in regard to the question whether the General Government is acting within the constitutional limit of its powers, or whether it is guilty of any usurpation of power, in any claim of authority it makes with reference to the affairs of the State. Because, in the case I have supposed, of a President elected from the State of Massachusetts, seeking to destroy the commerce of New York, and stationing a fleet off the harbor, it is not likely that a President who was guilty of such wickedness would avow that he did it for the purpose of building up the commerce of Boston and destroying that of New York. No; he would say that he had notice of a hostile invasion—a fleet leaving the coast of Great Britain or of some other maritime power to make a descent upon New York,—that he had notice of some threatened injury to New York, which would make it necessary to station a fleet there, and to prevent vessels from entering or leaving. The Governor alone would have the means of ascertaining whether there was any foundation in truth for that, or whether it was a mere pretence to cover his iniquitous purpose; and in determining the case whether the Federal Government is exceeding its power or not, or acting within the constitutional limit of its power, the Governor has to deal with a compound question of law and fact. He must first read the Constitution of the United States, and ascertain its grant of power, and then compare that with the facts as presented to him; and upon that comparison the jurisdiction is placed in him to decide whether the act of the General Government is within its power, or a transgression of it.

He decides the question, and what more have we then? He is, by his office, commander-in-chief of the military and naval forces of the State; for the State can have both military and naval forces. It has its militia at all times. It is authorized expressly by the Constitution to keep ships of war, in time of war. There is, certainly, a prohibition in the Constitution of the United States against a State granting letters of marque; but that is a prohibition against its granting letters of marque in a war against foreign States; it has no reference whatever to any possible collision that may take place between the State and the Federal Government. And that rule is laid down by *Grotius* and *Vattel* both; for they both maintain and assert the right of the people, under every limited Constitution, in the case of a palpable infringement of power by the chief of the State, forcibly to resist it; and GROTIUS puts the case of a State with a limited Constitution, having both a King and a Senate, in which the power of declaring war was in express terms reserved to the King alone, and he says that by no means prevents the Senate, in case of an infringement of the Constitution by the King, from declaring and making war against him; because the phrase is to be understood of a war with foreign nations and not of an internal war. I say, therefore, that in a case of that kind—a palpable infringement by the General Government of the Constitution—the Governor of the State, in the first place, has the only means and the only right of deciding whether that infringement has taken place.

In each State the Governor is commander-in-chief of the naval and military forces; he has a right to give military orders to citizens; he has a right to order them to muster in the service of the State; and if they disobey him they can be punished the same as they can in any civilized country.

And more than that: suppose a case arises of that kind, in which the General and State Governments come into forcible collision, and suppose a citizen should take arms against the State; there is the law of the State which punishes for treason every citizen of the State who adheres to its enemies, giving them aid and comfort; and, under the theory of the prosecution, if he adheres to the State, and the Federal Government should happen to be the victor in the contest, there is the law of the Federal Government which punishes him for adhering to the State. So that the poor citizen of the State, if this theory be correct, is to be punished and hanged, whichever party may succeed in the unhappy contest.

But, gentlemen, the law perpetrates no such absurdity as that; for the very moment the doctrine for which I contend is admitted, the citizen, in a conflict like that between the Federal Government and the State, is not liable to be considered a traitor or punished as such, let him adhere to which of the two parties he pleases, in good faith. The reason of which is clear. He is the subject of two sovereigns,—the one the Federal Government and the other the State in which he lives. Either of these sovereigns has jurisdiction to decide for him the question whether the other is committing a usurpation of power or not; and it inevitably follows that if these two sovereigns decide that question differently, the citizen is not to be punished as a traitor, let him adhere to which he pleases in good faith. And I submit to you, gentlemen, that is the only doctrine, under the Constitution of the United States, and under our complex system of government, which can be admitted for a moment. I will give you a confirmation of that. I have already stated to you the clause of the Constitution of the United States which defines the punishment of the crime of treason against the United States,—and by looking at the reports of the debates in the Convention which adopted the Constitution, you will find that the clause, as originally reported to the Convention, read: "Treason against the United States shall consist in levying war against the United States *or any of them*, or in adhering to the enemies of the United States, *or any of them*, giving them aid and comfort,"—and the clause, as reported, was amended by striking out the words, "or any of them," and making it read: "Treason against the United States shall consist in levying war against them or in adhering to their enemies," &c. Therefore, under our Constitution, treason against the United States must be levying war against all the States of this Confederacy. It does not mean the Government. The amendment which I have spoken of shows it must be an act of hostility which is, in judgment of law, an act of hostility against all the States of the Union. Therefore I say that a citizen who owes allegiance to a State of the Union, when he acts in good faith, under the jurisdiction of one of the sovereigns to whom he owes allegiance—to wit, the State—does not levy war against the United States. He levies war against the Government which claims to represent him, in that case,—his other sovereign, to whom he equally owes allegiance, deciding that that Government is committing an usurpation of power; and he is acting under the authority of those in whom he rightly and justly reposes faith,—to whom has been delegated the right to decide; and however the Governor of the State may be punished by impeachment, if he has acted in bad faith, the citizen cannot be subject to the halter for doing that which he was under a legal obligation to do.

Then, gentlemen, to show the application of the rule for which I have been contending—and with the necessary details of which I fear I must have wearied you—to the case in hand: The moment it is conceded that any possible case can arise in which a State would have the right to resist by force the General Government,—the moment it is conceded that it is the Governor of the State, who, co-ordinately with the President of the Union, has a right to decide that question for himself,—then I say we have nothing whatever to do with the question, whether, under the unhappy circumstances which have arisen, the Governor of the State, or of any of the States, decided right or wrong. We know they did claim that the General Government was usurping power which did not belong to it. In fact, I think we have the confession of the President of the United States that, with an honest heart and with honest purposes, which I believe have actuated him all through, he has, as he says, for the preservation of the Union, the hope of humanity in all ages, and the greatest Government, as I shall ever believe, that man has ever created,—that he has been compelled to, and did, usurp power which did not belong to him. President Buchanan, before and after this controversy arose, asserted plainly and unequivocally that he had searched the Constitution and laws of the United States for the purpose of finding any color of authority for the invasion of a State by military force, or the using of force against it; and that he could find no such warrant in the Constitution. He was right. There was nothing of the kind in the Constitution; but he failed to see (in my humble judgment) that the law of nature gave him the power to enforce the legitimate authority of the Union, as it gave to the State government the power to repel usurpation. President Lincoln, when he assumed the reins of power, admitted that there was a doubt on that subject. He declared at first that it was not expedient to exercise that power, and that he would not exercise it. He changed his mind afterwards, and did exercise it; and on the 13th of April he issued a proclamation calling for 75,000 volunteers, the first duty assigned to whom, as he stated in his proclamation, would be to invade the Southern States, for the purpose of recapturing the forts and retaking the places that had passed out of the jurisdiction of the United States. And in a subsequent proclamation he declared that he had granted to the military commanders of these forces, without the sanction of an Act of Congress, authority to suspend the writ of *habeas corpus*, within certain limits and in certain cases, in those States. And he makes the frank admission that, in his own belief at least, some of the powers which he had found himself compelled to exercise were not warranted in the Constitution of the United States.

Now these acts of hostility complained of in the indictment took place long subsequent to that. This proclamation was in the month of April. These commissions were not issued, and the Act of the Confederate States to authorize their issue was not passed, until some time afterwards—after they had learned of this proclamation; and this commission was not granted until the month of June subsequent.

I say, therefore, a case was presented for the exercise of the jurisdiction of the Government of the United States, to decide whether it was exercising its rightful powers, under the Constitution, and for the Governor of the State to decide, for the State, that same question; and that an unhappy case of collision, ever to be regretted and deplored, had arisen between the Government of the United States and the Government of those States; and I say that the citizens of any one of those States owing the duty of allegiance to two sovereigns—to the government of their State and to the Government of the United States—had a right honestly to make their election to which of the two sovereigns they would adhere, and are not to be punished as traitors or pirates if they have decided not wisely, nor as we would have done in the section of the country where we live.

I am sorry, gentlemen, to detain you on the question; but it is a most important one—one that enters into the very marrow of this case; and we do claim that the issuing of this commission, whether on the footing of its having been issued by a *de facto* Government, or by authority from the State, considering it as remaining under the Constitution, was a commission that forms a protection to the defendants, and one which is not within the purview of the Act of 1790; because it was not, in the language of that section, a commission taken by a citizen of the United States to cruise against other citizens of the United States, either from a *foreign* Prince or State, or a person merely.

You will observe that if the claim of the Confederate States, that the ordinances of secession are valid, be correct, then it is true that they are foreign States; but their citizens have ceased to be citizens of the United States, and are therefore not within the purview of the ninth section of the Act of 1700.

If, on the contrary, the claim on the part of the Government of the United States, that these ordinances are absolutely void, be correct, then the States are still States of this Union, and the commission, being issued by their authority, is not a commission issued by a *foreign* State, and therefore the case is not within the purview of the ninth section of the Act of 1790.

I must allude very briefly, before closing, to another ground on which this defence will be placed: and that is, that conceding (if we were obliged to concede) that this was not an authority, such as contemplated, to give protection to cruisers as privateers, there was a state of war existing in which hostile forces were arrayed against each other in this country, and which made this capture of the Joseph a belligerent act, even obliterating State lines altogether, for the purpose of the argument.

But before I pass from what I have said to you on the subject of the claim of authority of the States of this Union to come into collision with the General Government, allow me to call attention to the forcible precedents shown in the history of our own glorious Revolution, when the thirteen Colonies, numbering little more than three millions, instead of thirty, separated from Great Britain. At the time when that occurred, in 1776, this very statute of 1790 was in force in England, as I have shown you. It was passed in England, if I recollect right, in 1694. The position of the thirteen Colonies towards the mother country, at that time, was precisely the position that those States which call themselves the "Confederate States" now occupy towards the General Government of the Union.

Appealing to God, as the Supreme Ruler of the Universe, for the rectitude of their intentions, and acknowledging their accountability to no other power, they had claimed to resist the usurpation of the King of Great Britain. They had not even claimed, at the time of which I speak—for I speak of the end of the year 1775 and the beginning of 1776—to declare their independence and to throw off their subjection to Great Britain. At that very early day there were very few in these Colonies that contemplated a thing of that kind, or whose minds could be brought to contemplate such an act. They had risen in resistance against what they claimed to be arbitrary power; they claimed that the King of Great Britain had encroached upon their rights and privileges in a manner not warranted by the Constitution of Great Britain. They did not claim to secede from Great Britain; they did not claim to make themselves independent of subjection to her rule; they claimed to stop the course of usurpation which, they held, had been commenced; and they proposed to return under subjection to the British crown the very moment that an accommodation should be made, yielding allegiance to the King of Great Britain as in all time before. And now, gentlemen, on the 23d March, 1776, on a Saturday, the little Continental Congress was sitting in the chamber, of which you have often seen the picture, composed of the great, wise, and good men, who sat there in deliberation over the most momentous event that has ever occurred in modern times, if we except that now agitating and convulsing our beloved country. I never heard one of those men stigmatized as a pirate. I never heard one of those men calumniated as an enemy of the human race. I have often heard them called the greatest, wisest, and best men that ever lived on the face of God's earth. I will read to you what occurred on the 23d March, 1776;—they being subjects of the King of Great Britain, and having never claimed to throw off allegiance to him, but claiming that he was usurping power which did not belong to him, and that they, as representatives of the thirteen Colonies of America, were the judges of that question and those facts, as we claim that the States are now the judges of this question and these facts. They adopted the following preamble and resolutions:

"The Congress resumed the consideration of the Declaration, which was agreed to, as follows:

"WHEREAS, The petitions of the United Colonies to the King for the redress of great and manifold grievances have not only been rejected, but treated with scorn and contempt, and the opposition to designs evidently formed to reduce them to a state of servile subjection, and their necessary defence against hostile forces actually employed to subdue them, declared rebellion;

"AND WHEREAS, An unjust war hath been commenced against them which the commanders of the British fleets and armies have prosecuted and still continue to prosecute with their utmost vigor, in a cruel manner, wasting, spoiling, and destroying the country, burning houses and defenceless towns, and exposing the helpless inhabitants to every misery, from the inclemency of the winter, and not only urging savages to invade the country, but instigating negroes to murder their masters;

"AND WHEREAS, The Parliament of Great Britain hath lately passed an Act, affirming these Colonies to be in open rebellion; forbidding all trade and commerce with the inhabitants thereof until they shall accept pardons, and submit to despotic rule; declaring their property wherever found upon the water liable to seizure and confiscation, and enacting that what had been done there by virtue of the royal authority were just and lawful acts, and shall be so deemed; from all which it is manifest that the iniquitous schemes concerted to deprive them of the liberty they have a right to by the laws of nature, and the English Constitution, will be pertinaciously pursued. It being, therefore, necessary to provide for their defence and security, and justifiable to make reprisals upon their enemies and otherwise to annoy them according to the laws and usages of nations; the Congress, trusting that such of their friends in Great Britain (of whom it is confessed there are many entitled to applause and gratitude for their patriotism and benevolence, and in whose favor a discrimination of property cannot be made) as shall suffer by captures will impute it to the authors of our common calamities, Do Declare and Resolve as follows, to wit:

"*Resolved*, That the Inhabitants of these Colonies be permitted to fit out armed vessels to cruise on the enemies of these United Colonies.

"*Resolved*, That all ships and other vessels, their tackle, apparel and furniture, and all goods, wares and merchandize belonging to any inhabitant of Great Britain, taken on the high seas, or between high and low water-mark, by any armed vessel fitted out by any private person or persons, and to whom commissions shall be granted, and being libelled and prosecuted in any Court erected for the trial of maritime affairs in any of these Colonies, shall be deemed and adjudged to be lawful prize, and after deducting and paying the wages which the seamen and mariners on board of such captures as are merchant ships and vessels shall be entitled to, according to the terms of their contracts, until the time of their adjudication, shall be condemned to and for the use of the owner or owners, and the officers, marines, and mariners of such armed vessels, according to such rules and proportions as they shall agree on. Provided, always, that this resolution shall not extend to any vessel bringing settlers, arms, ammunition or warlike stores to and for the use of these Colonies, or any of the inhabitants thereof who are friends to the American cause, or to such warlike stores, or to the effects of such settlers.

"*Resolved*, That all ships or vessels, with their tackle, apparel and furniture, goods, wares and merchandize, belonging to any inhabitant of Great Britain, as aforesaid, which shall be taken by any of the vessels of war of these United Colonies, shall be deemed forfeited; one-third, after deducting and paying the wages of seamen and mariners, as aforesaid, to the officers and men on board, and two-thirds to the use of the United Colonies.

"*Resolved*, That all ships or vessels, with their tackle, apparel and goods, wares and merchandizes, belonging to any inhabitant of Great Britain, as aforesaid, which shall be taken by any vessel of war fitted out by and at the expense of any of the United Colonies, shall be deemed forfeited and divided, after deducting and paying the wages of seamen and mariners, as aforesaid, in such manner and proportions as the Assembly or Convention of such Colony shall direct."

There are two or three other resolutions, which it is not necessary for me to trouble you with the reading of. You will bear in mind that there were no two sovereignties over these United Colonies at that time. They had no sovereignty or independence whatever; they were mere Provinces of the British Crown; the Governors derived their appointment from the Crown itself, or from the proprietors of the Colonies; and these wise and good men, on the 23d March, 1776, claimed that the King of Great Britain had usurped powers which did not belong to him under the Constitution of Great Britain, and that they had the right to resist his encroachments; and they authorized letters of marque to cruise against the ships and property of their fellow subjects of Great Britain, because of the state of things which arose from a collision between them and the Crown. They were enemies, and although they regretted that they had to injure in their property men who were their friends, they trusted they would excuse them, owing to the inevitable necessity that existed and the impossibility of discriminating between friends and foes in the case of inhabitants of Great Britain.

And now, gentlemen, to trouble you with one more brief reference, let me show you what took place before that Act of the Provincial Congress was passed in the Province of Massachusetts. They had already passed a Provincial Act of the General Assembly, couched in similar language, authorizing cruisers and privateers against the enemies of that Province; and you will see what occurred. I read again from Cooper's Naval History, 1st Vol., p. 42. He is speaking of the year 1775:

"The first nautical enterprise that succeeded the battle of Lexington was one purely of private adventure. The intelligence of this conflict was brought to Machias, in Maine, on Saturday, the 9th of May, 1775. An armed schooner, in the service of the Crown, called the Margaretta, was lying in port, with two sloops under her convoy, that were loading with lumber on behalf of the King's Government.

"The bearers of the news were enjoined to be silent,—a plan to capture the Margaretta having been immediately projected among some of the more spirited of the inhabitants. The next day being Sunday, it was hoped that the officers of the schooner might be seized while in church; but the scheme failed, in consequence of the precipitation of some engaged. Captain Moore, who commanded the Margaretta, saw the assailants, and, with his officers, escaped through the windows of the church to the shore, where they were protected by the guns of their vessel. The alarm was now taken; springs were got on the Margaretta's cables, and a few harmless shot were fired over the town by way of intimidation. After a little delay, however, the schooner dropped down below the town to a distance exceeding a league. Here she was followed, summoned to surrender, and fired on from a high bank, which her own shot could not reach. The Margaretta again weighed, and running into the bay, at the confluence of the two rivers, anchored. The following morning, which was Monday, the 11th of May, four young men took possession of one of the lumber sloops, and, bringing her alongside of a wharf, they gave three cheers as a signal for volunteers. On explaining that their intentions were to make an attack on the Margaretta, a party of about thirty-five athletic men was soon collected. Arming themselves with firearms, pitchforks, and axes, and throwing a small stock of provisions into the sloop, these spirited freemen made sail on their craft, with a light breeze at northwest. When the Margaretta observed the approach of the sloop, she weighed and crowded sail to avoid a conflict that was every way undesirable,—her commander not yet being apprised of all the facts that had occurred near Boston. In jibing, the schooner carried away her main-boom, but, continuing to stand on, she ran into Holmes' Bay, and took a spar out of a vessel that was lying there. While these repairs were making, the sloop hove in sight again, and the Margaretta stood out to sea, in the hope of avoiding her. The breeze freshened, and, with the wind on the quarter, the sloop proved to be the better sailer. So anxious was the Margaretta to avoid a collision, that Captain Moore now cut away his boats; but, finding this ineffectual, and that his assailants were fast closing with him, he opened a fire—the schooner having an armament of four light guns and fourteen swivels. A man was killed on board the sloop, which immediately returned the fire with a wall-piece. This discharge killed the man at the Margaretta's helm, and cleared her quarter-deck. The schooner broached to, when the sloop gave a general discharge. Almost at the same instant the two vessels came foul of each other. A short conflict now took place with musketry,— Captain Moore throwing hand-grenades, with considerable effect, in person. This officer was immediately afterwards shot down, however, when the people of the sloop boarded and took possession of their prize. The loss of life in this affair was not very great, though twenty men, on both sides, are said to have been killed and wounded. The force of the Margaretta, even in men, was much the most considerable; though the crew of no regular cruiser can ever equal, in spirit and energy, a body of volunteers assembled on an occasion like this. There was, originally, no commander in the sloop; but, previously to engaging the schooner, Jeremiah O'Brien was selected for that station. This affair was the Lexington of the sea,—for, like that celebrated land conflict, it was a rising of the people against a regular force; was characterized by a long chase, a bloody struggle, and a triumph. It was also the first blow struck on the water, after the war of the American Revolution had actually commenced."

And that is the act, gentlemen, which, instead of being the act of desperadoes, pirates, and enemies of the human race, is recorded in history as an act of spirited freemen. You will remember that the act was done without any commission; it was done while these Provinces were Colonies of the British Crown; it was done long before the Declaration of Independence. The Act of the Provincial Congress, so far as that could have any validity, authorizing letters of marque, was not passed until afterwards, on the 23d of March. The Declaration of Independence was passed on the 4th July, 1776. According to the theory on the other side, call this lawful secession—call it revolution— call it what you please,—these Confederate States, as they are called, are not independent. They have not any Government—they cannot do any thing until their independence is acknowledged by the United States. Therefore, according to the theory of the other side, no act of the Provincial Congress, no act of any of the United Colonies, had any validity in it until the treaty of peace between them and Great Britain was signed, in 1783. But, I need not tell you, gentlemen, that in this country, in all public documents, in all public proceedings, in the decisions of our Courts, the actual establishment of the independence of the United States is dated as having been accomplished on the 4th July, 1776. All the state papers that run in the name and by the authority of the United States of America, run in their name, and by their authority, as of such a year of their independence, dating from the 4th July, 1776. Let me, therefore, show you what was done by the Colonies, in 1776, before and after the date of the Declaration of Independence; and let me show how many piracies our hardy seamen of those days must have committed, on the theory of the prosecution in this case. I read again from Cooper's Naval History:

"Some of the English accounts of this period state that near a hundred privateers had been fitted out of New England alone, in the two first years of the war; and the number of seamen in the service of the Crown, employed against the new States of America, was computed at 26,000.

"The Colonies obtained many important supplies, colonial as well as military, and even manufactured articles of ordinary use, by means of their captures,—scarce a day passing that vessels of greater or less value did not arrive in some one of the ports of their extensive coast. By a list published in the 'Remembrancer,' an English work of credit, it appears that 342 sail of English vessels had been taken by American cruisers, in 1776; of which number 44 were recaptured, 18 released, and 4 burned."

Well, gentlemen, with these facts staring you in the face, I ask you if it is not flying in the face of history—if it is not rejecting and trampling in the dust the glorious traditions of our own country—to be asked seriously to sit in that jury box and try these men for their lives, as pirates and enemies of the human race, on the state of things existing here? Gentlemen, my mind may be under a strong hallucination on the subject; but I cannot conceive the theory on which the prosecution can come into Court, on the state of things existing, and ask for a conviction. Remember that, in saying that, I am speaking as a Northern man,—for I am a Northern man; I am speaking as a subject and adherent to the Government of the Union; I am speaking as one who loves the flag of this country—as one who was born under it—as one who hopes to be permitted to die under it; and I am speaking with tears in my eyes, because I do not want to see that flag tarnished by a judicial murder, and by an act cowardly and dastardly, as I say it would be, if we are to treat these men as pirates, while we are engaged in a hand-to-hand conflict with them with arms in the field, and while they are asserting and maintaining the rights which we claimed for ourselves in former ages. In God's name, gentlemen, let us, if necessary, fight them; if we must have civil war, let us convince them, by the argument of arms, and by other arguments that we can bring to bear, that they are in the wrong; let us bring them back into the Union, and show them, when they get back, that they have made a great mistake; but do not let us tarnish the escutcheon of our country, and disgrace ourselves in the eyes of the civilized world, by treating this mighty subject, when States are meeting in mortal shock and conflict, with the ax and the halter. In God's name, let us have none of that!

I have but one word more to say, gentlemen, before I close. I have already said that we claim that this commission is an adequate protection, considering that this is an inter-state war. It has been so considered, and is now so considered by the Government of the United States itself, because, after the conflict had commenced and had gone on for some time, it being treated by the Government at Washington as a mere rebellion or insurrection by insurgent and rebellious citizens in some of the Southern States, it was found that it had assumed too mighty proportions to be treated in that way, and therefore, in the month of July last, the Congress then in session passed an Act, one of the recitals of which was that this state of things had broken out and still existed, and that the war was claimed to be waged under the authority of the governments of the States, and that the governments of the States did not repudiate the existence of that authority. Congress then proceeded to legislate upon the assumption of the fact that the war was carried on under the authority of the governments of the States. There is a distinct recognition by your own Government of the fact that this is an inter-state war, and that the enemies whom our brave troops are encountering in the field are led on under authority emanating from those who are rightfully and lawfully administering the Government of the States.

You will recollect, gentlemen, that in most of those States the State governments are the same as they were before this condition of things broke out. There has been no change in the State constitutions. In a great many of them there has been no change in the personnel of those administering the government. They are the recognized legitimate Governors of the States, whatever may be said of those claiming to administer the Government of the Confederate States.

But, gentlemen, let us pass from that, and let us suppose it was not a war carried on by authority of the States. It is, then, a civil war, and a civil war of immense and vast proportions; and the authorities are equally clear in that case, that, from the moment that a war of that kind exists, captures on land and at sea are to be treated as prizes of war, and prisoners treated as prisoners of war, and that the vocation of the ax and the halter are gone. I refer you to but a single authority on this subject, because I have already occupied more of your time than I had intended doing, and I have reason to be very grateful to you for the patience and attention with which you have listened to me in the extended remarks that I was obliged to make. I refer to Vattel, Book 3, cap. 18, secs. 287, 292 and 293:

"*Sec. 287.* It is a question very much debated whether a sovereign is bound to observe the common laws of war towards rebellious subjects who have openly taken up arms against him. A flatterer, or a Prince of cruel and arbitrary disposition, will immediately pronounce that the laws of war were not made for rebels, for whom no punishment can be too severe. Let us proceed more soberly, and reason from the incontestible principles above laid down."

The author then proceeds to enforce the duty of moderation towards mere rebels, and proceeds:

"*Sec. 292.* When a party is formed in a State who no longer obey the sovereign, and are possessed of sufficient strength to oppose him; or when, in a Republic, the nation is divided into two opposite factions, and both sides take up arms, this is called a civil war. Some writers confine this term to a just insurrection of the subjects against their sovereign to distinguish that lawful resistance from rebellion, which is an open and unjust resistance. But what appellation will they give to a war which arises in a Republic, torn by two factions, or, in a Monarchy, between two competitors for the Crown? Custom appropriates the term of civil war to every war between the members of one and the same political society. If it be between part of the citizens on the one side, and the sovereign with those who continue in obedience to him on the other, provided the malcontents have any reason for taking up arms, nothing further is required to entitle such disturbance to the name of civil war, and not that of rebellion. This latter term is applied only to such an insurrection against lawful authority as is void of all appearance of justice. The sovereign, indeed, never fails to bestow the appellation of rebels on all such of his subjects as openly resist him; but when the latter have acquired sufficient strength to give him effectual opposition, and to oblige him to carry on the war against them according to the established rules, he must necessarily submit to the use of the term civil war.

"*Sec. 293.* It is foreign to our purpose, in this place, to weigh the reasons which may authorize and justify a civil war; we have elsewhere treated of the cases wherein subjects may resist the sovereign. (Book 1, cap. 4.) Setting, therefore, the justice of the cause wholly out of the question, it only remains for us to consider the maxims which ought to be observed in a civil war, and to examine whether the sovereign, in particular, is on such an occasion bound to conform to the established laws of war.

"A civil war breaks the bonds of society and Government, or at least suspends their force and effect; it produces in the nation two independent parties, who consider each other as enemies, and acknowledge no common judge. Those two parties, therefore, must necessarily be considered as thenceforward constituting, at least for a time, two separate bodies—two distinct societies. Though one of the parties may have been to blame in breaking the unity of the State, and resisting the lawful authority, they are not the less divided in fact. Besides, who shall judge them? Who should pronounce on which side the right or the wrong lies? On each they have no common superior. They stand, therefore, in precisely the same predicament as two nations who engage in a contest, and, being unable to come to an agreement, have recourse to arms.

"This being the case, it is very evident that the common laws of war—those maxims of humanity, moderation and honor, which we have already detailed in the course of this work—ought to be observed by both parties in every civil war. For the same reasons which render the observance of those maxims a matter of obligation between State and State, it becomes equally and even more necessary in the unhappy circumstances of two incensed parties lacerating their common country. Should the sovereign conceive he has a right to hang up his prisoners as rebels, the opposite party will make reprisals; if he does not religiously observe the capitulations, and all other conventions made with his enemies, they will no longer rely on his word; should he burn and ravage, they will follow his example; the war will become cruel, horrible, and every day more destructive to the nation."

After noticing the cases of the Duc de Montpensier and Baron des Adrets, he continues:

"At length it became necessary to relinquish those pretensions to judicial authority over men who proved themselves capable of supporting their cause by force of arms, and to treat them not as criminals, but as enemies. Even the troops have often refused to serve in a war wherein the Prince exposed them to cruel reprisals. Officers who had the highest sense of honor, though ready to shed their blood on the field of battle for his service, have not thought it any part of their duty to run the hazard of an ignominious death. Whenever, therefore, a numerous body of men think they have a right to resist the sovereign, and feel themselves in a condition to appeal to the sword, the war ought to be carried on by the contending parties in the same manner as by two different nations, and they ought to leave open the same means for preventing its being carried into outrageous extremities and for the restoration of peace."

Now, gentlemen, can anything be more explicit on this subject, leaving out of view all questions of the authority of the States or of the Confederate

Government to issue this commission? Can anything be more pointed or more direct on the question? Treat this as a mere civil war—treat it as though all State lines of the Union were obliterated, and as though this was a common people, actuated by some religious or political fanaticism, who had set themselves to cutting each others' throats—treat it as a purely civil strife, without any question of State sovereignty or State jurisdiction connected with it,—and still you have the authority of Vattel, an authority than which none can be higher, as the Court will tell you—and I could multiply authorities on that point from now until the shadows of night set in—that even in that case it is obligatory to observe the laws of war just the same as if it was a combat between two nations, instead of between two sections of the same people. Even if there was no commission whatever here, by any one having a color or pretence of right to issue it, but if those belonging to one set of combatants, in a civil strife which had reached the magnitude and proportions of which Vattel speaks, had set out to cruise, and had captured this vessel, I submit to you that it could not be treated as a case of piracy.

I have closed, gentlemen, the argument which, on opening the case, I have thought it necessary to advance in order that you may be able to apply the evidence. Every word that Vattel says there endorses the entreaty which I have made to you, as you love your country and as you love her prosperity, to view this case without passion and without prejudice created by the section in which you live, as I know and trust by your looks and indications that you will. And I say to you, gentlemen, that a greater stab could not be inflicted on our Government—not a greater wound could be given to the cause in which we all, in this section of the country, are enlisted—than to proclaim the doctrine that these cases are to be treated as cases for the halter, instead of as cases of prisoners of war between civilized people and nations. The very course of enlistment of troops for the war has been stopped in this city by that threat. As I said before, the officers and soldiers on the banks of the Potomac, if they could be appealed to on that question, would say, "For God's sake, leave this to the clash of arms, and to regular and legitimate warfare, and do not expose us to the double hazard of meeting death on the field, or meeting an ignominious death if we are captured." And as history has recorded what I have called your attention to as having occurred in the days of the Revolution, so history will record the events of the year and of the hour in which we are now enacting our little part in this mighty drama. The history of this day will be preserved. The history of your verdict will be preserved. You will carry the remembrance of your verdict when you go to your homes. It will come to you in the solemn and still hours of the night. It will come to you clothed in all the solemn importance which attaches to it, with the lives of twelve men hanging upon it, with the honor of your country at stake, with events which no one can foresee to spring from it. And I have only to reiterate the prayer, for our own sake and for the sake of the country, that God may inspire you to render a verdict which will redound to the honor of the country, and that will bring repose to your own consciences when you think of it, long after this present fitful fever of excitement shall have passed away.

DOCUMENTARY TESTIMONY.

Mr. Brady, for the defence, put in evidence the following documents:

1. Preliminary Chart of Part of the sea-coast of Virginia, and Entrance to Chesapeake Bay.—Coast Survey Work, dated 1855.

2. The Constitution of Virginia, adopted June 29, 1776. It refers only to the western and northern boundaries of Virginia—Art. 21—but recognizes the Charter of 1609. That charter (Hemmings' Statutes, 1st vol., p. 88) gives to Virginia jurisdiction over all havens and ports, and all islands lying within 100 miles of the shores.

3. The Act to Ratify the Compact between Maryland and Virginia, passed January 3, 1786—to be found in the Revised Code of Virginia, page 53. It makes Chesapeake Bay, from the capes, entirely in Virginia.

Mr. Sullivan also put in evidence, from *Putnam's Rebellion Record*, the following documents:

1. Proclamation of the President of the United States, of 15th April, 1861. (*See Appendix.*)

2. Proclamation of the President, of 19th April, 1861, declaring a blockade. (*See Appendix.*)

3. Proclamation of 27th April, 1861, extending the blockade to the coasts of Virginia and North Carolina.

4. Proclamation of May 3d, for an additional military force of 42,034 men, and the increase of the regular army and navy.

5. The Secession Ordinance of South Carolina, dated Dec. 20, 1860.

Mr. Smith stated that, in regard to several of the documents, the prosecution objected to them,—not, however, as to any informality of proof. He supposed that the argument as to their relevancy might be reserved till the whole body of the testimony was in.

Judge Nelson: That is the view we take of it.

Mr. Brady suggested that the defence would furnish, to-morrow, a list of the documents which they desired to put in evidence.

The Court then, at half-past 4 P.M., adjourned to Friday, at 11 A.M.

THIRD DAY.

Friday, Oct. 25, 1861.

The Court met at 11 o'clock A.M.

Mr. Brady stated to the Court that two of the prisoners—Richard Palmer and Alexander Coid—were exceedingly ill, suffering from pulmonary consumption, and requested that they might be permitted to leave the court-room when they wished. It was not necessary that they should be present during all the proceedings.

Mr. Smith: It would be proper that the prisoners make the application.

Mr. Brady: They will remain in Court as long as they can; and will, of course, be present when the Court charges the Jury.

The Court directed the Marshal to provide a room for the prisoners to retire to, when they desired.

Mr. Sullivan: Before adjourning yesterday it was stated that the different ordinances of the seceded States were all considered in evidence without being read.

Mr. Smith: Are any of them later in date than the commission to the Savannah?

Mr. Sullivan: No, sir. Some States have seceded since the date of the commission, and have been received into the Confederacy.

Mr. Evarts: We will assume, until the contrary appears, that there are no documents of date later than the supposed authorization of the privateer.

Mr. Larocque: With this qualification,—that there are a great many documents from our own Government which recognize a state of facts existing anterior to those documents.

Mr. Sullivan read in evidence from page 10 of *Putnam's Rebellion Record*:

Letter from Secretary of War, John B. Floyd, to President James Buchanan, dated December 29, 1860.

President Buchanan's reply, dated December 31, 1860.

Also, from page 11 of *Rebellion Record*:

The Correspondence between the South Carolina Commissioners and the President of the United States.

[Considered as read.]

Also, referred to page 19 of *Rebellion Record*, for the Correspondence between Major Anderson and Governor Pickens, with reference to firing on the *Star of the West*.

Read Major Anderson's first letter (without date), copied from *Charleston Courier*, of Jan. 10, 1861. (*See Appendix.*)

Governor Pickens' reply, and second communication from Major Anderson. (*See Appendix.*)

Also, from page 29 of *Rebellion Record*, containing the sections of the Constitution of the Confederate States which differ from the Constitution of the United States.

Also, from page 31 of *Rebellion Record*: Inaugural of Jefferson Davis, as President of the Confederate States.

Also, page 36 of *Rebellion Record*: Inaugural of Abraham Lincoln, President of the United States, (for the passages, *see Appendix.*)

Also, page 61 of *Rebellion Record*: The President's Speech to the Virginia Commissioners. (*See Appendix.*)

Also, page 71 of *Rebellion Record*: Proclamation of Jefferson Davis, with reference to the letters of marque, dated 17th April, 1861.

Also, page 195 of *Rebellion Record*: An Act recognizing a state of war, by the Confederate Congress,—published May 6, 1861.

[Read Section 5.]

Mr. Lord read from pages 17, 19, and 20, of *Diary of Rebellion Record*, to give the date of certain events:

1861,	February	8.	The Constitution of the Confederate States adopted. February 18. Jefferson Davis inaugurated President.
	February	21.	The President of the Southern Confederacy nominates members of his Cabinet.
	February	21.	Congress at Montgomery passed an Act declaring the establishment of free navigation of the Mississippi.
	March	19.	Confederates passed an Act for organizing the Confederate States.

	April	8.	South Carolina Convention ratified the Constitution of the Confederate States by a vote of 119 to 16.

Mr. Sullivan: We propose now to introduce the papers found on board the Savannah when she was captured. The history of these papers is, that they were captured by the United States officers, taken from the Savannah, and come into our hands now, in Court, through the hands of the United States District Attorney, in whose possession they have been;—and they have been proceeded upon in the prize-court, for the condemnation of the Savannah. The first I read, is—

The Commission to the Savannah, dated 18th May, 1861.

Also, put in evidence, copy of Act recognizing the existence of war between the United States and the Confederate States, and concerning letters of marque,—approved May 6, 1861.

Also, read *President Davis' Instructions to Private Armed Vessels,*—appended to the Act.

Also, an Act regulating the sale of prizes, dated May 6, 1861,—approved May 14, 1861.

Also, an Act relative to prisoners of war, dated May 21, 1861.

Mr. Sullivan also read in evidence three extracts from the Message of President Lincoln to Congress, at Special Session of July 4, 1861. (*See Appendix.*)

Also, extracts from the Message of President Buchanan, at the opening of regular Session of Congress, December 3d, 1860. (*See Appendix.*)

Also, from page 245 of *Rebellion Record:* Proclamation of the Queen of Great Britain, dated May 13, 1861.

Mr. Evarts objected to this, on the ground that it could not have been received here prior to the date of the commission.

Objection overruled.

Also, from page 170 of *Rebellion Record:* Proclamation of the Emperor of France,—published June 11, 1861.

Also, the Articles of Capitulation of the Forts at the Hatteras Inlet, dated August 29th, on board the United States flagship Minnesota, off Hatteras Inlet.

Mr. Evarts remarked that this latter document was not within any propositions hitherto passed upon; but he did not desire to arrest the matter by any discussion, if their honors thought it should be received.

Judge Nelson: It may be received provisionally.

Mr. Brady also put in evidence the *Charleston Daily Courier*, of 11th June, 1861, containing a Judicial Advertisement,—a monition on the filing of a libel in the Admiralty Court of the Confederate States of America, for the South Carolina District, and an advertisement of the sale of the Joseph, she having been captured on the high seas by the armed schooner Savannah, under the command of T. Harrison Baker,—attested in the name of Judge Magrath, 6th June, 1861.

And containing, also, a judicial Act, relating to the administration of an estate in due course of law.

Mr. Brady stated that the reference was to show that they had a judicial system established under their own Government.

Lieutenant D. D. Tompkins recalled for the defence, and examined by *Mr. Sullivan.*

Q. State your knowledge as to the sending of any flags of truce while your vessel, the Harriet Lane, was lying at Fortress Monroe?

(Same objection; received provisionally.)

A. I have seen flags of truce come down from the direction of Norfolk.

Q. Did your vessel have any communication with the officer bearing the flag of truce?

A. No, sir.

Q. Did they come with the Confederate flag flying on the same vessel with the flag of truce?

A. Yes. One vessel came down with the Confederate flag flying, and a flag of truce, also.

Q. Where was it received, and by what officer?

A. I am not positive whether it was received by the Cumberland or the Minnesota. They communicated with either of those vessels.

Q. Were any vessels or boats, with flags of truce, ever sent from Fort Monroe toward the Confederate forces?

A. I have seen vessels go up the Roads with a flag of truce.

Q. And the United States flag on the same vessels?

A. Yes.

Q. You saw Captain Baker and the other prisoners—were they uniformed?

A. No, sir; I do not think they had any regular uniform. Captain Baker had a uniform, with metal buttons on his coat. I did not notice what was on the buttons.

Q. He had on such a dress as he wears to-day?

A. Something similar to that. He was the only one who had a uniform.

Q. Do you know anything as to the exchange of prisoners between the forces of the United States and of the Confederate States on any station where you have been?

A. No, sir.

The defence here closed.

The District Attorney stated that the prosecution had no rebutting evidence to offer.

Judge Nelson: Before counsel commence summing up the case to the Jury, they will please present the propositions of law on both sides.

Mr. Lord: I was going to ask my friends on the other side to give us their authorities, so that we shall know what we are to go to the Jury upon. We would then be able to lay our views before the Court and to divide the labor of summing up—some of us addressing ourselves entirely to the Court.

Mr. Evarts: I would have no objection to taking that course if I had been prepared for it. In the presentation of the case, we rely on the statute of the United States—on the fact that the defendants are within the terms of the statute; and that the affirmative defence, growing out of the state of things in this country, does not apply in a Court of the United States, and under a statute of the United States, which still covers the condition of the persons brought in. Whether they are citizens or aliens, nothing has been shown which takes them out of the general operation of our laws. On the question of the ingredients of the crime of piracy—which is a particular inquiry, irrespective of the considerations connected with the state of war—I do not know that we need refer to anything which is not quite familiar. The cases referred to by the learned counsel for the prisoners—the United States *vs.*

Jones, the United States *vs.* Palmer, and the United States *vs.* Tully—contain all the views in reference to the ingredients of the crime of piracy, or to the construction of the statutes, that we need to present. In the general elementary books to which the learned counsel have referred—the various books on the Pleas of the Crown—there are passages to which we shall have occasion to refer.

Judge Nelson: The counsel for the Government should give to the counsel on the other side, before the summing up is commenced, all the authorities on which they intend to rely.

Mr. Evarts: That we shall do, of course.

Judge Nelson: We will take them now.

Mr. Evarts: I refer to 1st East's Pleas of the Crown, 70-1.

It is under the title of Treason, but it is on the point of the character of the crime as qualified by the influence on the party, of force, or of the state of the population by which the accused was surrounded. I read from page 70:

"Joining with rebels freely and voluntarily in any act of rebellion is levying war against the King; and this, too, though the party was not privy to their intent. This was holden in the case of the Earl of Southampton, and again in Purchase's case, in 1710. But yet it seems necessary, in this case, either that the party joining with rebels, and ignorant of their intent at the time, should do some deliberate act towards the execution of their design, or else should be found to have aided and assisted those who did. * * * But if the joining with rebels be from fear of present death, and while the party is under actual force, such fear and compulsion will excuse him. It is incumbent, however, on the party setting up this defence, to give satisfactory proof that the compulsion continued during all the time that he stayed with the rebels."

The case of Axtell, one of the regicides, is referred to. The defense was set up for him that he acted by command of his superior officer; but that was ruled to be no defence. I now read from page 104:

"One species of treason, namely, that of committing hostilities at sea, under color of a foreign commission, or any other species of adherence to the King's enemies there, may be indicted and tried as piracy, by virtue of the statutes."

That is, that although being guilty of treason, in its general character of adhering to the enemy, yet it also falls within the description of piracy, and may be proceeded against as such. On the question of the element of force or intimidation as entering into the crime of robbery, I refer to 1st Hawkins' Pleas of the Crown, page 235:

"Wherever a person assaults another with such circumstances of terror as put him into fear, and cause him, by reason of such fear, to part with his money, the taking thereof is adjudged robbery, whether there were any weapon drawn, or not, or whether the person assaulted delivered his money upon the other's command, or afterwards gave it him upon his ceasing to use force, and begging an alms; for he was put into fear by his assault, and gives him his money to get rid of him.

"But it is not necessary that the fact of actual fear should either be laid in the indictment or be proved upon the trial; it is sufficient if the offence be charged to be done *violenter et contra voluntatem.* And if it appear upon the evidence to have been attended with those circumstances of violence or terror which in common experience are likely to induce a man to part with his property against his consent, either for the safety of his person or for the preservation of his character and good name, it will amount to a robbery."

I refer to Hale's Pleas of the Crown, vol. I., p. 68, on the question of double or doubtful allegiance:

"Though there may be due from the same person subordinate allegiances, which, though they are not without an exception of the fidelity due to the superior Prince, yet are in their kind *sacramenta ligea fidelitatis,* or subordinate allegiances, yet there can not, or at least should not, be two or more co-ordinate allegiances by one person to several independent or absolute Princes; for that lawful Prince that hath the prior obligation of allegiance from his subject can not lose that interest without his own consent, by his subject's resigning himself to the subjection of another."

I refer to the case of the United States *against* Tully, 1st Gallison's Reports, p. 253-5, to show that the statute does not, in terms, require that there shall be any personal violence or putting in fear to constitute robbery, provided the offence is committed *animo furandi.*

I also refer to the case of the United States *vs.* Jones, 3 Washington C.C.R., p. 219, on the point of the justification given by a commission; to the case of United States *vs.* Hayward, 2 Gallison, 501; to the observations of Chancellor Kent, vol. I., p. 200, marginal page 191; to the United States *vs.* Palmer, 3 Wheaton, p. 634, as to the manner in which our Courts deal with international questions respecting the recognition of nationalities; to the case of the Santissima Trinidad, Kent's Commentaries, vol. I., p. 27, marginal page 25; to the case of Rose *vs*. Hinely, 4 Cranch, 241. I refer to the latter case for the general doctrines therein contained on the proposition that although a parent or original Government may find the magnitude and power of the rebellion such as to induce or compel it to resort to warlike means of suppression, so as that toward neutral nations there will grow up such a state of authority as will compel the recognition by neutral nations of the rights of war and belligerents, that is not inconsistent with or in derogation of the general proposition that the parent Government still maintains the sovereignty, and can enforce its municipal laws, by all those sanctions, against its rebellious subjects. In other words, that the flagrancy of civil war, which gives rise to the aspect and draws after it the consequences of war, does not destroy either the duty of allegiance or the power of punishing any infraction of law which the rebels may be guilty of, either in reference to the principal crime of treason, or in reference to any other violation of municipal rights.

I also ask your honors' attention to a recent charge of Judge Sprague, to the Grand Jury in the Massachusetts District, in reference to the crime of piracy.

On the question of jurisdiction, I refer to the case of the United States *vs*. Hicks, decided in this Court.

I refer to the case of the Mariana Flora, to show that the arrest of a pirate at sea arises under a general principle of the law of nations, which authorizes either a public or a private vessel to make the arrest. It is analogous to the common-law arrest of a felon. The point in the case of the Mariana Flora is, that any public or private vessel has a right to arrest a piratical vessel at sea and bring it in. It differs in that respect from the authority to arrest a slaver.

On the general question of the ingredients of robbery, I refer to Archbold's Criminal Practice and Pleadings, 2 vol., p. 507, marginal pages 417, 510, 526.

In political connections I shall have occasion to refer to the Constitution of the United States and to the Articles of the Confederation, to the Virginia and Kentucky resolutions, and the answers of the other States of the Union, which will be found collected in Ellett's Debates, vol. 4, pages 528 to 545.

I may refer also to Mr. Pinckney's speech in the Convention of South Carolina which adopted the Constitution, same volume, p. 331; to the formal ratifications of the Constitution by the different States of the Union, same volume, p. 318; and I may have occasion to refer to Grotius in connection with the discussion of the general state of war. The citations will be—book 1st, chap. 1, secs. 1 and 2; chap. 3, secs. 1 and 4; and chap. 4, sec. 1.

MR. LORD'S ARGUMENT.

Mr. Lord, of counsel for the defence, said:

May it please your honors,—The distribution of duties which counsel for the defence have made among themselves is, that I shall briefly present the propositions of law, somewhat irrespective of the wide political range which my friends seem to think is to be involved. I shall not pursue even the field which Mr. Larocque has opened, knowing that he has cultivated it to a far greater degree than I have, and therefore I will leave it to him to till. My friend, Mr. Brady, will address the Jury on any questions of fact that may be supposed to be involved.

Before I enter upon the discussion, and with the view that this case may be relieved from one prejudice which probably every man has felt on first hearing of it, I beg leave to set ourselves all right on the idea that there is something different in a private armed ship from a public armed vessel, in the law, and in the view of the people of the country. I desire to read on that subject a letter from Mr. Marcy to the Count de Sartiges.

Mr. Lord read the letter, and continued:

Therefore in this discussion, so far from a private armed vessel being regarded with disfavor, it is regarded, and has to be regarded, with all the favor which would belong to it as a regularly commissioned cruiser, belonging to the State, and not to the individual.

I now approach, with all the brevity due to your valuable time, the question of jurisdiction. It seems to me to be very clear indeed that after Harleston and the crew, of the Savannah were taken by the Perry, he was confined as a prisoner, as one of a crew of a piratical vessel, for an act charged as piratical, on board the United States ship-of-war Minnesota, by order of its commander. That Harleston was taken by the said commander into the District of Virginia, within a marine league of its shores, where the said ship remained; and the said Harleston and the other prisoners could have been there landed and detained for trial. If the facts are so, the Circuit Court of this District has no jurisdiction, and the prisoners should be acquitted.

The evidence of our friend, Commodore Stringham, on that subject, leaves us no doubt as to the character of the arrest. After seeing the Perry close in to Charleston, she having been ordered by him to cruise further off, and he, wondering what she was doing there—he says:

"She hailed us and informed us she had captured a piratical vessel. The vessel was half a mile astern. Captain Parrot, of the Perry, came and made to me a report of what had taken place. I ordered him to send the prisoners on board, and I sent a few men on board the Savannah to take charge of her during the night. The vessels were then anchored. Next morning I made arrangements to put a prize crew on board the Savannah and send her to New York, and I directed the Captain of the Joseph to take passage in her. I took the prisoners from the Perry, and directed the Perry to proceed," &c.

Again he testifies:

"*Q.* What was your object in transferring the prisoners from the Perry to the Minnesota?

"*A.* Sending them to a Northern port. The port of New York was the port I had in my mind to send them to, in the first ship from the station."

The prisoners, thus taken from a piratical vessel, he determined to carry to Norfolk, and to send them thence to the North for trial.

Now, if your honors please, my learned friend (Mr. Evarts) seems to say that there is no authority in law for a United States vessel to arrest pirates at sea; but if you will read the President's proclamation of 19th June you will find that he speaks of dealing with the persons who may be taken on board private armed ships as pirates. I will then ask to direct your attention to the Act of 1819 (3d Vol. Statutes, p. 510), where the President is authorized to employ public armed vessels to arrest offenders against that law. Therefore the capture of the prize was not only a part of the general law of nations, but it was particularly a thing which the commanders of ships of the United States were charged by the proclamation of the President, and by Act of Congress, to do.

I now approach the other question, as to where these prisoners were apprehended, or into what District they were first brought. That they were apprehended by a warrant from the United States Commissioner in New York, is not in dispute. The question, however, is, where they were first brought. If an officer having them in charge could anchor his vessel at Baltimore, and then at Philadelphia, and then bring his prisoners to New York, it would be putting the law entirely in his hands and dissipating all its force. In ordinary cases of crime the jurisdiction is local; and that for many reasons. One is, that a man is to be tried by his peers—meaning those of his own neighborhood,—and that it is easier to procure evidence at the place where the crime is committed. The law does not give to any man the power of assigning the place of trial. In the case of offences committed on the high seas, the law declares that the accused shall be tried in the District into which he is first brought.

Now, that tnese men were held by Capt. Stringham for the purpose of being tried as pirates, the evidence is clear. They were transferred from the Perry to the Minnesota, taken to the Norfolk station, and there kept in irons on board the Minnesota till they were transferred to the Harriet Lane. Could they have been detained there for trial? It might be an inconvenience if there was no Court. They might have had to be detained for a long time, or Congress might pass some law varying the jurisdiction. But as the law stood, if these men could have been landed and detained for trial, then that was the District in which they were necessarily to be tried. Can any one say that it was not as easy to have landed these men at Fortress Monroe, or at Hampton, as to transfer them to the Harriet Lane? And could they not have been detained there? You did not need a Court to detain them. They were taken by force, and might have been detained in the fortress till a trial should be had. There was no difficulty in their being landed in Virginia; and, moreover, there were in Western Virginia loyal Courts, where they could be tried.

Now, what is there that takes away the jurisdiction which belongs to that part of the country and not to this? "Why," says Captain Stringham, "I wanted to send them to New York." But had he any right to do so, when he had actually brought them to that station where his ship belonged, and where he was bound to keep her unless he returned her to the cruising ground? Remember that his ship remained there some time before the transfer was made. They were detained as prisoners there, and might as well have been detained on shore. Therefore, it seems to me, that unless the capturing officer, and not Congress, has the right to determine the place where the trial shall be had, these men were to be tried in the District of Virginia.

Now, it is no answer to this to say that, where a vessel is sailing along the shores of a District, a prisoner on board is not brought there in the proper sense of the word. The ship is not bound to stop and break up her voyage in order to have the Court designated where he is to be tried; but where the ship comes into port—where she stops at a port—I submit to your honors that this is the bringing contemplated by the statute.

I now approach, if your honors please, the merits of this case. The indictment is founded on two sections of the Crimes Act, originally two separate and very distinct statutes. It is the eighth section which makes robbery on the high seas piracy. That embraces the first five counts of the indictment, which are varied in mere circumstances. The remaining counts rest on the transcript into the legislation of this country, from the Act of 11 and 12 William III., to the effect, substantially, that if any citizen of the United States shall, under color of a commission from any foreign Prince or State, or under pretence of authority from any other person, commit acts of hostility against the United States, or the citizens thereof, that shall be piracy. In the argument which I shall address to your honors I will beg leave to characterize the first as piracy by the laws of nations, and the second as statutory piracy. But, before I discuss that subject, permit me to say that, as to eight of these prisoners, it is conceded that they do not come under that section, as the evidence for the prosecution shows that they were not citizens of the United States. So that, as to these eight, unless they are adjudged pirates under the eighth section, they must be acquitted, if they can justify themselves under the commission.

Judge Nelson: Then the other four, you say, can only be convicted under the ninth section?

Mr. Lord: Yes; that is the statutory process, if I may be permitted to give it that name.

The act is charged as an act of robbery, not as an act of treason. It is not alleged to have been done treasonably. If the prosecution wanted to give it that character, they must have alleged it to be treason. They must have alleged that this act, done on the high seas, was done treasonably, traitorously, and therefore piratically. They have alleged no such thing. I take pleasure in saying that the District Attorney, in opening this case, did it with great fairness, and disavowed any idea of introducing treason into the case. There are many reasons why, if that were pretended, this whole trial should stop. The requisites of a prosecution for treason have not been, in any degree, complied with. The charge is robbery. It may be charged as done piratically, involving *animus furandi*. Let us see, for an instant, what piratical is. Piracy is, by all definitions, a crime against all nations. It enters into every description of a pirate that he is *hostis humani generis*. That is the common-law idea of piracy. It is not a political heresy that will make piracy. It is not a political conformity that will always exempt from the charge of piracy. For instance, if the officer of a Government vessel, with the most full and complete commission, such as my friend Commodore Stringham had, should invade a ship at sea, and should, under pretence of capture, take jewels and secrete them, not bringing them in for adjudication, he would be a pirate, because, though he held a commission, he did the act *animo furandi,*—did it out of the jurisdiction of any particular country,—did it against the great principles of civilization and humanity.

Again, if a commissioned vessel hails a private ship, and, on the idea that she is a subject of prize, captures her, and it turns out that that capture is illegal and unwarranted, that fact does not make the act piracy. Although the act might be ever so irregular—although it might subject the officer to the severest damages for trespass—yet it is not piratical, and the officer is not to be hung at the yard-arm because he mistakes a question of law. Your honors therefore see how utterly it enters into the whole subject that the thing shall be done *animo furandi*, piratically, as against the general law of nations and the sense of right of the civilized world.

Well, now, we are at once struck with this consideration: Suppose the act is regarded as not piratical by millions of people having civilized institutions, having Courts of Justice, giving every opportunity for a trial of the question of forfeiture or no forfeiture—why, it shocks the moral sense to say that that is done *animo furandi*, that it is a theft and a robbery, and that the man who does it is an enemy to the human race. Carry the idea a little further, and you find that the commission under which a man acts in seizing a vessel with a view of bringing it in as a prize is regarded by all the great commercial nations of the world as regular, and that the act is regarded not as a piratical, but as a belligerent act. Does it not shock the very elements of justice to have it supposed that in such a case the man acting under the commission, and within its powers, is to be deemed an enemy of the whole human race, while all the human race, except the power which seeks to subject him to punishment, says the act is not piratical?

Now, upon this subject my learned friends have cited many authorities, which all bear on the effect of what should give validity to the transfer of captured property under the circumstances of rebellions in States. Now I beg leave, at the outset of the consideration of this case, to say that the question of passing title to property is a thing entirely different from the question of hanging a man for committing a crime. In the first place, look at the numerous acts of trespass which are committed on the high seas by vessels of every nation. The books are full of cases of marine trespass, and of damages against captors for their irregularities; but are the authorities which bear upon that subject, which is a mere question of property—a question of title—of the mere transfer of title—are they authorities which decide the question that a man should be hanged if he mistakes the law, or if he acts under the impulse of a wrong judgment as to the sovereign which he should serve? I would call your attention to the case of Klintock, reported in the 5th of Wheaton, where the Court say that they will not regard the commission of General Aubrey as sufficient to give title to the property, "although it might be sufficient to defend him from a charge of piracy." I also refer to Phillimore on International Law, vol. 3, p. 319. [Counsel read from the authority.]

Now, under what circumstances was this done? And in the discussion I give to this question I am entirely free from the necessity of considering how the Government of this country shall regard the seceded States,—as having a Government, or not. I am under the law of nations, because this act which I am now discussing, of robbery on the high seas, was evidently a transcript of the law of nations upon the subject of piracy. What are the undeniable facts?—the facts about which, in this case, there is not any dispute, either in this country or in the whole world—about which there is but one opinion—what are they? At the time the crew of the Savannah shipped for this cruise, and at the time of the capture of the Joseph, the authorities of the State of South Carolina (for the State of South Carolina had an organization from its beginning, as a part of this country, and, as a government, was well known to the Government of the United States)—the authorities of the State of South Carolina, where the Savannah was fitted out and the crew resided, had become parties to a confederation of others of the United States. Now it is immaterial to me, in the light in which I view this case, whether that was politically right or not—whether it was legally right or not—whether this country could look at it as a source of title to property or not; the fact is there, that a State—one of the original, recognized States of the Union—united itself, under an assumption of authority, revolutionary if you please, with other similar States, and formed a league and a Government. That fact is undoubtedly so. Under such confederation a Government, in fact, existed, and exercised, in fact, the powers of civil and military Government over the territories and peoples of those States, or a principal part of them. Here we have eleven recognized States, doing, if you please, an illegal thing, when you come to submit it to the just principles of law. They form a league,—against an Act of Congress,—but they do form a league, and do constitute a Government; and this Government takes possession of a territory of some ten millions of people, all of whom submit to it. It maintains the Government in its domestic character of States, and originates a Government for its foreign relations. It assumes to make war, and declares war. The President's proclamation says that the said Confederated States had in fact declared war against the United States of America, and were openly prosecuting the same with large military forces, under the military and civil organization of a Government; and had assumed, and were in the exercise of, the power of issuing commissions to private armed ships to make captures of the property of the United States, and the citizens thereof, as prize of war, and to send them into Court for adjudication as such. Now, all that is beyond any doubt; and is it possible that it can be contended that an act of that vast extent, of that wide publicity and great power, should fail even to justify the killing of a chicken, without charge of petty larceny? Does it not shock the common sense of mankind that, in the case of men dwelling there, and acting in subordination to the existing Government (you cannot say whether voluntarily or not), for every shot fired and man killed you could have a trial for murder; that for every horse shot you could have an action of trover; and for every trespass you could have an action of trespass? This practically shocks us. How is it in view of the doctrine of *hostis humani generis*? Here are ten millions of people doing acts which, if done only by three or four, would be murders and treasons. But justice must be equal. If required to execute justice upon three or four, you are bound to execute it on tens of millions?

Why, that is the very thing which publicists tell us constitutes civil war. A civil war is always a rebellion when it begins. In the first instance it commences with a few individuals,—the Catalines of the country; but when it gets to be formed, so that a large force is collected, and, instead of the Courts of Justice before existing, it substitutes Courts of its own, then comes up the doctrine of humanity which belongs to the laws of war,—that you can no longer speak of it as a rebellion. In the judgments of publicists when a rebellion gets to that head that it represents States, and parts of a nation, humanity stops the idea of private justice, and it goes upon the principle of public and international law. That will be found elaborately stated in Vattel; but I do not intend to trouble you with any lengthened reading of citations. I refer to the 18th chap. on the subject of civil war, page 424:

"When a party is formed in a State, who no longer obey the sovereign, and are possessed of sufficient force to oppose him; or when, in a Republic, the nation is divided into two opposite factions, and both sides take up arms,— this is called a *civil war*. Some writers confine this term to a just insurrection of the subjects against their sovereign, to distinguish that lawful resistance from *rebellion*, which is an open and unjust resistance. But what appellation will they give to a war which arises in a Republic torn by two factions, or in a Monarchy, between two competitors for the crown? Custom appropriates the term of '*civil war*' to every war between the members of one and the same political society. If it be between the part of the citizens, on the one side, and the sovereign, with those who continue in obedience to him, on the other,— provided the malcontents have any reason for taking up arms, nothing further is required to entitle such disturbance to the name of *civil war*, and not *rebellion*. This latter term is applied only to such an insurrection against lawful authority as is void of all appearance of justice. The sovereign, indeed, never fails to bestow the appellation of *rebels* on all such of his subjects as openly resist him; but, when the latter have acquired sufficient strength to give him effectual opposition, and to oblige him to carry on the war against them according to the established rules, he must necessarily submit to the use of the term 'civil war.'"

The moment the term "civil war" comes up, the idea of punishing, as rebellion or as piracy, the capture of a vessel, is an abuse of justice; and it is not only an abuse of justice, but it is an abuse of the fact, to say that those who are large enough to be a nation are to be considered as the enemies of all nations, because they undertake to make civil war. The point is not founded upon any technical considerations; it is founded upon the great doctrines of humanity and civilization. Because, what is to be the end of it? If we hang twelve men, they hang one hundred and fifty-six. If we treat them as rebels, why they treat our captured forces as these rebels are treated. You bring on a war without any civilizing rules. You bring in a war of worse than Indian barbarity. You bring in a war which can know nothing except bloodshed, in battle or upon the block. This is not a technical notion. It is that, when civil war is found to exist (and that altogether comes from the magnitude of the opposition), then the rules of war apply, as much as in any public war, so far as to protect the individuals acting under them. What would be said if you should take a gentleman who was made prisoner at Fort Hatteras, and try him for treason, and hang him? What would be said in this country, or in Europe,—what would be said anywhere, in the present or in future ages,—as to an act like that? Well, why not? Because justice must be equal. If you do it to one, you must do it to all. If you do it to all, you carry on an extermination of the human race, against all the principles which can animate a Court of Justice, or find a seat in the human bosom. Therefore, if we have the fact of civil war, we have the rules of war introduced.

Now, is this a civil war? I do not ask the question of how this country simply should regard it; but on the question in a Criminal Court, as to whether a civil war exists so as to give protection to those who act on one side of it, I have the concurrent judgments of the Courts. Judge Dunlop, in the case of the Tropic Wind, says there can be no blockade except in a case of war; that this is a civil war, and therefore there is a blockade. Judge Cadwalader says this is a civil war, and in civil war you may make captures; and Judge Betts, in a vastly profitable judgment, delivered in the other room, confiscating millions of property of Union men in the South, says that this is civil war. Now, if the Government of the United States forfeits the property of persons residing in these seceded States, without the formality of a trial for treason, because it is simply enemy's property, with what pretence can they set up the principle that they will not treat them as enemies? They will treat them as enemies, for the purpose of confiscation, and not as enemies, but as traitors and pirates, for the purpose of execution? Why, it is a glaring inconsistency. It strikes us off our feet as a people fit to be looked at by any impartial or rational person, in political jurisprudence.

We submit, therefore, that there was a civil war. Then what was the taking of the Joseph? I now pass by the Savannah's commission for a moment. The capture of the Joseph was in this way: The Joseph was approached by the Savannah, and her Captain ordered on board. I make no question about its being a taking by force; I make no question but that, if it was done piratically, there was force enough to make it piratical. But when asked, Why do you do it? Captain Baker replied, "I take this by authority of the Confederated States. I am sorry for it; but you make war upon us, and we have, in retaliation, to make war upon you." The vessel is taken; nothing is removed from her; and she is sent in as a prize, and reaches Georgetown. Nothing is then taken from her, but she is proceeded against in Court, and men are examined there as to the vessel, just as fairly, and probably just as good men, as have been examined in the other room. The question is tried. It is an undeniable case that, if this is a civil war, they having declared war, the vessel belongs to a belligerent, and she is taken, condemned and sold, according to the laws which have dominion over that country—a proceeding (erroneous as it may be in the ultimate object of it) according to all the course of every civilized country. And yet, we are told, that is piratical! I submit that this cannot be so. We cannot, with any approach to consistency, hold that we can treat them both as enemies and rebels at the same time. Not so. Treat them as rebels, and confiscate the property by due course of law, and you can get nothing; because it is a singular thing that in this country there is no such thing as forfeiture for treason. You cannot forfeit the chattels, but only the land, and that for life; and as the penalty of treason is death, leaving no life estate for the forfeiture to act on, there is, practically, no forfeiture for treason. When these men come and say, we have taken this property as an enemy, you treat them as rebels. It seems to me this is indulging a private animosity; it is indulging a fanatical principle, an unworthy principle, that cannot be carried out without disregarding the great rules that belong to civilized nations with regard to war.

Again, if your honors please, piracy and robbery always have secrecy about them. The open robber, who meets you in noonday, yet secretes the plunder. He does not go into a Court of Justice and say, "Behold what I have taken! here are the jewels, and here the gold; adjudge if they are lawful prize!" The robber never does that. Here there is nothing secret or furtive. The vessel and cargo are taken before a Court and adjudicated to be a prize. Let us take a case which, although unlikely to happen, might occur. A man goes from seceding Virginia with an execution to levy upon a man in loyal Virginia. The man there says, "You are superseded; you have no authority;" and it is tried there. The Court hold that the execution and levy from the seceded State does not pass the property; but would it be possible to say, there was anything furtive in the taking on the part of the officer? There is nothing more plain, in criminal law, than that, if you act under color of authority, although you may be ruined by suits in trespass, yet you are not to be subjected to punishment as having done what was felonious.

But there is one other consideration which I would present on the subject of piracy: it is robbery upon the high seas,—an act *hostis humani generis*. It is made an offence in this country, because it is an offence against the law of nations; for this is a question on which civilized nations do not differ. All the nations of Europe look on at this controversy. Here comes a man that the District Attorney of New York says is *hostis humani generis*. What says the great commercial nation of Great Britain? We do not treat you as pirates, but as belligerents. We do not recognize your independence, because you have not achieved it; but when the question arises, whether we shall consider you as pirates, whom we, in common with all other nations, have a right to take up, we say it is no such thing. Judge Sprague says, that they say it is no such thing. So, too, with France. Here is the authority of a great Empire that this is not a piratical but a belligerent act. And again, Spain reiterates the same decision. Suppose I could bring the authority of the highest Court in Great Britain that, just in such a case as this, the Court acquitted a man of piracy; and suppose I could add to that a similar judgment under the law of France; and bring a case from the Courts in Spain, deciding the question in the same way; and so, too, from Holland,—and when I come down to New York, the District Attorney says the man is *hostis humani generis*! Is it not absurd? If piracy be a crime against public law, it is so. The recognition and the application of the doctrines of common humanity to this great struggle,—that they should be regarded as the determining point upon this great question—it seems to me your honors will never hesitate in admitting. I, therefore, present this point, and if your honors will permit me, after this discursive argumentation, I will read it as I think it ought to be decided in law:

"There is evidence that at the time of the crew of the Savannah shipping for the cruise, and at the time of the capture of the Joseph, the authorities of the State of South Carolina had become parties to a confederation of others of the United States of America, named in the President's proclamation. That under such confederation a Government, in fact, existed; and exercised, in fact, the powers of civil and military Government over the territories and people of those States, or the principal part thereof. That the said Confederate States had, in fact, declared war against the United States of America, and were openly prosecuting the same, with large military forces, and the military and civil organization of a Government; and had assumed, and were in the exercise of, the power of issuing commissions to private armed ships, to make captures of the property of the United States, and the citizens thereof, as prize of war, and to send them into port for adjudication as such. And that a civil war thus, in fact, existed. That the taking of the Joseph was under such authority of the Confederate States, and in the name of prize of war, and with the purpose of having the same adjudged by a Prize Court in South Carolina, or some other of the said Confederate States. And, if the facts are so found, then the taking of the Joseph was not piratical, under the eighth section of the Act of 1790, and the prisoners must be acquitted from the charge under this count."

Now I approach the case of the commission. I suppose that the District Attorney, by not proving the commission as a part of the charge, is not entitled to convict any of these prisoners under the commission which is shown. He does not prove his case; and it is no matter what we have proved,—he is not entitled to a conviction under evidence which he does not bring.

But now I take up the matter of the commission, and the consideration of *piracy by statute*, under the 9th section. If your honors please, it is right that I should give some history of that 9th section's coming into the law of piracy. The 8th section you will find to be the law of piracy, by the law of nations. All nations hold that to be piracy which is there described. But, in the 11th and 12th of William III., this state of things existed: King James had abdicated the Crown of England twelve years before; William and Mary reigned together six years; William survived her. Here, then, was a Government in England, with a pretender, whom the English Government had declared was an alien from the Throne; they had banished him. But he was at the Court of St. Germain, in France; and there, through his instrumentality, privateers were fitted out against English commerce. Then this Act was enacted which I will now mention. You find it in *Hawkins' Pleas of the Crown*, under the title *Piracy*, book I., chap. 37, sec. 7:

"It being also doubted by many eminent civilians whether, during the Revolution, the persons who had captured English vessels, by virtue of commissions granted by James II., at his Court at St. Germain, after his abdication of the Throne of England, could be deemed pirates, the grantor still having, as it was contended, the right of war in him, it is enacted—11 & 12 Wm. III., c. 7, s. 8—'That if any of His Majesty's natural-born subjects, or denizens of this Kingdom, shall commit any piracy or robbery, or any act of hostility against others, His Majesty's subjects, upon the sea, under color of any commission from any foreign Prince or State, or pretence of authority from any person whatsoever, such offender or offenders, and every of them, shall be deemed, adjudged, and taken to be pirates, felons, and robbers; and they, and every of them, being duly convicted thereof, according to this Act, or the aforesaid statute of King Henry VIII., shall have and suffer such pains of death, loss of lands, goods, and chattels, as pirates, felons, and robbers upon the seas ought to have and suffer.'"

When an Act of Congress, declaring the crime of piracy, was enacted, in 1790, it is perfectly apparent that those who drew up the Act were acquainted with *Hawkins' Pleas*, containing the 8th section, which is the recognized law of piracy by all nations, and from that book, then, took in this 9th section; because there was no exigency in our Government to call for it, and no reason for its introduction, except that it was found in a book familiar to those who were legislating for this country. In regard to the Act, there are some peculiarities which are very striking, and which bear strongly on this subject. The first is the fact that a commission, although from a foreign State, taken by a British subject or denizen of England, and committed against British commerce, protected the party against the charge of piracy,—because the thing was taken as prize, and for adjudication according to the principles of the laws of nations, for which national action the nation which took it was responsible. But, in the case and condition of James II., the English declared that he was no longer of England,—they declared him fallen from the Crown, and a foreigner. He had no dominions, and no place where the poor man could hold a Prize Court; and, if he could authorize a capture, there was no Court to adjudicate upon it; there was no sovereign to be responsible for the action of the Prize Court. He was a King without responsibility, and without the power of having Courts of Adjudication; and it was a necessity arising in the history of English law that that kind of action should be treated as piratical. The English adopted that, therefore, as the statute piracy. I refer your honors to Phillimore's International Law (vol. III., page 398), where all the discussion and reasons are contained; and they all are reasons applicable to a Prince without dominions, without Courts, without a country; and to a foreign Prince, in regard to English property and English subjects.

Now, then, let us see how these men stand. Under the 8th section, those men who were not citizens of the United States, are, of course, protected by a commission from a Government *de facto*. Their taking was not *animo furandi*, because there was a commission. The very enactment of the statute of William III. was upon the basis that it was not piracy where there was a commission, even of this questionable sort.

I say, then, in my third point, that if the facts are found as supposed in the preceding point, and if it also appears that the commission from the Confederated States, or the President thereof, had been issued for the Savannah, and that the capture was made under color thereof, then, as to the prisoners shown not to be citizens of the United States, the taking of the Joseph was not piratical under the eighth section of the Act of 1790,—*first*, because it was under color of authority; nor, *second*, was it piratical under the ninth section, because that only applies to citizens of the United States; and the prisoners, Del Carno, &c., must be acquitted under the ninth as well as under the eighth section.

But now we come to the American citizens who took that commission, and we are to see with some accuracy how the case stands as to them,—which involves two questions: One is, what kind of "other person" is embraced in that law? And the other is, whether this indictment is supported as under a commission from any *person* whatever? Let me call your attention to the form of the indictment in this last count of the declaration. They all run in this way: that these persons, "being citizens, did, *on pretence of authority from a person, to wit, one Jefferson Davis,*" &c. That is all that is said as to the pretence. Now there is no lack of skill in this indictment. The pleader under this indictment was surrounded with difficulties very grave indeed. He had the commission. If he had described it as a commission from certain foreign States, namely, South Carolina, Georgia, &c., the Government would have recognized the existence of those States in the most formal manner and by action of the most formal kind. If he said "Jefferson Davis, President of certain Confederate States," that would be simply that the pretence of authority was a pretence of authority from those States, and the same consequence would result. Well, what could he do? The only way in which he could make this stand at all was by saying that it is an authority from Jefferson Davis, as an individual. That is the meaning of this allegation.

Now, then, under the facts already stated, including now the commission and the action under it, the taking of the Joseph was not piratical, under the ninth section, because the commission was from the Confederate States, and not from "a person, to wit, one Jefferson Davis," as described in the indictment. Now that leads me to a consideration of this commission. We had something a little like it here yesterday, when the warrant issued by Mr. Buchanan Henry was given in evidence for the arrest of these men. I suppose I would be charged with ridicule in the last degree if I said they were arrested by the authority of Buchanan Henry, or under pretence of authority from Buchanan Henry; yet the warrant ran in the name of Buchanan Henry. Now let us see whether this commission supports the allegation of its being a commission from a private person. The allegation is, that the capture was made under pretence of authority from one Jefferson Davis. The commission runs just as the President's commission to your honors:

"JEFFERSON DAVIS,

"PRESIDENT OF THE CONFEDERATE STATES OF AMERICA.

"To all who shall see these presents, greeting:—Know ye, that by virtue of the power vested in me by law, I have commissioned, and do hereby commission, have authorized, and do hereby authorize, the schooner or vessel called the Savannah (more particularly described in the schedule hereunto annexed), whereof T. Harrison Baker is commander, to act as a private armed vessel in the service of the Confederate States, on the high seas, against the United States of America, their ships, vessels, goods, and effects, and those of her citizens, during the pendency of the war now existing between the said Confederate States and the said United States.

"This commission to continue in force until revoked by the President of the Confederate States for the time being.

"Schedule of description of the vessel:—Name, Schooner Savannah; tonnage, 53-41/95 tons; armament, one large pivot gun and small arms; number of crew, thirty.

"Given under my hand and the seal of the Confederate States, at Montgomery, this 18th day of May, A.D. 1861.

"JEFFERSON DAVIS.

"By the President—R. TOOMBS, Secretary of State."

Now I submit that, if they had framed an indictment for taking a commission under the King of England, and it had been under the Government of England as a foreign State, without naming the individual, such a commission as this would sustain it. If they had indicted as taking a commission out under any foreign State or nation, a commission in this way would have sustained that indictment; because the officer is merely the authenticator of the instrument; the authority is not his,—it is not under his authority; he is the mere ministerial officer, in fact, of the Government.

Now I submit, that this taking cannot be held piratical, under the ninth section, on this indictment; because it was a taking, not on pretence of authority from Jefferson Davis, but under authority of the Confederate States, exercised by Jefferson Davis. And, in a case of this kind, I must say that I consider it will prove the greatest Godsend to the Government, and to the prisoners on both sides who now anxiously await the result, if, without touching the other questions, this indictment shall fall to the ground on a mere technical point.

That is one reason. Another reason is this: The Act is for taking vessels under a commission from any foreign Prince or State, or on pretence of authority from any person. Now what is a foreign Prince or a foreign State? If your honors please, at the time this Act was enacted, within some three years of the United States coming together, is it conceivable that the thought entered into the heart of any man who had anything to do with it that it was to take effect against any man acting under the authority of any of the States of this Union? The States all were authorized, under certain circumstances, to have ships-of-war and to have armies. There was no telling what collision there might be; and the idea that this Act, almost a literal transcript from the English statute of 11 and 12 William III., contemplated that punishment for acting under the authority of domestic persons, is inconceivable.

In construing an Act so highly penal as this we must be very sure that we are not only within the letter, but within the very spirit and contemplation, of the Act; and can you think that the framers of this Government gravely provided for the offence of taking a commission under some of the persons acting as Governor, or in connection with the domestic institutions of this country? I submit that the Act was intended to operate against foreign States and nations, and a foreign person; and it is inconceivable that the Act should have been contemplated to embrace any such thing as is now brought up. I submit, therefore, as the third of my specifications under this point, that Jefferson Davis was not a foreign person, nor assuming the authority of a foreign Prince or Ruler. The statute was one against commissions under foreign authority of some kind or other, either Prince, or State, or person.

But I now draw your attention to another feature of the statute, which seems to me equally decisive. This statute is transmitted to us from England, and that which was the design and exigency of its adoption there is to bear with great, if not decisive, force, upon its construction here. We took it because they had it, and we took it, therefore, for reasons similar to theirs. Now what was the real difficulty there? It was this: that a Prince without dominion, a Prince having no Government *de facto*, a mere nominal Prince, undertook to issue commissions throughout the world against British commerce. Evils that are very manifest and plain, in regard to the law of prizes, apply to that case. The prizes could not be adjudicated in his Courts; he had none. This was an enactment against Princes who had abdicated and were without dominion. Such things were common, as well in the time of William III. as since. Abdicated Princes very soon turn to be robbers, whose only object is to get re-established, and they are not scrupulous as to means. They stand as mere fictions, undertaking to exercise authority, with none of the responsibilities which belong to Rulers. How different it is with this Jefferson Davis! I speak now in no degree of his merits, or as lessening that feeling which my fellow-citizens and I share alike upon the subject of this rebellion. But here is a man, not a nominal Prince or Ruler, but he is (if you please without right) Ruler of ten millions of people. Is this Act, which is intended to meet the case of a man without people, or dominion, or force—without any thing but the name and claim of Ruler—to be applied to a man who represents (rightfully or wrongfully) a large fraction of a great nation? To say that every man who takes a commission (applying as well to civil as to military commissions), that any man who takes a commission, from him, is either a robber or a pirate—if on land, a robber, if on sea, a pirate—is unjust and unreasonable—contrary to every principle that governs the laws of nations. Patriotic vituperation may go far—patriotic spirit and feeling may go far— but there is a limit to every thing that is real. The human mind, as it seems to me, and the human heart, cannot go to the extent of the doctrine that they can be treated as robbers who act under a Government extending *de facto* so far and doing *de facto* so many things throughout upon the principles of civilized warfare, and having a vast territory, and vast numbers of people acting as it dictates. It is perverting the law of piracy to apply it to a case so entirely different.

Now it comes back to the fact that this "pretence of authority" was the authority of all those States. Those States, when they come back to the Union, if they ever do, will come back with all their powers as original States. The Confederation you may call illegal and improper, but it is a Confederation *de facto*; its right may be questioned, but it is a *de facto* Government, with this gentleman presiding over it, and performing the duties which, as the Ruler of a great nation, devolve upon him—bringing out armies by hundreds of thousands, bringing out treasures by the million,— and yet you are to say it has no color of authority. It is idle, it seems to me, to say that a man situated as Jefferson Davis is was intended by a law against a mere nominal Prince. I submit that because Jefferson Davis was actually the Chief of a Confederation of States, not foreign, exercising actual power and government over large territories, with a large population, under an organized Government, having Courts within its territories for the adjudication of captures,—that upon each of these grounds Harleston, as well as the others who are citizens, should be acquitted under the 9th section.

That is all the argument which I address particularly; and I beg leave to read two or three general propositions on the construction of the law in this matter:

I.—The recognition, by the great commercial nations of the world, of the Confederate States as belligerents, and not pirates and robbers, prevents the captures under authority from being held piratical under the law of nations.

II.—1. The ninth section of the Act of 1790 has not in view any application to the States then recently united as the United States of America, or to the persons having authority *de facto* in them.

2. That section had in view foreign Princes and States, and foreign authority only.

3. The authority from any person in that section has reference to persons without the possession, in fact, of territory.

If your honors please, I have endeavored, so far as it was possible, to abbreviate what I have had to say on this subject. It is a very interesting one, undoubtedly, not only to the legal student, but to all persons in the country. This war is a war to reclaim those States. To attempt to reclaim them by prosecutions for piracy, or by acts of hostility which disregard them as having any form of society,—it seems to me that no national evil could be greater. The idea that in a commercial city it is very offensive that there should be privateers, is a trifle. The navy can regulate that. Let them look more to the privateers that want to get out than to the prizes that want to come in, and that will be provided for. We need not violate principles of law, or of humanity, or the common sense of the world, to produce an effect of that kind. We need to show that, in the midst of all this excitement and outcry against piracy—in the midst of a press that never names any of these people without calling them "pirates"—the men brought in always in chains, for the purpose of exciting public indignation against them and preventing their being treated as men of common rights and common interests with us—all which is very humiliating, it seems to me—in a Court of Justice no such feelings will be succumbed to.

Certain I am that, where I stand, no such principles will be put in use. Justice will come—severe and stern, it may be—but it will be justice, with truth, and reason, and humanity, and political tenderness accompanying all its acts and all its judgments.

Mr. Larocque: If the Court please, I had hoped to be saved the necessity of addressing your honors upon these propositions of law; but, in the distribution that has been made among the counsel, it has fallen to my lot to present the propositions in reference to which my opening was made, yesterday, to the Jury, and which will be adverted to by the counsel who, on our side, will close the case; and, simply, without detaining your honors, at this late hour, with any remarks upon them further than the reading of some extracts from authorities I have collected, I will present the propositions, leaving them to the action of your honors, and to the remarks of my associate, who will close this case, after we have ascertained the direction it will take before the Jury.

The first proposition I had stated, with reference to jurisdiction: "That the defendants, after their capture and confinement as criminals, for the acts charged in this indictment, having been taken within the District of Virginia, on board the vessel on which they were so confined before being brought within the Southern District of New York, cannot be convicted under this indictment."

In reference to that, there are a number of additional authorities that I will furnish to your honors. In the case of the *United States* vs. *Charles A. Greiner,* tried before Judge Cadwalader, in the Philadelphia District, the defendant had been arrested under a charge of treason committed in Georgia. It seems to have been understood, by the learned counsel on the other side, that the question of jurisdiction may be influenced by the fact of whether there was any possibility of these prisoners being tried in Virginia or not; and it is in reference to that point that I cite this case. Judge Cadwalader says:

"The questions in this case are more important than difficult. On the 2d of January last an artillery company of the State of Georgia, mustered in military array, took Fort Pulaski, in that State, from the possession of the United States, without encountering any forcible resistance. They garrisoned the post for some time, and left it in the possession of the government of the State. The accused, a native of Philadelphia, where he has many connections, resides in Georgia. He was a member of this artillery company when it occupied the fort, and, for aught that appears, may still be one of its members. He was not its commander. Whether he had any rank in it, or was only a private soldier, does not appear, and is, I think, unimportant. He is charged with treason in levying war against the United States. The overt act alleged is, that he participated, as one of this military company, in the capture of the fort, and in its detention until it was handed over to the permanent occupation of the authorities of the State.

"The primary question is whether, if his guilt has been sufficiently proved, I can commit him for trial, detain him in custody, or hold him to bail to answer the charge. The objection to my doing so is, that the offence was committed in the State of Georgia, where a Court of the United States cannot, at present, be held, and where, as the District Attorney admits, a *speedy* trial cannot be had. The truth of this admission is of public notoriety.

"The Constitution of the United States provides that in all criminal prosecutions the accused shall enjoy the right to a *speedy* trial by a Jury of the *State and District* wherein the crime shall have been committed. The only statute which, if the Courts of the United States for the State of Georgia were open, would authorize me to do more than hold this party to security of the peace, and for good behavior, is the 33d section of the Judiciary Act of the 24th September, 1789. That section, after authorizing commitments, &c., for trial, before any Court of the United States having cognizance of the offence, provides that if the commitment is in a District other than that in which the offence is to be tried, it shall be the duty of the Judge of the District where the delinquent is imprisoned *seasonably* to issue, and of the Marshal of the same District to execute, a warrant for the removal of the offender to the District in which the trial is to be had. The District Attorney of the United States does not ask me to issue such a warrant for this party's removal to Georgia for trial. Therefore I can do nothing under this Act of Congress. It does not authorize me to detain him in custody to abide the ultimate result of possible future hostilities in Georgia, or to hold him to bail for trial in a Court there, of which the sessions have been interrupted, and are indefinitely postponed."

In reference to the counts of the indictment founded upon the 8th section of the Act of 1790 and the Act of 1820, the propositions I have are these:

"*Second*, That to convict the defendants, under either of the first five counts of the indictment, the Jury must have such evidence as would warrant a conviction for robbery if the acts proved had been performed on land.

"*Third*, That the defendants cannot be convicted of robbery, in the capture of the Joseph, unless she was taken with a piratical and felonious intent.

"*Fourth*, That if the defendants, at the time of her capture, were acting under the commission in evidence, and, in good faith, believed that such commission authorized her capture, they did not act with a piratical or felonious intent, and cannot be convicted under either of the first five counts in the indictment."

There are one or two authorities I did not state yesterday, which I beg now to furnish, as some additional authorities have been handed up on the other side:

The Josefa Segunda, 5 Wheaton, 357. In this case Judge Livingston says:

"Was the General Arismendi a piratical cruiser? The Court thinks not. Among the exhibits is a copy of a commission, which is all that in such a case can be expected, which appears to have been issued under the authority of the Government of Venezuela. This Republic is composed of the inhabitants of a portion of the dominions of Spain, in South America, which have been for some time, and still are, maintaining a contest for independence with the mother country. Although not acknowledged by our Government as an independent nation, it is well known that open war exists between them and His Catholic Majesty, in which the United States maintain strict neutrality. In this state of things, this Court cannot but respect the belligerent rights of both parties, and does not treat as pirates the cruisers of either so long as they act under and within the scope of their respective commissions."

In the *United States* vs. *The Brig Malek Adhel* (2 Howard's U.S. Rep. 211), as to the Act of 1819, Judge Story (page 232) says:

"Where the Act uses the word piratical, it does so in a general sense,— importing that the aggression is unauthorized by the law of nations, hostile in its character, wanton and cruel in its commission, and *utterly without any sanction from any public authority or sovereign power. In short, it means that the act belongs to the class of offences which pirates are in the habit of perpetrating, whether they do it for purposes of plunder, or purposes of hatred, revenge, or wanton abuse of power. A pirate is deemed—and properly deemed*—HOSTIS HUMANI GENERIS. But why is he so deemed? *Because he commits hostilities upon the subjects and property of any or all nations, without any regard to right or duty, or any pretence of public authority.* If he willfully sinks or destroys an innocent merchant ship, without any other object than to gratify his lawless appetite for mischief, it is just as much piratical aggression, in the sense of the law of nations, and of the Act of Congress, as if he did it solely and exclusively for the sake of plunder, *lucri causâ*. The law looks to it as an act of hostility; and, being committed by a vessel not commissioned and engaged in lawful warfare, it treats it as the act of a pirate, and one who is emphatically *hostis humani generis*."

Then upon the question that this commission is only by color of authority from an unrecognized power, and that the authority to grant such a commission is disputed, I refer to the case of *Davison* vs. *Certain Seal Skins* (2 Paine's C.C.R. 332), which was a case of salvage of property after a piracy alleged to have been committed by Louis Vernet, at Port St. Louis, in the Eastern Falkland Islands, by taking them from a vessel,—he wrongfully and unlawfully claiming and pretending to be Governor of the Islands, under Buenos Ayres. The Court says:

"Robbery on the high seas is understood to be piracy by our law. The taking must be *felonious*. A commissioned cruiser, by exceeding his authority, is not thereby to be considered a pirate. It may be a marine trespass, but not an act of piracy, *if the vessel is taken as a prize*, unless taken feloniously, and with intent to commit a robbery: the *quo animo* may be inquired into. *A pirate is one who acts solely on his own authority, without any commission or authority from a sovereign State*, seizing by force and appropriating to himself, without discrimination, every vessel he meets with; and hence pirates have always been compared to robbers. The only difference between them is that the sea is the theatre of action for the one, and the land for the other."

By referring to this case, pp. 334, 335, your honors will find that Buenos Ayres had no lawful jurisdiction over the islands, and that our Executive Government had so decided; but Buenos Ayres avowed the acts of those claiming to act under her authority, and our Government discharged the prisoners who had been captured as pirates, disclaiming, under those circumstances, to hold them personally criminally responsible.

The next proposition which I state is this: "That, by the public law of the world, the law of nations, and the laws of war, the commission in evidence, supported by the proof in the case as to the color of authority under which it was issued, would afford adequate protection to the defendants against a conviction for piracy; and being an authority emanating neither from a foreign Prince nor foreign State, nor from a person merely, the offence charged in the last five counts of the indictment, is not within the purview of the 9th section of the Act of 1790, and the defendants cannot be convicted under either of those counts, if they acted in good faith under that commission."

I refer your honors to the case of the *Santissima Trinidad*, 7 Wheaton, 283, to the opinion of Judge Story, in which he says:

"There is another objection urged against the admission of this vessel to the privileges and immunities of a public ship, which may as well be disposed of in connection with the question already considered. It is, that Buenos Ayres has not yet been acknowledged as a sovereign independent Government, by the Executive or Legislature of the United States, and therefore is not entitled to have her ships-of-war recognized by our Courts as national ships. We have, in former cases, had occasion to express our opinion on this point. The Government of the United States has recognized the existence of a civil war between Spain and her Colonies, and has avowed a determination to remain neutral between the parties, and to allow to each the same rights of asylum, and hospitality, and intercourse. Each party is, therefore, deemed by us a belligerent nation, having, so far as concerns us, the sovereign rights of war, and entitled to be respected in the exercise of those rights. We cannot interfere to the prejudice of either belligerent, without making ourselves a party to the contest and departing from the posture of neutrality. All captures made by each must be considered as having the same validity; and all the immunities which may be claimed by public ships in our ports, under the laws of nations, must be considered as equally the right of each, and as such must be recognized by our Courts of Justice, until Congress shall prescribe a different rule. This is the doctrine heretofore asserted by this Court, and we see no reason to depart from it."

Your honors, by referring to the case of The Bello Corunnes, 6 Wheaton, 152, will see the doctrine laid down distinctly, that acts may be piratical for all civil purposes which would not authorize the conviction of the perpetrators criminally as pirates; *e.g.*, a citizen of the United States, taking from a State at war with Spain a commission to cruise against that power, contrary to the 14th art. of the Spanish Treaty;—and the Court held, in that case, that that would involve the consequences of a piracy, for the purpose of condemnation of property; but it would not be criminal piracy, under either the law of nations or of the United States.

On the general subject of privateers I had a reference to Vattel, but I do not think it necessary to read it, because the authorities on that subject cover it so fully.

I come now, if your honors please, to what my learned friend, when he addressed the Court on the part of the Government, has been pleased to call the political part of this case; and I have distinctly stated in my propositions what I contended for on that subject. In the first place, that the Federal Executive Government, and the executive governments of the States, under the Constitution of the United States, each possess the jurisdiction to decide whether their respective acts are within or exceed the limits of their respective constitutional powers, in cases of collision between them in their administrative acts, operating upon the public domain, or upon the State, or its citizens as a body politic.

I shall, without stopping for any discussion, simply state the subordinate propositions by which I think that is established, and give a reference to the authorities. I say, in the first place, as I said to the Jury, that citizens of the United States owe a divided allegiance, partly to the United States and partly to their respective States. They can commit treason against either; for the State constitutions and laws define and punish treason against the States, as the Constitution of the United States does treason against them.

The Federal and State Governments are each supreme and sovereign within the limits of their respective jurisdictions under the Federal and State Constitutions; each operates directly upon the citizen, and each also operates as a check and restriction upon the other, and upon the encroachments of the other, in seeking to extend beyond legitimate limits its jurisdiction over the citizen, or over the public domain common to both. Now, if your honors please, in regard to that, I will very briefly refer you to what I rely upon. I refer, in the first place, to sections 2 and 3, of Article 6th, of the Constitution of the United States.

"*Sec. 2.* This Constitution, and the laws of the United States, *which shall be made in pursuance thereof,* and all treaties made, or which shall be made, under the authority of the United States, shall be the supreme law of the land; and the Judges in every State shall be bound thereby, anything in the constitution or laws of any State to the contrary notwithstanding.

"*Sec. 3.* The Senators and Representatives before mentioned, and the members of the several State Legislatures, and all executive and judicial officers, both of the United States and of the several States, shall be bound by oath or affirmation to support this Constitution; but no religious test shall ever be required as a qualification to any office or public trust under the United States."

In the amendments to the Constitution of the United States, Articles 9 and 10, we find this language:

"The enumeration in the Constitution of certain rights, shall not be construed to deny or disparage others retained by the people. The powers not delegated to the United States by the Constitution, nor prohibited by it to the States, are reserved to the States respectively, or to the people."

I refer to the case of McCulloch *vs.* The State of Maryland, 4 Wheaton, p. 400, in which the opinion was delivered by Chief Justice Marshall. He says:

"No political dreamer was ever wild enough to think of breaking down the lines which separate the States, and of compounding the American people into one common mass."

I cite particularly from pp. 402 and 410. On page 410 his language is as follows:

"In America, the powers of sovereignty are divided between the Government of the Union and those of the States. *They are each sovereign with respect to the objects committed to it, and neither sovereign with respect to the objects committed to the other.* We cannot comprehend that train of reasoning which would maintain that the extent of power granted by the people is to be ascertained, not by the nature and terms of the grant, but by its date. Some State constitutions were formed before, some since, that of the United States. We cannot believe that their relation to each other is in any degree dependent upon this circumstance. Their respective powers must, we think, be precisely the same as if they had been formed at the same time."

The next I refer to is the case of *Rhode Island* agst. *Massachusetts*, 12 Peters, 889, where Judge Baldwin says:

"Before we can proceed in this cause, we must, therefore, inquire whether we can hear and determine the matters in controversy between the parties, who are two States of this Union, *sovereign within their respective boundaries, save that portion of power which they have granted to the Federal Government, and foreign to each other for all but federal purposes.*"

I now refer to the case of *Livingston* vs. *Van Ingen*, 9 Johnson, 574, where Chancellor Kent reasons thus:

"When the people create a single entire Government, they grant at once all the rights of sovereignty. The powers granted are indefinite and incapable of enumeration. Every thing is granted that is not expressly reserved in the constitutional charter, or necessarily retained as inherent in the people. *But when a Federal Government is erected with only a portion of the sovereign power, the rule of construction is directly the reverse, and every power is reserved to the members that is not, either in express terms or by necessary implication, taken away from them and rested exclusively in the Federal Head.*"

"This rule has not only been acknowledged by the most intelligent friends to the Constitution, but is plainly declared by the instrument itself. This principle might be illustrated by other instances of grants of power to Congress, with a prohibition to the States from exercising the like powers; but it becomes unnecessary to enlarge upon so plain a proposition, as it is removed beyond all doubt by the 10th article of the amendments to the Constitution. That article declares that 'the powers not delegated to the United States by the Constitution, nor prohibited by it to the States, are reserved to the States respectively, or to the people.' The ratification of the Constitution by the Convention of this State was made with the explanation and understanding that 'every power, jurisdiction and right which was not clearly delegated to the General Government remained to the people of the several States, or to their respective State governments.' There was a similar provision in the articles of Confederation, and the principle results from the very nature of the Federal Government, which consists only of a defined portion of the undefined mass of sovereignty vested in the several members of the Union. There may be inconveniences, but generally there will be no serious difficulty, and there cannot well be any interruption of the public peace in the concurrent exercise of those powers. *The powers of the two Governments are each supreme within their respective constitutional spheres. They may each operate with full effect upon different subjects, or they may, as in the case of taxation, operate upon different parts of the same subject.*"

I now refer to the Massachusetts Bill of Rights of 1780, art. 4. It reads:

"The people of this Commonwealth have the sole and exclusive right of governing themselves as a free, sovereign and independent State; and do, and forever hereafter shall, exercise and enjoy every power, jurisdiction and right, which is not, or may not hereafter be, by them expressly delegated to the United States of America, in Congress assembled."

I also refer to the New Hampshire Bill of Rights, of September, 1792:

"ART. 7. The people of this State have the sole and exclusive right of governing themselves as a free, sovereign and independent State; and do, and forever hereafter shall, exercise and enjoy every power, jurisdiction and right pertaining thereto, which is not, or may not hereafter be by them expressly delegated to the United States of America, in Congress assembled."

I next beg leave to refer your honors to No. 32 of the Federalist, by Hamilton, who says:

"An entire consolidation of the States into one complete national sovereignty would imply an entire subordination of the parts, and whatever power might remain in them would be altogether dependent on the general will. But as the plan of the Convention aims only at a partial union or consolidation, *the State governments would clearly retain all the rights of sovereignty which they before had, and which were not by that act exclusively delegated to the United States.*"

Also, to the Federalist, No. 39, by Madison, in which he says:

"The difference between a Federal and National Government, as it relates to the operation of the Government, is, by the adversaries of the plan of the Convention, supposed to consist in this, that in the former the powers operate upon the political bodies composing the Confederacy in their political capacities; in the latter, on the individual citizens composing the nation in their individual capacities. On trying the Constitution by this criterion, it falls under the national and not the federal character, though perhaps not so completely as has been understood. In several cases, and particularly in the trial of controversies to which States may be parties, they must be viewed and proceeded against in their collective and political capacities only. But the operation of the Government on the people in their individual capacities, in its ordinary and most essential proceedings, will, on the whole, in the sense of its opponents, designate it, in this relation, a National Government.

"But if the Government be national with regard to the operation of its powers, it changes its aspect again when we contemplate it with regard to the extent of its powers. The idea of a National Government involves in it not only an authority over the individual citizens, but an indefinite supremacy over all persons and things, so far as they are objects of lawful government. Among a people consolidated into one nation, this supremacy is completely vested in the National Legislature. Among communities united for political purposes, it is vested partly in the general and partly in the municipal

Legislatures. In the former case all local authorities are subordinate to the supreme, and may be controlled, directed or abolished by it at pleasure. *In the latter the local or municipal authorities form* DISTINCT AND INDEPENDENT PORTIONS OF THE SUPREMACY, *no more subject, within their respective spheres, to the general authority, than the general authority is subject to them within its own sphere. In this relation, then, the proposed Government cannot be deemed a national one, since its jurisdiction extends to certain enumerated objects only, and leaves to the several States a residuary and* INVIOLABLE *sovereignty over all other objects.* It is true that, in controversies relating to the boundary line between the two jurisdictions, the tribunal which is ultimately to decide is to be established under the General Government. But this does not change the principle of the case. The decision is to be impartially made according to the rules of the Constitution; and all the usual and most effectual precautions are taken to secure this impartiality. *Some such tribunal is clearly essential to prevent an appeal to the sword and a dissolution of the compact;* and that it ought to be established under the general rather than the local Governments, or, to speak more properly, that it could be safely established under the first alone, is a position not likely to be combated."

I will refer, also, to the letter of Gov. Seward, written to Gov. Gilmore, of Virginia, October 24th, 1839, taken from the Assembly Journal, 63d Sess., 1840, p. 55. That distinguished public man says:

"You very justly observe, 'that neither the Government nor the citizens of any other country can rightfully interfere with the municipal regulations of any country in any way;' and in support of this position you introduce the following extract from Vattel's Law of Nations, 'that all have a right to be governed as they think proper, and that no State has the smallest right to interfere in the government of another. Of all the rights that belong to a nation, sovereignty is doubtless the most precious, and that which other nations ought the most scrupulously to respect if they would not do her an injury.'

"It might, perhaps, be inferred, from the earnestness with which these principles are pressed in your communication, that they have been controverted on my part. Permit me, therefore, to bring again before you the following distinct admissions: 'I do not question the constitutional right of a State to make such a penal code as it shall deem necessary or expedient; nor do I claim that citizens of other States shall be exempted from arrest, trial and punishment in the State adopting such code, however different its enactments may be from those existing in their own State.' Thus you will perceive that I have admitted the sovereignty of the several States upon which you so strenuously insist. To prevent, however, all possible misconstruction upon this subject, I beg leave to add that no person can maintain more firmly than I do the principle that the States are sovereign and independent in regard to all matters except those in relation to which sovereignty is expressly, or by necessary implication, transferred to the Federal Government by the Constitution of the United States. I have at least believed that my non-compliance with the requisition made upon me in the present case would be regarded as maintaining the equal sovereignty and independence of this State, and by necessary consequence, those of all the other States."

I contend, then, that the people of the several States, in forming the State governments, have surrendered to the latter supreme and sovereign jurisdiction over all questions affecting the State, or its citizens as a body politic, not included in the grant of power to the General Government by the Federal Constitution. This surrender necessarily includes the power and jurisdiction to determine, co-ordinately with the Federal Government, whether the Federal Executive Government is acting within or transgressing the limits of its legitimate authority in any case affecting the State as such, or its citizens as a body politic, when the question is not one of the validity or constitutionality of a law of the United States, operating directly upon individual citizens, and conformity to which is to be enforced or resisted by suit or defence in the Federal or State Courts, with the right of ultimate appeal, in either case, to the Supreme Court of the United States; but, on the contrary, brings into collision the Federal and State Executive Departments of the Government, in the exercise of powers which, from their very nature and the mode in which they are exerted, never can be presented for the determination of a Court.

And with regard to that proposition I would cite Vattel, Book I., chap. 1, sec. 2, upon the proposition that jurisdiction to determine such a mixed question of law and fact has been ceded equally to the State as to the Federal Government. Vattel says:

"It is evident that, by the very act of the civil or political association, each citizen subjects himself to the authority of the entire body in everything that relates to the common welfare. The authority of all over each member therefore essentially belongs to the body politic or State; but the exercise of that authority may be placed in different hands, according as the society may have ordained."

I refer, also, to the Federalist, No. 40, by Madison. He uses this language:

"Will it be said that the fundamental principles of the Confederation were not within the purview of the Convention, and ought not to have been varied? I ask, what are those principles? Do they require that, in the establishment of the Constitution, the States should be regarded as distinct and independent sovereigns? They are so regarded by the Constitution proposed. * * * Do they require that the powers of the Government should act on the States, and not immediately on individuals? In some instances, as has been shown, the powers of the new Government will act on the States in their collective character. In some instances, also, those of the *existing* Government act immediately on individuals. In cases of capture, of piracy, of the post-office, of coins, weights and measures; of trade with the Indians; of claims under grants of land by different States; and, above all, in the cases of trial by Courts Martial, in the Army and Navy, by which death may be inflicted without the intervention of a Jury, or even of a Civil Magistrate,—in all these cases the *powers of the Confederation* operate immediately on the persons and interests of individual citizens."

I would also refer your honors to the Report of the Committee of the General Assembly of Connecticut, on a call for the militia, by the General Government, in 1812. The Report reads:

"The people of this State were among the first to adopt that Constitution; they have been among the most prompt to satisfy all its lawful demands, and to give facility to its fair operations; they have enjoyed the benefits resulting from the Union of the States; they have loved, and still love and cherish that Union, and will deeply regret if any events shall occur to alienate their affection from it. They have a deep interest in its preservation, and are still disposed to yield a willing and prompt obedience to all the legitimate requirements of the Constitution of the United States.

"But it must not be forgotten that the State of Connecticut is a free, sovereign and independent State,—that the United States are a Confederacy of States,—that we are a confederated and not a consolidated Republic. The Governor of this State is under a high and solemn obligation 'to maintain the lawful rights and privileges thereof as a sovereign, free and independent State,' as he is 'to support the Constitution of the United States,' and the obligation to support the latter imposes an additional obligation to support the former. The building cannot stand if the pillars upon which it rests are impaired or destroyed. The same Constitution which delegates powers to the General Government, forbids the exercise of powers not delegated, and reserves those powers to the States respectively."

And that was "approved by both Houses," and the following resolution passed:

"*Resolved*, That the conduct of His Excellency, the Governor, in refusing to order the militia of this State into the service of the United States, on the requisition of the Secretary of War and Major-General Dearborn, meets with the entire approbation of this Assembly."

I would also refer to the second speech of Mr. Webster on Mr. Foot's resolution, in reply to Mr. Hayne, in the Senate of the United States, where he thus expresses himself:

"The States are unquestionably sovereign, so far as their sovereignty is not affected by this supreme law (the Constitution). * * * The General Government and the State governments derive their authority from the same source. Neither can, in relation to the other, be called primary; though one is definite and restricted, and the other general and residuary."

Also, to the case of *Luther* vs. *Borden*, 7 Howard, 1—one of the Dorr rebellion cases. The Supreme Court of the United States there decided that the government of a State, by its Legislature, has the power to protect itself from destruction by armed rebellion by declaring martial law, and that the Legislature is the judge of the necessary exigency.

At this point the Court intimated that they would adjourn to the following day.

The District Attorney, Mr. E. Delafield Smith, stated that the case of the *United States* vs. *William Smith*, one of the ship's company of the privateer Jefferson Davis, the trial of which had been proceeding in Philadelphia, had terminated in a verdict. That case involved the main questions, and also the question of jurisdiction involved here. Mr. Smith further stated that he had sent for a copy of the charge of Mr. Justice Grier in that case, and expected to receive it by telegraph, and he desired to reserve the right to refer to that charge as one of his authorities in this case.

The Court assented.

Adjourned to Saturday, October 26th, at 11 A.M.

FOURTH DAY.

Saturday, Oct. 26, 1861.

The Court met at 11 o'clock, when—

Mr. Larocque resumed:

I will proceed very briefly, if your honors please, to close what I was submitting to the Court upon the propositions which, as I maintain, tend to show a colorable authority in the State government, in possible cases that might arise, to authorize the issuing of letters of marque. I will state them in their connection, in order that your honors may see what they are. The first is the one I considered yesterday, viz., that the Federal Executive Government and the executive governments of the States, under the Constitution of the United States, each possess the jurisdiction to decide whether their respective acts are within or exceed the limits of their respective constitutional powers in cases of collision between them in their administrative acts operating upon the public domain, or upon the State, or its citizens as a body politic.

I had concluded what I intended to submit upon that, and proceed to the others, which are—

2. That in such cases, the Constitution having erected no common arbiter between them, the right of forcible resistance to the exercise of unlawful power, which, by the law of nature, resides in the people, has been delegated by them, by the Federal and State Constitutions respectively, to the Federal and State Governments respectively, and each having the jurisdiction to judge whether its acts are within the constitutional limit of its own powers, has also necessarily the right to employ force in their assertion or defence, if needed.

3. That in such cases the citizen of a State which, in its political capacity, has come into forcible collision with the Federal Government, owing allegiance to both within the limits of their respective constitutional powers, and each possessing the jurisdiction to determine for him the compound question of law and fact, whether the constitutional limit of those powers has been exceeded by itself or the other in the particular case, is protected from all criminal liability for any act done by him, in good faith, in adhering to and under the authority of either Government.

I wish very briefly to refer your honors to a few authorities, which, I hold, sustain these propositions. I say, in the first place, that this right bears no analogy whatever to the right, once claimed and most successfully refuted, of the inhabitants of a State, in Convention, to decide by ordinance upon the unconstitutionally of a law of the Union, and to prevent by force its operation within the limits of the State, in a case legitimately falling within the cognizance of the Courts. The claim to collect duties under an Act of Congress alleged to be unconstitutional was strictly an instance of this latter class. The citizen from whom the duties were claimed could simply refuse to pay, and thereby refer the question of constitutionality of the law to the judicial tribunals to which it properly belonged, and which must necessarily pass upon the question before the duties could be collected. On the other hand, the claim to hold or retake forts or other public places within the limits of a State, as property of the United States, is one against which, if unauthorized, the State could not by possibility defend itself through the agency of the Courts.

Now, if your honors please, I have stated most distinctly, and admitted most fully, that, in whatever cases the judicial power of the United States extends to, it is supreme. That is to say, if a collision takes place in a suit in a State Court between the Federal and State laws, and the decision of the State Court is against the right, privilege, or exemption, as it is called in the judiciary Act, claimed under the authority of the Union, the Supreme Court of the United States can redress the error. But I am now speaking of that class of cases where the judiciary have nothing whatever to do, and in which, I contend, the Federal and State authorities are each supreme and sovereign, within the limits of their respective power, and neither has any right or authority beyond the lines which bound their respective jurisdiction. And, if your honors please, I refer to the Inaugural Address of Mr. Lincoln, not only for the proposition that the judicial authority has nothing to do whatever in a case such as that I am now supposing, but that, even in cases where the judiciary is competent to act, its decisions do not form precedents, do not form rules for the government of the co-ordinate departments of the Union, in future cases of State policy, and that the executive and the legislative departments are still left at liberty to act as if no decision had been made. I do not mean to be understood as acquiescing in that claim; I consider it as a doctrine infinitely more dangerous and destructive than the doctrine of constitutional secession; but it comes to us as the claim set up on the part of the President; and if that is at all correct, there is an end of all pretence that the judiciary is competent to afford any relief or protection in the other class of cases referred to.

He says:

"I do not forget the position assumed by some, that constitutional questions are to be decided by the Supreme Court; nor do I deny that such decision must be binding in any case upon the parties to a suit, while they are also entitled to very high respect and consideration in all parallel cases by all other departments of the Government; and while it is obviously possible that such decision may be erroneous in any given case, still the evil effect following it being limited to that particular case, with the chances that it may be overruled, and never become a precedent for other cases, can better be borne than could the evils of a different practice. At the same time the candid citizen must confess that, if the policy of the Government upon the vital questions affecting the whole people is to be irrevocably fixed by the decisions of the Supreme Court, the instant they are made in ordinary litigations between parties in personal actions, the people will have ceased to be their own masters, having to that extent practically resigned the Government into the hands of that eminent tribunal. Nor is there, in this view, any assault upon the Court or the Judges. It is a duty from which they may not shrink, to decide cases properly brought before them, and it is no fault of theirs if others seek to turn their decisions to political purposes."

I have not the document at this moment; but your honors will probably bear in mind that the Executive also lately consulted the law-officer of the Government upon the question of suspending the privilege of *habeas corpus*, and I well remember the clause in the opinion which was delivered by that eminent legal gentleman and high officer of the Government on that occasion, and which was afterwards communicated by the President to Congress as the basis of his action. In that opinion the present learned Attorney-General used this language: "To say that the departments of our Government are co-ordinate, is to say that the judgment of one of them is not binding upon the other two, as to the arguments and principles involved in the judgment. It binds only the parties to the case decided." And your honors will recollect that, acting upon that enunciation of the law of the land and of the construction of the Constitution, although he admitted that the Supreme Court of the United States had decided that the privilege of *habeas corpus* could not be suspended by the Executive, without the interposition of Congress, the legal adviser of the Government held, at the same time, that that decision of the Supreme Court was not binding upon the Executive.

Now, for the purpose of showing what I mean by the right of resistance reserved to the people by the law of nature, which, as I say, is delegated by them to these two sovereigns, for the purpose that each may maintain its own authority and prevent encroachment by the other, I beg to refer your honors to *Rutherforth's Institutes of Natural Law, vol. 1, page 391*, commencing with section 10. And as a proof than I broach no novel or revolutionary doctrine, your honors will bear in mind that these Institutes of Natural Law were a course of lectures delivered in one of the great seminaries of learning of England, and their doctrines thought fit and proper to be instilled into the minds of the youth of that Kingdom, the loyalty of whose people to their Government has become proverbial among all the nations of the world.

The author says:

"It is a question of some importance, and has been thought a question not easily to be determined, whether the members of a civil society have, upon any event, or in any circumstances whatsoever, a right to resist their governors, or rather the persons who are invested with the civil power of that society."

Then he states several cases in which the civil governors, as he calls them, lose their power over their subjects, and continues:

"Fourthly, Though the governors of a society should be invested by the constitution with all civil power in the highest degree and to the greatest extent that the nature of a civil power will admit of, yet this does not imply that the people are in a state of perfect subjection. Civil power is, in its own nature, a limited power; as it arose at first from social union, so it is limited by the ends and purposes of such union, whether it is exercised, as it is in democracies, by the body of the people, or, as it is in monarchies, by one single person. But if the power of a Monarch, when he is considered as a civil governor, is thus limited by the ends of social union, whatever obedience and submission the people may owe him whilst he keeps within these limits, he has no power at all, and consequently the people owe him no subjection, when he goes beyond them.

"Having thus taken a short view of the several ways in which the authority of the governors of a society fails, and the subjection of the people ceases, we may now return to the question which was before us.

"If you ask whether the members of a civil society have a right to resist the civil governors of it by force? your question is too general to admit of a determinate answer.

"As far as the just authority of the civil governors and the subjection of the people extend, resistance by force is rebellion.

"Subjection consists in an obligation to obey; as far, therefore, as the people are in subjection, they can have no right to resist; because an obligation to obey, and a right to resist, are inconsistent with one another.

"But the power of civil governors is neither necessarily connected with their persons, nor infinite whilst it is in their possession.

"It ceases by abdication; it is overruled by the laws of nature and of God; and it does not extend beyond the limits which either the civil constitution or the ends of social union have set to it.

"Where their power thus fails in right, and they have no just authority, the subjection of the people ceases; that is, as far as of right they have no power, or no just authority, the people are not obliged to obey them; so that any force which they make use of, either to compel obedience or to punish disobedience, is unjust force; the people may perhaps be at liberty to submit to it, if they please; but, because it is unjust force, the law of nature does not oblige them to submit to it.

"But this law, if it does not oblige the people to submit to such force, allows them to have recourse to the necessary means of relieving themselves from it, and of securing themselves against it, to the means of resistance by opposing force to force, if they cannot be relieved from it and secured against it by any other means."

I continue my citation at—

"Sec. XV. In the general questions concerning the right of resistance, it is usually objected that there is no common judge who is vested with authority to determine, between the supreme governors and the people, where the right of resistance begins; and the want of such a judge is supposed to leave the people room to abuse this right; they may possibly pretend that they are unjustly oppressed, and, upon this pretence, may causelessly and rebelliously take up arms against their governors, although they are laid under no other restraints, and no other compulsion is made use of, but what the general nature of civil society or the particular circumstances of their own society require.

"But, be this as it may, the possibility that the right may be abused, does not prove that no such right subsists.

"If we would conclude, on the one hand, that the people have no right of resistance, because this right is capable of being abused, we might, for the same reason, conclude, on the other hand, that supreme governors have no authority.

"Whatever authority these governors have in any civil society, it was given them for the common benefit of the society; and it is possible that, under the color of this authority, they may oppress the people in order to promote their own separate benefit.

"Sec. XVI. It is a groundless suggestion, that a right of resistance in the people will occasion treason and rebellion, and that it will weaken the authority of civil government, and will render the office of those who are invested with it precarious and unsafe, even though they administer it with the utmost prudence and with all due regard to the common benefit.

"The right of resistance will indeed render the general notion of rebellion less extensive in its application to particular facts.

"All use of force against such persons as are invested with supreme power, would come under the notion of rebellion, if the people have no right of this sort; whereas, if they have such a right, the use of force to repel tyranical and unsocial oppression, when it cannot be removed by any other means, must have some other name given to it. So that, however true it may be that, in consequence of this right of resistance, supreme government will be liable, of right, to some external checks, arising out of the law of nature, to which they would otherwise not be liable, yet it cannot properly be said to expose them to rebellion."

I beg, in the next place, to read to your honors, from the opinion of Mr. Justice Johnson, a short paragraph. It is to be found in 1st Wheaton, 363, in the case of *Martin* vs. *Hunter's Lessee.* I believe a paragraph from that has been already read, on the other side, and I wish to give you, in connection with it, what he says, speaking of the power of the judiciary, and the consequences that would result in any case to which that power did not reach. He says:

"On the other hand, so firmly am I persuaded that the American people no longer can enjoy the blessings of a free Government, whenever the State sovereignties shall be prostrated at the feet of the General Government, nor the proud consciousness of equality and security, any longer than the independence of judicial power shall be maintained consecrated and intangible, that I could borrow the language of a celebrated orator, and exclaim, 'I rejoice that Virginia has resisted.'"

I also wish to read a sentence from the case of *Moore* vs. *The State of Illinois*, in 14 Howard, p. 20—the opinion by Mr. Justice Grier. He says:

"Every citizen of the United States is also a citizen of a State or Territory. He may be said to owe allegiance to two sovereigns, and may be liable to punishment for an infraction of the laws of either."

And Mr. Justice McLean, in speaking of the same subject, in the same case, at page 22, says:

"It is true the criminal laws of the Federal and State Governments emanated from different sovereignties; but they operate on the same people, and should have the same end in view. In this respect the Federal Government, though sovereign within the limitation of its powers, may, in some sense, be considered as the agent of the States, to provide for the general welfare by punishing offences under its own laws within its jurisdiction."

I wish also to refer to the case of the *United States* vs. *Booth*, in 21 Howard— the opinion of CHIEF JUSTICE TANEY—in connection with the question of what the result is where the judiciary has not power to act. He says:

"The importance which the framers of the Constitution attached to such a tribunal, for the purpose of preserving internal tranquillity, is strikingly manifested by the clause which gives this Court jurisdiction *over the sovereign States which compose this Union,* when a controversy arises *between them.* Instead of reserving the right to seek redress for injustice from another State by their sovereign powers, they have bound themselves to submit to the decision of this Court, and to abide by its judgment. And it is not out of place to say, here, that experience has demonstrated that this power was not unwisely surrendered by the States; for, in the time that has already elapsed since this Government came into existence, several irritating and angry controversies have taken place between adjoining States, in relation to their respective boundaries, and which have sometimes threatened to end in force and violence, but for the power vested in this Court to hear them and decide between them.

"The same purposes are clearly indicated by the different language employed when conferring supremacy upon the laws of the United States and jurisdiction upon its Courts. In the first case, it provides that 'this Constitution, and the laws of the United States, *which shall be made in pursuance thereof,* shall be the supreme law of the land, and obligatory upon the Judges in every State.' The words in italics show the precision and foresight which marks every clause in the instrument. The sovereignty to be created was to be limited in its powers of legislation; and, if it passed a law not authorized by its enumerated powers, it was not to be regarded as the supreme law of the land, nor were the State Judges bound to carry it into execution."

And further on, speaking of the claimed right of the State of Wisconsin to discharge a prisoner convicted in the United States Court upon a criminal conviction, and to refuse afterwards to obey a writ of error issued out of the Supreme Court of the United States to review that judgment, he uses language of this kind:

"This right to inquire by process of habeas corpus, and the duty of the officer to make a return, grows necessarily out of the complex character of our Government, and the existence of two distinct and separate sovereignties within the same territorial space, each of them restricted in its powers, and each, within its sphere of action prescribed by the Constitution of the United States, independent of the other."

Now, if your honors please, upon that question still further—that where there is no possibility of the power of the judiciary being exercised, there being, as the learned Chief Justice expresses it in his own language, "two distinct and separate sovereignties within the same territorial space" exercising jurisdiction, the right of forcible resistance exists in the State governments. I beg to refer to the Federalist, No. 28, by Alexander Hamilton, p. 126. He says:

"It may safely be received as an axiom in our political system, that the State governments will in all possible contingencies afford complete security against invasions of the public liberty by the federal authority. Projects of usurpation cannot be masked under pretences so likely to escape the penetration of select bodies of men as of the people at large. The Legislatures will have better means of information; they can discover the danger at a distance, and, possessing all the organs of civil power and the confidence of the people, they can at once adopt a regular plan of opposition; they can combine all the resources of the community. They can readily communicate with each other in the different States, and unite their common forces for the protection of their common liberty."

I refer also to the *Federalist*, No. 46, by James Madison, where he uses this language:

"Were it admitted, however, that the Federal Government may feel an equal disposition with the State governments to extend its power beyond the due limits, the latter would still have the advantage in the means of defeating such encroachments. If the act of a particular State, though unfriendly to the

National Government, be generally popular in that State, and should not too grossly violate the oaths of the State officers, it is executed immediately, and of course by means on the spot, and depending on the State alone. * * * On the other hand, should an unwarrantable measure of the Federal Government be unpopular in particular States, which would seldom fail to be the case, or even a warrantable measure be so, which may sometimes be the case, the means of opposition to it are at hand. * * *

"But ambitious encroachments of the Federal Government on the authority of the State governments would not excite the opposition of a single State, or of a few States only. They would be signals of general alarm. Every government would espouse the common cause; a correspondence would be opened; plans of resistance would be concerted; one spirit would animate and conduct the whole. The same combination, in short, would result from an apprehension of the *federal* as was produced by the dread of a *foreign* yoke; and, unless the projected innovations should be voluntarily renounced, the same appeal to a trial of force would be made in the one case as was made in the other. But what degree of madness would ever drive the Federal Government to such an extremity? * * * But what would be the contest in the case we are supposing? Who would be the parties? A few Representatives of the people would be opposed to the people themselves; or, rather, one set of Representatives would be contending against thirteen sets of Representatives, with the whole body of their common constituents on the side of the latter. The only refuge left for those who prophesy the downfall of the State governments is the visionary supposition that the Federal Government may previously accumulate a military force for the projects of ambition. * * * Extravagant as the supposition is, let it, however, be made. Let a regular army, fully equal to the resources of the country, be formed, and let it be entirely at the devotion of the Federal Government; still it would not be going too far to say that the State governments, with the people on their side, would be able to repel the danger. The highest number to which, according to the best computation, a standing army can be carried in any country, does not exceed 1/100th of the whole number of souls, or 1/25th part of the number able to bear arms. This proportion would not yield to the United States an army of more than 25 or 30,000 men. To these would be opposed a militia amounting to near 500,000 citizens, with arms in their hands, officered by men chosen from among themselves, fighting for their common liberties, and united and conducted by governments possessing their affections and confidence."

I shall not spend the time of your honors by reading the Virginia and Kentucky resolutions—the one the production of James Madison, and the other of Thomas Jefferson—with which you are so familiar. They fully bear out the doctrine for which I contend, and much more than I contend for. I wish, however, to read, from the American State Papers, vol. 21, p. 6, a series of resolutions adopted by the Legislature of Pennsylvania, on the 3d April, 1809. They are as follows:

"*Resolved*, by the Senate and House of Representatives of the Commonwealth of Pennsylvania:

"That, as a member of the Federal Union, the Legislature of Pennsylvania acknowledges the supremacy, and will cheerfully submit to the authority, of the General Government, as far as that authority is delegated by the Constitution of the United States. But while they yield to this authority, when exerted within constitutional limits, they trust they will not be considered as acting hostile to the General Government *when, as the guardians of the State rights*, they cannot permit an infringement of those rights by an unconstitutional exercise of power in the United States Courts.

"*Resolved*, That in a Government like that of the United States, where there are powers granted to the General Government and rights reserved to the States, it is impossible, from the imperfection of language, so to define the limits of each that difficulties should not sometimes arise from a collision of powers; and it is to be lamented that no provision is made in the Constitution for determining disputes between the General and State Governments by an impartial tribunal, when such cases occur.

"*Resolved*, That, from the construction which the United States Courts give to their powers, the harmony of the States, if they resist the encroachments on their rights, will frequently be interrupted; and if, to prevent this evil, they should on all occasions yield to stretches of power, the reserved rights of the States will depend on the arbitrary powers of the Courts.

"*Resolved*, That should the independence of the States, as secured by the Constitution, be destroyed, the liberties of the people in so extensive a country cannot long survive. To suffer the United States Courts to decide on State rights, will, from a bias in favor of power, necessarily destroy the federal part of our Government; and, whenever the Government of the United States becomes consolidated we may learn from the history of nations what will be the event."

To prevent the balance between the General and State Governments from being destroyed, and the harmony of the States from being interrupted—

"*Resolved*, That our Senators in Congress be instructed, and our Representatives be requested, to use their influence to procure amendment to the Constitution of the United States, that an impartial tribunal may be established to determine disputes between the General and State Governments; and that they be further instructed to use their endeavors that, in the meantime, such engagements may be made between the Governments of the Union and of the State as will put an end to existing difficulties."

Those resolutions were transmitted to Congress by President Madison. They were never acted upon.

My next reference is to the Remonstrance of the State of Massachusetts against the War of 1812, adopted June 18th, 1813—from the *American State Papers*, vol. 21, page 210:

"The Legislature of Massachusetts, deeply impressed with the sufferings of their constituents, and excited by the apprehension of still greater evils in prospect, feel impelled by a solemn sense of duty to lay before the National Government their views of the public interests, and to express, with the plainness of freemen, the sentiments of the people of this ancient and extensive Commonwealth.

"Although the precise limits of the powers reserved *to the several State sovereignties* have not been defined by the Constitution, yet we fully concur in the correctness of the opinions advanced by our venerable Chief Magistrate, that our Constitution secures to us the freedom of speech, and that, at this momentous period, it is our right and duty to inquire into the grounds and origin of the present war, to reflect upon the state of public affairs, and to express our sentiments concerning them with decency and frankness, and to endeavor, so far as our limited influence extends, to promote, by temperate and constitutional means, an honorable reconciliation. * * * *The States, as well as the individuals composing them, are parties to the National Compact; and it is their peculiar duty, especially in times of peril, to watch over the rights and guard the privileges solemnly guaranteed by that instrument.*"

There were also a set of resolutions, which I will not take time to read, passed by the Legislature of New Jersey, November 27th, 1827, which will be found in the *American State Papers*, vol. 21, page 797. They were based upon the then prevalent opinion that the Constitution had not conferred upon the Supreme Court of the United States the power to decide disputed questions of boundary, or similar questions, between States of the Union, and proposed an amendment to remedy that difficulty, expressly recognizing that the right to resort to force in such cases necessarily resulted from the omission. The decision of the Supreme Court, in the case of *Rhode Island* vs. *Massachusetts*, that it possessed that jurisdiction, conjured that danger. The greater one, however, of there being no tribunal to administer justice between the federal and State sovereignties, remains.

I will also refer to one other resolution, passed by the Legislature of the State of New York, on the 29th January, 1833, upon the Nullification Ordinances, as they were called:

"*Resolved*, That we regard the right of a single State to make void within its limits the laws of the United States, as set forth in the Ordinance of South Carolina, as wholly unauthorized by the Constitution of the United States, and, in its tendency, subversive to the Union and the Government thereof."

I do not know that any sane man will now dispute that truth; but this follows. The present Secretary of State of the United States, at that time a member of the Senate of this State, then moved:

"That this Legislature do adhere, in their construction of the Constitution, to the principle that the reserved rights of the States, not conceded to the General Government, ought to be *maintained and defended.*"

This latter resolution was indefinitely postponed.

I will not now stop to read what was said by President Buchanan, in his Message to Congress, on December 4th, 1860, as to the consequences of a refusal by the States to repeal the obnoxious laws which had been enacted. You will recollect that he said that, if that was not done, the injured States would be justified, standing on the basis of the Constitution, in revolutionary resistance to the Government of the Union. I do not need to claim that, for I have nothing to do, on this trial, with the justice of these mighty questions, debated between the General Government and the governments and people of these States. The question of their justice or injustice does not arise upon this trial. I was simply making these citations to show that, by the ablest writers cotemporaneous with the Constitution, and who performed the work of framing it—by the proceedings of legislative bodies and the decisions of the Supreme Court—the principle has been recognized that, in all cases in which jurisdiction has not been given to the judiciary over questions between the General Government and the State, they are equal, co-ordinate, each possessed of the right to decide for itself as to the excess by the other, if it is claimed that there is an excess of constitutional power, and to assert its own right or repel the encroachments of the other by force.

I say, in further confirmation of this, that the offence of treason against the United States, under the 3d section of the 3d article of the Constitution of the United States, must be a levying of war against them all. The words, "United States," in that section, mean the States, and not merely the Government of the Union. This is evident from the fact that the section, as originally reported (being sec. 2 of art. 7), read: "Treason against the United States shall consist only in levying war against the United States, OR ANY OF THEM; and in adhering to the enemies of the United States, OR ANY OF THEM," &c. (Journal of the Convention, page 221). It was amended so as to read collectively only, and not disjunctively. When, however, the act done is not under authority of a State, I concede that levying war against the General Government is levying war against all the States.

And, in this connection, I wish to refer to the proceedings, which I have hastily adverted to in opening to the Jury, upon the adoption of the section of the Constitution relating to treason. I refer to the *Madison Papers*, vol. 3, page 1370:

"Art. 7, sec. 2, concerning treason, was then taken up.

"*Mr. Gouverneur Morris* was for giving to the Union an exclusive right to declare what should be treason. In case of a contest between the United States and a particular State, the people of the latter must, under the disjunctive terms of the clause, be traitors to one or other authority.

"*Dr. Johnson* contended that treason could not be both against the United States and individual States, being an offence against the sovereignty, which can be but one in the same community.

"*Mr. Madison* remarked that as the definition here was of treason against the United States, it would seem that the individual States would be left in possession of a concurrent power, so far as to define and punish treason particularly against themselves, which might involve double punishment."

The words, "or any of them," were here stricken out by a vote.

"*Mr. Madison*: This has not removed the difficulty. The same act might be treason against the United States, as here defined, and against a particular State, according to its laws.

"*Dr. Johnson* was still of opinion there could be no treason against a particular State. It could not, even at present, as the Confederation now stands—*the sovereignty being in the Union*; much less can it be under the proposed system.

"*Colonel Mason:* *The United States will have a qualified sovereignty only. The individual States will retain a part of the sovereignty.* An act may be treason against a particular State, which is not so against the United States. He cited the rebellion of Bacon, in Virginia, as an illustration of the doctrine.

"*Mr. King:* No line can be drawn between levying war and adhering to the enemy, against the United States, and against an individual State. Treason against the latter must be so against the former.

"*Mr. Sherman:* Resistance against the laws of the United States, as distinguished from resistance against the laws of a particular State, forms the line."

Mr. Ellsworth, afterwards Chief Justice of the Supreme Court of the United States, closed the debate in these memorable words:

"The United States are sovereign on one side of the line dividing the jurisdictions; the States, on the other. *Each ought to have power to defend their respective sovereignties.*"

Now, if your honors please, it will probably be attempted to be answered to the argument, that by section 10 of article 1 of the Constitution of the Union, the States are forbidden to enter into any treaty, alliance, or confederation, or to grant letters of marque and reprisal; or, without the consent of Congress, to enter into any agreement or compact with another State; or to engage in war, unless actually invaded, or in such imminent danger as will not admit of delay. This does not conflict with, but, on the contrary, confirms, the views I have presented, for the following reasons:

The prohibition against entering into any treaty, alliance, or confederation, and against granting letters of marque and reprisal, has clearly no reference whatever to the relations which the States of the Union sustain to each other. It refers solely to their relations towards foreign powers.

I beg to cite, upon that subject, from Grotius, Lib. 1, chap. 4, sec. 13. He says:

"In the sixth place, when a King has only a part of the sovereignty, the rest being reserved to the people, or to a Senate, if he encroaches upon the jurisdiction which does not belong to him he may lawfully be opposed by force, since in that regard he is not at all sovereign. This is the case, in my opinion, even when in the distribution of the sovereign power the power of making war is assigned to the King. *For the grant of such a power must in that case be understood only in its relation to wars with foreign powers, those who possess a part of the sovereignty necessarily having at the same time the right of defending it*, and when a necessity arises of having recourse to forcible resistance against the King, he may, by right of war, lose even the part of the sovereignty which incontestibly belonged to him."

I say, then, in the next place, that if any of the States, having come into collision with any of their sister States, or with the General Government, and being threatened with invasion or overthrow in the contest, resort to letters of marque as a means of weakening their adversary, and thereby preventing or retarding the threatened invasion, their right to do so is not at all affected or impaired by that provision of the Federal Constitution. The right of resistance includes it as well as every other means of rendering resistance effectual.

So also with regard to the prohibition against entering into any treaty, alliance, or confederation, which is coupled with the prohibition against granting letters of marque in the first paragraph of the tenth section. That that prohibition is restricted to compacts or agreements with foreign powers, is manifest from the whole structure of the section.

The second paragraph of the section provides that no State shall, without the consent of Congress, enter into any agreement or compact with another State. It follows that, conceding the invalidity of the State acts of separation from the Union, which the whole of the preceding argument admits, the Confederation of the States claiming to have separated is not valid against the authority of the Union; but the individual States, in ratifying the Constitution of the so-called Confederate States, have done more than to make an agreement or compact with each other. Each one of them, separately, has conferred upon the same agent the authority to issue the commission in question, as its act.

Moreover, this second paragraph of the tenth section strongly confirms the doctrine of the right of forcible resistance of the States in the Union. It permits a State, without the consent of Congress, to engage in war when actually invaded, or in such imminent danger as will not admit of delay. This, it will be remembered, is in the paragraph of the section imposing restrictions upon the States, and clearly justifies forcible resistance, rising even to the dignity of war, by one State, to aggressive invasion, from another or others, when the danger is so imminent that it will not admit of delay.

The same paragraph also permits individual States to keep troops and ships of war, in time of war. The word "troops" here is evidently used in the sense of regular troops, forming an army, in contradistinction to the ordinary State militia.

To apply, then, these principles to the facts of this case: The President of the United States had, by proclamation, on the 15th April last, called for military contingents from the various States of the Union, to put down resistance to the exercise of federal authority in the State of South Carolina and other Southern States.

Those States had, by their Legislatures and Conventions of their people, decided that a proper case for resistance to the federal authority claimed to be exercised within their borders had arisen, and had authorized and commanded such resistance.

The 5th section of the Act of July 13th, 1861, and the President's Proclamation of August 16th, under that Act, concede that the resistance was claimed to be under authority of the State governments; that that claim was not disavowed by the State governments; and Congress thereupon legislated, and the President exercised the authority vested in him by the Act, on the assumption that such was the fact,—prohibiting commercial intercourse with those States, authorizing captures and confiscations of the property of their citizens without regard to their political affinities, and placing them, as we contend, in all respects, upon the footing of public enemies.

They were, moreover, threatened with immediate invasion. The Proclamation of the President assigned, as their first probable duty, to the military contingents called for from other States, to repossess the Federal Government of property which it could not repossess without an actual invasion of the discontented States.

The Congress of the Union was not then in session. It had adjourned, after having omitted to confer upon the Federal Executive the power to resort to measures of coercion, which had been under discussion during its sitting.

The commission in question was issued as one of the measures of forcible resistance to this exercise of federal power, claimed—whether rightfully or wrongfully, is not the question here—to be unlawful by the governments of all the States against which it was directed, and to which those governments enjoined forcible resistance upon, and authorized it by, their citizens.

I contend, therefore, that whether the action of the Federal Government or of the State government was justifiable or unjustifiable, no citizen of any of the States which authorized and enjoined such resistance is criminally responsible, whether he espoused one side or the other in the unhappy controversy, either to the General Government or to the government of the State of which he is a citizen, so long as he acted in good faith, and in the honest belief that the government to which he adhered was acting within the legitimate scope of its constitutional powers. We contend that every sovereign has necessarily power to defend its sovereignty, and to decide the mixed question of law and fact as to whether it has been infringed; that there can be no sovereign, or defence of sovereignty, without subjects to whom the sovereign's mandate and authority are a protection; and that as one sovereign cannot lawfully punish another, who is his equal, by personal pains and penalties, for resistance, after he is subdued, so neither can punish the subject of both who, in good faith and under honest convictions of duty, adhered to either in the struggle.

Now, if your honors please, I pass to the next proposition, which is:

That the defendants, who are citizens of the States calling themselves Confederate States, cannot be convicted under this indictment, if they in good faith believed, at the time of the capture of the Joseph, that the political *status* of those States, as members of the Federal Union, had been legally terminated, and that they had thereby ceased to be citizens of the United States, and made the capture in good faith, under the commission in evidence, as a belligerent act,—such States being, as they supposed, at war with the United States.

It is not necessary for me, if your honors please, to enlarge upon that. I rely, for that proposition, on the same authorities that I have already cited to the point, that robbery or piracy cannot be committed, unless it is committed with felonious or piratical intent. But I say, with reference to the validity or invalidity of those acts of separation from the Union, that the counsel for the prisoners, whatever their private convictions may be, are not at liberty to concede their invalidity, so long as that concession may affect the lives of their clients. Their validity has been maintained by some of the ablest lawyers of the country, and in the Senate of the United States itself, and by all the authorities, legislative, executive and judicial, of the States which have adopted them. If, as they undoubtedly did, the prisoners *bona fide* believed in their validity, the argument in favor of the protection afforded by the commission, or, by what comes to the same thing, the absence of criminal intent, becomes so much the more irresistible. And even though wholly invalid, such illegal action could not deprive the citizen of the State of the shield and protection afforded him by the action of the State government authorizing resistance, and regarded as still continuing a member of the federal Union.

The next proposition is:

That under the state of facts existing in South Carolina, as established by the public documents and other evidence in the cause, those administering the Government of the so-called Confederate States constituted the *de facto* Government which replaced the Government of the United States in those States before and at the time of the commission of the acts charged in the indictment; and the defendants who are citizens of those States were justified by overpowering necessity in submitting to that Government, in yielding their allegiance to it, and thenceforth in actively aiding and supporting it; and that the capture of the Joseph, having been a belligerent act in a war between such *de facto* Government, and the people of the States which had submitted to its authority on the one side, and the United States on the other, such defendants cannot be convicted under this indictment.

Now, with reference to that, allow me to call your honors' attention to but a single authority, in addition to those which I cited in my opening remarks to the Jury. It is the case of *The United States* vs. *The General Parkhill*, decided by Judge Cadwalader, in the United States District Court, in Philadelphia, in July, 1861. He says:

"The foregoing remarks do not suffice to define the legal character of the contest in question. It is a civil war, as distinguished from such unorganized intestine war as occurs in the case of a mere insurrectionary rebellion.

"Civil war may occur where a nation without an established Government is divided into opposing hostile factions, each contending for the acquisition of an exclusive administration of her Government. If a simple case of this kind should occur at this day, the Governments of the nations not parties to the contest might regard it as peculiarly one of civil war. As between the contending factions themselves, however, neither could easily regard their hostile opponents in the contest otherwise than as mere insurgents engaged in unorganized rebellion. Thus, in the language of Sir M. Hale, every success of either party would subject all hostile opponents of the conqueror to the penalties of treason. A desire to prevent the frequency of such a result was the origin of the rule of law, that allegiance is due to any peaceably established Government, though it may have originated in usurpation. The statute of 11 H. 7, c. 1 (A.D. 1494), excusing an English subject who has yielded obedience, or who has even rendered military service to a Ruler who was King in fact, though not in law, was declaratory of a previous principle of judicial decision."

After referring to Bracton, Coke, Hawkins, and Foster, the learned Judge proceeds:

"It has already been stated that a King in whose name justice was administered in the Courts of law was usually regarded as in actual possession of the Government.

"Civil war of another kind occurs where an organized hostile faction is contending against an established Government, whose laws are still administered in all parts of its territory except places in the actual military or naval occupation of insurgents or their adherents.

"In such a case the question has been, whether a place in the actual military occupation of the revolutionary faction, or of its adherents, may, under the law of war, be treated by that Government as if the contest was a foreign war and the place occupied by public enemies. In the case of a maritime blockade of such a place, the affirmative of this question was decided in England, in the year 1836. It had previously been so decided by the Supreme Tribunal of Marine, at Lisbon (3 Scott, 201; 2 Bingh., N.C., 781)."

Judge Cadwalader then refers to Grotius (Proleg., sec. 23), citing with approval the statement by Demosthenes of the rule of public law in the case of the invasion by Deiopeithes, the Athenian commander in the Chersonese, of the dominions of Philip of Macedon, who had sent a military force to the relief of Cardia, when sought to be reduced to submission by Deiopeithes—that wherever judicial remedies are not enforceable by a Government against its opponents, the proper mode of restoring its authority is war,—and continues:

"This doctrine is of obvious applicability to civil war of a third kind, which occurs where the exercise of an established Government's jurisdiction has been revolutionarily suspended in one or more territorial Districts, whose willing or unwilling submission to the revolutionary rule prevents the execution of the suspended Government's laws in them, except at points occupied by its military or naval forces. The present contest exemplifies a civil war of this kind. It was also, with specific differences, exemplified in the respective contests which resulted in the independence of the United Netherlands and of the United States."

He then proceeds:

"Within the limits of two of the States in which so-called ordinances of secession have been proclaimed the execution of the laws of the United States has not been wholly suppressed. They are enforceable in the Western Judicial District of Virginia, and perhaps in the adjacent Eastern Division of Tennessee. In the other nine States which profess to have seceded, including South Carolina, those laws are not enforceable anywhere.

"The Constitution of the United States prohibits the enactment by Congress of a bill of attainder, and secures, in all criminal prosecutions, to the accused, the right to a speedy public trial, by Jury of the State and District wherein the crime shall have been committed, which District must have been previously ascertained by law. Therefore if a treasonable or other breach of allegiance is committed within the limits of one of these nine States, it is not at present punishable in any Court of the United States. This was practically shown in a recent case (Greiner's case, *Legal Intelligencer*, May 10, 1861). War is consequently the only means of self-redress to which the United States can, in such a case, resort, for the restoration of the constitutional authority of their Government.

"The rule of the common law is, that when the regular course of justice is interrupted by revolt, rebellion, or insurrection, so that the Courts of justice cannot be kept open, civil war exists, and hostilities may be prosecuted on the same footing as if those opposing the Government were foreign enemies invading the land. The converse is also regularly true, that when the Courts of a Government are open, it is ordinarily a time of peace. But though the Courts be open, if they are so obstructed and overawed that the laws cannot be peaceably enforced, there might perhaps be cases in which this converse application of the rule would not be admitted. (1 Knapp, 346, 360, 361; 1 Hale, P.C. 347; Co. Litt. 249 *b*.)"

Now, if your honors please, the last proposition with which I am compelled to trouble you is:

That the Acts of Congress and the Proclamations of the President since the outbreak of the present struggle evidence the existence of a state of war between the Federal Government and the States calling themselves the Confederate States from a time anterior to the performance of the acts charged in the indictment, in which all the citizens of those States are involved and treated as public enemies of the Federal Government, whether they had any agency in initiating the conflict or not; and that the natural law of self-preservation, under these circumstances, justified the defendants, who are citizens of those States, in the commission of the acts charged in the indictment, as a means of weakening the power of destruction possessed by the Federal Government.

Now the counsel on the other side, from the intimation which he gave when he addressed the Court, intended to treat that subject of a *de facto* Government, or whatever it was, on the footing of men under duress, not in danger of their lives, joining with rebels and aiding them in a treasonable enterprise. Your honors will perceive that was not the footing on which we put it at all. It was the footing on which it stood at one time, when rebellion first broke out, when forts were seized—acts which it is no part of the duty of counsel on this trial to justify or say anything about, because there is no act connected with that part of the struggle which is in evidence on this trial.

But on that I wish to refer to what Judge Cadwalader said in another case— that of *Greiner*—which undoubtedly the learned counsel for the Government had in his mind when he drew that distinction. Shortly before the late so-called secession of Georgia, a volunteer military company, of which *Greiner* was a member, by order of the Governor, took possession of a fort within her limits, over which jurisdiction had been ceded by her to the United States, and garrisoned it until her ordinance of secession was promulgated, when, without having encountered any hostile resistance, they left it in the possession of her Government. A member of this company, Charles A. Greiner, who had participated in the capture and detention of the fort, afterwards visited Pennsylvania, at a period of threatened if not actual hostilities between the Confederate States and the United States. He was arrested in Philadelphia, under a charge of treason. Your honors will very readily perceive what a difference there was between that case and this. Judge Cadwalader applies the rule in reference to that; and, speaking of this doctrine of allegiance due to a Government in fact, he says:

"This doctrine is applicable wherever and so long as the duty of allegiance to an existing Government remains unimpaired. When this fort was captured, the accused, in the language of the Supreme Court, owed allegiance to two Sovereigns, the United States and the State of Georgia (see 14 How. 20). The duty of allegiance to the United States was co-extensive with the constitutional jurisdiction of their Government, and was, to this extent, independent of, and paramount to, any duty of allegiance to the State (6 Wheaton, 381, and 21 Howard, 517). His duty of allegiance to the United States continued to be thus paramount so long at least as their Government was able to maintain its peace through its own Courts of Justice in Georgia, and thus extend there to the citizen that protection which affords him security in his allegiance, and is the foundation of his duty of allegiance. Though the subsequent occurrences which have closed these Courts in Georgia may have rendered the continuance of such protection within her limits impossible at this time, we know that a different state of things existed at the time of the hostile occupation of the fort. The revolutionary secession of the State, though threatened, had not then been consummated. This party's duty of allegiance to the United States, therefore, could not then be affected by any conflicting enforced allegiance of the State. He could not then, as a citizen of Georgia, pretend to be an enemy of the United States, in any sense of the word 'enemy' which distinguishes its legal meaning from that of traitor. *Future cases may perhaps require the definition of more precise distinctions and possible differences under this head. The present case is, in my opinion, one of no difficulty, so far as the question of probable cause for the prosecution is concerned.*"

Having decided that, in the present state of things, he could not commit the prisoner for trial, to be conveyed to Georgia, because there were no Courts of the United States there, and because it would be a violation of the Constitution of the United States—that he could not have a speedy trial—he decided that, under a subsequent act of Congress, he had a right to require the prisoner to find sureties to be of good behavior towards the United States.

I have thus ended what I had to say upon this subject, with but one single exception.

A great deal will be said, undoubtedly, on the part of the prosecution, here, with reference to this being a revolutionary overthrow of the Government of the United States in the States which have taken these steps. I have only to ask, in reference to that—conceding it, for the sake of argument, in its fullest extent—what was the adoption of the Constitution of the United States but a revolutionary overthrow of the previously existing Confederation? It was done by nine States, without the consent of four, whose consent was necessary, and the Government of the United States went into operation; and it was a long time before at least two of them came in under the new Government.

Mr. Evarts: Will my learned friend allow me to ask him, in that part of his argument which proceeds upon the right of a State, yet being a State, to justify the acts of its citizens, to explain the proposition that a State can oppose the United States, within and under the Constitution, in regard to any law of the United States about which this essential right of judgment, whether the aggression of the United States has carried it beyond the powers of the Constitution, or not, is claimed to exist?

Mr. Larocque: I thought I had been very explicit on that. I said, in the first place, that I had nothing to do with the question of right or wrong. I said this: That a collision had occurred between the government of the State and the Federal Government; that each being sovereign, within the limitation of its powers, had a right to judge for itself whether the occasion for such a collision had occurred, or not; that these prisoners, citizens of the States which had decided that such a case had occurred, as subjects owing allegiance to two equal and co-ordinate sovereigns, which had come into hostile collision with each other, must exercise, upon their consciences, their election to which Sovereign they would adhere; and that, whatever may be the unfortunate consequences, they are not responsible before the tribunal of the other sovereignty because they adhered to one of them; that they would be no more responsible before the criminal tribunals of South Carolina if, in this contest, they had adhered to the General Government and borne arms against their native State, than they are responsible in the tribunals of the Federal Government because, exercising their own consciences, they had adhered to the State and not to the Federal Government. I say it is like the case of a child whose parents disagree, and who is obliged to adhere either to his father or his mother; and that he violates no law of God or of man in adhering to either.

Mr. Smith: If the Court please, I rise for a purpose different from the remark that I wish to make in reply to the last illustration of my learned friend. I might say that the instance of a child is one very parallel to that we might have given—that the father is the superior authority, where there is a difference between two parents.

I rise, however, to present to the Court, as one of the authorities, or rather a citation which will receive its respectful consideration, the Charge of Mr. Justice Grier, in the case tried in Philadelphia; and also the opinion of Judge Cadwalader, in the same case.

Mr. Brady: Who reported this?

Mr. Smith: I received it, by telegraph, from the District Attorney of Philadelphia; and it is also printed in a newspaper published last evening in Philadelphia. I have compared them, and the two accounts perfectly agree. I do not cite them as authority, but as entitled to the respectful consideration of the Court.

Mr. Brady: As, now-a-days, what the newspapers publish one day they generally contradict the next, I think any report should be taken with some grains of allowance, at least. I suppose I would recognize the style of Judge Grier.

Mr. Blatchford: I think you will, on examining it. It is evidently printed from the manuscript.

Mr. Smith read the charge of Judge Grier in the case of the privateers tried in Philadelphia.

Mr. Brady: Tell me what question of fact was there left to the Jury?

Mr. Smith: I refer you to Judge Cadwalader's opinion, which is much longer.

Mr. Brady: I do not see that there was anything left for the Jury. Judge Grier decided that case,—which undoubtedly he could do, for he is a very able man.

Mr. Sullivan put in evidence the log-book of the Savannah.

ARGUMENT OF MR. MAYER, OF COUNSEL FOR THE DEFENCE.

MR. MAYER said:—May it please your honors,—A foreign-born citizen now rises, on behalf of eight of the defendants, who, as it has been conceded by the prosecution, are subjects of foreign States. It might appear almost superfluous, after the full and eloquent argument of our venerable brother— I was almost tempted to say father (Mr. LORD)—for one of the junior counsel for the defence to say anything. Still, I thought it incumbent on me to anticipate a construction or interpretation which the prosecution may attempt to make, by offering, myself, a proposition. But before reading it, I will, as briefly as my proposition is brief, state my comment thereon.

Let us, in the first place, look at the aspect of the relations in which these foreigners stood at the time of their committing this alleged offence. They are all sea-faring men. Their various crafts had been locked up in the port of Charleston by the blockade there. Business, as we have heard here in evidence, was prostrated. Nothing was left for them but to enlist in the army of the Confederacy, or to become privateers. It is certainly a pity that they did not choose the first alternative; for, even if they had been caught with arms in their hands, their fate would now be far better than it is. They would not now be in jeopardy of their lives, threatened with the pains and penalties of a law that is not applicable to them. But being, as I said before, inured to the life of seafarers, they chose to become privateers.

We must, however, in judging of their act, place ourselves in their position. They were foreigners. As foreigners, they brought to this country views and notions as regards their act which are widely different from those sought to be enforced here. They knew the practice and theories of Europe in regard to their act. What are those views and theories? I can state them in a very few words, and am sorry that the authorities to which I shall refer are in a language which may not be familiar to your honors. I will, however, state their effect. It is this: Whenever a rebellion in any country has assumed such extensive magnitude as no longer to be a simple insurrection, which may be put down by police measures or regulations, but has come to such a degree that mighty armies are opposed to each other, although the revolted portion may not have been acknowledged by any nation, yet belligerent rights must be granted to it. This is the notion, or theory, which has entered into the mind of every European, to whatever State or nation he may belong. I may be permitted to quote a few historical facts to show why this is so. When the Netherland Colonies revolted against Spain the privateers of the Prince of Orange, even before he was elected Admiral General by those Colonies, were by most nations recognized. They were only not recognized by some of those nations against which they committed depredations; and it is a historical fact that a great many of those privateers commissioned by the Prince of Orange became pirates.

Another case is furnished by our own Revolution. It is known to all Europeans that, although in the beginning of the American Revolution England did not recognize the belligerent rights of America, yet, after some time, she did recognize those rights, even by a Parliamentary Act. I refer to 16 George the Third, ch. 5. The same was the case in the French Revolution; and there I may refer to a very curious fact. England recognized the privateers of the revolutionary Government of France, so far as those privateers went against other nations; but when they cruised against her own commerce she did not recognize them. She remonstrated with Denmark because Denmark had recognized them, and Denmark simply pointed to her (England's) own course.

All these facts are very well known to every European, and it is with a knowledge of these facts that every European looks upon a revolution. To express it in a very short sentence, it is the theory of "Let us have fair play."

If your honors please, I may say that this notion of belligerent rights in revolution has entered into the flesh and blood of every European to such an extent, that the only nation which does not allow, in revolution, that fair play, is despised and hated, except by these United States. I mean Russia. Russia is now very friendly towards this Union; not, however, I may be permitted to state—reversing an oft-quoted passage of Shakspeare—not because she loves Rome more, but that she loves Cæsar less. It is not out of love for this country, but because the diplomatists of Russia—the farthest-seeing diplomatists of Europe—hope that England and France will interfere in the contest between these States, and that she may get an opportunity to return the compliment to these two powers which she received from them at Sebastopol. With a knowledge of these facts, and with these European theories, these foreigners, now indicted under the Act of 1790, entered into this privateering business.

They saw, as I said before, Charleston blockaded. To them a blockade is an act of belligerent rights. They saw a constitutional government adopted in the Confederate States. They never dreamed that, if they wished to embark in this privateering business, they should be treated as pirates. They knew well, as every European knows who has any knowledge of international law, that there are two kinds of piracy—piracy by international law, and piracy under municipal law—municipal piracy, or, as Mr. LORD called it yesterday, statutory piracy.

And now I refer, as to the right of one nation making anything piracy that is not piracy by the law of nations, to Wheaton, volume 6, page 85; 1st Phillimore, 381; and to 1st Kent, 195. I will not take up the time of your honors in reading all these passages, but I hold here the last work on international law. It is, however, written in the German language. It is of unbounded authority on the Continent, and has been translated into French and Greek. It is very frequently referred to by all those authors whom I have just quoted. It states this theory in two lines, which I will read to your honors in a translation:

"Laws of individual nations (as, for instance, the French law of the 10th April, 1825) may, so far as their own subjects are concerned, either alter the meaning of piracy, or extend its operation; but they are not allowed to do that to the prejudice of other States."

I refer to Hefter on Modern International Law, 4th ed., page 191.

From this we can see that there are two kinds of piracy—national piracy and municipal piracy. No State can be prevented by any law of nations from making anything piracy which that State pleases. For instance, there is a law of piracy in Spain that any person committing frauds in matters of insurance is a pirate; or that any one even cutting the nets of a simple fisherman is a pirate. I might quote other instances. In our own country the slave-trade is a piracy; but that does not make it piracy everywhere. In some of the States of Germany slave-trade is kidnapping, and is punished as such.

What, now, is the relation of these foreigners to this municipal piracy, under the indictment with which they stand charged? That it is municipal piracy, I need not say anything further, after the full argument of our friend and father, Mr. Lord. The law is very distinct. It is, "if any *citizen* shall do so and so." But how do these men come in? Here I come to the point why I thought it fit and incumbent on me to offer my propositions. The prosecution will certainly stretch, as I said before, the construction and interpretation of the law in this way: It will say, "These men were apprehended on an American bottom, and, being on an American bottom, they were on American soil, and as, according to criminal law, they are protected by our law, so they are bound by our law." This, I apprehend, is the theory on which the prosecution will urge that these foreigners—notwithstanding the distinct expression of the law, "if any citizen"—shall be found guilty under this indictment. But as they are foreigners to this law, so is this law foreign to them. And there is a principle in criminal law which says—I read from section 238 of Bishop's Criminal Law, vol. I.—

"It is a general principle that every man is presumed to know the laws of the country in which he dwells, or, if resident abroad, transacts business. And within certain limits, not clearly defined, this presumption is conclusive. Its conclusive character rests on considerations of public policy, and, of course, it cannot extend beyond this foundation, though we may not easily say, on the authorities, precisely how far the foundation of policy extends. We may safely, however, lay down the doctrine that in no case may one enter a Court of Justice to which he has been summoned, in either a civil or criminal proceeding, with the sole and naked defence that when he did the thing complained of he did not know of the existence of the law he violated. *Ignorantia juris non excusat* is, therefore, a principle of our jurisprudence, as it is of the Roman, from which it is derived."

This rule, so essential to the ordinary administration of justice, cannot be deemed strange in criminal cases generally, because most indictable wrongs are *mala in se*, and, therefore, offenders are still conscious of violating the law "written in every man's heart."

But—and now I refer to the note to this section, which says—"ignorance of the law of foreign countries is, with the exception noticed in the text, ignorance of fact which persons are not held to know." The author cites the following authorities: Story's Equity Jurisprudence, sections 110, 23; American Jurisprudence, sections 146 and 347; to which I would add 8 Barbour's Supreme Court Reports, 838 and 839, and the case of Rex *versus* Lynn, 2d Term Report, 233.

Now, I contend that, as this law under which the indictment is drawn is a law creating municipal piracy, so it is a law foreign to these foreigners; that, therefore, as to them, it is a matter of fact, and, according to the criminal theory, *ignorantia facti excusat*, these foreigners cannot be found guilty under this law. Municipal piracy, to carry out the doctrine of this theory, is not *malum in se*; for, as I said before, international law does not acknowledge it as such, but is opposed to it as to foreigners; and if I understand well the decision of the Supreme Court, it is even acknowledged, in the case of the United States *versus* Palmer, 3d Wheaton, 610, that the Congress of the United States cannot make that piracy which is not piracy by the law of nations, in order to give jurisdiction to its Courts over such offences.

Besides, this knowledge of facts enters a good deal into the theory of intent. So much has been said about the piratical intent, that I can pass this by in silence. But, with reference to the theory that foreigners are to be taken as ignorant of facts, I will give an illustration that was suggested to me this morning by an incident which occurred on my way to the Court. A little boy in the street handed to me a card of advertisement which had all the appearance of a bank note. Now, I remembered at the moment that about three years ago the Legislature of South Carolina passed a law making the issuing and publication of such advertisements—such business cards—an offence, punishable, if I am not mistaken, both by fine and imprisonment. Now suppose that the great American showman at the corner of Ann and Broadway should carry his "What is it" or Hippopotamus down to Charleston, and issue such an advertisement, and he should be brought before the Court of South Carolina; would it not be unjust, as the offence is not *malum in se*, to find him guilty? Certainly it would be; and, according to the same theory, I cannot imagine, by any possible process of reasoning, that these prisoners should be deemed guilty under an indictment, when the law was entirely foreign to them. They may justly say, as they might have known, and did perhaps know, that our country, too, holds to this simple doctrine: "Let us have fair play." So when certain provinces rose up in revolt against the parent or original Government, to conquer, as it were, their independence, this country maintained a state of neutrality, and granted to both parties belligerent rights. Many such cases have been cited; but the most striking one, I am astonished, has not been cited. I will refer to it now. It is the case of the United States against the Miramon and the Havana, tried before the District Court of New Orleans. These two steamers were commissioned vessels, belonging to an authority not only not recognized by the Government of the United States, but opposed to the Government which had been recognized by ours. They were commissioned ships of General Miramon, and were seized and libeled; yet they were released. Perhaps it would have been better for us if they had not been released, because they have since given us some trouble—one of them (the Havana) having been converted into the ubiquitous Sumter, which is rather a terror to our mercantile marine.

I will not further trespass upon your honors' time, but will immediately read my proposition. That proposition is, that, "As to the defendants who are shown to have been citizens of foreign States at the date of the alleged offence, the law is, that they cannot be found guilty of piracy under the present indictment, which includes only piracy by municipal law—the ignorance of which, as to foreigners, is not *ignorantia legis*, but *ignorantia facti*. Therefore the defendant Clarke, and the other foreigners, should be acquitted."

Before, however, I close my few remarks, I must, in justice to my immediate client, William Charles Clarke, add another observation. I have, by submitting to your honors the proposition, separated, as it were, his case and that of the other foreigners from the rest of the prisoners. I did so on my own responsibility; for he let me understand that he did not wish to see his case separated from the others. He expressed that sentiment to me in a very forcible German proverb. It was, "*Mitgegangen, mitgefangen, mitgehangen!*" [3] Yet I thought it incumbent on me, as his counsel, to urge all those circumstances that might be beneficial to him and to those in the same position,—trusting that the unity and identity of the fate of all thus severed by me may be restored in this wise: that the case of these foreigners may be made also the case of the four citizens, both by the ruling of your honors and the verdict of general acquittal of the Jury.

Mr. *Brady*—Before Mr. Evarts proceeds to close the legal considerations involved in the case I feel it proper to advise him of a point for which I will contend, and on the discussion of which I do not now intend to enter. I will not admit that Congress had the power, under the Constitution of the United States, to pass the ninth section of the Act of 1790, which, upon my construction of it, would punish as piracy the act of an American citizen who should take a commission from England or France and then commit an act of hostility on an American ship or on an American citizen on the high seas. The argument is in a nutshell; though, of course, I shall give some illustrations at the proper time. It is this—that there is no common-law jurisdiction of offences in this Government; that it can take cognizance of no crimes except those which are created by Act of Congress, including piracy; and that the authority of the Constitution conferred upon Congress, to pass laws defining piracy and to punish offences against the law of nations, relates only to such offences as were then known, and does not invest the Legislature of the Federal Government with authority, under pretence of defining well-known offences, to create other and new offences, as is attempted to be done in the Act of 1790.

ARGUMENT OF MR. EVARTS.

Mr. *Evarts* said: If the Court please, I shall hardly find it necessary, in stating the propositions of law for the Government, to consume as much time as has been, very usefully and very properly, employed by the various counsel for the prisoners in asking your attention to the views which they deem important and applicable in defence of their clients. The affirmative propositions to which the Government has occasion to ask the assent of the Court, in submitting this case to the Jury, are very few and simple. Your honors cannot have failed to notice that all the manifold, and more or less vague and uncertain, views of ethics, of government, of politics, of moral qualifications, and of prohibited crimes, which have entered into the discussion of the particular transaction whose actual proportions and lineaments have been displayed before the Court and Jury, are, in their nature, affirmative propositions, meeting what is an apparently clear and simple case on the part of the Government, and requiring to be encountered on our part more by criticism than by any new and positive representation of what the law is which is to govern this case under the jurisprudence of the United States.

I shall first ask your honors' attention to the question of jurisdiction, which, of course, separates itself from all the features and circumstances of the particular crime. Your honors will notice that this question of jurisdiction does not, in the least, connect itself with the subject or circumstances of the crime, as going to make up its completeness, under the general principles which give the *locality* of the crime as the *locality* of the trial. With these principles, whether of right and justice, or of convenience for the adequate and complete ascertainment of the facts of an alleged crime, we have no concern here. The crime complained of is one which has no locality within the territorial jurisdiction of the United States, and assigns for itself, in its own circumstances, no place of trial. From the fact that the crime was completed on the high seas, equally remote, perhaps, from any District the Courts of which might have cognizance of the transaction, there are no indications whatever, in its own circumstances, pointing out the jurisdiction for its trial. It is, therefore, wholly with the Government, finding a crime which gives, of itself, no indication of where, on any principle, it should be tried, to determine which of all the Districts of the United States in which its Courts of Judicature are open,—all having an equal judicial authority, and all being equally suitable in the arrangement of the judicial establishment of the Union,—it is entirely competent, I say, for the Government to determine, on reasons of its own convenience, which District, out of the many, shall gain the jurisdiction, and upon what circumstances the completeness of that jurisdiction shall depend.

It is not at all a right of the defendant to claim a trial before a particular tribunal, nor are there any considerations which should prevent the selection of the place of jurisdiction through whatever casual agency may be employed in that selection. In the eye of the law, the Judges are alike, and the Districts are alike. Congress, considering the matter thus wholly open, in order that there might be no contest open for all the Districts, and assuming that there would be some natural circumstance likely to attend the bringing of the offender within the reach of civil process, when a crime had been committed outside of the civil process of every nation, determined, by the 14th section of the Crimes Act of March 3d, 1825, which gives the law of jurisdiction in this case, that the trial should be "had in the District where the offender is apprehended, or into which he may be first brought." Nor is it a true construction of this statute to say that the law intends that the cognizance of the crime—all of the Districts being equally competent to try it, and there being nothing in the crime itself assigning its locality as the place of trial—shall belong exclusively to that Court which shall first happen to get jurisdiction by the actual bringing of the offender within its operation. If that be true, it is apparent that neither one of the Districts thus differently described has jurisdiction exclusively of the other. Now, the language of the statute certainly gives this double place of trial in the alternative; and it is very difficult to say what principle either of right, of convenience, or of judicial regularity, is offended by such a construction and application of the statute. Accordingly, I understand it to have been held by Mr. Justice Story, in the case of *The United States* vs. *Thompson* (1 *Sumner*, 168), that there were these alternative places of trial; and, as a matter of reasoning, he finds that such arrangement is suitable to the general principles of jurisprudence, and to the general purposes of the statute. Now, if this be so, then, as we come, in this District, within one of the alternatives of the statute, and as this District is confessedly the one in which the apprehension of the offenders took place, we are clear of any difficulty about jurisdiction.

The case of Hicks, decided here, was, perhaps, not entirely parallel to the one now under consideration. But, let us see how far the views and principles there adopted go to determine this case, in the construction of the statute in any of its parts. Hicks had committed a crime on the high seas—in the immediate vicinity, I believe, of our own waters. Making his way to the land, he proceeded unmolested to Providence, in Rhode Island. The officers of justice of the United States, getting on his track, pursued him to Rhode Island, and there he was found, unquestionably within the District of Rhode Island. They did not obtain his apprehension by legal process there, and thus bring him within the actual exercise of the power of a Court of the District of Rhode Island; but they persuaded him, or in some way brought about his concurrence, to come with them into the District of New York, and here the process of this Court was fastened upon him, and he was brought to trial on the capital charge of piracy. On a preliminary plea to the jurisdiction of the Court, and on an agreed state of facts, to the effect, I believe, of what I have stated, the matter was considerably argued before your honor, Judge Nelson, on behalf of the prisoner; but your honor, as I find by the report, relieved the District Attorney from the necessity of replying, considering the matter as settled, under the facts of the case, in the practice of the Court. Now, the argument there was, that the District of Rhode Island was the District where the offender was apprehended; and it could not be contended that the Southern District of New York was the one into which he was first brought by means other than those of legal process. And the argument was, that the crime for which he was to be tried here, being a felony, any control of his person by private individuals was a lawful apprehension, and one which might be carried out by force, if necessary; and that, therefore, there was, in entire compliance with the requisition of the statute, an apprehension within the District of Rhode Island. If, under the circumstances of that case, that view had been sustained by the Court, it could not have been, I think, pretended that the Courts of this District had concurrent jurisdiction, because of Hicks having been first brought into this District. The whole inquiry turned on the question whether he was apprehended in the District of Rhode Island.

In considering the case, your honor, Judge Nelson, recognized, as I suppose, the view of the alternative jurisdiction which I have stated. You said to the District Attorney: "We will not trouble you, Mr. Hunt. The question in this case is not a new one. It is one that has been considered and decided by several members of the Supreme Court, in the course of the discharge of their official duties. It has repeatedly arisen in cases of offences upon the high seas, and the settled practice and construction of the Act of Congress is, that in such cases the Court has jurisdiction of the case, in the one alternative, in the District into which the offender is first brought from the high seas—meaning, into which he is first brought by authority of law and by authority of the Government. In cases where the offender has been sent home under the authority of the Government, the Courts of the District into which he is first brought, under that authority, are vested with jurisdiction to try the case. The other alternative is, the District in which the prisoner is first apprehended—meaning an apprehension under the authority of law—under the authority of legal process. This interpretation of the Statute rejects the idea of a private arrest, and refers only to an arrest under the authority of law and under legal process. It is quite clear, in this case, that no District except the Southern District of New York possesses jurisdiction of the offence; for here the prisoner was first apprehended by process of law. We do not inquire into anything antecedent to the arrest under the warrant in this District, because it has no bearing whatever upon the question of the jurisdiction of the Court. We have no doubt, therefore, that the Court has jurisdiction of the case, and that this is the only District in which the prisoner can be tried."

Now I owe the Court and my learned friend, Mr. Lord, an apology for having supposed and stated that the provisions of the Act of March 3d, 1819, giving certain powers to the naval officers of the United States "to protect the commerce of the United States," as is the title of the Act, were not now in force. I was misled. The Act itself was but temporary in its character, being but of a year's duration. By the Act of May 15th, 1820, the first four sections of the Act of March 3d, 1819, were temporarily renewed. But afterwards, by the Act of January 30th, 1823, those four sections were made a part of the permanent statutes of the country. The substantial part of the Act of March 3d, 1819, namely, the fifth section, which defined and punished the crime of piracy, was repealed, and replaced by the Act of May 15th, 1820, and has never reappeared in our statutes.

Judge Nelson: It is the fifth section of the Act of 1819 that is repealed.

Mr. Evarts: Yes; that Act is found at page 510 of the 3d volume of the Statutes at Large.

Mr. Lord: All that relates to the apprehension of offenders is in force.

Mr. Evarts: Yes; that is all in force. The Act is entitled, "An Act to protect the Commerce of the United States, and punish the Crime of Piracy." The first section provides, that "the President of the United States be, and hereby is, authorized and requested to employ so many of the public armed vessels as, in his judgment, the service may require, with suitable instructions to the commanders thereof, in protecting the merchant vessels of the United States and their crews from piratical aggressions and depredations." There is nothing in that section which is pertinent to this case. The second section provides, "that the President of the United States be, and hereby is, authorized to instruct the commanders of the public armed vessels of the United States to subdue, seize, take, and send into any port of the United States, any armed vessel or boat, or any vessel or boat, the crew whereof shall be armed, and which shall have attempted or committed any piratical aggression, search, restraint, depredation, or seizure, upon any vessel of the United States or of citizens thereof, or upon any other vessel, and also to retake any vessel of the United States or its citizens which may have been unlawfully captured upon the high seas."

This, your honors will notice, is entirely confined to authority to subdue the vessel and take possession of it, and send it in for the adjudication and forfeiture which are provided in the fourth section.

The third section gives the right to merchant vessels to defend themselves against pirates.

There is nothing in the Act which gives to the officers of the Government the power, or enjoins on them the duty, of apprehending the pirates. I will now ask your honors' attention to the distinction between this Act and the powers conferred by the slave-trading Act.

Judge Nelson: The Act of 1819 gives to the commanders authority to bring home prisoners,—does it not?

Mr. Evarts: It does not, in terms, say anything about them. That is the point to which I ask your honors' attention. The Act instructs the commanders of public armed vessels to subdue, seize, take, and send into any port of the United States, any armed vessel or boat, or any vessel or boat, the crew whereof is armed, and that may have attempted or committed any piratical aggression, &c. There is nothing said as to the arrest of the criminals. It is a question of construction.

Judge Nelson: It is not specific in that respect.

Mr. Evarts: No, sir, it is not specific. Now, in the Act of March 3d, 1819, entitled, "An Act in addition to the Acts prohibiting the slave trade," which will be found at page 532 of the 3d volume of the Statutes at Large, a general authority is given to the President, "whenever he shall deem it expedient, to cause any of the armed vessels of the United States to be employed to cruise on any of the coasts of the United States or Territories thereof, or on the coast of Africa, or elsewhere," "and to instruct and direct the commanders of all armed vessels of the United States to seize, take, and bring into any port of the United States, all ships or vessels of the United States, wheresoever found," engaged in the slave trade. And then comes this distinct provision in reference to the apprehension and the bringing in for adjudication of persons found on board of such vessels. It is the last clause of the first section: "And provided further, that the commanders of such commissioned vessels do cause to be apprehended and taken into custody every person found on board of such vessel so seized and taken, being of the officers or crew thereof, and him or them convey, as soon as conveniently may be, to the civil authority of the United States, to be proceeded against in due course of law, in some of the Districts thereof."

This Act is the one referred to by Judge Sprague in the case of *The United States* vs. *Bird (Sprague's Decisions, 299)*

Judge Nelson: There is limitation to that Act, is there?

Mr. Evarts: No, sir; it is unlimited in duration, and a part of the law now administered. Now, I need not ask your honors' attention to the familiar act which gives to Consuls of the United States direct authority to take offenders into custody and detain them, and send them by the first convenient vessel to the United States, to be delivered to the civil authorities to be proceeded against.

Now, my proposition is this,—that neither under the slave-trading Act, nor under the Act for the prevention and punishment of piracy passed in 1819, does the extra-territorial seizure, control and transmission of offenders, exclude the plain terms of the alternative of the statute, which makes jurisdiction dependent, not on apprehension merely, but on apprehension within a District; and that, even though there is a governmental introduction of the offender into a District, making that District, in a proper sense, the one into which he is first brought, yet that does not in the least displace the alternative of jurisdiction of an apprehension within a District, there having been no prior apprehension, by process, within any other District, as the consummation and completion of the delivery of the offender to the civil authorities for the purpose of a trial, the transaction having been instituted on the high seas or in a foreign port.

Now, on the facts in this case, there is no room for disputing that the first apprehension was within this District. Nor can I deny that the seizure of these persons on the high seas was made by an armed vessel of the United States, either under the general right which the law of nations gives both to public and private vessels to seize pirates, or under the implied right and power to do so, certainly so far as to make it justifiable on the part of commanders of cruisers, by virtue of the provision of the Act of 1819 which authorizes them to send in a piratical vessel. These men were sent in, in the course of such active intervention, by an armed vessel of the United States. But I submit to your honors, that the provisions of that Act, which thus incidentally include, as it were, the transmission of the ship's company of a pirate, because they are to be subdued, and the ship is to be sent in, cannot be turned, by any process of reasoning, into anything that can be called a legal apprehension. I am satisfied that your honor, Judge Nelson's view, that the term "apprehension" is only meant to apply to the service of judicial process within a District, is entirely sound.

The principal argument and the principal authority relied on to displace the jurisdiction thus plainly acquired under one alternative of the statute, denies, really, that there is any alternative, or that there can possibly be two Districts, either one of which may rightfully have jurisdiction. That, I take it, is the substance of the proposition. It is, that the alternative gives to one of the two exclusive jurisdiction; and that, whenever facts have occurred—whether jurisdiction has been exercised or not—which give to the one District jurisdiction and an opportunity to exercise it, then, by the prior concurrence of all the circumstances which fix the statutory jurisdiction on that District, the possibility of the occurrence of any new circumstances to give jurisdiction in the other and alternative District is displaced.

The case of *The United States* vs. *Townsend* has been brought to your honors' attention in the manuscript record of the preliminary proceedings. The prisoner, who had been taken and brought into Key West, where the vessel stopped, as we are told, for the temporary purpose of supplies, was thence brought into Massachusetts. It is the record of a proceeding wherein Judge Sprague, with the concurrence of his associate, Mr. Justice Clifford, of the Supreme Court, sent the prisoner, in that predicament, back to Key West for trial, and would not permit an indictment to be found against him in the District of Massachusetts. We have no knowledge of the facts of that case, except what are contained in this record. Now, your honors will notice, in the first place, that this is not a judicial determination as to the right of jurisdiction of the Massachusetts Court, necessarily; but that, on the theory which I present, that there are two alternative jurisdictions, it may have been only a prudent and cautious exercise of the discretion of that Court, preliminary to indictment, that this man should be sent, on his own application, to the District of Florida for trial. In other words, he interposed an objection that he was entitled to a trial in Key West; and the Court, affirming the opinion that that District had jurisdiction of the crime, determined that it would send him there for trial, and that it would not exercise its own jurisdiction, which might be made subject to some question. And yet it is not to be denied that Judge Sprague is apparently of the opinion that there are not two alternative places of jurisdiction, neither one exclusive of the other; but that they are only alternative as respects the one or the other which is the first to gain jurisdiction. It is a little difficult to see, on this view, how there can be any two places, rightfully described as separate places, one of which is the place into which the prisoner is first brought, and the other of which is the place where he is first apprehended; because, in the very nature of the case, the moment you raise the point that the offender has been in two Districts, and that in the latter of them he is apprehended, then it follows that he has passed through the former; and the statute is really reduced to this—that the offender must be indicted in the District into which he is first brought. There cannot then be two different Districts, into one of which he is brought, within the meaning of the law, and in the other of which he is apprehended; because, that into which he is first brought must necessarily precede, in time, that in which he is first apprehended, and he could not have been apprehended before, in a District other than that into which he is first brought. So that you necessarily reduce the statute to a fixing of the place of trial in the District into which the offender is first brought.

The case of Smith—the trial just terminated in Philadelphia, in which the prisoner was tried and convicted before the Circuit Court of the United States—is an authority of the two Judges of that Court on this very point, the circumstances of a prior introduction of the prisoner within the Eastern District of Virginia being much more distinct than in this case. The capturing vessel was a steamer, which took the prize into Hampton Roads. The defendant and the others of the prize crew were kept as prisoners on board this war steamer, which, after anchoring in Hampton Roads, near Fortress Monroe, went a short distance up the Potomac, returned, and again anchored in Hampton Roads, after which she brought the prisoners, including the defendant, into Philadelphia, where they were taken into the custody of the Marshal. Now, unquestionably, geographically, that prisoner was within the State of Virginia, and within the Eastern District of Virginia, rather more distinctly than in the case now on trial. In that case, the Court said—"One of the points of law on which counsel for the defence requests instruction to the Jury is, that the Court has no jurisdiction of the case; because, after his apprehension on the high seas, he was first brought into another District, meaning the Eastern District of Virginia, and ought to be there tried. This instruction cannot be given. When he was taken prisoner, and was detained in the capturing vessel, he was not apprehended for trial, within the meaning of the Act of Congress. His first apprehension for that purpose, of which there is any evidence, was at Philadelphia, after his arrival in this District. Whether he had been previously brought into another District, within the meaning of the Act, is immaterial"—recognizing the doctrine of two alternative jurisdictions, neither exclusive of the other. "It has been decided that, under this law, a person, first brought into one District, and afterwards apprehended in another, may be tried in the latter District. Therefore, if you believe the testimony on the subject, this Court has jurisdiction of the case."

Now, your honors very easily understand, that without any election or purpose on the part of any authority, civil or naval, representing the

Government, a prisoner may be brought into a District, yet never come, in any sense, under the judicial cognizance of that District. In this case, these prisoners might have escaped from the Harriet Lane, and have fled to Massachusetts, or Pennsylvania, or wherever else their fortune should have carried them, and might there have been first apprehended. Now, what is there in the nature of the jurisprudence of the United States, in respect of a crime committed outside of both Districts, which should prevent the jurisdiction of Massachusetts being just as effective as the jurisdiction of New York? If such be the law, I have no occasion to argue any further. But the decision of Judge Sprague is, in my judgment, quite opposed to that view of the law; and I, must, therefore, present to your honors some considerations which, in my judgment, make this the District, in the intendment of the statute, into which these offenders were first brought, as well as the District in which they were first apprehended.

The alleged prior introduction of these persons within any other Judicial District of the United States, within the meaning of the statute, is shown by the evidence of what occurred in reference to the transit of the Minnesota, after she had taken them on board from the capturing vessel, the Perry, off the coast of South Carolina. She anchored off Fortress Monroe, just opposite Hampton Roads, and there transferred these prisoners to the Harriet Lane, which brought them into this District.

Now, it is said that that incident of the anchorage of the Minnesota in or near Hampton Roads, and the transhipment of the prisoners to another vessel, which the exigencies of the naval service sent to New York, did fulfill the terms of the law in reference to the introduction of those offenders within a District of the United States, and that they were, therefore, first brought into the Eastern District of Virginia; and, if that circumstance displaces the alternative jurisdiction, and thereby Virginia became the exclusive District of jurisdiction, this trial cannot be valid, and must result in some other disposition of these prisoners than a verdict of guilty, if, on the merits of the case, such a verdict should be warranted.

What are the traits and circumstances of that transmission? I understood my learned friend, Mr. Lord, to concede that he would not argue that the mere transit of the keel of the vessel transporting the prisoners, in the course of its voyage to a port of destination, through the waters of another District, was an importation or introduction of the offenders into that District, so as to make it the place of trial. Take, for instance, the case of a vessel making a voyage from Charleston to New York. For aught I know, certainly, within the practicability of navigation, her course may be within a marine league of the shore of North Carolina, of the shore of Virginia, of the shore of Maryland, and of the shore of New Jersey, before making the port which is the termination of her transit. Well, my learned friends say that they do not claim that this local position of a vessel within a marine league while she is sailing along, is, within any sensible view of the statute, an introduction into the District, so as to found a jurisdiction.

Let us see, if your honors please, whether the transit of these prisoners from the capturing vessel to the Marshal's office in New York was not simply part of the continuous voyage of the vessel from one point to the other. Where was the Minnesota, and on what employment and duty, at the time she received these prisoners on board? She was the flag ship, as the Commodore has told us, of the Atlantic Blockading Squadron, and her whole duty was as a cruiser or blockading ship, at sea, in discharge of the duty assigned to her.

I take it for granted that my learned friends will not contend that a vessel, pursuing her voyage continuously along the coast of North Carolina and the coast of Virginia, introduces an offender within a District by stopping, either under any stress of navigation, or for any object unconnected with any purpose to terminate her voyage, or that the fact of her being becalmed, or of her having anchored off the coast to get water or supplies, and having then pursued her voyage continuously to New York, would alter the character of the transit, in any legal construction that it should receive.

Now, what did the Minnesota do? The Commodore took the prisoners on board that vessel, as he tells you, for the purpose of sending them to New York by the first naval vessel that he should be able to detach from the service. Did he, in the interval between the capture and the complete transmission and reception of the prisoners here, ever make a port or a landing from his vessel, or ever depart from the design of the voyage on which he was engaged? No. He was on his cruise, bound to no port, always at sea, and only in such relations to the land as the performance of his duty to blockade at such points as he saw fit, whether at Charleston or the Capes of Virginia, required him to be in. And there is no difference, in the quality of the act, arising from his having stopped at Hampton Roads, and thence sent forward the prisoners by the Harriet Lane, because she was the first vessel that was going to New York—going, as has been stated, for a change of her armament and for repairs.

Now, I submit to your honors, that there is nothing, either in the design or the act of this blockading vessel, the Minnesota, or of the Harriet Lane, that causes the course of transmission of these prisoners to the point of their arrest in this District to differ from what it would have been if, with an even keel, and without any interruption, the capturing vessel, the Perry, had started for New York, and had, in the course of her navigation, come within the line of a marine league from the shore of some District of the United States, and had, perchance, anchored there, for the purpose of replenishing her supplies for the voyage. In other words, in order to make out, within the terms of the statute, a bringing into a District of the United States, so as to make it a District of jurisdiction, within the sense of the statute, it is impossible for the Court to fail to require the ingredient of a voyage into a port, at least as a place of rest and a termination of the passage of the vessel, temporary or otherwise. That is requisite, in order to make an introduction within a District. And I cannot imagine how his honor, Judge Sprague, or his honor, Judge Clifford, could, in the case before them, have given any such significance to the prior arrival of the vessel of the United States at Key West; for, it was but a stopping at an open roadstead for the purpose, not of a port, but of continuing at sea or in the sea service of the country.

Your honors will notice that, by such a construction of the Act, instead of making the place where jurisdiction shall be acquired dependent on some intelligent purpose, in the discretion of the officers who control the person of the prisoner, as to where he shall be landed, you make the question of jurisdiction dependent upon the purest accident in the navigation of the vessel. Thus, in this particular case, the Captain of the Minnesota tells us he had not coal enough to come directly to New York, if he had designed to do so, and that he stopped at his blockading station and sent the prisoners on by another vessel, which the exigencies of the service required to make the voyage.

There is another proposition upon this question of jurisdiction which I deem it my duty to make to your honors, although I suppose the whole matter will be disposed of on considerations which have been presented on one side or the other, and, as I suppose, in favor of the jurisdiction. Yet I cannot but think that the rules of jurisprudence and the regular and effective administration of criminal justice will suffer if these questions are to be interposed and to be passed upon by the Court at the same time as the indictment itself. Where the question of the locality of the trial forms no part of the body of the crime, and has nothing to do with the place where the crime was committed, but is wholly a question of the local position of the prisoner, then the exception to the jurisdiction can only be taken as a preliminary plea, or in the shape of a plea in abatement. That was the construction in the Hicks case, and is the general rule in reference to jurisdiction in civil cases which are dependent upon the proper cognizance of the person of the defendant. I refer to the cases of *Irvine* vs. *Lowry*, (14 *Peters*, 293;) *Sheppard* vs. *Graves*, (14 *Howard*, 505;) and *D'Wolf* vs. *Rabaud*, (1 *Peters*, 476.)

Mr. Larocque: I ask what particular point is decided by those cases?

Mr. Evarts: They are wholly on the point that where the jurisdiction of a Court of the United States depends, not on the subject matter of the suit, but on the District where the defendant is found, or on the citizenship of the parties, an objection to the jurisdiction must be taken by a plea in abatement.

Mr. Larocque: But suppose it depends upon the place where the crime was committed, whether in New York or Ohio, whether on land or at sea?

Mr. Evarts: It is not necessary to ask that question, for I have expressly excluded that consideration by the preliminary observation, that the locality of the trial forms no part of the body of the crime. In this case, the crime having been committed outside of any locality, it is wholly a question of the regularity and legality of the means whereby the criminal has been brought into the jurisdiction—nothing else.

Mr. Larocque: Does the counsel cite these cases to show that want of jurisdiction must be pleaded in abatement?

Mr. Evarts: It is the rule in civil cases. Now, your honors will see that the question forms no part of the issue of guilty or not guilty.

Mr. Larocque: Will you look at the last averment in your indictment?

Mr. Evarts: I repeat, that it forms no part of the body of the crime, and no part of the issue of guilty or not guilty, that is to be determined by the Jury. If the Jury, upon the issue of guilty or not guilty, should pass upon the question as to what District the defendant had been first brought into, or as to what District he was apprehended in, and should find that this Court had no jurisdiction, he would be entitled to an acquittal on that ground, and that acquittal would be pleadable in bar if he were put on trial in the proper District; for, there is no mode, that I know of, of extricating this part of the issue from the issue on the merits of the case, when it is decided by a verdict. There is no possibility of discriminating in the verdict. There is no special verdict and no question reserved. It is a verdict of not guilty. And, therefore, on the question of regularity of process, the crime itself is disposed of—the whole result of the judicial investigation being that the trial should have been in another District.

But, where the locality of the crime forms a part of its body, of course, the Government, undertaking to prove a crime to have been committed within a District, rightly fails if the crime is shown not to have been committed within that District.

Mr. Larocque: And then can they not try it where it was committed?

Mr. Evarts: I should not like to be the District Attorney who would try it.

Now, if the Court please, upon the matters connected with the merits of this trial, the first proposition to which I ask your honors' attention is—that the Act of April 30th, 1790, in the sections relating to piracy, is constitutional, and that the evidence proves the crime as to all the prisoners under the eighth section, and as to the four citizens under the ninth section. The crime is also charged and proved against all the prisoners under the third section of the Act of May 15th, 1820.

I do not know that your honors' attention has been drawn to the distinction between the eighth section of the Act of 1790 and the third section of the Act of 1820. The counts in the indictment cover both statutes, and both statutes are in force. The words of the eighth section of the Act of 1790 are these:

"If any person or persons shall commit, upon the high seas," "murder or robbery," "every such offender shall be deemed, taken and adjudged to be a pirate and felon, and, being thereof convicted, shall suffer death."

The whole description of the crime is "murder or robbery" "upon the high seas."

The third section of the Act of 1820 adds to that simple description of criminality certain words not at all tautological, but making other acts equivalent to the same crime. The section provides that, "if any person shall, upon the high seas, or in any haven, &c., commit the crime of robbery in or upon any ship or vessel, or upon any of the ship's company of any ship or vessel, or the lading thereof, such person shall be adjudged to be a pirate, and, being thereof convicted," "shall suffer death." Beyond the simple word, "robbery," is added, "in or upon any ship or vessel, or upon any of the ship's company of any ship or vessel, or the lading thereof."

Judge Nelson: The fifth section of the Act of March 3d, 1819, provides for piracy on the high seas according to the law of nations. The previous Act of 1790, and the third section of the Act of 1820, prescribe the punishment of the crimes of murder and robbery on the high seas.

The District Attorney: The Act of 1820 does not refer to murder, only to robbery on the high seas.

Judge Nelson: It denominates as a pirate a person guilty of robbery on the high seas.

Mr. Evarts: But the body of the crime is the robbery, and not the epithet.

Mr. Brady: That is the question.

Mr. Evarts: But, in the fifth section of the Act of 1819, the provision is, that "if any person shall, on the high seas, commit the crime of piracy as defined by the law of nations."

- 220 -

Judge Nelson: That is a different offence.

Mr. Evarts: Yes, and is open always to the inquiry, what the law of nations is.

Now, that Act of 1790 is, we say, constitutional. And here I may as well say what seems to be necessary in reference to the point made by Mr. Brady on behalf of the prisoners. He will contend, he says, that the ninth section of the Act of 1790 is beyond the constitutional power of Congress—its constitutional power in the premises being limited, as he supposes, to the right to define and punish the crime of piracy.

Mr. Brady: "And offences against the law of nations."

Mr. Evarts: To that explicit clause in the Constitution.

Now, your honors will notice what the crime in the ninth section of the Act of 1790 is. It is not piracy so described, nor robbery so described merely, but it is a statutory definition of the crime, which includes a particular description and predicament of the offender (the eighth section having included all persons), and also defines the subject of the robbery, or the object of the piratical aggression. It is this: "If any citizen shall commit any piracy or robbery aforesaid, or any act of hostility against the United States, or any citizen thereof," &c. "Piracy or robbery aforesaid" would, of course, include the definition of the crime as embraced in the eighth section. But, the ninth section proceeds to add a new and substantive completeness of crime, not described either as piracy or robbery, to wit: "Or any act of hostility against the United States, or any citizen thereof, upon the high seas, under color of any commission from any foreign Prince or State, or on pretence of authority from any person, such offender shall, notwithstanding the pretence of any such authority, be deemed, adjudged, and taken to be a pirate, felon, and robber, and, on being thereof convicted, shall suffer death."

Now, it is quite immaterial whether this statute is accurate in declaring the offender to be "a pirate, felon, and robber." It has made the offence a crime. Under what restrictions has it made it a crime? Has it undertaken to extend the jurisdiction of the Federal Government, as supported by the law of nations respecting piracy, which is a right on the part of every nation to legislate not only for its own citizens—not only in protection of its own property—but in punishment of all pirates, of whatever origin, and in protection of all property on sea, and wherever owned? Now that, undoubtedly, is the jurisdiction under the law of nations, and neither by the Constitution has Congress received any greater power under the law of nations than that, nor, I respectfully submit, can it receive any greater power under the law of nations; that is, Congress cannot receive any power greater than that which other nations, not bound by our municipal statutes, would be bound to respect, as sustained by the law of nations. Now I agree that "any act of hostility against the United States, or any citizen thereof," would not necessarily be up to the grade and of the quality of piracy under the law of nations; and that the Congress of the United States, in undertaking to make laws which would create an offence, and punish it as piracy, which was not piracy by the law of nations, and in seeking to enforce its jurisdiction and inflict its sanctions on a people who owed it no municipal obedience, and in protection of property over which it had no municipal control, and no duty to perform, could not control foreign nations; and that foreign nations would not be bound to respect convictions obtained under such a municipal extension of our law over persons never subject to us, and in respect to property never under our dominion.

And thus your honors see that, just in proportion as the ninth section has extended the crime, it has limited both the persons to whom the statute is applied, and the property in respect of which the crime is defined. It is wholly limited to our own citizens, subject to whatever laws we choose to make for our own government, and in respect of the marine property of the United States, and of its citizens when at sea, which, by every rule of the extension or limit of municipal authority, is always regarded, on general principles of public jurisprudence, as a part of the property and of the territory of the nation to which the ship and cargo belong, wherever it may be on the high seas.

Now, this ninth section, I suppose, if your honors please,—and such I understand to be the views of Judge Sprague, as expressed by him to the Grand Jury, at Boston,—proceeds and is supported on the general control given by the Constitution to Congress over all external commerce, which, I need not say, must, to be effective, extend to the criminal jurisprudence which protects against wrong, and the criminal control which punishes crime perpetrated by our citizens on our own commerce on the high seas. My learned friend would certainly not contend that the different States had this authority in reference to crimes on the high seas. And, if they have not that authority, then, between these jurisdictions, we should have omitted one of the most necessary, one of the most ordinary, one of the wisest and plainest duties of Governments in regard to the protection of their commerce. For, it is idle to say that there are no crimes which may be committed at sea which are not piracy, and that there is no protection needed for our own commerce against our own citizens which does not fall within the international law of piracy.

Mr. Brady: I ask Mr. Evarts' permission to make a suggestion upon this point, which it is due to him, and to myself, also, that I should present, that I may hear his views in respect to it. I would ask the learned gentleman, and the Court, to suppose the case of an American citizen who, on the breaking out of a war between the United States and England, should be residing in

England as a denizen, and who had resided there for many years, and who should take a commission for privateering from the British Government, regularly issued, having about it all the sanctions belonging to such an authority, and who, in the prosecution of a war, should take an American prize,—would he be liable to be convicted in the Courts of the United States of piracy or robbery, under the act of 1790? He clearly would, on its language. And then the question occurs—Had Congress any authority to pass such a law?

Now, I will put a case which is stronger, and which comes equally within the plain terms, purview, and spirit of that Act, upon a literal construction. Suppose that two American vessels should come into collision on the Pacific Ocean, each manned and officered exclusively by American citizens, and, an angry feeling being engendered, the Captain of one of them should direct a sailor to throw a belaying-pin at the Captain of the other, and the sailor should do it. That would clearly be an act of hostility against one citizen of the United States perpetrated by another, and would be perpetrated under pretence of authority from a person, to wit, the Captain of the ship who gave the violent order. Would the sailor be liable to a conviction for that offence, as a pirate or robber? and would Congress have the authority to pass such a law? I doubt it very much.

Mr. Evarts: I agree with my learned friend that the case which he first stated is not only within the words, but within the intent, of the ninth section.

Mr. Brady: That an American citizen cannot take a commission from a foreign Government without being a pirate?

Mr. Evarts: To serve against the United States, he certainly could not; and, if the law of nations and the rights of citizens require that a Government which demands allegiance and repays it by protection cannot make penal the taking of service from a foreign power against itself, I do not know what a Government can do. So much for the general right or power of a Government. If the particular and clipped interpretation of our Constitution has shorn our Government of that first, clearest, and most necessary power, why, very well. Such a result follows, not from that power or its exercise being at variance with the general principles or powers of Government, but because, as I have said, in the arrangement of the Government, there has fallen out of the general fund of sovereignty this plain, and clear, and necessary right.

But, on the second instance which my learned friend has put, I am equally clear in saying, that the case he there suggests is not within the statute of 1790, simply because, although by a forced and literal construction, if you please, about which I will not here quarrel, my learned friend thinks he places it within the general terms of the ninth section, yet I imagine your honors will at once come to the conclusion, which seems to my poor judgment a sensible one, that the case he puts has nothing to do with the subject matter of the statute, within its intent or purpose—and that, simply, because the statute has not chosen to cover the case proposed, by applying to it so extravagant a penalty. It is not from any defect in the power of Congress. Congress does punish just such an offence as the one suggested, whenever the weapon and the assault make it of the gravity of offences to which Congress has chosen to apply its penal legislation. The statute covering such an offence is enforced every day in this Court. And, certainly, I do not need to argue that, if Congress had the right to pass a statute prohibiting an assault with a belaying-pin, it had the right to call the offence piracy, if it pleased, and might punish it by hanging, if it saw fit; and, for that, it is not amenable to the law of nations, nor is its power exercised with reference to piracy under the law of nations when it deals with that class of offences.

I certainly do not need to fortify my answer to the case first put by my learned friend, in regard to the right of a nation to punish its citizens for taking service against its own country and commerce, by the practice or the legislation of other nations. But your honors will find, in the statutes of Great Britain—the statutes of 11 and 12 William III., and 2 George II.—precisely the same exercise of power and authority, and to the same extent, as respects the gravity of the crime and the punishment prescribed for it. And it would seem to me to be one of the plainest rights and most necessary duties of the Government, if its attention is called to any proclivity of its citizens to take service against itself, to punish them not as prisoners of war, and not under the laws affecting privateers.

Mr. Brady: I will only mention to you that, when I argue the question hereafter, and answer your suggestions, I will refer to the case of *The United States* v. *Smith,* (5 *Wheaton,* 153,) where Mr. Webster conceded, in the Federal Court, that this original Act defining piracy was, as respects the language I have referred to, not a constitutional exercise of the power conferred on Congress. He took the ground that the statute made a general reference to the law of nations as defining piracy, whereas, in his view, Congress should have proceeded to state what were the elements of the offence. I want to use that, in my argument, as an illustration of how strictly the Courts have held that it was never intended that even the case of taking a commission in a foreign service and making war against the United States, which might be treason, should be converted into piracy by any necromancy or alchemy of the law, such as the gentleman seems to have in view.

Mr. Evarts: Whenever a statute declares an offence to be a certain offence, that offence the Courts must hold it to be. The nomenclature of the Legislature is not to be quarreled with by the Courts which sit under its authority. They are to see that the crime is proved. What the crime is called is immaterial.

Mr. Brady: Then the Legislature might say that speaking offensive words on the high seas by our citizens is piracy.

Mr. Evarts: They can call it piracy, and punish it.

Mr. Brady: Yes, by death!

Mr. Evarts: It does not come under the law of nations as piracy, but under the general control of Congress over our citizens at sea. In other words, no nation depends, in the least, on the law of nations and its principles for the extent of its control over its own citizens on the high seas, or for the extent of the penalties by which it protects its own commerce against the acts of its own citizens on the high seas. It takes cognizance of such offences by the same plenary power by which it takes cognizance of offences on land. The difference with us would be, that the State government would have the control of these offences when committed on the land, as a general rule, and they would come within the Federal jurisprudence and the Federal legislation only by their being committed on the high seas. Now, what was said by Mr. Webster in the case of *The United States* v. *Smith,* a case arising under the Act of 1819? Mr. Webster argued that the special verdict did not contain sufficient facts to enable the Court to pronounce the prisoner guilty of the offence charged—that his guilt could not be necessarily inferred from the facts found, but that they were, on the contrary, consistent with his innocence—but that, even supposing the offence to have been well found by the special verdict, it could not be punished under the Act of 1819, because that Act was not a constitutional exercise of the power of Congress to define and punish piracy,—that Congress was bound to define it in terms, and was not at liberty to leave it to be settled by judicial interpretation. That was Mr. Webster's criticism upon the statute—that while the Constitution had said that the law must define what was piracy, Congress had left it to the Courts to define. Mr. Justice Story delivered the opinion of the Supreme Court in that case, to the effect, that the crime of piracy was constitutionally defined by the Act of Congress, and the point was so certified to the Circuit Court.

The authority which this Court has for punishing the crime which has come under consideration in this case is the law of the United States, supported by the Constitution of the United States, in respect to both branches of the statute under inquiry. As the indictment follows the law, and the law follows the Constitution, the subject for your cognizance is rightfully here, and the proofs and the evidence in the case show that the crime has been committed, and that the acts of the prisoners which resulted in the seizure of the Joseph on the high seas include all the ingredients that enter into the completeness of the crime of robbery on the high seas, as named in the eighth section of the Act of 1790, and in the third section of the Act of 1820. I am confining myself, in these observations, to the crime of the whole twelve, not affected by the question of citizenship, and not falling under the ninth section of the Act of 1790.

It is certainly not necessary for me here to insist, with much of detail, on the question of the completeness or effect of the evidence as showing that the seizure of the Joseph was attended by all the circumstances of force, and was stimulated by all the purposes of robbery, which the law makes an ingredient of this offence. So far as the sufficiency of the evidence is to pass under the judgment of the Jury, it is entirely out of place for me to comment on it here. And, so far as any purpose of instruction to the Jury by your honors requires any consideration now, it is sufficient for me to say, that there is no trait of violence, and threat, and danger which, within the law of robbery,—and the law of piracy, if there be any difference,—makes up the necessary application of force, that is not present here. And I understand my learned friend, Mr. Lord, to concede, that there was force enough to make up the crime, if the element of intent, the vicious purpose of robbery, was present, as part of the body of the crime.

My learned friends have treated this latin phrase, *animo furandi*, as if it meant *animo fruendi*—as if the point was, not the intent to despoil another, but the intent to enjoy the fruits of the crime themselves. Now, I need not say that a man who robs his neighbor to give the money to charity, despoils him, *animo furandi*, just as much as if he did it with the intention of using the money for his own purposes of pleasure or profit. That is the point, and all the cases cited only touch the question of whether, in the violent taking, or the fraudulent taking, imputed as a crime, there could be supposed by the Jury to be, on any evidence introduced, any honest thought, even the baseless notion, on the part of the offender, that the property was not that of the man from whom he took it, but was his own. I have not seen anything in this evidence which should lead us to suppose that Mr. Baker and his crew thought that this vessel, the Joseph, belonged to them, and that they took her under a claim of right, as property of their own. The right under which they acted was a supposed right to make it their own, it then and there being the property of somebody else—to wit, of the United States of America, or of some of its citizens. So, your honors will find, that except so far as the considerations of the moral quality of this crime, in regard to its not being furtive and stealthy, are raised and supported by the general considerations which are to change this transaction from its private quality and description into a certain public dignity, as part of a wider contest, and which considerations are to be disposed of by the views which your honors may take of the affirmative proposition of the defence, which would make this privateering at least an act of hostility in flagrant war—except so far, I say, as these considerations are concerned, I need not say anything more as to the completeness of the ingredients, both of force, and of robbery or despoiling another, necessary to make up the crime.

We come, now, if the Court please, to a variety of considerations, many of them, I think, not at all pertinent to a judicial inquiry; many of them ethical; many of them political; many of them addressed to the consciences of men; and many of them addressed to the policy of Governments—and which, in the forum where they are debatable, and which for the most part is a forum which can never make a decision, may be useful and interesting. Some of them do approach, doubtless, the substance and shape of legal propositions; and I am sure I do no injustice either to the nature, or purpose, or character of these manifold views, when I say that they all centre on the proposition, that this transaction, which, in its own traits and features as a private act of these parties, is a crime of piracy, is transferred into the larger range of a conflict of force, authorized by the laws of war, and with no arbiter and no avenger, but in the conscience, and before the common Judge of all. Now, if the Court please, the legal notion to which we must bring this down, is this— that the acts here complained of are, within the law and jurisprudence which this Court administers, acts of privateering, not falling within the law of piracy.

Now, what is privateering? My learned friends have spoken of privateering as if it were one of the recognized, regular, suitable public methods of carrying on hostilities between nations, and as if it fell within the general protection which makes combatants in the field, fighting as public enemies, and against public enemies, amenable only to the laws of war. And my learned friend, Mr. Lord, has read, with much satisfaction, the very pointed observations made by Mr. Marcy in his letter to the French Minister, which were very just and very appropriate as a home argument against France; that is, the encomiums of certain French commanders on the dignity and nobility of the conduct of privateers who rushed to the aid of their country when at war. Now, my view, and I believe the view of the law books and of the publicists of the present day, is this—that privateering is the last relic of the early and barbarous notions of war, that a trial of force between nations involved a rightful exercise of personal hostility by every individual of one nation against every individual of the other, and against every portion of the property of the other. That law of war which authorizes the attack on peaceful persons by armed bands on land, and the robbery, devastation, and destruction of private property wherever it may be found, has been long since displaced by those principles of humanity, of necessity, and of common sense, which make war an appeal, when there is no other arbiter, to the strength of the parties, to be determined with as little injury to property and life as possible. Now, privateers have never been looked upon as being themselves entitled to the least comparison with the regularly enrolled military power, or with the regular naval service, in respect to their motives, or the general rules of their conduct, or the general effect which their depredations are expected to produce. And the tendency of all movements in the public laws of nations, as affecting the maintenance of war, has been at least to discourage and to extirpate, if possible, this private war on sea, in both of its forms—to wit, in the form of public armed vessels taking private and peaceable property on sea, and in the still more aggravated form of private armed vessels, with crews collected for the purposes of gain and plunder, under the license which war may give. So far from this Government having, on the general principles, moral and social, which should govern such a discussion, desired to maintain or extend privateering, it was among the first and the earliest to concede in its treaties, and to gain from the other contracting parties the concession, that if war should arise between the parties to the treaty, privateers should not be commissioned or tolerated on either side. And, if this Government has failed to yield to the attempt made on the part of certain European powers to crush this single branch of private war on the ocean, to wit, war by private parties on the ocean, it has only been because it saw that that design, not including the destruction of that other branch of private war at sea—the war of public vessels against private property—was not a design clearly stimulated by the purposes and interests of humanity. While the European Governments chose to destroy that branch which was least important to them—the use of private armed vessels—they claimed to continue in full force the right of public armed vessels to make aggressions on private property on every sea. The one point was quite as important to have ameliorated as the other, which permits us to recruit the small navy which our republican institutions justify us in maintaining, by the vigor of our mercantile marine in the time of naval war. Therefore, there is nothing in the history of the country which can, in the least, support the idea that we look with favor on the notion of privateering.

Some sensible observations upon the subject are to be found on marginal page 97, in the first volume of Kent's Commentaries, to which I ask your honors' attention:

"Privateering, under all the restrictions which have been adopted, is very liable to abuse. The object is not fame or chivalric warfare, but plunder and profit. The discipline of the crews is not apt to be of the highest order, and privateers are often guilty of enormous excesses, and become the scourge of neutral commerce. They are sometimes manned and officered by foreigners, having no permanent connection with the country or interest in its cause."

I agree that there is still left, under the license and protection of the law of nations, the prosecution of hostilities on the high seas by privateers and private armed vessels. And I agree that, although the crime proved in this case does come within the description and punishment of robbery and piracy, in its own actual traits and features, yet if it be shown that what is thus made piracy and robbery by the statute was actually perpetrated by a privateer, under the protection of the law of nations, with a commission from a sovereign nation, within the scope of the authority of that commission, it is an answer to an indictment, the terms of which had been otherwise proved. And that is undoubtedly what is claimed here. You have proved piracy and robbery under the eighth section, say these defendants, if we cannot impart to the circumstances and features of this crime some public quality and authority which saves the transaction from condemnation and punishment.

Mr. Brady: We say no such thing. We say that, if they acted in good faith, however mistaken, and though the commission may be void, they have not committed any offence whatever.

Mr. Evarts: This is the extent of my concession, as matter of law,—that it is an answer to a charge of piracy which is otherwise complete, that the crime was committed under conditions which, by the law of nations, relieve it from punishment. Now, what are the conditions that the law of nations requires?

First, there must be a war. We do not allow private armed vessels to prosecute general marauding hostilities in support of the views of their Governments. We do not allow the interruption of the freedom of the seas by such marauding vessels, except in cases of flagrant war, which neutral nations are compelled to recognize.

Secondly. The privateer must have received its commission from a public, national, sovereign power. You cannot make a privateer, and turn private acts that, by the law of nations and by municipal law, are piratical, into acts of war, which are of the same intrinsic quality and have the force of national acts, unless by this *sine qua non* of public authority and adoption.

Now, if the Court please, when it comes up for judicial inquiry, whether a case of privateering, under the law of nations, is fairly made out, and where the case arises during flagrant war between two separate, independent, established nations, whose nationality is a part of the order of things in the world, the Court has only really to inquire, judicially, into two subjects— whether the vessel had a lawful privateer's commission from one of the contending parties—and whether the acts committed by her were within its scope, either actually or in the sense of a fair construction of the authority, and of good faith in the exercise of the power. But, even in these cases, where the only points are, whether there be war, and whether there be nationalities on each side which can convey this public authority, the Court is all the while governed by, dependent upon, and subordinate to, the views of the Government from which the Court derives its authority. No judicial tribunal has a right to recognize a nation, of its own motion. No judicial tribunal has authority to recognize a Government which the Government from which it derives its authority does not recognize. I have never heard it proposed, as a view either of public or of domestic law, that when a Government has declined to recognize a nation, it was within the jurisdiction of a Court of that Government to determine differently, and reverse the decision of the political power. In the cases of France and England, which are recognized Governments that have placed themselves as firmly among the nations of the world as private individuals are planted in the rights of man, our Courts intermit this inquiry. A privateer of England which confines itself within the scope of its commission, can not be proceeded against as a pirate, although it commits acts which would of themselves be piracy. But, there do arise questions which come under the jurisdiction of the Courts, under circumstances of doubt and obscurity as to the course or view which our Government has taken in relation to the alleged nationalities of alleged belligerents; and I need not say to your honors, that by an unbroken series of the decisions of the Supreme Court, as well as by the necessary subordination of the judicial authority to the political power of the Government, our Courts always take the view which their Government takes in respect to struggles and hostilities which arise between uncertain, indefinite and unascertained powers. Thus, whenever there occur, between Colonies and the parent Government,—between disaffected regions or populations and the sovereign to which they have been subject—dissensions which, arising from the region of discontent, sedition and turbulent disorder, reach the proportion of military conflict and appeal to arms, then, when acts in the nature of war are assumed to be performed, under circumstances that bring them within judicial cognizance in our Courts, and in the Courts of any other civilized nation, as to whether they still retain their quality and character of private acts, attended by the private responsibility of the criminals, or whether they are transferred to the wider theatre and looser responsibility of warlike engagement, our Courts, as do the Courts of other civilized nations, look to the Government to see what is its policy and its purpose. The instances in which these unhappy contests and these obscure questions have been presented before the Courts, have been almost entirely connected with the separation of the South American Colonies from the mother country of Spain. In all these cases, the new Governments of the revolted Colonies gave commissions to privateers, and undertook to put themselves before the nations of the world as belligerents, claiming from neutral nations, not a recognition of their independence, or of their completed nationality, but of their right to struggle, through the forms of force and war, to establish that nationality. They presented to the discretion and the policy of every other civilized Government precisely this question—Is there enough of substance, of good faith, of power, to justify us, as equal expounders and equal defenders and protectors of the laws of nations, although there be now no present nationality that can support, under the rules of the law of nations, by mere right, the exercise of warlike powers—is there enough, in the transaction, to justify us in considering it to be so substantial and *bona fide* an effort for the assertion of independence and the creation of a new nation, that we shall give to it the opportunity, and turn what would be piracy and marauding into an act of belligerents, so far as we neutrals are concerned?

When a nation is an independent nation, all other nations of the earth are, by public law, bound to recognize it, and bound to recognize its right to make war. The most powerful nation in the world has no more right to make war than the smallest nation in the world; and, each being judge of its own conduct, when a state of war exists, such war must, by the public law of the world, be recognized. But when new, unformed, inchoate, tentative consolidations or efforts of nationalities present themselves, every nation has, by the public law, a right to exercise its own wisdom, its own policy and its own sense of justice, to determine whether or not it will recognize them; and, in every one of the cases I have referred to that came before our Courts, arising for their consideration as between two parts of a foreign country, our Courts said—Our Government has done so and so; it has recognized them as belligerents, and we follow our Government. In other cases, as in that of the Commander Aury, the Court said—We do not understand that there is any such power known in the world; our Government has never in any way recognized, not its independence, for that is not necessary, but its position as a war-making power, or as a struggling power, fighting for nationality, and we cannot recognize that condition of things.

Now, unhappily, there arises a conflict in our own country, which presents the case of an armed military rebellion—a revolt of certain portions of population, maintaining, if you please, to a certain extent, the mastery over a certain portion of our soil, using against us the actual means and processes of war, and compelling from our Government, in maintaining dominion against their aggressive assaults, the means of military power, naval and land forces, and all the authority and violence of war. Foreign nations have had, in regard to us and to this conflict, the same kind of questions presented that have been presented to us in the contests between the dismembered parts of other countries. And every nation was free to determine, upon this exact question of the right of private war, as belonging to those rebellious portions of this country—to determine whether it would tolerate privateering as a warlike proceeding, or would regard privateers as marauders or pirates without just right or cause, and without the pretence of sufficient force and dignity, in a movement to disturb the peace of the world.

My learned friends have said, using the force of the argument in aid of their cause, that France and England have recognized the insurgents as belligerents, and have precluded themselves from treating as pirates private armed vessels that shall derive authority from these rebellious powers. Well, by the same law of nations that gave to France and England this right thus to elect, they had the right to determine, and to announce by proclamation, that the peace of the world upon the ocean should not be disturbed, under pretence of war, by these insurgents, and that, if they should resort to private armed vessels to inflict aggressions and disturb the commerce of the world, they would be treated as pirates. And if, under the law of nations, the political authorities of France and England had thus announced their policy that these insurgents should be treated as pirates, I would like to know if advocates would be heard, in the Court of Queen's Bench or in the Courts of France, to urge that the Court, wiser than its Government, should, in the exercise of sovereign discretion under the law of nations, tolerate, as an act of war, what is piracy by municipal statute or the law of nations, unless accredited as part of a warlike movement. Would those Courts permit the defence to be made, that what were declared to be acts of piracy were acts of war,—the Government having so elected and so announced, that it would regard them as acts of piracy and not as acts of war?

Now, I am arguing this case altogether on this point, as if the Government from which this Court derives its authority—whose laws we are administering—whose authority is vested in your honors on this trial—stood as a stranger to and spectator of this contest, and it was really a controversy between parts of another nation. And all I have claimed is, that our Government, in common with the other nations of the world, has, by the law of nations, the right, in its discretion, to determine how this proceeding shall be treated, and what consequences shall follow from it. Now, I need not say that, treating our Government as if it stood *ab extra*, and as if, passing its judgment on what was going on, it had determined that these privateers should be regarded as pirates, they should not be recognized as having the right of war, or the right, as an inchoate nationality, to perfect their independence.

The Proclamation of the President of the United States, of the 19th of April, 1861, is a complete and perfect denunciation of this threatened crime of piracy, the purpose to recur to which had been manifested by a public declaration of Jefferson Davis, which had invited, from all quarters of the globe, privateers to prey upon the commerce of the United States. I need not say to your honors that when our Government has pronounced this to be piracy, and to be not within the law of nations, under its discretion to determine whether it will recognize an inchoate nationality, this Court has not, any more than has a Court of England or France, the power to say that

- 232 -

what its Government does not choose to recognize, even in the quality of belligerents, it will recognize. What our Government has said shall remain in the quality of criminality, must so remain, notwithstanding this proclamation of Jefferson Davis, or any commission that may issue in pursuance of it.

I apprehend that even if we were to bring ourselves into the paradoxical condition of passing judgment on this question as a disinterested, yet sovereign nation, your honors would find in the acts of the Government a complete denunciation against this proceeding as a crime of piracy, and a complete policy, which the Court must follow, leaving any diplomatic considerations of the results which may follow its mistaken, if you please, construction of its duty, to be disposed of by the authorities that are responsible for it.

Mr. Brady: I believe there is no proof of any such action by the legislative branch of this Government.

Mr. Evarts: I apprehend that the whole course of the legislation of this country shows that we do not recognize or tolerate this contest as a thing that is rightfully to go on. That is all that is necessary.

I say, if the Court please, that the course of an external sovereignty, in these intestine quarrels, turns upon the point whether it will give its sanction to an intrusion upon the peace of the world by an inchoate nation, and I am trying to consider that question as if our Government had passed judgment upon it *ab extra*; and I say that the action of our Government shows that we do not intend to recognize it as something that should be allowed to go on. These considerations, as to any recognition by this Court of rights derivable from *quasi*, pretended, nascent, public powers, would induce this Court to follow the decision of the Government, in case we were judging of the question as a controversy between parts of another nation.

I am now brought to the consideration of who are the parties to this controversy, and what are the relations of this Court and of the laws we are administering to the subject and the inquiry. The Government of the United States still stands. The old Constitution, the whole system of its statutes, the whole power of its army and of its navy, stand. It has its Courts of judicature; it has its commerce still on the seas; its laws are still operative, and still to be administered. And when this Court considers this case, it finds it brought before it as every other criminal case is, and limited to the considerations that belong to every criminal case. The Government of the United States, by the ordinary exercise of the process of judicature,—by seizure under public authority,—by arrest within this District, through the criminal process of this Court,—by the indictment of a Grand Jury,—by the prosecution of the District Attorney,—has proposed to this Court the naked and narrow inquiry of whether these men have committed a crime against the statutes of the

United States. Now, I would like to know whether there is anything in these occurrences, that have secured, if you please, for the present, (and the future may be uncertain,) in large portions of our territory, a practical control over great portions of our population,—I would like to know if there is anything in these transactions that has displaced the constitutional legislation of the United States of America over crimes on the high seas, and over its citizens committing crimes on the high seas, or over subjects or citizens, of whatever country, committing crimes on the high seas against our property? I take it, not. Therefore, if your honors please, whatever may be said, in one form or another, of the political right, as respects these States, either constitutionally or by the right of force, to be independent, or to attempt to be independent of the United States, or to engage in this struggle for the settlement of some question of dispute under the Constitution,—whatever may be said of that, your honors cannot fail to discover that nothing which has occurred has destroyed the organism of our Government, or altered for a moment the judicial authority or the force and supremacy of the Constitution and the laws, within the territory where the Courts are open, over the subjects of our Government, and the subjects of whatever Government, in respect to whatever property, upon the high seas.

I understand that my learned friend, Mr. Larocque, supposes that the ordinance of repeal of South Carolina, constitutionally or unconstitutionally supported by the strength to maintain its independence, has changed these four men who are indicted here and are proved to be citizens of the United States, from their condition of citizens of the United States; and he holds, and asks as legal proposition from your honors, that, at the time of the commission of this crime, these men were not citizens of the United States, by reason of the constitutional right of South Carolina to carry itself out of the Union, by force of ordinances, or supported by military power that had maintained itself up to the first of June in the possession of independent power. Your honors will charge, or refuse to charge, accordingly as you may find that the old Government has sovereignty and has attempted to exercise it, and that there has been no severance of our territory to the extent of a permanent division,—whether these men are citizens of the United States, or of a foreign country. If they are held to be citizens of a foreign country, to wit, of South Carolina, or of the Confederate States, then they fall back under the eighth section of the Act, as having committed piracy under that section.

But, to come back to the attitude of our Government, which this Court must follow, towards these rebels,—towards these malcontents,—towards these combinations, which are exercising the processes of war, undoubtedly,— what is the attitude of our Government? Does it recognize their right—does it recognize their independence—does it recognize their authority, so that you find that our Government has adopted the policy of not punishing them under the laws of the United States?

And this brings me to the consideration of another general subject, which Mr. Lord adverted to, and upon which he cited the authority of Vattel—that it would be monstrous, and would expose this Government to the execration of the world, if the criminal laws against murder and robbery on land, and the civil laws against trespass, were to be executed to the letter, and to the full extent of the vengeance of the law against the multitudinous enemies that are arrayed against this Government. Now, I must decline to be led out of a Court of Justice, by this argument, to considerations that appeal to the wisdom, or humanity, or policy of the Government. I would like to know whether my learned friend would contend that, if a private soldier, found in arms, and part of a military force, against the Government of this country, is arrested by that Government, and is indicted, and put upon his trial for treason, which the Constitution of the United States limits to the overt act of levying war against the Government, and if, under the indictment, he pleads in bar that he was levying war against the United States of America,— that would relieve him? For that is the whole nature of the proposition put forward in a Court of Justice,—that, because there are armies, there is no treason! Why, if your honors please, how absurd to present for the recognition of a Government, in its Courts of Judicature, the proposition that there is no treason, from the number of the confederates in the treachery! Your honors see at once that, the idea of setting up such a defence, on a trial for treason, against a private soldier, found in arms against the Government, is absurd. And yet, your honors recognize what is laid down by the publicists, that when the dimensions of a rebellion have been aggravated into the proportions of flagrant war, for a Government to insist upon the decimation or extermination of the population by the gallows or the axe, would be inconsistent with those general principles of humanity and justice that actuate, by necessity, the affairs of men.

It is not necessary for me to discuss these questions. It belongs to the Government, after it has procured a conviction, either for piracy or for treason, to decide, in its own discretion, whether the penalty of the law shall be inflicted. Let us confine ourselves to our duties. Let us not be asked here, as a learned Bench, or as honest Jurymen, to recognize a Government or a state of belligerency that our nation does not recognize. And let us not be asked to repeal statutes of treason because the number of the traitors is so great that we cannot carry out the penalties of the law against the whole. I would like to know if in the face of any Court of Justice,—if in the face of the public opinion of the world,—if in the face of the principles of eternal justice,—it is to be set forward as a shield over the heads of the rebel leaders and traitors, that they have inflamed and misled so large a body of the common people, that they, the leaders, cannot be punished. I would like to know if, when in advance, immediately upon the rebel proclamation inviting privateers, our Government, through every newspaper in the land, proclaimed that whoever should voluntarily take up this form of piracy would be treated as a pirate, and you find the first privateer, with the first commission taken out under this proclamation of sovereignty, and the first band that volunteer—Mr. Baker and his crew, collected from all the quarters of the globe,—the first engaged in this new and flagrant form of outrage, against which they had been warned,—I would like to know if these bold outlaws, stretching forward a ready hand to grasp the license of war for plunder, the whole proceeds of which are to fill their pockets, are to be presented in this Court as being special objects of protection, under the principles of humanity, and as being shielded against public justice in enforcing the laws of piracy.

Now, if your honors please, treating, as I do, this question as one to be passed upon, not with the coolness of a neutral power looking upon these contending parties as independent nations, but by this Court as the Government's own judicial organ for administering the public justice, I would like to know what pretence there is that, under the laws of the United States, the crime of piracy having been proved, there is anything in this notion of a commission from a nationality recognized by our Government, or of a belligerent right recognized by our Government, that this Court can adopt as a merger of the private crime in the public conflict. We contend, therefore, that in the conflict now raging, the Constitution and the laws of the United States make every person levying war against the Government a rebel and traitor, and, if the war thus levied take the form of piratical aggression, a pirate, within the statute.

Now, let me consider the ninth section of the statute. I will readily concede to my learned friends whatever advantage they can gain from the proposition that, when the ninth section was drawn, in the year 1790, one year after the adoption of the Constitution, it was never supposed that a pretended commission or authority to prey upon the commerce of the United States and violate its laws would come from any part of the people or of the territory of the United States. And I claim that there is nothing in this commission which, if there had been no statute recognizing a possible protection from a commission—there is nothing in this commission from a citizen of the United States, Jefferson Davis, to another citizen of the United States, Thomas Harrison Baker, to prey upon the commerce of the United States, that can be regarded for a moment as a license which makes him a privateer, instead of a pirate. My learned friends have even sought to find occasion for a variance between the proof and the indictment because we have alleged, under the ninth section, that the pretended authority comes from "one Jefferson Davis," and have proved a commission which says, "I, Jefferson Davis, in the name of the Confederate States," have given such authority. Why, if your honors please, this indictment was drawn by an officer of the United States Government, to be tried in a Court of the United States; and, having a fear of the law and a sense of his duty to his country, he describes things as they are. And I would like to have my learned friends point out to me any place, any office, any title, any description, any addition, any qualification, that, under the laws of the United States of America and its Constitution, describes Jefferson Davis, except "one Jefferson Davis." He has precisely that port and dignity before the law and the Constitution that every other individual in the United States has, not filling an office and post of authority under our Government and under our laws. He does fill the place of citizen of the United States, and no measures of separate State action, or of Confederate authority, have relieved him from that full and complete description of him, under the Constitution of the United States, as the measure of his allegiance and of the penalties for its forfeiture. How could we have found a legal phrase or term, if we regard the Government of the United States and its Constitution, by which we could designate any such thing as "Confederate States," or a foreign state, within the accredited territory of the United States? The terms and intent of this ninth section were framed so as to cover every imaginable authority, in the nature of a commission from a State, from a nation, from a power, or from any person, under the law of nations, for the conversion of private marauders into public enemies with the rights of war; and, although it never entered into the imagination of the framers of this statute that it would ever have to be applied to exclude protection under a commission from a citizen of the United States, its terms are absolutely fitting. I contend that the statute is complete, and that this commission is not a pretence of authority, even under the law of nations establishing and recognizing privateers for struggling communities. It is nothing but an authority from one citizen of the United States to another citizen of the United States to prey upon the property of the United States.

There are, if the Court please, some political considerations which were, it appears to me, more appropriately urged by my learned friend, Mr. Larocque, in his first address to the Jury, than in his argument to the Court. The point made by him was this—that, under the Constitution of the United States, every citizen of every State held what was called the position of divided allegiance, having two sovereign masters over him; that they were equal and co-ordinate sovereigns; and that it was his duty to obey both of them. Now, with the necessary limitation that each one is sovereign over him in some respects, and has not the least power over him in others, and that the other is sovereign over him in other respects, and does not include the first topic or line of duty, there is a speculative support for this general notion. And, whenever it is not urged into any absurd consequences, it serves, in the language of the Courts and of public men, to describe the complex Government under which we live. But, if my learned friend means to assert that there are, under the Government of the United States, according to its form and method of organic operation, two equal sovereigns over every citizen on the same subjects, why then he has flown in the face of a fundamental proposition, coming from higher authority than the Convention of 1790—that no man can serve two masters. It is not in the nature of things that there can be two sovereigns having equal rights and authority over one subject; and my learned friend illustrates the absurdity of the proposition when he comes to consider what would be the result if the two sovereigns should disagree. He says it is the duty of the subject to adhere to one side or the other; that, it being his complete duty to adhere to one side, the other side cannot complain of it as a breach of duty that he does not adhere to him, but to the other; and that, therefore, the general rule, that when you have a sovereign and are unfaithful to him you may be hanged, cannot apply to the case, because you would, in either case, be hanged. And his wise, and suitable, and certainly humane solution of this difficulty is, that when one of the sovereigns indicts you for treason, it is a good bar to say you elected in good faith to serve the other sovereign. Thus, so far from there being two sovereigns, the nature of the term sovereign including the right to hang you for unfaithfulness, there is not one that has the right to hang you, and you are master of both; for, whatever you do in good faith is a supreme answer to both.

Now, if the Court please, this is the point of the whole thing—that, under this peculiar Constitution of ours, and under this division of the subjects of Government, each sovereign is judge of when the other has passed the limits of his authority, and that the States possess the right to compel the obedience of their citizens, and the United States possess the right to compel the obedience of their citizens. It is sufficient for us to say that we represent, as Federal citizens, the Government of the United States in its interpretation of its own position towards those its citizens, or those persons not its citizens, who are alleged to have perpetrated crimes against its commerce; and, whether there be, or not, speculations of political and theoretical and ethical and conscientious right, in good faith, to put yourself at variance with the Government of the United States because other people do so, or because the State authority does so, it follows that the United States, its authorities, its Courts, and its population, have the right to think, and feel, and act, as if its Government were in the right and you were in the wrong; and you, being brought within the criminal justice of their law, can find no support and no protection upon the good faith or upon the speculative political theories upon which you have rested for your protection and for your authority.

It is said, that outside of this question of the political and legal qualifications of this act which we say is criminal, the circumstances, actual and moral, which surround these actors, and are shown by their actions, have deprived their acts of the criminal quality which the statute affixes to them; and that if, in good faith, they thought there was a commission, and in good faith thought there was a rightful Government, that good faith, which has despoiled the American merchant of his property, is a plea in bar to the criminal jurisdiction of the United States of America, whose laws they have violated, although all this pretence, all this show, all this form of political and legal support qualifying their acts, comes from men whom the Constitution pronounces to be in the category of rebels and traitors, every one of them amenable to the final jurisdiction of our laws. This is but another form of saying that criminals joining hand in hand shall go unpunished. Make the number of them what you will, if in the eye of the law they assume authority which is on its face criminal and illegal, and even though it is a part of a general scheme and organization for violent military resistance to the authority of the country, no Court can dispense from the punishment, but must inflict it through the general and ordinary criminal authority in respect to the crime in question, leaving the question of dispensation to the clemency, the humanity, and the policy of the Government.

I believe that all the cases have been cited, either on the one side or the other, from the Reports of the Supreme Court of the United States, that have had to do with the question as to the political character of the revolted South American States. Those which were cited by my learned friend, Mr. Larocque, *The Josefa Segunda* (5 *Wheaton*, 338), *The Bello Corunnes* (6 *Wheaton*, 152), and *The Santissima Trinidad* (7 *Wheaton*, 283), are all authorities, as we suppose, for the view which the Courts adopt, even when they are Courts of a neutral nation—that they follow the decisions of their Government as to the public quality and character of belligerents.

Adjourned to Monday, 28 Oct., at 11 o'clock, A.M.

FIFTH DAY.

October 28, 1861.

ARGUMENT OF MR. DUKES FOR THE DEFENCE.

Mr. Evarts said: Perhaps it is unnecessary that I should say to the Court and learned counsel, that I shall refer to the Statute of treason, as well as to the Constitutional provision as to treason. The Statute of treason is found in the first section of the Crimes Act of 1790.

Mr. Dukes said:

May it please your honors and gentlemen of the Jury.

It has been said by one of the most eminent statesmen that ever lived, that "civil wars strike deepest into the manners of the people,—they vitiate their politics; they corrupt their morals; they pervert the natural taste and relish of equity and justice."

If this be so, one would think that this was a singularly unfortunate time for the Government to bring on the trial of these prisoners at your bar, who are entitled to that right which the Constitution offers to the meanest citizen— that of a fair and impartial trial.

Is it to obtain that fair and impartial trial that the case is brought on now, when the flame of civil war lights the land, and when, in every stage and condition of society, the bitterest sentiments of hostility prevail?

Is it in order to afford the prisoners a fair and impartial trial that the case is brought on now, when tender infancy and gentle woman unite with stern and selfish man in uttering the deepest imprecations on their enemies?

Is it in order to obtain a fair and impartial trial that the case is brought on now, when, on God's holy day, in his holy temple, his chosen ministers officiating at his holy altar, utterly unmindful of the injunction of their meek and lowly Master, "to forgive their enemies, and to pray for those who despitefully use them"—offer up to Heaven prayers for its severest vengeance upon the heads of their enemies?

If so, gentlemen, I beg at least, (as one of the counsel,) to offer my dissent.

It does, indeed, seem to me that this is a singularly unfortunate time to bring on this trial. But yet, gentlemen, I feel buoyed up with hope, because I know the unbending integrity of the Judges that officiate, and I know that the Jury, which sits in judgment over the lives of these men, is chosen from the citizens of New York—a city in which, if any city in the world possesses large, liberal, and enlightened views, we may hope to find them. But, still, the officers of the Government must excuse me for saying that I think it

- 240 -

unfortunate, and somewhat illiberal in them, considering the character of the charge made against these men, to try them now. It does seem to me that it is, at best, but trying treason with an odious name.

Gentlemen, this is no new thing. Years ago this very question, as to the propriety of trying men situated as these men are, was brought before the mind of that liberal and enlightened statesman, Edmund Burke—the long-tried and faithful friend of America; and I trust that I may be pardoned for referring to his words on this occasion, and for reading to you a passage from his celebrated letter to the Sheriffs of Bristol, in 1777, which, perhaps, will more fully illustrate my views than anything I can say. Speaking about American privateersmen, then in the same position as these men now are, he says:

"The persons who make a naval warfare upon us, in consequence of the present troubles, may be rebels; but to treat and call them pirates is confounding, not only the natural distinction of things, but the order of crimes; which, whether by putting them from a higher part of the scale to the lower, or from the lower to the higher, is never done without dangerously disordering the whole frame of jurisprudence.

"Though piracy may be, in the eye of the law, a less offence than treason, yet, as both are, in effect, punished with the same death, the same forfeiture, and the same corruption of the blood, I never would take from any fellow-creature whatever any sort of advantage which he may derive to his safety from the pity of mankind, or to his reputation from their general feelings by degrading his offence, when I cannot soften his punishment.

"The general sense of mankind tells me, that those offences which may possibly arise from mistaken virtue are not in the class of infamous actions.

"Lord Coke, the oracle of the English law, conforms to that general sense, where he says, 'That those things which are of the highest criminality may be of the least disgrace.' * * * * *

"If Lord Balmerine, in the last rebellion, had driven off the cattle of twenty clans, I should have thought it would have been a scandalous and low juggle, utterly unworthy of the manliness of an English judicature, to have tried him for felony as a stealer of cows.

"Besides, I must honestly tell you that I could not vote, or countenance in any way, a statute which stigmatizes with the crime of piracy these men, whom an Act of Parliament had previously put out of the protection of the law.

"When the legislature of this Kingdom had ordered all their ships and goods, for the mere new-created offence of exercising trade, to be divided as a spoil among the seamen of the navy—to consider the necessary reprisal of an unhappy, proscribed, interdicted people as the crime of piracy, would have appeared, in any other legislature than ours, a strain of the most insulting and unnatural cruelty and injustice. I assure you, I never remember to have heard any thing like it, in any time or country."

Gentlemen, I read this extract because it is the testimony of an eminently wise man, and an eminently just one. Such were his views at that day, and I am inclined to believe that those words spoken by him then have a better application to the state of things at present than any remarks I can make, or that can be made by any one of us who are in the midst of this whirl of excitement.

But, gentlemen, the Government has chosen to make the issue. It was at liberty to do so; and that issue is piracy.

Piracy, gentlemen of the Jury, you have heard defined by the eminent counsel who preceded me. The parties here occupy, as it were, a two-fold capacity. The eighth section of the Act of 1790 applies to piracy under the common law; the ninth section of that Act creates what we have called statutory piracy. The eighth section of the Act only alludes to piracy as it is acknowledged under the law of nations, and as known to the common law. The ninth section, however, differs from the eighth, because it applies peculiarly to citizens of the United States, and is supposed to be more enlarged in its character than the eighth section. Now, with reference to a portion of the prisoners here,—to those who are not citizens,—eight of them come entirely under the eighth section; and we shall contend that, under that section, they cannot be convicted. As regards the other four, it will be contended, that not only are they embraced by the first, but likewise by the second of these sections—that of statutory piracy, which applies peculiarly to them.

Well now, gentlemen, in regard to the eighth section, the learned counsel who very ably addressed the Court on last Saturday, stated that intent had little or nothing to do with the offence; that he did not choose to be held to the *animus fruendi*, but that the charge was the *animus furandi*, and that when a person committed robbery it was but of very little consequence to what purpose he applied the proceeds of the robbery, or for whom he committed it. Now, with all due deference to the learned counsel, I think this is putting the case rather unfairly, because he is quietly assuming the very point we are discussing; for it is the fact of the *animus furandi*—the fact whether or not this is robbery—that we are discussing.

We have distinctly said, and shown by the books, that that which he says is not the characteristic of the crime, is really its characteristic, and that intent in this, as in every other offence, peculiarly constitutes the crime.

It is just because the taking is not for the party himself—is not an appropriation for his own purpose, and for his own ends, and for his own object, that there is a difference between piracy and privateering. And why is this so? Because the party who goes forth on a privateering expedition, goes forth under the sanction of a nation. It may be a nation only *de facto*, but still it is a nation. He goes by the authority of that nation, armed with a commission under its sanction, after having given the most ample security to be responsible to the nation itself for any act of misconduct on his part; that nation holding itself out to the civilized world as responsible for every excess on the part of the citizen to whom it grants letters of marque. Well, gentlemen, the taking of property on the part of the privateer is not for himself. The taking is in the name of the State. The title which the privateer has in the captured property is no title at all, nor does he pretend to claim it. The title is in the State, and up to the very moment of condemnation, although the property may have been acquired by his blood, and by his treasure, the State has the right to release it. So important is this fact of intention, as entering into the transaction, that it has been held that no excess on the part of a person carrying letters of marque from a regular Government could be punished as piracy—the Government being liable, and he himself being referred to his own Government for punishment.

It has been even held in England, that where the act of taking a commission from a foreign prince was so unlawful in its character as to amount under the law to a felony, yet still the party having letters of marque, should not be charged with piracy.

Now, gentlemen, there was an attempt made by the learned counsel to cast odium upon privateering and upon this transaction, by speaking of these men as going out for their own plunder. Well, I have nothing to say about that; but there is one thing to be remarked: that in times of hostility the plunder does not belong to one side, nor does it belong to the privateersman alone, but the regularly armed vessels of every nation in the world, as well as privateersmen, are enriched by the capture of prizes at sea; and I suspect that the members of the bar now present can tell you how extensively our own navy has been enriched within the last few weeks by the condemnation of prizes. If the spoils derived from enemies' property be plunder, and if it be disgraceful to take it, then the highest names in England have been associated with such plunder, for you have but to look into the English books to find the name of the great and distinguished Arthur, Duke of Wellington, as connected with such cases.

But, gentlemen, there is another thing which would prevent the parties from being convicted of piracy, that is, the state of enmity existing between the two nations. It is a general rule that enemies can never commit piracy against each other, their depredations being deemed mere acts of hostility. This is as far back as the days of Lord Coke; and the rule has been carried so far as to protect the citizen of one of the belligerents, who, without any letter of marque at all, goes on the ocean and seizes the property of the enemy. It is true, it has been said that in such cases citizens act at their peril, and are liable to be punished by their own sovereign; but the enemy is not warranted in considering them as criminals.

That the people of the Confederate States, under whose commission these men have acted, stand in the light of enemies, the learned decisions of Judges Cadwalader and Betts; the blockade of the Southern ports, which is a hostile measure; the confiscation of the property of their citizens—not only of the property of the men who have arms in their hands, but of the citizens at large; the captures at sea; the vessels condemned here; the virtual dissolution of partnerships; the admission of the plea of alien enemy; the President's proclamation of non-intercourse; the arrest of citizens of those States returning from Europe; and the opinion of my learned friend, the District Attorney himself, showing that it is treason for the banks here to pay over the bank balances to Southern customers,—all these things go to establish, thoroughly and sufficiently, the condition of enmity or hostility, which forms a protection to these parties. They fix the status of war; they decide that the two powers are enemies, and that, too, without any declaration of war, for no declaration of war is needed. It seems to me that it is all useless to attempt to evade the admission that there is war. We cannot by legal enactments— we cannot by judicial decisions—we cannot by Presidential Proclamations— establish the condition of war and all the consequences of war, and yet shrink from its open avowal. And yet that is precisely what is attempted here. It may do with those that are strong to oppress their own subjects, but it will not do when you come to deal with foreign nations. When you come to deal with these eight men who are here, the subjects of foreign powers, those powers have a right to put in a word. Gentlemen, it is impossible for this Government to do less than acknowledge that, in fact, there is a state of hostility; and you may as well call it by its proper name—we are in the midst of war.

It will not do for the Government, like the ostrich, to put its head under its wing, and fancy that because it sees nobody, nobody sees it. The Government has enacted all the consequences of war without making an open or decided declaration of it. Under such circumstances, however, the status of enmity is sufficiently fixed to protect the prisoners.

But there is another test of piracy, gentlemen, and it is this—Is the privateer a universal enemy? Is he a universal plunderer? Is his hand against every man? Has he not a nation?

Now a pirate has no nation. He is an outlaw, and is justiciable everywhere. His is the law of might—

"For why? Because the good old rule

Sufficeth him: the simple plan

That they should take who have the power,

And they should keep who can."

But it is not necessary that the nation under whose commission he acts, shall be one which is already established and acknowledged among the family of nations. It may be a colony struggling for independence, and not yet recognized by the nations of the earth. Our own Courts years ago decided this case with a liberality which has eminently distinguished them, and established the principle in respect to the South American colonies— colonies at that time not acknowledged by our Government as independent nations.

So, gentlemen, it was with regard to the powers of Europe during the days of the American Revolution. Every power in the world respected the letters of marque issued by Congress; and if there is an instance of a single case in which, in any land in the civilized world, there was a criminal trial of an American privateersman, I have not been able to find it. Their letters of marque were recognized because they were the letters of a *de facto* Government.

Now, gentlemen, what are the tests sufficient to form such a nationality as will cover these commissions? Are the Confederate States, in this instance, competent to maintain the relations of war and of peace? Gentlemen, if the South American provinces were, I think it can hardly be disputed that the people of ten great States like these certainly are. They are very far beyond them in civilization, in information, in wealth, and in all the means by which nations sustain their independence.

So important, however, is the fact of a commission, that even a commission from the Barbary powers—states which subsisted entirely, I may say, by plunder and piracy—was regarded as sufficient, in the Courts of England, to protect an Algerine who was taken with letters of marque. And that opinion comes with the authority of one of the greatest masters of the science of jurisprudence—Sir William Scott—a name that can never be mentioned without feelings of reverence by any man who respects the sentiments of justice and their application to the principles of international law. In the case I allude to, the Barbary subject was taken in an attempt to seize an English vessel. The crew was composed of foreigners, men of different nations, most of them belonging to Spain and France. It was held that as to all the rest of the parties they should be treated as outlaws, but the Algerine was allowed the plea of *respondeat superior*. In other words, he had but to point to his country, and say she was responsible; that she gave him authority, and assumed the responsibility; and upon that plea he was allowed to go. I mention this to show how far the doctrine has been carried.

But, gentlemen, if the commission from a Government *de facto* generally is a plea in bar (and that it is, I have no doubt the Court will charge you), it certainly holds good in a case of this kind, where the authority is much less questionable. Now, are the United States bound to recognize the Confederate States as belligerents? Not as an independent nation,—that is an entirely different question. We say, gentlemen, not only that the United States are bound to recognize the Confederate States as belligerents, but we think we have shown that they have done so. The capitulation between Commodore Stringham, General Butler, and Commodore Barron, recognized the existence of a state of war, and recognized the prisoners as prisoners of war; and not one word has been said, and not one act done, by the Government, to disavow their authority in so doing. It is the principle of civilized nations—and we belong to the family of civilized nations—to recognize parties, even in the midst of civil war, as belligerents; and this country is too just, too powerful, and too elevated in sentiment, to shrink from that which civilization, decency and honor compel her to stand to. She must recognize even those who are her children—struggling against her authority though they be—as fair and honest antagonists. From the time of our own struggle, in the days of the Revolution, we professed the principles of international law. They are now a part of the law of the land. There is a moral obligation upon us to occupy our position in the great family of nations; to hold it, as we have always done, with honor and with distinguished consideration. Sorry, indeed, would I be to think that there should be, on this occasion, any eminent departure from it, as there certainly would be if these men were held in any other light than as mere privateersmen, and not pirates.

But if these principles are true, as applying between the people of this country and the people of England during the days of the Revolution,—if the mother country then considered us as belligerents where there could be no subtle political question such as may be raised here, and has already been raised— the doctrine of the two sovereignties,—there is then, at least, a reason which applies in this case, and never could have applied in that case; for the allegiance of the colonies to the mother country was firm, fixed, and undivided: it never was, and never could be, questioned.

I say, then, that these parties are not pirates; and I further say that the municipal laws of a State, or of a number of States, cannot constitute that offence to be piracy which is not so characterized by international law; and for this principle I refer to 1st Phillimore, 381 (International Law).

I come now to the 9th section, and I will read that section:

"And be it further enacted, that if any citizen should commit any piracy or robbery aforesaid, or any act of hostility against the United States or any citizen thereof, on the high seas, under color of any commission of any foreign Prince or State, or on pretence of authority from any person, such offender shall, notwithstanding the pretence of any such authority, be deemed, adjudged, and taken to be a pirate, felon, and robber, and on being convicted thereof shall suffer death."

This section applies particularly to the citizens of the United States. Now, I contend that this section does not change the character of the offence. It differs only by stating that the commission shall not form a pretext. The words "piracy and robbery" explain the words "acts of hostility," which follow immediately afterwards. Where particular words are followed by general words, the latter are held as applying to persons and things of the same kind as those which precede. The coupling of words together shows that they are to be understood in the same sense. Take these two principles with the other principle, that penal statutes are to receive a strict interpretation. The general words of a penal statute must be restrained for the benefit of him against whom the penalty is inflicted.

To the same effect is the case of *The United States* vs. *Bevins* (5 *Wheaton*):

"Penal statutes, however, are taken strictly and literally only in point of defining and setting down the *crime* and the *punishment*; and not literally in words that are but circumstances and conveyance in the putting of the case.

"Thus, though by the statute 1 Ed. 6, C. 12, it was enacted that those who were convicted of stealing *horses* should not have the benefit of clergy, the Judges conceived that this did not extend to him that should steal but one horse, and therefore procured a new Act for that purpose in the following year.

"But upon the Statute of Gloucester, that gives the action of waste against him that holds *pro termino vitæ vel annorum*, if a man holds but for a year he is within the statute; while, if the law be that for a certain offence a man shall lose his right hand, and the offender hath had his right hand before cut off in the wars, he shall not lose his left hand, but the crime shall rather pass without the punishment which the law assigned than the letter of the law shall be extended.

"A penal law, then, shall not be extended by equity; that is, things which do not come within the words shall not be brought within it by construction.

"The law of England does not allow of constructive offences, or of arbitrary punishments. No man incurs a penalty unless the act which subjects him to it is clearly both within the spirit and the letter of the statute imposing such penalty.

"'If these rules are violated,' said Best, C.J., in the case of *Fletcher* vs. *Lord Sondes, 3 Bing., 580,* 'the fate of accused persons is decided by the arbitrary discretion of Judges, and not by the express authority of the laws. *2d Dwarris Stat., 634.*'

"By another restrictive rule of construing penal statutes, if general words follow an enumeration of particular cases, such general words are held to apply only to cases of the *same kind* as those which are expressly mentioned. By the 14 Geo. 2, C. 1, persons who should steal sheep *or any other cattle* were deprived of the benefit of clergy. The stealing of any cattle, whether commonable or not commonable, seems to be embraced by these general words, "*any other cattle,*" yet they were looked upon as too loose to create a capital offence. By the 15 George 2, C. 34, the Legislature declared that it was doubtful to what sorts of cattle the former Act extended besides sheep, and enacted and declared that the Act was made to extend to any bull, cow, ox, steer, bullock, heifer, calf, and lamb, as well as sheep, and to no other cattle whatsoever.

"Until the Legislature distinctly specified what cattle were meant to be included, the Judges felt that they could not apply the statute to any other cattle but sheep.

"The Legislature, by the last Act, says that it was not to be extended to horses, pigs, or goats, although all these are cattle.

"3 Bingh., 581.
"2 Dwarris, Statutes, 635."

By the English law, and by the principles of general law, may it please the Court, the offence must be clearly defined—it must be limited, ascertained, fixed. It must be clear to the accuser. It must be clear to the accused. It must be equally clear to the Judge. It must leave him no discretion whereby he can enlarge or alter it. And, may it please the Court, this is the safe and true principle of construction—to give as little as possible to the discretion of the Courts; for it has been well said, that the arbitrary discretion of any man is the law of tyrants. It is always unknown; it is different in different men; it is casual, and depends on constitution, temper, and passion. In the best of us it is oftentimes caprice; in the worst of us it is every vice, folly and passion to which human nature is liable. It is by defining crime clearly that the citizen has his strongest guarantee for his personal safety. Let us see the opinion of perhaps the greatest master that ever touched the subject of jurisprudence— I mean *Montesquieu.*

"It is determined," he says, "by the laws of China, that whoever shows any disrespect to the Emperor is to be punished with death. As they do not mention in what this disrespect consists, every thing may furnish a pretext to take away a man's life, and to exterminate any family whatsoever.

"If the crime of high treason be indeterminate, this alone is sufficient to make the Government degenerate into arbitrary power."—*Montesquieu, Spirit, Book* 12, *c.* 7.

Now, may it please the Court, it is through statutes in which crimes are ill-defined—are not clearly and distinctly designated—that tyrants in every age have been able to crush their victims. Hence, in the noble system of laws that it is your honors' privilege to dispense, safeguards have been put in the strongest degree, and bulwarks have been erected around the life, the liberties, and the rights of the citizen.

Now, what is an "act of hostility"? Suppose these men had gone out with a commission instructing them to go on the seas, to board vessels, and to beat the captains of vessels, and to do no more—to abandon them then, and take to their own ships—would that be an act of piracy? Is it not plain that the law meant piracy or robbery, or any "act of hostility" *ejusdem generis*, that is, *animo furandi?* To show that this construction is not forced, your honors will find in the Act of March 3d, 1825 (Dunlop's Laws, p. 723, sect. 6), that a special law was passed for the very purpose of punishing *acts of hostility* against the United States and its citizens by *forcibly attacking* and *setting upon vessels* owned in part or wholly by either of them, *with intent to plunder and despoil the owners of moneys, goods,* &c., &c. If, therefore, this construction of these words, which I respectfully submit to the Court, has any weight in it, they amount to no more than what has been already decided in Clintock's case—the clear and well-settled principle of law that the commission shall not form a pretext for robbery.

But, may it please the Court, as to the ninth section of the Act, it never was contemplated as applying to organized States. It was an Act which was intended to apply to individuals alone. States are not the subjects of criminal law, nor can you legislate against them; and this has been distinctly decided. If the Confederate States have been guilty of a gross breach of faith in the attempt to withdraw from the Confederation, they may be coerced; but the citizen himself must go unpunished. They are States—recognized by yourselves as States. They are not a collection of piratical hordes; and under such circumstances the law will not apply to the citizen of any of these States who acts fairly and honestly under his commission.

The learned counsel who spoke last Saturday, referred to privateering as a relic of the barbarous age. No one agrees with the learned counsel in that respect more than I do; and from the bottom of my heart I hope that he may be yet able to take his share in banishing from the world this relic of the olden time. But, really, I see very little chance of advancement in that line, so long as a vessel of war is allowed to take private property on the seas. There should be perfect immunity for all property on the ocean belonging to individuals; but the letter of Mr. Marcy shows that we are not yet exactly up to that point.

The learned counsel stated that, before he could concede the commission in this case to be a justification, two things must be shown: First, there must be a state of war; and, second, the privateer must have received his commission from some public, national, sovereign power. Well, we think we have shown the existence of war sufficiently strongly; and as to this point, I fancy that few gentlemen of the bar can forget the pointed and admirable allusion of the learned counsel himself (Mr. Evarts), in his argument in the District Court, some time since, to the absent clerk, in illustrating the fact of the existence of war. I remember how forcibly it struck me when I read it. The decisions in the case of the South American privateers settles the point as to the nationality.

But, gentlemen, there is another subject to which I will briefly allude—that is, the abstract right of these States legally to secede. Now, gentlemen, we do not deny that there is no such right. I concede all that. Yet, still, these men have ever held different notions; and, on this subject, a line has been drawn for many years through an immense tract of this our country. The right or the wrong of it does not affect us here. You have failed to convince them, and they have failed to convince you. There is no common arbiter between you, because they contend that, being sovereigns, they cannot submit to the Courts questions between themselves and the United States. Now, they may be wrong, but have you the right to declare them so? You ought to be perfectly certain. Justice, reason, and duty prompt that there ought to be no mistake. When you hold a party for a criminal charge, there ought not to be a reasonable doubt. Is there no possibility that, in the course of the proceedings between the Federal and State Governments, you may be wrong? Does truth only consort with one side of the line, and falsehood with the other? May you not be mistaken? Look at the different lights in which, for years, you have respectively viewed various questions. See how gradually the change has been effected; and yet how stronger and stronger it has grown day by day. Can any one forget the deep and intense anxiety with which that great statesman, Mr. Clay, just before his death, regarded the division between the Methodist and Baptist Churches of the North and the South? And yet no man was a truer or firmer patriot, or an abler advocate of the Government; and no man saw with more unerring certainty that the line, sooner or later, was destined to be drawn between the two sections, unless some compromise was effected.

Now, the doctrine in which these men have been brought up may be political heresy; but, do you crush a heresy with chains? Does history not tell us how utterly vain and futile such an attempt is? Have you to go back farther than the days of James the Second, to see the attempt of that despot to enforce upon the English people a religion which they did not choose to adopt? Can you forget the bloody assizes of Jeffreys, when hundreds were carried to the block and thousands were sent into exile to all parts of the world? Can you forget the great scene, when the noble Duke of Argyle, with his head bared and his limbs in chains, was led through Edinburgh amidst the reproaches and contempt of the populace; and do you forget the cold and manly dignity with which he endured it all? And do you reflect that, with all these things, the religion of England to-day is the same as it was then? Can you expect, by a system like this, to mould the human mind as you would mould potter's clay? Oh, no! gentlemen, the human heart is a different thing; love and tenderness may melt and control it, but chains and manacles never yet subdued it. Call this piracy! why this is, indeed, confounding the order of things; and when the real piracy comes, you will feel no dislike or contempt for the offence. You give it a dignity by thus confounding it with crimes of a different nature. If these men are pirates, all are pirates who have taken naval commissions from the Confederate States, and all are robbers who have served them on land. Pirates! Is Tatnall a pirate—Tatnall who, by his skill, and valor, and daring, succeeded in landing your gallant army in Mexico, challenging on that occasion the admiration alike of the army and navy? Tatnall a pirate! Tatnall, whose name has been for forty years the synonym of all that is high and noble and brave in the American navy! Is Hartsteine a pirate—Hartsteine, the modest but hardy sailor, who carried your ensign into the far, remote, and unfriendly regions of the frigid zone? Is Ingraham a pirate—Ingraham, who, when the down-trodden naturalized refugee from Austria asked for the protection of the American flag said, "Do you want the protection of this flag?—then you shall have it!" Are these men pirates? Oh, no! gentlemen; there is some mistake about this. Is Lee a robber—Lee, the chosen and bosom friend of your venerable commander in Washington, and who, but a few months ago, parted from him with an aching heart and eyes brimful of tears? Lee, a robber! Lee, whose glory is yours, and whose name is written on every page of your country's history which attests the triumphant march of your army from Vera Cruz to the gates of Mexico? Methinks I see the flash of fire light the eye, and the curl of contempt play upon the lips, of the old hero of Lundy's Lane, as he hears the foul imputation upon the stainless honor of the well-tried friend of many years. No, gentlemen, these men are not pirates! they are not robbers! Your own hearts tell you they are not. Truly, it may indeed be said, that civil war does pervert the natural taste, and relish of equity and of justice.

But, gentlemen, what is the object of this prosecution? Can the united States desire revenge on these men? That is a passion not attributable to States. States have no passion. The dignity and the power of a State ought to make it tolerant. Is it because the President's proclamation has pronounced these men pirates? Certainly, the respected Chief Magistrate of these United States has no disposition to enforce this law, simply because he has declared it, as in the case of King Ahasuerus. Is their punishment sought for the good of the community? If it is designed for such a purpose, its effect is very questionable.

It is extremely strange, gentlemen, that the prosecution should have been, any how, brought on now, and under this Act. Is it a strange fact, gentlemen, that, under the Act of William the Third, which has been cited to you, there was not, during the American Revolution, a single American privateersman ever brought to trial in England. And yet the English Government repeatedly captured them, and put them in prison. That Act is just as strong as this, for the ninth section of our Act of 1790 is copied from it. I suppose the truth is, gentlemen, that the English Government felt the utter inapplicability of that law to a case of this kind.

But, it is time that I should draw to a close. If these men have been brought into the position in which they now stand, much depends upon their political education—much depends upon the different views with which they have regarded this question from ourselves. It is the part of humanity to err. These men are the representatives of those who were once united with us in the gentle tie of brotherhood. That tie is now rent, and it may be years before the kindly and good feeling which once subsisted between the sections is restored. God grant that the hour may not be far distant! But, gentlemen, to treat these men with kindness; to treat them with humanity; to have respect for that great principle which underlies the bottom of our own Government—the right of resistance (and I mean here legal resistance, and not that revolutionary resistance which the Courts of justice do not adopt, and never have, and cannot sanction),—I say, to treat them with kindness and humanity will do more, in my honest belief, to knit together the two sections than a hundred battle-fields would do.

Gentlemen, if there has been a division between you, remember that that division has sprung up from honest conviction. Can you think otherwise? Shoulder to shoulder with your fathers, in the days of the Revolution, their fathers fought the battles of freedom. Side by side with you, they trod the burning plains of Mexico, and encountered, in hostile strife, the foes of your country; and when the shock of battle was over, wrapped in the same honored flag, their dead and yours were borne to their final resting place. Is it for a light and a trifling cause that they have thus separated from you?

In conclusion, gentlemen, let me beg you to meet this issue like men. No matter what the pressure upon you is, stand firm, do justice, and discharge these prisoners. In so doing, you will but do your duty, and God himself will sanction the act. But, gentlemen, if deaf to the promptings of reason, of justice, and of humanity—if, impelled by political rancor and passion—you condemn these prisoners, and execution follows condemnation, be assured that they will meet their fate like men; and that these manacled hands, which you have so often disported through your streets to excited crowds, will, "though impotent here," be lifted, and not in vain, to a far more august tribunal than this, before whose unerring decrees Courts and nations alike must bow with awful reverence.

ARGUMENT OF MR. SULLIVAN.

Mr. Sullivan, of Counsel for the prisoners, said:

May it please the Court: Gentlemen of the Jury:

This case has brought to my mind an interesting episode in ancient history, to which I beg permission to refer. For many years, the States of Greece had been engaged in bloody civil strife, which ended in the discomfiture of Athens. The Spartans and their allies assembled in council to consider and determine on her fate. Animated by resentful passion, the Thebans urged extreme and vindictive measures: that Athens should be razed to the ground, that the hand of the victorious States should fall heavy, and the Athenians be proclaimed exiles from their homes and outlaws in Greece. This proposal was applauded by the Corinthians and some others, but at that moment the deputy of the Phocians, who owed a debt of gratitude to the Athenians, sang in the assembly the mournful Choral Ode from the Electra of Sophocles, which moved all present in such a manner that they declared against the design. The poem had lifted them from the passion of the hour, and invoked the memories and ancestral glories of their common nation. The spirits of departed heroes now lent the inspiration of their presence, and yielding to it the members of that council and jury became great Greeks, as of old their fathers were. Marathon and Salamis, Platæa and Mycale, were pictured in the chambers of their souls, with Miltiades, Themistocles and Aristides for their counselors; and then, and not until then were they fit to render a verdict upon Athens, the loveliest sister of them all.

And gentlemen, before we touch upon the details of this case, may we not contemplate some examples and sentiments which will enlighten and strengthen our spirits as guardians of the important interests committed to our hands this day? I am sure it will be agreeable to you and to seek them in the annals of our forefathers,

"The great of old,

The dead but sceptred sovereigns, who still rule

Our spirits, from their urns."

It may be that a voice like that of the Theban delegate, and like the voice of Corinth, is sounding in your ears, and appealing, by sophistries, and passion, and prejudices, to you to lay the hand of your Government with all possible severity upon those of her enemies who are now in her power and arraigned at her bar. But I entreat you to lift yourselves to that stand-point from which our ancestors, who founded this Union, who enacted the law upon which this prosecution is founded, would have regarded a case analogous to that of Captain Baker and the other defendants herein. What was the central and distinguishing idea of Government, blazing like another sun on the world, which our fathers established and made honorable? Was it not the imperishable doctrine of revolutionary right—and that without special regard to the names, and forms, and paths through which it might be sought? For many other causes they may have pledged their fortunes; there were many for which they periled their lives; but only for this is it recorded by them, "We pledge our sacred honor." It is their incommunicable glory that they consummated their purpose; and if for anything we have a place in history and a name in the world, it is that we have hitherto professed to be the special guardians of that principle among the nations. Will you rise with me to the dignity and affecting associations that surrounded and auspicated the struggle of our forefathers for this principle? Shall their memory be your guiding light, and their honorable purpose that upon which your thoughts will linger? Let us subject our hearts to their influence, for it will not mislead us. And, now, would our fathers with casuistry and technical constructions of a statute which they never meant should apply to such a case as the present, pronounce judgment of piracy and outlawry against any people who were making an effort, by the recognized forms of war, to assert revolutionary right and independent self-government for themselves? Never! And while the page on which our fathers' history is written is lustrous, it would be readorned with all the beauty of immortal splendor, if under it were written to-day, "That which the American people of 1776 claimed for themselves (the right to 'dissolve the political bands that bound them to another'), they possessed the greatness of soul, in 1861, to acknowledge against themselves, when another portion of the same race sought the same end. Beguiled by the almost omnipotent sophistries of interest and passion, they have nevertheless adhered in loyal faith to their time-honored doctrine of free government. In the faithful devotion of the Sons, the principles of the Fathers have been revindicated. Henceforth the nation must stand unapproachable in their greatness."

Why I make these observations, gentlemen, is, that when the officers of the United States ask you to-day to find a verdict of guilty against these prisoners, they ask you to do that which, shape it and distort it and reason about it as they may, is asking you to lift an impious hand and strike a parricidal blow, conspicuous in the eyes of the world, against the ever sacred doctrine which our ancestors transmitted to us as their best legacy and a part of their own good name. Will you abandon it? Nay, rather cling to it,

"As one withstood clasps a Christ upon the rood,

In a spasm of deathly pain."

I wish now, gentlemen, to ask you to go with me a moment to the deck of the *Perry*, when she captured the *Savannah* and her crew. Let us recall the historical incidents of the capture, and the preparations for the trial, that we may introduce this case as justice requires.

The *Savannah* was captured on the Atlantic Ocean, about fifty-five miles from Charleston. The Commander of the *Perry*, who at that moment represented the United States Government, virtually said to the defendants herein, "We propose to try you as *citizens* of the United States, who, by acting under a commission of letter of marque from the Confederate States, have become liable to the penalties of the United States law against piracy." The prisoners at once reply, "If that is true, take us into the nearest ports for trial. They are in South Carolina. You claim that she is a part of the United States, and that her citizens (*i.e.*, ourselves) are amenable to your laws, and that the United States are sovereign there. Take us before one of your Courts in that State and try our case." "Oh! no, (say the United States) we cannot, with all our guns, land upon the shores of South Carolina." "Well, take us into the adjoining State, Georgia." "No; there is not an officer of the United States in Georgia. We cannot protect or sustain a single law in Georgia." "Well, take us to Florida, Alabama, Mississippi, Louisiana or Texas—any place along that extended coast of over two thousand miles." "No, (say the United States) throughout all that coast, we confess to you, Capt. Baker, that we have not a Court, not an officer, we cannot execute a single law." "Well, take us north, into North Carolina, or into Virginia." The reply of the United States is still, "We have no place there. But, notwithstanding we admit that throughout that territory we have no practical existence; we have no Court; we have no civil functionaries; we have no protection for allegiance to us; we have not a citizen who acknowledges his allegiance to us; we admit that the people in those States have excluded our government and established another, which is in active and exclusive control—notwithstanding all this, you are still our citizens; and none, nor all of these facts, relieve you from the guilt and liability to punishment."

The defendants are accordingly put in chains and brought to the District of New York for trial. The witnesses for the prosecution prove all the facts that are in the case, and we stand willing to be tried by them. They prove that the defendants did capture a brig on the high seas, which brig belonged to citizens of the United States. They prove, further, that the defendants at the time of the capture, and in the act, alleged that they did so, in the name and on behalf of the "Confederate States of America," and by authority derived from them, as an act of war between the two Governments.

The authority and intent thus alleged for the capture, were they honestly, or only colorably alleged? Were they a justification of the act, so far as this prosecution is concerned, or not?

First: Was it true that the capture of the Joseph was in the name of the Confederate States? The fact is, that when the Savannah approached and summoned the Joseph to surrender, the captain of the Savannah stated his purpose to be as I have repeated; he hoisted the Confederate flag; he wore the uniform and insignia of an officer of the Confederate States; he had, as the paper upon which his vessel was documented, a paper which has been produced before us, and which bears the broad seal of the "Confederate States of America," which authorizes him to take the Savannah as a private armed vessel, and, in the name and authority of the Confederate States, to "make war" against the United States and her vessels. The facts preclude any possible suggestion, that the defendants made any false pretence on the subject. The defendants had every adequate and sufficient warrant for what they did, if the "Confederate States of America" could give any authority which would constitute a defence, or if there was anything in the state of the contest between the United States and the Confederate States which constitutes *war*. But, the question will present itself, even if the defendants had this warrant from the Confederate States—Did they intend to, and did they in fact comply with its requirements, or were they abusing and transgressing its license, and engaged in freebooting? Did they intend to infract the regulations prescribed for their control by the Government of the Confederate States and imposed imperatively by the law of nations upon legitimate privateers, or did they intend to rob and steal? I think I may safely assert that the law officers of the United States will admit that the defendants intended in good faith to comply strictly and literally with all the conditions of their authority, prescribed by their own Government for their conduct, and also with the code of war in the law of nations. And not only was this their general intention, but as a fact, their conduct furnishes not a single deviation from these requirements. I read to the Court and Jury the Regulations published by the Confederates, for the privateers, and which were found to be on board of the Savannah at the time of her capture. They are similar, in all of their provisions, to those usually prescribed by civilized nations at war. In substance, they permitted the privateers to capture the vessels and cargoes belonging to the United States and her citizens, the capture to be made in the name of the Confederate States; they forbade, after capture, any disturbance or removal of the furniture, tackle, or cargoes of the captured prizes, and required immediate transmission, to a proper Court, of the prize, for adjudication. Did the defendants comply with these terms? The evidence is too plain that they did, to admit the slightest doubt.

As soon as the Joseph was captured, a prize crew was put on board of her and she was sent to the care of an Admiralty Court in a home port, and her papers, books and crew were sent along, that the Court might have the fullest evidence of the ownership and character of the captured vessel, and be able to decide properly, whether or not she was liable to capture. If the defendants had any corrupt or furtive motives, or if they had been indifferent to their assumed obligations, would they have been so scrupulous in furnishing all the evidence to the Court? Did they destroy, alter or erase any evidence, or offer to do so? Did they evince the least desire to have any other than the full facts appear with regard to all their acts? Your answer, with mine, is No! And when the vessel arrived in port, observe what proceedings were instituted by the agent of the captors. He did not offer to sell the vessel and cargo at private sale; he did not offer to submit her disposition to the adjudication of any merely State Court; but caused her to be libeled in a Prize Court, constituted on precisely the same basis, and enforcing the identical rules of law with the United States Prize and Admiralty Court, which convenes in the room adjoining to that in which we now are. In fact, I am safe in saying that the decisions of our Courts here are controlling precedents in the Court wherein the brig Joseph was tried and condemned as a prize of war. The trial was in a Court known to and recognized by the law of nations. Now, gentlemen, I certainly need do no more than thus re-advert to the facts in evidence to remove from your minds the slightest suspicion that the defendants ever intended to violate the laws of war or the instructions received from their Government when they received their letter of marque.

Perhaps, however, the question may arise,—whether the defendants did regard the commission under which they sailed as competent and adequate authority to justify their acts; or were they distrustful of its sufficiency? I do not admit, gentlemen, that that is a consideration to which in this trial we should recur, for your decision must rest on other grounds. But, I will not hesitate to say, that it is morally impossible for any man who has heard the evidence, and who is familiar with the course of events in the South, to believe that the defendants did not act in the fullest confidence that the authority of the Confederate States was ample and just authority for their undertaking. Even that one of the Savannah's crew who has become a witness for the prosecution, under a *nolle prosequi*, asserted on the stand, that at the time the Savannah was being fitted out for her cruise as a privateer, no one in the community of the South seemed to have any other idea but that the Government of the Confederate States was completely and legally established, and that every citizen of those States owed to it supreme allegiance. They believed that a letter of marque from the Confederate States constituted as good authority for privateering as the letters which were issued by our revolutionary fathers in '76, or as if they were issued by the United States. But, gentlemen, we are to proceed one step further, for under the theory presented by attorneys for the prosecution, they virtually admit that there was good faith on the part of the prisoners, and that they intended to comply with the restrictions imposed by the authority which they carried out of port with them. But they say that, inasmuch as the Confederate States were not a recognized Government, they could not confer any right upon the defendants to act as privateers, which could justify them in a plea to the pending charge. That is a proposition which enfolds the real issue in this trial. The difficulties in respect to its solution do not appear to me to be great, and I am satisfied that the more they are examined the less they will appear to candid minds.

Had the Government of the Confederate States a right to issue letters of marque; or, in other words, to declare and wage war? The denial of that right, by the attorneys for the United States, involves them in inextricable embarrassments, and must expose the fallacies which lie at the bottom of the erroneous reasonings of the prosecution.

In the first place, it is substantially an assertion, on the part of the United States, of the doctrine, "*Once a sovereign always a sovereign,*"—that the United States Government cannot—by revolution accomplished—by the Act of the States repealing their ordinances of union—by any act of the people establishing and sustaining a different Government—be divested of their former sovereignty. Or, in the language of Mr. Evarts, until there has been some formal acquiescence, some assent, some acknowledgment by the executive authority of the United States of the independence of the Confederate States, there can be no other plea, and no progress in any line of investigation, with a view to a defence of these defendants in a Court of justice of the United States. Upon that point, I beg to be understood as taking an issue as wide as it is possible for human minds to differ; and I am bold to assert that the doctrine cannot be maintained successfully in a capital case of this kind. It is not true that a recognition of the Confederate States by the United States executive, in a formal and distinct manner, is requisite to entitle them and their citizens to the rights belonging to a nation, in the eye of this Court. An acknowledgment of independence would be one way of proving the fact, but is far from being the only way. Proof of such an acknowledgment by a formal State paper would, of course, terminate this prosecution; but, in the absence of that fact, there may be a recurrence to others, which will suffice as well, and satisfy the Court and Jury that the Confederate States must, at least, to a certain extent, be regarded as a nation, entitled to the usual consideration belonging to a nation at war. To show how unreasonable the proposition is, and to illustrate how impossible it is to accept it, let me submit a supposition:

If, for fifty years to come, the United States shall not re-establish her sovereignty and restore her laws and power over the seceded States, and the latter shall continue to maintain an open and exclusive Government; and if the United States shall still refuse to recognize the new Government by formal documentary record, would the refusal then warrant the United States in capturing Confederate armies of a new generation, and punishing them for treason and piracy? And, if so fifty years hence, would it continue twice or thrice fifty years? Or what is the limit? The difficulties in the answer can be avoided in only one way, and that is, to conclude that the acknowledgment of the independence of the revolutionizing section is of no consequence at all, for all the purposes of this case, provided the fact of independence and separate Government really exists, and is proven. A *de facto* Government, merely, must be allowed by every sound jurist to possess in itself, for the time being, all the attributes and functions of a Government *de jure*. It may properly claim for itself, and the citizen may rightfully render to it, allegiance and obedience, as if the Government rested on an undisputed basis.

This is a rule never denied in the law of nations. History has scarcely a page without its record of revolution and dynastic struggle to illustrate this rule. The official acts of a *de facto* Government affecting personal rights, title to property, the administration of justice, the organization of its society, and imposing duties on the citizens, receive that consideration which belongs to acts of long-established Governments.

The successor does not pronounce the laws of the predecessor null. He simply repeals them, with a clause protecting all vested rights. This principle is correct, even in case of an usurping monarch; but how much more, if it shall appear that the people who are to be governed, have, for themselves, with mutual concurrence and choice, cast off the former Government, and organized a new one, avowing to the world their purpose to maintain it, and at the same time yielding to it the obedience which it requires?

When that state of facts shall occur, and a people sufficiently numerous to enable them to fulfill the duties of a nation, and with a territory sufficiently compact to enable its Government to execute its functions without inconvenience to the world, shall evince its purpose and a fair assurance of its ability to maintain an independent Government, it will be a surprise, indeed, to hear, in this country, that such a people are still liable to felons' punishment and pirates' doom. It is no longer a case of insurrection or turbulent violence. It has ceased to be a tumult or a riot. The war between the original Government and the revolutionary Government may still continue, but no longer can it, with propriety, be said that the army is merely the *posse comitatus*, dispersing and arresting offenders against the law. The conflicting parties must, at least for the time, be deemed two distinct people—two different nations. The evidence in this case and the public history of the day, show that such is the condition of the United States and the Confederate States. In addition thereto, the United States have, by repeated acts, indicated that they so regarded the fact. The principal witness for the prosecution testified that he repeatedly saw the officers of the United States negotiating, through flags of truce, with the officers of the Confederate States; and that always the flag of truce from the Confederate States was displayed with their Government flag, but that fact never prevented the negotiation. This was well known to our Government. We have in evidence, also, the agreement of capitulation at the surrender of the Forts at Hatteras Inlet. The representative of the United States signed that official document and accepted it for his Government, with the signature of Commander Barron to it as "commanding the forces of the Confederate States," etc. That was a virtual recognition that there is such a Government, *de facto*.

A few days since our Government published another general order, or document, directing that a certain number of prisoners, captured in arms against the United States, and when fighting under regular enlistment the army of the Confederate States, should be released as "prisoners of war," because the Confederate States had released a similar number. That was an exchange of prisoners of "war," and another virtual acknowledgment that the Confederate States constitute a Government. Remember that these "prisoners of war" had, if they were citizens of the United States, violated the law in the first section of the statute under the eighth and succeeding sections of which this prosecution is founded. One class were fighting on land against the United States, and the penalty is death by the statute. The defendants here fought on water; and there is the same penalty, if either is liable to the penalties of the statute. Both classes fought under the same flag and received their commission from the same Government. If one class are "prisoners of war" in the opinion of the Government of the United States, so must the other be. It is impossible to recede from the consequences of the virtual recognition of belligerent rights involved in the exchange of these captives, under the chosen designation of "prisoners of war." How, then, doth the dignity of our Government suffer by this prosecution! It evinces an indecision, a caprice, a want of consistency and character on the part of the Government. It is an unfortunate, and I hope an unpremeditated one. The good name of the nation is involved, unnecessarily, by the mere fact of arraignment of these defendants under an indictment; but your verdict of "not guilty" may yet save it.

The Jury will and must accept the construction which the Government has in fact put on the law, viz., that it does not apply, and was never intended to apply, to such a state of affairs as the present revolution has brought about.

Let me illustrate further the absence of all reason to support the proposition that, until a formal acknowledgment of the existence of the Confederate States by the United States, the official acts of the former cannot be regarded as having any validity, or as affording protection to their citizens. Go beyond our own borders, to countries where the sovereign is an individual, with fixed hereditary right to reign, and where the doctrine established is that which I repudiate, "Once a sovereign, always a sovereign," and that the sovereign rules by divine right and cannot innocently be superseded. If the doctrine affirmed in this case be true, that to give validity to the acts of a Government established by a revolution the preceding Government must have recognized its existence, then the world will be sadly at fault. Show me where the King of Naples has acknowledged the kingship of Victor Emanuel? Show me where the sovereigns of Parma and Modena and Tuscany have consented to the establishment of the new government in their territory?

But the people have voted in the new Government, and they maintain it; and Victor Emanuel is, in spite of King Bomba, *de facto*, King of Naples; and Victor's commissions to his army and navy, and his letters of marque, will be recognized in every court in every enlightened nation.

Even in Italy, the Courts of Justice would, when the case arose that required it, enforce the same regard to the existing Government as if the former sovereigns had formally relinquished their claims to sovereignty. Again, I say, the act of the people is entitled to more weight in an inquiry, "what is the Government?" than the seal and recognition of the former sovereign.

As Americans, imbued with correct opinions upon the relation of the governed to the governing, your hearts reject the theory propounded by this prosecution, and concur with me.

To vindicate your opinion you will find the defendants herein "not guilty."

Come to our own recent history. Texas was one of the States of the Union which is called Mexico. Texas seceded from that Union. She declared her independence, and during a struggle of arms became a *de facto* Government. Mexico would not recognize her independence, and continued her intention to restore her to the old Union. The United States, however, recognized the right of Texas to her independence, and invited her to enter into our Union, and did incorporate her in that Union in defiance of the doctrine of Mexico, "once a sovereign, always a sovereign until independence shall be acknowledged." We then denounced that doctrine, but now we seem ready to embrace its odious sentiments. We placed our declaration on record before the world, that Texas, by her act alone, unauthorized and unrecognized by the central Government of Mexico, had become a sovereign and independent State, invested with full power to dispose of her territory and the allegiance of her citizens, and, as a sovereign State, to enter into compacts with other States.

Have not the Courts of the United States sanctioned that proceeding? Suppose that Hungary, or Venice, or Ireland shall separate from their present empires and establish Governments for themselves, what will be our position? Let your verdict in this case determine.

It is, perhaps, well, now, to recur to the law of nations. That is a part of the common law of England and of this country. We may claim in this Court the benefit of its enlightened and humane provisions, as if they were embodied in our statutes. There are circumstances in the history of every nation, when the law of nations supervenes upon the statutes and controls their literal interpretation.

If the case becomes one to which the law of nations is applicable, it thereby is removed from the pale of the statute. Such is the present case. In the seceded States a Government has been established. It has been hitherto maintained by force, it is true, as against the United States, but by consent of the people at home; and both sides have taken up arms, and large armies now stand arrayed against each other, in support of their respective Governments. It is all-important to the cause of justice, and to the honor of the United States, to see that in their official acts, in their treatment of prisoners, either of the army or captured privateers, they conform to the rules recognized as binding, under similar circumstances, by civilized and Christian nations, and sanctioned by the authoritative publicists of the world. I will recall your attention to extracts from Vattel, and with the firmest confidence that they will vindicate my views, that the defendants are entitled to be held as prisoners of war, and not as criminals awaiting trial:

Vattel, Book III., chapter 18, sec. 292:

"When a party is formed in a State, which no longer obeys the sovereign, and is of strength sufficient to make a head against him, or when, in a Republic, the nation is divided into two opposite factions, and both sides take arms, this is called a *civil war*. Some confine this term only to a just insurrection of subjects against an unjust sovereign, to distinguish this lawful resistance from *rebellion*, which is an open and unjust resistance; but what appellation will they give to a war in a Republic torn by two factions, or, in a Monarchy, between two competitors for a crown? Use appropriates the term of civil war to every war between the members of one and the same political society."

Subsequent clause in same section:

"Therefore, whenever a numerous party thinks it has a right to resist the sovereign, and finds itself able to declare that opinion, sword in hand, the war is to be carried on between them in the same manner as between two different nations; and they are to leave open the same means for preventing enormous violences and restoring peace."

Last clause in section 295:

"But when a nation becomes divided into two parties absolutely independent and no longer acknowledging a common superior, the State is dissolved, and the war betwixt the two parties, in every respect, is the same with that in a public war between two different nations. Whether a Republic be torn into two factious parties, each pretending to form the body of the State, or a Kingdom be divided betwixt two competitors to the Crown, the nation is thus severed into two parties, who will mutually term each other rebels. Thus there are two bodies pretending to be absolutely independent, and who having no judge, they decide the quarrel by arms, like two different nations. The obligation of observing the common laws is therefore absolute, indispensable to both parties, and the same which the law of nature obliges all nations to observe between State and State."

"If it be between part of the citizens, on one side, and the sovereign, with those who continue in obedience to him, on the other, it is sufficient that the malcontents have some reasons for taking arms, to give this disturbance the name of *civil war*, and not that of *rebellion*. This last term is applied only to such an insurrection against lawful authority as is void of all appearance of justice. The sovereign, indeed, never fails to term all subjects rebels openly resisting him; but when these become of strength sufficient to oppose him, so that he finds himself compelled to make war regularly on them, he must be contented with the term of civil war."

Clause of section 293:

"A civil war breaks the bands of society and government, or at least it suspends their force and effect. It produces in the nation two independent parties, considering each other as enemies, and acknowledging no common judge. Therefore, of necessity, these two parties must, at least for a time, be considered as forming two separate bodies—two distinct people. Though one of them may be in the wrong in breaking up the continuity of the State— to rise against lawful authority—they are not the less divided in fact. Besides, who shall judge them? On earth they have no common superior. Thus they are in the case of two nations who, having dispute which they cannot adjust, are compelled to decide it by force of arms."

First clause in sec. 294:

"Things being thus situated, it is evident that the common laws of war, those maxims of humanity, moderation and probity which we have before enumerated and recommended, are, in civil wars, to be observed on both sides. The same reasons on which the obligation between State and State is founded, render them even more necessary in the unhappy circumstance when two incensed parties are destroying their common country. Should the sovereign conceive he has a right to hang up his prisoners as rebels, the opposite party will make reprisals; if he does not religiously observe the capitulations and all the conventions made with his enemies, they will no longer rely on his word; should he burn and destroy, they will follow his example; the war will become cruel and horrid; its calamities will increase on the nation."

Remember you are an American Jury; that your fathers were revolutionists; that they judged for themselves what Government they would have, and they did not hesitate to break off from their mother Government, even though there were penalties of statutes with which they were threatened. And remember, also, that from the beginning of your fathers' revolution, they claimed that they were not liable to the treatment of offenders against British statutes, but that the Colonies were a nation, and entitled to belligerent rights—one of which was, that if any of their army or navy fell into the hands of the British army, they should be held as prisoners of war.

Your fathers never admitted that the *continental army* were liable to punishment with the *halter*, if taken prisoners.

To be sure, the statute of Great Britain, literally construed, so provided, but the law of nations had supervened, and rendered that statute no longer applicable. Vindicate your respect for your fathers' claims, by extending the same immunities to the prisoners at the bar, whose situation is analogous to that of our fathers.

At the commencement of the Revolution, preceding the Declaration of Independence in 1776, the Colonies became each a separate sovereignty. That became the *status*, with some, without documentary declaration to that effect; but most of them have left on record positive enunciations of their assumption of independence and sovereignty as States, unconnected with the proceedings of any other State. [4]_They entered into a Confederation as independent States, declaring, however, distinctly, in a separate article, that each State retained its own sovereignty, freedom, and independence, and every power of jurisdiction and right not expressly delegated to the United States in Congress assembled. And at the close of the war, when the treaty of peace was made, recognizing the independence of the Colonies, each State was named individually. I have never been able to discover when and where, since that period, any State has surrendered its sovereignty, or deprived itself of its right to act as a sovereign. The Constitution suspends the exercise of some of the functions of sovereignty by the States, but it does not deprive them of their power to maintain their rights as sovereigns, when and how they shall think best, if that Constitution shall, in their judgment, be broken or perverted as a delegated trust of power.

Listen, therefore, to the better voices whispering to each heart. Remember, the honor and consistency of the United States are involved in this case. By a conviction of the defendants, you condemn the Revolution of your ancestors; you sustain the theories of the worst courtiers who surrounded George III. in his war to put down the rebellion; you will appear to the world as stigmatizing revolutionists with the names of outlaws and pirates, which is the phraseology applied to them by Austria and Russia; you will violate the law of nations; you will appear to be merely wreaking vengeance, and not making legitimate war; you will henceforth preclude your nation from offering a word of sympathy to people abroad who may be struggling for their independence, and who have heretofore always turned their hearts to you. You can never—having punished your revolutionists on the gallows—

send an invitation to the unfortunate champions of independent Government in the old world. Kossuth will reply: The American maxim is that of Francis Joseph, and of Marshal Haynau. You cannot say "Godspeed!" to Ireland, if she shall secede. No! as you love the honor of your country, and her place among nations, refuse to pronounce these men pirates.

Tell your Government to wage manly, open, chivalric war on the field and ocean, and thus or not at all; that dishonor is worse even than disunion. Stain not your country's hand with blood. If I were your enemy, I would wish no worse for your names, than to record your verdict against these prisoners. Leave no such record against your country in her annals; and when the passions of the hour shall have subsided, your verdict of acquittal of Thomas H. Baker and the other defendants herein, will be recalled by you with satisfaction, and will receive the approval of your countrymen.

ARGUMENT OF MR. DAVEGA.

May it please your Honors: Gentlemen of the Jury:

On the 25th of June last, when the startling intelligence was announced in our daily papers of the capture of the so-called *Pirates of the Savannah*, our community was thrown into a *furore* of excitement. Every one was anxious to get a glimpse of the "monsters of the deep," as they were carried manacled through our streets. Some expected to see in Captain Baker a "counterfeit presentment" of the notorious Captain Kidd; others expected to trace resemblances in Harleston and Passalaigue to Hicks and Jackalow; but what was their surprise when they discovered, instead of *fiends* in human shape, gentlemen of character, intelligence, refinement, and education! Captain Baker is a native of the Quaker City, Harleston and Passalaigue of the State of South Carolina,—all occupying the best positions in society, and respectably connected. The father of Harleston was educated in one of our Northern universities, and, by a strange coincidence, one of his classmates was no less a person than the venerable and distinguished counsel who now appears in behalf of his unfortunate son. (The counsel directed his eyes to Mr. Lord.) Another strange coincidence in the case is, that twelve men are sitting in judgment upon the lives of twelve men, and these men "enemies of the country, enemies of war," and as such are entitled to the rights of prisoners of war.

They do not belong to your jurisdiction; their custody belongs exclusively to the military and not the civil power. Instead of being incarcerated as felons, in the Tombs, they should have been imprisoned in Fort Lafayette, as prisoners of war. They are your enemies to-day; they were your friends yesterday. It is no uncommon occurrence that when two men engage in a quarrel, ending in a fierce combat, they are afterwards better friends than they were before; the vanquished magnanimously acknowledging the superiority of the victor, and the victor in return receiving him kindly. And so, gentlemen, I hope the day is not far distant when the Stars and Stripes will float in the breeze upon every house-top and every hill-top throughout the length and breadth of our glorious Republic: then shall we establish the great principle, for which our forefathers laid down "their lives, their fortunes, and their sacred honor," that this is a Government of consent, and not of force; and "that free governments derive their just powers from the consent of the governed."

In this case some of the gravest and most complicated questions of political and international jurisprudence are involved.

The learned counsel who have preceded me have so fully and ably argued the political questions involved, that it would be the work of supererogation for me to go over them; but in this connection it is not inappropriate to refer to the fact that political opinions instilled into the minds of the prisoners may have influenced their conduct. They were indoctrinated with the principles of political leaders who advocated States' Rights, Nullification, and Secession; and without undertaking to justify or approve the soundness or correctness of their views, it is enough for me to show that the prisoners at the bar were actuated by these principles. The name of John C. Calhoun was *once* dear to every American; his fame is now sectional. Every Southerner believes implicitly in his doctrines; his very name causes their bosoms to swell with emotions of pride; his works are political text books in the schools. It has been facetiously said that when Mr. Calhoun took a pinch of snuff, the whole State of South Carolina sneezed. I do not mean to treat this case with levity, but merely intend to show the sympathy that existed between Mr. Calhoun and his constituents. Then what is the "*head and front of their offending*"? They conscientiously believed that *allegiance* was due to their State, and she in return owed them protection; and under such convictions enlisted in her behalf. If they have erred, it was from mistaken or false notions of patriotism, and not from criminality. It is the *intent* that constitutes the crime. And this is the only just rule that should obtain in *human* as well as *divine* tribunals.

The prisoners at the bar stand charged with the offence of piracy. I contend that they do not come within the intention and purview of the statute against piracy. To understand and properly interpret a law, we must look to the intention of the legislator, and the motives and causes which give rise to the enactment of the law. In the construction of a will, the intention of the testator is to be ascertained; and the same rules apply in the just interpretation of every law. These laws were enacted at a period when peace and prosperity smiled upon this country. If they had been passed during Nullification in 1832, when the disruption of the Union was threatened, then we might reasonably infer that they were intended to apply to the existing state of affairs; so that the irresistible conclusion is, that they were applicable only to a state of peace, and not to a state of war.

The question then arises, Does a state of war exist? The learned counsel for the prosecution (Mr. Evarts), in an able and elaborate argument for the Government, when this question arose in the trial of prize causes, in the other part of this Court (when it was the interest of the Government to assume that position), demonstrated clearly, to my mind, that a state of war did exist, and confirmed his views by citations from the best authorities on international law.

Vattel, who ranks among the first of authors, and whose work on the law of nations is recognized by every enlightened jurist throughout the civilized world, defines "war to be that state, where a nation prosecutes its rights by force." That this is a nation no one will doubt; that it is prosecuting its rights can not be denied; and no one will doubt that it is using force upon a stupendous scale—requiring four hundred millions of dollars, and 500,000 men, with the probability of additional requisitions of men and treasure for a successful termination of this fratricidal war.

It may be said that this is a civil war. Admitting it to be so, the only distinction between this and an international war is, that the former is an intestinal war between the people, where the Republic is divided into two factions, and the latter is where two nations are opposed to each other. All the rules of civilized war, therefore, should govern equally, and it is to soften and mitigate the horrors of civil war that an exchange of prisoners is recognized.

I have endeavored to show that the prisoners at the bar are not guilty of piracy, as defined by the Acts of Congress; and if they are not guilty of municipal piracy, they are certainly not guilty of piracy by the law of nations. What is a pirate? He is defined to be an enemy of the human race—a common sea rover, without any fixed place of residence, who acknowledges no sovereign, no law, and supports himself by pillage and depredation. Do the prisoners come within the meaning of this definition? Did they not encounter a British vessel upon the high seas? Could they not have captured her? But, no, gentlemen of the Jury, as soon as they ascertained that she belonged to a nation in amity with theirs, they allowed her to depart in peace. With the permission of the Court, I would beg leave to refer to an authority entitled to high respect—the works of Sir Leoline Jenkins, 4th Institutes, p. 154, where this principle is laid down: "If the subjects of different States commit robbery upon each other upon the high seas, if their respective States be in amity, it is piracy; if at enmity, it is not, for it is a general rule that enemies never can commit piracy on each other, their depredations being deemed mere acts of hostility."

The prisoners were acting in good faith, by virtue of a commission under the seal of the Confederate States. It is said, by the learned counsel for the prosecution, that the prisoners were acting under the authority of a person named Jefferson Davis. This does so appear nominally, but it is virtually and actually a commission issuing from eight millions of people, who recognize and sanction it under the hand of their President and the seal of their Government—each one being *particeps criminis*, and each one being amenable to the laws of the country, and liable to the penalties of treason and piracy, if evenhanded justice is to be meted out.

I have not yet been able to perceive the distinction between this offence as committed upon sea or land, except that it is attended with more danger. Why, then, have not the prisoners captured by our armies, who are now in Fortress Monroe and Fort Lafayette, been brought to the bar of justice? Because the Government has come to the conclusion that it would be unwise, impolitic, and impracticable; our tribunals would be inadequate in the administration of the laws. But justice should be equal.

One of the learned Judges who charged the Jury in the case of the privateers who were tried in Philadelphia, has undertaken to establish the doctrine that rebellion is wrong, and that it is only justifiable when it acquires the form of a successful revolution. To analyze this doctrine, it means no more nor less than this: that that which was originally wrong, success makes right. To carry out the metaphor, a certain insect in its chrysalis state is the loathsome and detestable caterpillar, but when it assumes the form and variegated hues of the butterfly, it is glorious and beautiful to behold. With equal force of reason it might be said, that if the Father of his country had been unsuccessful in consummating our independence, his name, instead of going down to posterity in glory and honor, would have descended in infamy and disgrace to all succeeding generations. Such notions are unworthy of refined and enlightened civilization.

It was intimated by the learned District Attorney, in his opening remarks, that in the event of a conviction, the President would exercise the pardoning prerogative. Gentlemen, this is a delusion. I do not mean to insinuate that the learned counsel would willfully mislead you; for I am bound to admit, in all becoming candor, that the prosecution have acted with fairness and magnanimity highly creditable, and not in any manner inconsistent with the *performance of their arduous* and responsible duties; but I do say that it should not have the slightest weight in your deliberations upon the important questions involved in this case. Is this a mere form—a farce? is your time, and the valuable time of the Court, to be consumed in the investigation of a long and tedious case like the present as a mere pastime? It is a reflection upon the good sense and intelligence of a Jury, for the Executive to exercise the pardoning power, except in special cases, where new evidence is discovered after conviction which may go to establish the innocence of the party so convicted.

Gentlemen of the Jury, you have a duty to perform that requires almost superhuman nerve and moral courage—requiring more prowess than to face the cannon's mouth. You have it in your power to prove to the nation, and to the whole civilized world, that in the administration of the criminal laws of the country, in a case involving the rights and interests of this Republic, before a Jury of New York citizens, that "*justice can triumph over passion, and reason prevail over prejudice.*" If there is no other feeling which can influence your judgment, if you have no sympathy in common with these men, there is a sympathy you should have—a sympathy for those brave and valiant spirits who fought so nobly for the Union, the Constitution, and the enforcement of the laws, and who are now prisoners of war in the power of the enemy; and it would be expecting too much clemency from the hands of the enemy to suppose that they would allow the sacrifice of these men to go unavenged.

I repeat, you have a solemn duty to perform, and public opinion should not have the slightest influence upon your mind. You are to be governed by a "higher law;" a law based upon the sacred precepts of Holy Writ—its teachings emanating from God himself; and therein you are commanded to observe that golden rule, "Do unto others as you would that they should do unto you."

ARGUMENT OF JAMES T. BRADY, ESQ.

Mr. Brady inquired of Mr. Evarts for what purpose he intended to refer to the statute against treason.

Mr. Evarts: Not in any other light than I have already referred to the doctrine of treason, to wit, that a party cannot be shielded from indictment for the crime of piracy by showing a warrant or assumed authority for acts which made out that his crime was treason; that showing a treasonable combination did not make out a warrant or authority for that which was piracy or murder.

Mr. Brady then proceeded to address the Jury on behalf of the accused:

May it please the Court: Gentlemen of the Jury:

I feel quite certain that all of you are much satisfied to find that this important trial is rapidly drawing to a close; and I think it would be unbecoming in me, as one of the counsel for the accused, to proceed a step farther in my address to you without acknowledging to the Court the gratitude which we feel for their kindness in hearing so largely discussed the grave legal questions involved in this controversy; to the Jury, for their unvarying patience throughout the investigation; and to our learned opponents, for the frank and open manner in which the prosecution has been conducted. Our fellow-citizens at the South—certainly that portion of them who cherish affection for this part of the Union—will find in the course of this trial most satisfactory evidence that respect for law, freedom of speech, freedom of discussion, liberty of opinion, and the rights of all our countrymen, here exist to the fullest extent. All of us have heretofore been connected with interesting and exciting trials. I am warranted in saying that, considering the period at which this trial has occured, and all the facts and circumstances attending it, the citizens of New York have reason to be proud that such a trial could proceed without one word of acerbity, without one expression of angry feeling, or one improper exhibition of popular sentiment. At the same time, as an American citizen, loyal to the Union,—one who has never recognized as his country any other than the United States of America; who has known and loved his country by that name, and will so continue to know and love it to the end of his existence,—I deeply regret that, for any purpose of public policy, it has been deemed judicious to try any of these "piratical" cases, as they are denominated, at this particular juncture. I am not to assume that good reasons for such a proceeding have not in some quarters been supposed to exist; and I certainly have no right to complain of the officers of the law, charged with a high duty, who bring to trial, in the usual course, persons charged with crime. I have not a word to say against my friend the District Attorney, for whom I feel a respect I am happy to express; nor against his learned associate, Mr. Evarts, for whom I have high regard; nor our brother Blatchford, who always performs the largest amount of labor with the smallest amount of ostentation. Still I regret the occurrence of this trial at a time when war agitates our country; for, apart from all theories of publicists, all opinions of lawyers, for you or me to say that there is not a war raging between two contending forces within our territory, is to insult the common sense of mankind. A war carried on for what? What is to be its end, gentlemen of the Jury? This war to which you, like myself, and all classes and all denominations of the North have given a cheerful and vigorous support—pouring out treasure and blood as freely as water—what is it for? Not to look at the result which must come out of it is folly; and it is the folly that pervades the whole American people. Suppose it were now announced that the entire Southern forces had fled in precipitate retreat before our advancing hosts, and that the American flag waved over every inch of American soil—what then? Are we fighting to subjugate the South in the sense in which an emperor would make war upon a rebellious province? Is that the theory? Are we fighting to compel the seceded States to remain in the Union against their will? And do we suppose such a thing practicable? Are we fighting simply to regain the property of the Federal Government of which we have been despoiled in the Southern States? Or are we fighting with a covert and secret intention, such as I understand to have been suggested by an eloquent and popular divine, in a recent address to a large public audience, some of them, like himself, from the Bay State, "that Massachusetts understands very well what she is fighting for"? Is it to effect the abolition of slavery all over the territory of the United States? I will do the Administration the justice to say that, so far as it has given the country any statement of its design in prosecuting the war, it has repelled any such object as negro emancipation. Who can justify the absurd aspect presented by us before the enlightened nations of the Old World, when they find one commander in our army treating slaves as contraband of war; another declaring that they belong to their masters, to whom he returns them; and another treating them all as free. I am an American, and feel the strongest attachment to my country, growing out of affection and duty; but I cannot see that we present before the world, in carrying on this war, anything like a distinct and palpable theory. But I tell you, and I stand upon that prophecy, as embodying all the little intelligence I possess, that if it be a war for any purposes of mere subjugation—that if it be for the purpose of establishing a dictatorship, or designedly waged for the emancipation of all the slaves, our people never will sustain it at the North. (Applause, which was checked by the Court.)

You will see presently, gentlemen, why I have deemed it necessary, at the very outset, to speak thus of what I call a state of civil war,—a condition which, if the learned Judges on the bench, in their charge to you, shall, as matter of law, declare to have existed, then this commission, under which the acts charged in the indictment were perpetrated, forms an absolute legal protection to the accused. Whether such a war exists, is one of the great questions with which the Jury have to deal; and I understand that the Jury *have* to deal with this case—that they are not mere *automata*—that we have not had twelve men sitting in the jury-box for several days as puppets.

The great question for this Jury, absorbing all others, is, Have the twelve men named in the indictment, or has either of them, committed piracy, and thus incurred the penalty of death? It is a very interesting inquiry, gentlemen,—interesting in its historical, national, judicial, and political aspects,—interesting, too, because of the character and description of the accused. We discover that eight of them are foreigners, who have never been naturalized, and do not judicially come under the designation of citizens of the United States. Four of them are what we call natural-born citizens—two from the State of South Carolina, one from North Carolina, and one from Philadelphia. Two of them are in very feeble health; and I am sorry to say, some are not yet of middle age—some quite young, including Passalaigue, who has not yet attained his eighteenth year. I know my fellow-citizens of New York quite well enough to be quite sure that even if there had been any exhibition of popular prejudice, or feeling, or fury, with a view to disturb their judgments in the jury-box, the sympathy that arises properly in every well-constituted heart and mind, in favor of the accused, their relatives and friends, would overcome any such wrong impulse as might be directed to deprive them of that fair trial which, up to this point, they have had, and which, to the end, I know they will have.

Are they pirates and robbers? Have they incurred the penalty of death? Gentlemen, it is a little curious, that during the present reign of Victoria, a statute has been passed in England softening the rigor of the punishment for piracy, and subjecting the person found guilty to transportation, instead of execution, unless arms have been used in the spoliation, or some act done aggravating the offence. I have used the term "pirate," and the term "robber." There is another which, strangely enough, was employed by a Judge of the Vice Admiralty Court in South Carolina, in 1718, who calls these pirates and robbers, as we designate them, "sea thieves;" and I am very glad to find that phrase, because the words robber and pirate have fallen into mere terms of opprobrium; while the word "thief" has a significance and force understood by every man. You know what you thought a "thief" to be, when a boy, and how you despised him; and you are to look at each prisoner mentioned in this indictment, and say, on your consciences as men, in view of the facts and of the law, as expounded by the learned Court, do you consider that the word "thief" can be applied to any one of the men whom I have the honor to assist in defending? That is the great practical question which you are to decide.

[Here Mr. Brady briefly alluded to the question of jurisdiction as already discussed fully enough, and made some observations on the Hicks case, which had been referred to. He then continued as follows:]

This indictment charges two kinds of offence: Piracy, as that crime existed by the *law of nations*,—which law may be said to have been incorporated into the jurisprudence of the United States,—and Piracy *under the ninth section of the Act of 1790*. Piracy by the law of nations is defined by Wheaton, the great American commentator on international law, on page 184 of his treatise on that subject. "*Piracy*" says that eminent gentleman, who was an ornament to the country which gave him birth, and an honor to my profession, "*Piracy is defined by the text writers, to be the offence of depredating on the seas* WITHOUT BEING AUTHORIZED BY ANY SOVEREIGN STATE, *or with commissions from* DIFFERENT SOVEREIGNS *at war with* EACH OTHER." The last part of the definition you need not trouble yourselves about as I only read it so as not to quibble the text. I will read the passage without the latter part. "*Piracy is defined to be the offence of depredating on the seas* WITHOUT BEING AUTHORIZED BY ANY SOVEREIGN STATE." Other definitions will hereafter be suggested.

This leads me to remark upon certain judicial proceedings in Philadelphia against men found on board the Southern privateer "Jefferson Davis," and who were convicted of piracy for having seized and sent away as a prize the "Enchantress." Now my way of dealing with juries is to act with them while in the jury box as if they were out of it. I never imitate that bird referred to by the gentleman who preceded me—the ostrich, which supposes that when he conceals his head his whole person is hidden from view. I know, and every gentleman present knows, that a jury in the city of Philadelphia has convicted the men arrested on the "Jefferson Davis," of piracy. We are a nation certainly distinguished for three things—for newspapers, politics, and tobacco. I do not know that the Americans could present their social individualities by any better signs. Everybody reads the papers, and everybody has a paper given him to read. The hackman waiting for his fare consumes his leisure time perusing the paper. The apple-woman at her stall reads the paper. At the breakfast table, the dinner table, and the supper table, the paper is daily read. I sometimes take my meals at Delmonico's, and have there observed a gentleman who, while refreshing himself with a hasty meal, takes up the newspaper, places it against the castor, and eats, drinks and reads all at the same time. Gentlemen, I say that a people so addicted to newspapers must have ascertained that the men in Philadelphia were convicted; and how the jury could have done otherwise upon the charge of Justices Grier and Cadwalader I am incapable of perceiving. I have the pleasure of knowing both those eminent Judges. My acquaintance with Judge Cadwalader is slight, it is true, but of sufficient standing to ensure him the greatest respect for his learning and character. With Judge Grier the acquaintance is of longer duration; and as he has always extended to me in professional occupations before him courtesies which men never forget, I cannot but speak of him with affection. I have nevertheless something to say about the law laid down by those Judges on that case. No question on the merits was left to the jury, as I understand the instructions. The jurymen were told that *if they believed the testimony, then the defendants were guilty of piracy.* Now, as to the aspect of this case in view of piracy by the law of nations, the question for the jury is, in the first place, *Did these defendants, in the act of capturing the "Joseph," take her by force, or by putting the captain of her in fear,* WITH THE INTENT TO STEAL HER? That is the question as presented by the indictment, and in order to convict under either of the first five counts, the jury must be satisfied, beyond all reasonable doubt, *that in attacking the "Joseph" the defendants were actuated* as described in the indictment, from which I read the allegation that they, "with *force* and *arms, piratically, feloniously, and violently,* put the persons on board in *personal fear and danger of their lives,* and in seizing the vessel did, as aforesaid, *seize,* ROB, STEAL and carry her away." In this the indictment follows the law. Another question of fact, in the other aspect of the case, under the ninth section of the act of 1790, will be, substantially, *whether the existence of a civil war is shown.* That involves inquiry into the existence of the Confederate States as a *de facto* Government or as a *de jure* Government.

The *animus furandi*, so often mentioned in this case, means nothing but the intent to *steal*. The existence of that intent must be found in the evidence, before these men can be called pirates, robbers, or thieves; and whether such intent did or did not exist, is a question entirely for you.

To convict under the ninth section of the Act of 1790, the prosecution must prove that the defendants, being at the time of such offence *citizens of the United States of America*, did something which by that Act is prohibited. You will bear in mind that the Act of 1790, in its ninth section, has no relation except to American-born citizens, and as to that part of the indictment the eight foreigners charged are entirely relieved from responsibility.

Well, on page 104, 5 Wheaton, in the case of *The United States* vs. *Smith*, the Jury found a special verdict, which I will read to illustrate what is piracy and what is not piracy.

[Here Mr. Brady commented on the case referred to, saying, amongst other things,—]

According to the evidence in the case of Smith, the defendants were clearly pirates. They had no commission from any Government or Governor, and were mere mutineers, who had seized a vessel illegally, and then proceeded to seize others without any pretence or show of authority, but with felonious intent. For these acts they were justly convicted.

Now, we say, that this felonious intent as charged against these defendants, must be proved. But what say my learned friends opposed? Why (in effect), that it need not be proved to a Jury by any evidence, but must be *inferred*, as a matter of law, or by the Jury first, from the presumption that every man knows the law; and these men, in this view, are pirates—though they *honestly believed that there was a valid Government called the Confederate States, and that they had a right to act under it*—because they *ought* to have known the law; *ought* to have known that, although the Confederate States had associated for the purpose of forming, yet they had not *completed* a Government; *ought* to have known that, though Baker had a commission signed by Jefferson Davis, the so-called President of the Confederate States, under which he was authorized to act as a privateer, yet the law did not recognize the commission.

There is, indeed, a rule of law, said to be essential to the existence of society, that all men must be taken to know the law, except, I might add, lawyers and judges, who seldom agree upon any proposition until they must.

The whole judicial system is founded upon the theory that judges will err about the law, and thus we have the Courts of review to correct judicial mistakes and to establish permanent principles. Yet it is true that every man is presumed to know the law; and the native of Manilla (one of the parties here charged), *Loo Foo*, or whatever his name may be, who does not, probably, understand what he is here for, is presumed to know the law as well as one of us. If he did not know it better, considering the differences between us, he might not be entitled to rate high as a jurist. One of my brethren read to you an extract from a recent German work, which presents a different view of this subject as relates to foreign subjects in particular cases. I was happy to hear MR. MAYER on the law of this case, more particularly as he declared himself to be a foreign-born citizen; for it is one of the characteristics of this Government—a characteristic of our free institutions—that no distinction of birth or creed is permitted to stand in the way of merit, come from what clime it may.

There is another presumption. Every man is presumed to *intend the natural consequences of his own acts.* Now, what are the natural consequences of the acts done by these defendants? The law on this point is illustrated and applied with much effect in homicide cases. Suppose a man has a slight contention with another, and one of the combatants, drawing a dagger, aims to inflict a slight wound, say upon the hand of the other; but, in the struggle, the weapon enters the heart, and the injured party dies. The man is arrested with the bloody dagger in his hand, the weapon by which death was unquestionably occasioned; and the fact being established that he killed the deceased, the law will presume the act to be murder, and cast upon the accused the burthen of showing that it was something other than murder. I hope, gentlemen, to see the day when this doctrine of law will no longer exist. I never could understand how the presumption of murder could be drawn from an act equally consistent with murder, manslaughter, justifiable or excusable homicide, or accident, but such is the law, and it must be respected.

I say, that neither of the defendants intended, as the ordinary and natural consequence of his act, *to commit piracy or robbery,* though what he did might, in law, amount to such an offence. He intended to take legal prizes, and no more to rob than the man in the case I supposed designed to kill.

The natural consequences of his acts were, to take the vessel and send her to a port to be adjudicated upon as a prize. Now, I state to my learned friends and the Court this proposition—that though a *legal presumption* as to intent might have existed in this case if the prosecution had proved merely the forcible taking, yet if, in making out a case for the Government, any fact be elicited which shows that the actual intent was different from what the law in the absence of such fact would imply, the presumption is gone. And when the prosecution made their witness detail a conversation which took place between Captain Baker and the Captain of the Joseph, with reference to the authority of the former to seize the vessel, and when you find that Captain Baker asserted a claim of right, that overcomes the presumption that he despoiled the Captain of the Joseph with an intent to steal. The *animus furandi* must, in this case, depend on something else than presumption. I will refer you for more particulars of the law on this point, to *1 Greenleaf on Evidence*, sections 13 and 14, and I make this citation for another purpose. When an act is in itself illegal, sometimes, if not in the majority of cases, the law affixes to the party the intent to perpetrate a legal offence. But this is not the universal rule. In cases of procuring money or goods under false pretences, where the intent is the essence of the crime, the prosecution must establish the offence, not by proving alone the act of receiving, but by showing the act and intent; so both must be proved here. Now, I ask, has the prosecution entitled itself to the benefit of any presumption as to intent? What are the facts—*the conceded facts?* Baker, and a number of persons in Charleston, did openly and notoriously select a vessel called the "Savannah," then lying in the stream, and fitted her out *as a privateer*. Baker, in all of these proceedings, acted under the authority of a commission signed by Jefferson Davis, styling and signing himself President of the Confederate States of America. Baker and his companions then went forth as privateersmen, and in no other capacity, for the purpose of despoiling the commerce of the United States, and *with the strictest injunction not to meddle with the property of any other country*. The instructions were clear and distinct on this head, as you know from having heard them read. They went to sea, and overhauled the Joseph; gave chase with the American flag flying—one of the ordinary devices or cheats practiced in naval warfare; a device frequently adopted by American naval commanders to whose fame no American dare affix the slightest stigma. On nearing the Joseph, the Savannah showed the secession flag, and Baker requested Captain Meyer to come on board with his papers. The Captain asked by what authority, and received for answer: "The authority of the Confederate States." The Captain then went on board with his papers, when Baker, helping him over the side, said: "I am very sorry to take your vessel, but I do so in retaliation against the United States, with whom we are at war." Baker put a prize crew on board the Joseph, and sent her to Georgetown; the Captain he detained there as a prisoner. She was then duly submitted for judgment as a prize. These are the facts upon which they claim that piracy at common law is established.

My learned associate, Mr. Larocque, cited a number of cases to show that though a man might take property of another, and appropriate it to his own use, yet if he did so under color of right, under a *bona fide* impression that he had authority to take the property, he would only be a trespasser; he would have to restore it or pay the value of it, but he could not be convicted of a crime for its conversion.

Let me state a case. You own a number of bees. They leave your land, where they hived, and come upon mine, and take refuge in the hollow of a tree, where they deposit their honey. They are your bees, but you cannot come upon my land to take them away; and though they are in my tree, I cannot take the honey. Such a case is reported in our State adjudications. But, suppose that I did take the bees and appropriate the honey to my own use: I might be unjustly *indicted* for larceny, because I took the property of another, but I am not, consequently, a thief in the eye of the law; the absence of intent to steal would ensure my acquittal.

That is one illustration. I will mention one other, decided in the South, relating to a subject on which the South is very strict and very jealous. A slave announced to a man his intention to escape. The man secreted the slave for the purpose of aiding his escape and effecting his freedom. He was indicted for larceny, on the ground that he exercised a control over the property of the owner against his will. The Court held that the object was not to steal, and he could not be convicted. In *Wheaton's Criminal Proceedings*, page 397, this language will be found, and it is satisfactory on the point under discussion.

"There are cases where taking is no more than a trespass: Where a man takes another's goods *openly before him*, or where, having otherwise than by *apparent robbery*, possessed himself of them, he *avows the fact* before he is questioned. This is *only a trespass.*"

Now all these principles are familiar and simple, and do not require lawyers to expound them, for they appeal to the practical sense of mankind. *It is certainly a most lamentable result of the wisdom of centuries, to place twelve men together and ask them, from* FICTIONS *or* THEORIES *to say, on oath, that a man is a thief, when every one of them* KNOWS THAT HE IS NOT. If any man on this Jury thinks the word pirate, robber or thief can be truly applied to either of these defendants, I am very sorry, for I think neither of them at all liable to any such epithet.

But, suppose that the intent is to be inferred from the act of seizing the Joseph, and the defendants must be convicted, unless justified by *the commission issued for Captain Baker,* let us then inquire as to the effect of that commission. We say that it *protects the defendants against being treated as pirates.* Whether it does, or not, depends upon the question whether the Confederate States have occupied such a relation to the United States of America that they might adopt the means of retaliation or aggression recognized in a state of war.

It is our right and duty, as advocates, to maintain that the *Confederate Government was so situated;* and to support the proposition by reference to the political and judicial history and precedents of the past, stating for these men the principles and views which they and their neighbors of the revolting States insist upon; our personal opinions being in no wise called for, nor important, nor even proper, to be stated at this time and in this place.

If it can be shown that the Confederate States occupy the same position towards the Government of the United States that the thirteen revolted Colonies did to Great Britain in the war of the Revolution, then these men cannot be convicted of piracy.

I do not ask you to decide that the Southern States had the *right* to leave the Union, or secede, or to revolt—to set on foot an insurrection, or to perfect a rebellion. That is not the question here. I will place before the Jury such views of law and of history as bear upon the case—endeavoring not to go over the ground occupied by my associates. I will refer you to a small book published here in 1859, entitled, "The History of New York from the Earliest Time," a very reliable and authentic work. In this book I find a few facts to which I will call your attention, one of which may be unpleasant to some of our friends from the New England States, for we find that New York, so far as her people were concerned—exclusive of the authorities—was in physical revolt against the parent Government long before our friends in New England, some of whom often feel disposed to do just what they please, but are not quite willing to allow others the same privilege. I will refer to it to show you what was the condition of things long before the 4th of July, 1776, and to show that, though we now hurl our charges against these men as pirates,—who never killed anybody, never tried to kill anybody,—who never stole and never tried to steal,—yet the men of New York city who committed, under the name of "Liberty Boys," what England thought terrible atrocities, in New York, were never touched by justice—not even so heavily as if a feather from the pinion of the humming bird had fallen upon their heads. I find that, about the year 1765, our people here began to grumble about the taxes and imposts which Great Britain levied upon us. And you know, though the causes of the Revolutionary war are set forth with much dignity in the Declaration of Independence, the contest originated about taxes. That was the great source of disaffection, directing itself more particularly to the matter of tea, and which led to the miscellaneous party in Boston, at which there were no women present, however, and where salt water was used in the decoction. I find that the governor of the city had fists, arms, and all the means of aggression at his command; but at length, happily for us, the Government sent over a young gentleman to rule us (Lord Monckford), who, when he did come, appears to have been similar in habits to one of the accused, who is described as being always idle. The witness for the prosecution explained that separate posts and duties were assigned to each of the crew of the Savannah; one fellow, he said, would do nothing. But he will be convicted of having done a good deal, if the prosecution prevail. A state of rebellion all this time and afterwards existed in this particular part of the world, until the British came and made themselves masters of the city. In the course of the acts then committed by the citizens, and which the British Government called an insurrection, a tumultuous rebellion and revolution, they offered, or it was said they offered, an indignity to an equestrian statue of George III. The British troops, in retaliation, and being grossly offended at the conduct of Pitt, who had been a devoted friend of the Colonists, mutilated the statue of him which stood on Wall street. The remains of the statue are still with us, and can be seen at the corner of West Broadway and Franklin street, where it is preserved as a relic of the past—a grim memento of the perfect absurdity of charging millions of people with being all pirates, robbers, thieves, and marauders.

When the British took possession of this city, they had at *one time in custody five thousand persons*. That was before any formal declaration of independence—before the formation of a Government *de jure* or *de facto*—and yet did they ever charge any of the prisoners with being robbers? Not at all. Was this from any kindness or humane spirit? Not at all: for they adopted all means in their power to overcome our ancestors. The eldest son of the Earl of Chatham resigned his commission, because he would not consent to fight against the colonies. The Government did not hesitate to send to Germany for troops. They could not get sufficient at home. The Irish would not aid them in the fight. The British did not even hesitate to employ Indians; and when, in Parliament, the Secretary of State justified himself, saying that they had a perfect right to employ "all the means God and nature" gave them, he was eloquently rebuked. Even, with all this hostility, such a thing was never thought of as to condemn men, when taken prisoners, and hold them outside that protection which, according to the law of nations, should be extended to men under such circumstances, even though in revolt against the Government.

In October, 1774, the King, in his Message to Parliament, said that a most daring spirit of resistance and disobedience to the laws existed in Massachusetts, and was countenanced and encouraged in others of his Colonies.

Now, I want you to keep your minds fairly applied to the point, on which the Court will declare itself, as to whether I am right in saying, that the day when that Message was sent to Parliament the Colonies occupied towards the old Government a position similar to that of the Confederate States in their hour of revolt to the United States. But we will possibly see that the Confederate States occupy a stronger position.

In the course of the discussion which ensued upon the Message, the famous Wilkes remarked: "Rebellion, indeed, appears on the back of a flying enemy, but revolution flames on the breastplate of the victorious warrior."

If an illegal assemblage set itself up in opposition to the municipal Government, it is a mere insurrection, though ordinary officers of the law be incapable of quelling it, and the military power has to be called out. That is one thing. But when a *whole State* places itself in an attitude of hostility to the other States of a Confederacy, assumes a distinct existence, and has the power to maintain independence, though only for a time, that is quite a different affair.

We remember how beautifully expressed is that passage of the Irish poet, so familiar to all of us, and especially to those who, like myself, coming from Irish ancestry, know so well what is the name and history of rebellion:

"Rebellion—foul, dishonoring word,

Whose wrongful blight so oft hath stained

The holiest cause that tongue or sword

Of mortal ever lost or gained!

How many a spirit born to bless

Has sunk beneath thy withering bane,

Whom but a day's—an hour's success,

Had wafted to eternal fame!"

A remarkable instance, illustrating the sentiment of this passage, is found in the history of that brave man, emerging from obscurity, stepping suddenly forth from the common ranks of men, whose name is so generally mentioned with reverence and love, and who so lately freed Naples from the rule of the tyrant. This brave patriot was driven from his native land, after a heroic struggle in Rome. History has recorded how he was followed in this exile by a devoted wife, who perished because she would not desert her husband; and how he came to this country, where he established himself in business until such time as he saw a speck of hope glimmer on the horizon over his lovely and beloved native land. Then he went back almost alone. Red-shirted, like a common toiling man, he gathered round him a few trusty followers who had unlimited confidence in him as a leader, and accomplished the revolution which dethroned the son of Bomba, and placed Victor Emanuel in his stead. You already know that I speak of Garibaldi. And yet, Garibaldi, it seems, should have been denounced as a pirate, had the sea been the theatre of his failure; and a robber, had he been unsuccessful upon land!

What do you think an eminent man said, in the British Parliament, about the outbreak of our Revolution, and the condition of things then existing in America? "*Whenever oppression begins, resistance becomes lawful and right.*" Who said that? The great associate of Chatham and Burke—Lord Camden. At that time Franklin was in Europe, seeking to obtain a hearing before a committee of Parliament in respect to the grievances of the American people. It was refused.

The Lords and Commons, in an address to the King, declared in express terms, that a "REBELLION *actually existed in* MASSACHUSETTS;" and yet, in view of all that, no legal prosecution of any rebel ever followed. So matters continued till the war effectively began, Washington having been appointed Commander-in-chief. Then some Americans were taken by the British and detained as prisoners. Of this Washington complained to General Gage, then in command of the British army. Gage returned answer that he had treated the prisoners only too kindly, seeing that they were rebels, and that "their lives, by the law of the land, were destined for the cord." Yet not one of them so perished.

In view of these things, even so far as I have now advanced; in view of the sacrifices of the Southern Colonies in the Revolution; in view of the great struggle for independence, and the great doctrine laid down, that, whenever oppression begins, resistance becomes lawful and right,—is it possible to forget the history of the past, and the great principles which gleamed through the darkness and the perils of our early history? Are we to assert that the Constitution establishing our Government is perfect in all its parts, and stands upon a corner stone equivalent to what the globe itself might be supposed to rest on, if we did not know it was ever wheeling through space? Is all the history of our past, its triumphs and reverses, and the glorious consummation which crowned the efforts of the people, all alike to be thrown aside now, upon the belief that we have established a Government so perfect, and a Union so complete, that no portion of the States can ever, under any circumstances, secede, or revolt, or dispute the authority of the others, without danger of being treated as pirates and robbers? The Declaration of Independence has never been repudiated, I believe, and I suppose I have a right to refer to it as containing the political creed of the American people. I do not know how many people in the old world agree with it, and a most eminent lawyer of our own country characterized the maxims stated at its commencement as "glittering generalities." But I believe the American people have never withdrawn their approbation from the principles and doctrines it declares. Among those we find the self-evident truth, that man has an inalienable right to life, liberty, and the pursuit of happiness; that it is to secure these rights that Governments are instituted among men, deriving their just powers from the consent of the governed; and that whenever any form of Government becomes destructive of those ends, it is right and patriotic to alter and abolish it, and to institute a new Government, laying its foundations on such principles, and conferring power in such a form, as to them may seem most likely to secure their safety and happiness. Is this a mockery? Is this a falsehood? Have these ideas been just put forward for the first time? There has been a dispute among men as to who should be justly denominated the author of this document. The debate may be interesting to the historian; but these principles, though they are embodied in the Constitution, were not created by it. They have lived in the hearts of man since man first trod the earth. I can imagine the time, too, when Egypt was in her early glory, and in fancy see one of the poor, miserable wretches, deprived of any right of humanity, harnessed, like a brute beast, to the immense stone about being erected in honor of some monarch, whose very name was destined to perish. I can imagine the degraded slave pausing in his loathsome toil to delight over the idea that there might come a time when the meanest of men would enjoy natural rights, under a Government of the multitude formed to secure them.

Now, what says *Blackstone (1st vol., 212)*, the great commentator on the law of England, when speaking of the revolution which dethroned James II.: *"Whenever a question arises between the society at large and any magistrate originally vested with powers originally delegated by that society, it must be decided by the voice of the society itself. There is not upon earth any other tribunal to resort to."*

Prior to the 23d March, 1776, the legislature of Massachusetts authorized the issuing of letters of marque to privateers upon the ocean, and when my learned friend, Mr. Lord, in his remarks so clear and convincing, called attention to the lawfulness of privateering, my brother Evarts attempted to qualify it by designating the granting of letters of marque as reluctantly tolerated, and as if no such practice as despoiling commerce should be permitted even in a state of war. I will not again read from *Mr. Marcy's* letter, but I will say here that the position he took gratified the heart of the whole American people. He said in substance, If you, England and France, have the right to despoil commerce with armed national vessels we have a right to adopt such means of protection and retaliation as we possess. We do not propose, if you make war upon us, or we find it necessary to make war upon you, that we, with a poor, miserable fleet, shall not be at liberty to send out privateers, but yield to you, who may come with your steel-clad vessels and powerful armament to practice upon us any amount of devastation. No. We never had a navy strong enough to place us in such a position as that with regard to foreign powers. Look at it. Do you think that France or England has any feeling of friendship towards this country as a nation? I do not speak of the people of these countries, but of the cabinets and governments. No. Nations are selfish. Nearly all the laws of nations are founded on interest. Nations conduct their political affairs on that basis. They never receive laws from one another—not even against crime. And when you want to obtain back from another country a man who has committed depredations against society, you do it only by virtue of a treaty, and from no love or affection to the country demanding it. And if this war continues much longer, I, for one, entertain the most profound apprehension that both these powers, France and England, will combine to break the blockade if they do not enter upon more aggressive measures. If they for a moment find it their interest to do so, they will, and no power, moral or physical, can prevent them. I say, then, the right of revolution is a right to be exercised, not according to what the Government revolted against may think, but according to the necessities or the belief of the people revolting. If you belonged to a State which was in any way deprived of its rights, the moment that oppression began resistance became a duty. A slave does not ask his master when he is to have his freedom, but he strikes for it at the proper opportunity. A man threatened with death at the hands of another, does not stop to ask whether he has a right to slay his assailant in self-defence. If self-preservation is the first law of individuals, so also is it of masses and of nations. Therefore, when the American Colonies made up their minds to achieve independence, whether their reasons were sufficient or not, they did not consent to have the question decided by Great Britain, but at once decided it for themselves. Very early in our history, in 1778, France recognized the American Government. England, as you know, complained, and the French Government sent back an answer saying, Yes, we have formed a treaty with this new Government; we have recognized it, and you have no right to complain; for you remember, England, said France, that during the reign of Elizabeth, when the Netherlands revolted against Spain, you, in the first place, negotiated secret treaties with the revolutionists, and then recognized them; but, when Spain complained of this, you said to Spain—The reasons which justify the Netherlands in their revolt entitle them to our support. Was success necessary? Was the doctrine of our opponents correct, that, though people may be in absolute revolt against the parent Government, with an army in the field, and in exclusive possession of the territories they occupy, yet they have no right to be recognized by the law of nations, and are not entitled to the humanities that accompany the conditions of a war between foreign powers? Is success necessary? Why was it not necessary in the case of the Colonies when recognized by France? Why not necessary in the case of the Netherlands when recognized by England? Never has been put forward such a doctrine for adjudication since the days of *Ogden and Smith*, tried in this city in 1806. That was a period when we were in profound peace with all the world. Our new country was proceeding on the march towards that greatness which every one hoped would be as perpetual as it was progressive. We had invited to our shores not only the oppressed of other lands, but all they could yield us of genius, eloquence, industry and wisdom. Among others who came to assist our progress and adorn our history was that eminent lawyer and patriot—that good and pure man whose monument stands beside St. Paul's Church, on Broadway, and may be considered as pointing its white finger to heaven in appeal against the severe doctrines under which these prisoners are sought to be punished. I refer to THOMAS ADDIS EMMETT.

In 1806, two men, Smith and Ogden, were put upon trial, charged with aiding Miranda and the people of Caraccas to effect a revolt against the Government of Spain, which, it was said, was at peace with the United States. They were indicted under a statute of the United States; and if it had turned out on the trial that the United States was certainly in a condition of peace with Spain, they might have been convicted. However, that was a question of fact left to the Jury. The learned Judges, pure and able men, entertained views very hostile to the notions of the accused, and were quite as decided in those views as his honor Judge Grier in the summary disposition he made of the so-called pirates in Philadelphia. The trial came on, and, with the names of the Jurors on that trial, there are preserved to us the names of Counsel, whose career is part of history. Among them were NATHAN SANFORD, PIERPOINT EDWARDS, WASHINGTON MORTON, CADWALLADER D. COLDEN, JOSIAH OGDEN HOFFMAN, RICHARD HARRISON, and MR. EMMETT, already named. Well, there was an effort made to disparage any such enterprise as Miranda's, and any such aid thereto as the accused were charged with giving. The Counsel endeavored to prove that the intent was a question of law, and the fact had nothing to do with it. COLDEN, in his argument, said, "Gentlemen, all *guilt* is *rooted in the mind*, and *if not to be found there, does not exist, and whoever will contend against the proposition* MUST FIGHT AGAINST HUMAN NATURE, AND SILENCE HIS OWN CONSCIENCE."

We do not often find an opportunity, gentlemen, to regale ourselves with anything that emanated from the mind of Mr. Emmett. It is peculiar to the nature of his profession that most of what the advocate says passes away almost at the moment of its utterance. When Mr. Emmett comes to allude to the disfavor sought to be thrown on revolutionary ideas by the eminent counsel for the prosecution, he says:

"In particular, I remember, he termed Miranda a fugitive on the face of the earth, and characterized the object of the expedition as something audacious, novel, and dangerous. It has often struck me, gentlemen, as matter of curious observation, how speedily new nations, like new made nobility and emperors, acquire the cant and jargon of their station.

"Let me exemplify this observation by remarking, that here within the United States, which scarcely thirty years ago were colonies, engaged in a bloody struggle, for the purpose of shaking off their dependence on the parent State, the attempt to free a colony from the oppressive yoke of its mother country is called 'audacious, novel, and dangerous.' It is true, General Miranda's attempt is daring, and, if you will, '*audacious*,' but wherefore is it novel and dangerous?

"Because he, a private individual, unaided by the public succor of any state, attempts to liberate South America. Thrasybulus! expeller of the thirty tyrants! Restorer of Athenian freedom! Wherefore are *you* named with honor in the records of history?

"Because, while a fugitive and an exile, you collected together a band of brave adventurers, who confided in your integrity and talents—because, without the acknowledged assistance of any state or nation, with no commission but what you derived from patriotism, liberty, and justice, you marched with your chosen friends and overthrew the tyranny of Sparta in the land that gave you birth. Nor are Argos and Thebes censured for having afforded you refuge, countenance, and protection. Nor is Ismenias, then at the head of the Theban government, accused of having departed from the duties of his station because he obeyed the impulse of benevolence and compassion towards an oppressed people, and gave that private assistance which he could not publicly avow."

Mr. Emmett, remembering the history of his own name, and the fate of that brother who perished ignominiously on the scaffold for an effort to disenthrall his native land, after that outburst of eloquence, indulged in the following exclamation:

"In whatever country the contest may be carried on, whoever may be the oppressor of the oppressed, may the Almighty Lord of Hosts strengthen the right arms of those who fight for the freedom of their native land! May he guide them in their counsels, assist them in their difficulties, comfort them in their distress, and give them victory in their battles!"

I have thought proper to fortify myself, gentlemen, by reference to this man of pure purpose, finished education, and thorough knowledge of international law, in what I said to you, that the principles which lie at the base of this American revolution, call it by what name you please, have been known and recognized at least as long as the English language has been spoken on the earth, and will be known forever—they furnishing certain rules, the benefit of which, I hope and trust, under the providence of God, after the enlightened remarks of the Court, and through your intervention, may be extended to our clients.

Some people in New England take particular offence at applying these doctrines to the present state of affairs. Has New England ever repudiated them? Has the South ever maintained with more unhesitating declaration, more vigorous resolve, more readiness for the deadly encounter, than the North, these views which I present? Gentlemen, when we look at history, we must take it as we find it. In the war of 1812, the New England States, which had taken offence before at the embargo of 1809, were found, to a very great extent among her people, in an attitude of direct resistance to the war; and they were not afraid to say so. New England said so through her individual citizens. She said so in her public associations. She said so in the form of conventions and solemn resolves. To one of these I will call attention. I do this for no other purpose than to present analogies, principles, and precedents showing what rights belong to those who oppose the Government, or to a state of civil war, or revolution,—that men situated like our clients are not to be treated as pirates and robbers.

I have here a book called "THE UNION FOREVER; THE SOUTHERN REBELLION, AND THE WAR FOR THE UNION." It is an excellent compilation, prepared and published under the superintendence of *James D. Torrey*, of this city. I read from it:

"The declaration of war against Great Britain, June, 1812, brought the excitement to its climax. A peace party was formed in New England, pledged to offer all possible resistance to the war. * * * The State Legislatures of Massachusetts, Connecticut, Vermont, &c., passed laws forbidding the use of their jails by the United States for the confinement of prisoners committed by any other than judicial authority, and directing the jailors at the end of thirty days to discharge all British officers, prisoners of war, committed to them. The President, however, applied to other States of the confederacy for the use of their prisons, and thus the difficulty was, in a measure, obviated."

Thus these men set themselves up pretty strongly against the Government. It is an act of which I do not approve, gentlemen; but, suppose I should say that the men who did that were, because their political sentiments differed from mine, fools or idiots, knaves or traitors, what would you think of the taste or justice of such an observation? It is the intolerance, gentlemen, which abides in the heart of almost every man, woman, and child, and the diffusion of it over the land, that has led to our present dreadful condition. It is the endeavor of one party, or of one set, to set itself up in absolute judgment over the opinions, rights, persons, liberties and hearts of other men. It is that notion which CROMWELL expressed when he said (I quote from memory alone), "I will interfere with no man's liberty of conscience; but, if you mean by that, solemnizing a mass, that shall not be permitted so long as there is a Parliament in England." I have no doubt that the men who did these acts in New England, which we would call unpatriotic, were actuated by conscientious motives; and I want to claim the same thing for the men who, in the South, are doing what is very offensive to you and very offensive to me, and the more offensive because I honestly and conscientiously believe that it is unnecessary and wanton. I know that I differ with very eminent men who belonged to the same political organization as myself when I make that remark; but it is the result of the best judgment that I can form, after a careful and just review of the circumstances attending the present unfortunate breach in our relation to each other. And certainly, gentlemen, it is in no spirit of anger that we, in this sacred temple of justice, should deal with our erring brethren. We do not mean to pronounce, through the forms of justice, from this jury-box, any anathema or denunciation against our fellow-men, *merely* for holding erroneous opinions. All the dictates of every enlightened religion on earth are against any such conduct. I take for granted that there is not one of you who has not some friend engaged in the war, on one side or the other. I took up a newspaper the other morning, and discovered that two men, with whom I had been in the most intimate relations of personal friendship, were in the same engagement, each commanding as colonel, and fighting against each other. They were men who had been close friends during a long series of years—men whom you and I might well be proud to know—each of them a graduate of West Point. One of them is said to have been seen to fall from his saddle, and the fate of the other (COLONEL COGSWELL) is at this moment uncertain. You or I, while we remain loyal to our flag and our country—while we wish and hope for success to our arms in all the conflicts that may occur—may regard with pity men born on the same territory, as well educated, as deftly brought up, as generous and as high minded as ourselves, because we consider them wrong. But, to look upon them as mere outlaws and outcasts, entitled to no protection, sympathy, or courtesy, is something which I am perfectly sure this Jury will never do, and which no community would feel justified or excusable in doing.

Now, let me read more to you from this book:

"On the 18th of October, twelve delegates were elected to confer with delegates from the other New England States. Seven delegates were also appointed by CONNECTICUT, and four by RHODE ISLAND. NEW HAMPSHIRE was represented by two, and VERMONT by one. The Convention met at Hartford, Connecticut, on the 15th of December, 1814. After a session of twenty days a report was adopted, which, with a slight stretch of imagination, we may suppose to have originated from a kind of *en rapport* association with the South Carolina Convention of 1861. We may quote from the report."

Listen to this, gentlemen, and say how much right we have to stigmatize as novel, unprecedented, base, or wicked, the notions on which the Southern revolt is, in a certain degree, founded:

"Whenever it shall appear" (says this Report, the result of twenty days' labor among calm and cool men of New England) "that the causes are radical and permanent, *a separation, by equitable arrangement* will be *preferable to an alliance by constraint among nominal friends, but real enemies, inflamed by mutual hatred and jealousy, and inviting, by intestine divisions, contempt and aggressions from abroad; but a severance of the Union by one or more States against the will of the rest, and especially in time of war, can be justified* ONLY BY ACTUAL NECESSITY."

The report then proceeds to consider the several subjects of complaint, the principal of which is the national power over the militia, claimed by Government. We will not agree, say they, that the general Government shall have authority over the militia; we claim that it shall belong to us. The report goes on to say:

"In this whole series of devices and measures for raising men, this Convention discerns a total disregard for the Constitution, and a disposition to violate its provisions, demanding from the individual States a firm and decided opposition. An iron despotism can impose no harder service upon the citizen than to force him from his home and occupation to wage offensive war, undertaken to gratify the pride or passions of his master. *In cases of deliberate, dangerous and palpable infraction of the Constitution, affecting the sovereignty of a State and the liberties of the people, it is not only the right but the duty of such State to interpose its authority for the protection, in the manner best calculated to secure that end. When emergencies occur, which are either beyond the reach of the judicial tribunals or too pressing to admit of the delay incident to their forms, States which have no common umpire must be their own judges and execute their own decisions.*"

I think that is pretty strong secession doctrine. I do not see that it is possible, in terms, to state it more distinctly. Well, it is true that candid people in that section of the country did not approve these views, but disapproved them; and yet they were the views, clearly and forcibly expressed, of a large number of intelligent and moral people.

Now, this enables me to repeat, with a clearer view derived from history, the proposition that the Confederate States are—*under the law of nations*, and the principles embodied in the Declaration of Independence, sustained in the Revolution, and recognized by our people—in a condition not distinguishable from that of the Colonies in '76, except that, if there be a difference, the position of the Confederates, *in reference to legality, as a judicial question*, is more justifiable, as it is certainly more formidable. This word "secession" is, after all, only a word; a word, as MR. WEBSTER said in one of his great speeches, answering Mr. Calhoun, of fearful import; a word for which he could not according to his views, too strongly express condemnation. But whether you use the word "secession," or the familiar expression, "going out of the Union," or, "not consenting to remain in the Union," the idea is one and the same. Much acumen and ingenuity have been displayed, even by a mind profound as that of Mr. Calhoun—a most acute man and a pure man, as Mr. Webster eloquently attested in the Senate chamber, after the decease of that South Carolina statesman—I say a good deal of acumen has been spent on the question whether a State, or any number of States, have *a* RIGHT UNDER THE CONSTITUTION *to secede from the Union*. It is a quarrel about phrases. It is not necessary in any point of view, political, philological or moral, to use the word "secession" as either excusing or justifying the act of the Confederate States. Suppose I grant, as a distinct proposition, in accordance with what I admit to be the opinion of the great majority of jurists, and orators, and statesmen at the North, that there is no right in a State, under the Constitution, to recede from the Union—what then? I shall not stop to give you the argument with which the South presents a view of the question entirely different from that of the North. Of what consequence is it, practically, whether the right of the State to go out be found in any part of the compact called the Constitution, or be derived from a source extrinsic of it? You (let me suppose) are twelve States, and I am the thirteenth. There is the original Confederacy of States, pure and simple, under the agreement with each other; and there, according to the views of Mr. Webster and the prosecution here, we became constituted in a general Government, or, as Wheaton says, in a "composite Government," giving great power to the general center. Now, what difference does it make, if you twelve States conclude to leave me, whether you do it by virtue of anything contained in the Constitution, or inferable from the Constitution, or in virtue of some right or claim of right that resides out of the Constitution? It is not of the least consequence. I do not care for the word "secession." It would be, at the worst, revolution. In that same great speech of Mr. Webster's against Calhoun, in which I think I am justified in saying he exhausts the subject and makes the most formidable argument against the theory of secession that was ever uttered in the United States, all the conclusion he comes to is this:—"*'Peaceable* secession!' I cannot agree to such a name. I cannot think it possible. *It would be* REVOLUTION." Very well. Of what consequence is the designation? Who cares for the baptism or the sponsors? It is the *thing* you look to. And if they have either the *right* or the *power* to secede or revolutionize, they *may do it*, and there is no tribunal on earth to sit in judgment upon them; though we have the right and the power, on the other hand, to battle for the maintenance of the whole Union. Our friend, *Mr. Justice Grier*, says: "*No band of* CONSPIRATORS *can overcome the Government* MERELY *because they are dissatisfied with the result of an election.*" Now, gentlemen, with the deference he deserves, I would ask the learned Justice Grier, or any other Justice, or my learned friend, Mr. Evarts, how he will proceed to dispose of the case which I am about to put? Suppose that all but one of our States meet in their Legislatures, and, by the universal acclaim, and with the entire approval of all the people, resolve that they will remain no longer in association with the others—what will you do with them? That solitary State, which may be Rhode Island, says: "I have in me the sovereignty; I have in me all the attributes that belong to empire or national existence; but I think I will have to let you go. Whether you call it secession, or rebellion, or revolution, you may go, because *you have the power to go*, if there be no better reason." And power and right become, in reference to this subject, the same thing in the end. Do they not? Is there any relation on earth that has a higher sanction than marriage? So long as two parties, who have contracted that holy obligation, have, in truth, no fault to find with each other, is there any *right* in either to go away from the other? There is no such right, either by the law of God or of man. But there is a *power* to do it, is there not? And if the wife flee from her husband, instead of towards him, or if a husband go from his wife, is there any law of society that can compel them to unite? And why not? Because mankind, though they have perpetrated many follies, have, at least, recognized that this was a remedy utterly impossible. In the relation of partnership between two individuals, does not the same state of things exist? and do not the same arguments suggest themselves? I ask my learned brother what he can do in reference to the ten States that have claimed to secede from the Union, and have organized themselves into a Government? I will give him all the army he demands, and will let him retain in the chair of State this honest, pleasant Mr. Lincoln, who is not the greatest man in the world— nobody will pretend that—but is as good and honest a person as there is in the world. There is not the slightest question but that, in all his movements, he only proposes what he deems consistent with the welfare and honor of the country. I will give my learned brother the army now on the banks of the Potomac, doing nothing, and millions of money, and then I desire him to tell us how, with all these aids, he can coerce those ten States to remain in the Confederacy. What was said by MR. BUCHANAN on the subject, in his Message of December last? "*I do not propose*" said he, "*to attempt any coercion of the States. I believe that it would be utterly impossible. You cannot compel a State to remain in the Union. They may refuse to send Senators to the Senate of the United States. They may refuse to choose electors, and the Government stops.*" Well, I grant you that this is not the view of other men quite as eminent as Mr. Buchanan. I grant you that the great CHIEF JUSTICE MARSHALL—a man to whom it would be bad taste to apply any other word than great, because that includes everything which characterized him—I grant you that brilliant son of Virginia met an argument like this with the great power that distinguished all his judgments, when a question arose in the Supreme Court of the United States, affecting the State of Virginia and a citizen. But of what importance is it what any man thinks about it? What is your theory as compared with your practice? Now, I will give my friend all the power he wants, and ask him to deal with these ten States. Do you believe it to be within the compass of a possibility to compel them to remain in the Union, as States, if they do not wish it?

Thus I reach the conclusion, on even the weakest view of the case for us, that the POWER to secede, and the POWER to organize a Government existing, there is no power on earth which, on any rule of law, can interfere with it, except that of war, conducted on the principles of civilized war.

Now, then, let us look at those Confederate States a little more closely. What says Vattel, in the passage referred to by my learned friend, Mr. Larocque, and which it is of the utmost importance, in this connection, to keep in mind?

[Here Mr. Brady read an extract, which will be found in the argument of Mr. Larocque. [5]]

Is not that clearly expressed, and easy to understand? All of us comprehend and can readily apply it in this case. That resolves the question, if indeed this be the law of the land, into this: *Have the Confederate States, on any show of reason, or without it—for that does not affect the inquiry—attained sufficient* STRENGTH, *and* BECOME SUFFICIENTLY FORMIDABLE, *to entitle them to be treated, under that law of nations, as in a condition of* CIVIL WAR, *even if they have not constituted a separate, sovereign,* and *independent nation?* Really, it seems to me, too clear for doubt, that they have. We had, in the Revolution, thirteen Colonies, with a limited treasury, almost destitute of means, and with some of our soldiers so behaving themselves, in the early part of the struggle, that General Washington, on one memorable occasion, threw down his hat on the ground and asked, "Are these the men with whom I am to defend the liberties of America?" And those of you, gentlemen, who have read his correspondence, know how constantly he was complaining to Congress about the inefficiency of the troops, and their liability to desertion. I remember that he says something like this: "There is no doubt that patriotism may accomplish much. It has already effected a good deal. But he who relies on it as the means of carrying him through a long war will find himself, in the end, grievously mistaken. It is not to be disguised that the great majority of those who enter the service do so with a view to the pay which they are to receive; and, unless they are satisfied, desertions may be expected." He also remarked, at another period, in regard to the troops of a certain portion of our country, which I will not name, that they would have their own way; that when their term of enlistment expired they would go home; and that they would sometimes go before that period arrived. That, I am mortified to say, has been imitated in the present struggle.

Such was the early condition of the Colonies.

Now, the Southern Confederacy have ten States—they had seven when this commission was issued—with about eight millions of people. They have separate State governments, which have existed ever since the Union was formed, and which would exist if this revolution were entirely put down. They have excluded us from every part of their territory, except a little foothold in the Eastern part of Virginia, and "debateable ground" in Western Virginia. We have not yet been able to penetrate farther into the Confederate States. We cannot send even food to the hungry or medicine to the afflicted there. We cannot interchange the commonest acts of humanity with those of our friends who are shut up in the South. I do think, with the conceded fact looking directly into the face of the American people that, with all the millions at the command of the Administration, there is yet found sufficient force and power in the Confederate States to maintain their territory, their Government, their legislature, their judiciary, their executive, and their army and navy, it is vain and idle to say that they are not now in a state of civil war, and that they ought to be excluded from the humanities incident to that condition. Such an idea should not, I think, find sanction in either the heart, the conscience, or intelligence of any right-minded man.

Not only are the facts already stated true, but the Confederate States have been RECOGNIZED AS A BELLIGERENT POWER by FRANCE and ENGLAND, as we have proved by the proclamations placed before you; and *they have been recognized* by OUR *Government as belligerents, at least.* That I submit, as *a distinct question of fact, to the Jury,* unless the Court conceive that it is a pure question of law,—in which case I am perfectly content that the Court shall dispose of it.

And where do I find this? I find it in the *admission of Mr. Lincoln, in his Inaugural Address, that there is to be no attempt at any physical coercion of these States*—a concession that it is a thing not called for, not consistent with the views of the Administration, or with the general course of policy of the American people. According to his view, there was to be no war. I find it in the *correspondence of General Anderson with Governor Pickens*, which has been read in the course of the trial—which of course has been communicated to the Government, will be found among its archives, and of which no disapprobation has been expressed. And here I borrow a doctrine from the District Attorney, who said, when I declared that the legislative branch of the Government had not given their declaration as to what was the true condition of the South, that their silence indicated what it was; and so, the silence of the Government, in not protesting against this correspondence, is good enough for my purpose.

The *proclamation of the President, calling for 75,000 troops*, and then calling *for a greater number*, would, in any Court in Christendom, outside of the United States, be regarded, under international law, as conclusive evidence that those troops were to be used against *a belligerent power*. Who ever heard of EIGHT MILLIONS of people, or of ONE MILLION of people, being ALL TRAITORS, and being ALL LIABLE TO PROSECUTION FOR TREASON AT ONCE. I find this recognition in the *exchange of prisoners*, which we know, as a matter of history, has occurred. I find it in the *capitulation at Hatteras*, at which, and by which, GENERAL BUTLER, of his own accord, when he refused the terms of surrender proposed by Commodore Barron, declared that the garrison should be taken as PRISONERS OF WAR; and that has been communicated to the Government, and no dissatisfaction expressed about it.

And, gentlemen, I rest it, also, as to the recognition by our Government, on the fact to which MR. SULLIVAN so appropriately alluded—*the exchange of flags of truce* between the two contending forces, as proved by one of the officers of the navy. A flag of truce sent to rebels—to men engaged in lawless insurrection, in treasonable hostility to the Government, with a view to its overthrow! Why, gentlemen, it is the grandest, as it is the most characteristic, device by which humanity protects men against atrocities which they might otherwise perpetrate upon each other—that little white flag, showing itself like a speck of divine snow on the red and bloody field of battle; coming covered all over with divinity; coming in the hand of peace, who rejoices to see another place where her foot may rest; welcome as the dove which returned to the ark; coming, I say, in the hand of peace, who is the great conqueror, and before whom the power of armies and the bad ambitions and great struggles of men must ultimately be extinguished. This, of itself, will be regarded by mankind, when they reflect wisely, as sufficient to show that our Government must not be brutal; and we seek to rescue the Administration from any imputation that it wants to deny to the South the common humanities which belong to warfare, by your refusing to let men be executed as pirates, or to make a distinction between him who wars on the deep and him who wars upon the land.

It is very strange if the poor fellows who had no means of earning a meal of victuals in the city of Charleston, like some of those who composed the crew of this vessel, shut up as if in a trap, should be hanged as pirates for being on board a privateer, under a commission from the Confederate States, and that those who have slain your brothers in battle should be taken as prisoners of war, carefully provided for, and treated with the benevolence which we extend to all prisoners who fall into our hands—the same humanities that, as you perceive, are provided for in the instructions from Jefferson Davis, found on board the privateer, directing that the prisoners taken should be dealt with gently and leniently, and to give them the same rations as were supplied to persons in the Confederate service.

But it seems to be suggested in Vattel, and certainly is promulgated in the opinion of Mr. Justice Grier, that, although the Confederate States have obtained any proportions however large, any power however great, there must be some *sound cause*, some *reasonable pretext*, for this revolt. Well, who is to judge of that? We do not, says the Government, admit that the cause is sufficient. The United States Government says there is none. Now, I propose to show you *what the South says on that subject*—to lay before you matters of history with which you are all acquainted—to show you what is supposed by men as able as any of us, as well acquainted with the history of the country, and as pure—what is supposed by them to have created this state of things, entitling the Confederate States to leave us and be a community by themselves. I will hereafter appeal to the late Daniel Webster as a witness that one of the causes assigned by the Southern States for their act is at least the expression and proof of a great wrong done them.

In the first place, a large proportion of our people at the North claim *the right to abolish slavery in places ceded to the United States, or formed by contributions from the States, such as the District of Columbia*. I do not know what my learned friends' views on that subject are, but I know that the two great political parties of the country have had distinct opinions on that subject. By one, it has been steadily maintained, and with great energy, that, so far as the nation has power over the subject of slavery, it shall exercise it to abolish slavery. And the South says: "If you undertake to abolish slavery in any fort, any ceded place, any territory that we have given you for the purposes of the National Government, we will regard that as a breach of faith; for, whether you abhor slavery, or only pretend to abhor it, it is the means of our life. I, a Southerner, whose mother was virtuous as yours—whom I loved as you loved your mother—received from her at her death, as my inheritance, the slaves whom my father purchased—whom I am taught, under my religious belief, to regard as property, and whom I will so continue to regard as long as I live." That is the argument of the South; and if men at the South conscientiously believe that, from their knowledge of the sentiments, factions, or agitations at the North, such as these, there is an intention to make a raid and foray on the institution of slavery, deprive them of all the property they have in the world, and condemn them to any stigma—is it any wonder that they should express and act upon such an opinion?

Next, gentlemen, in the category of their complaints, is the *agitation for the prohibition of what is called the inter-State slave trade*. Next is *the exclusion of slavery from new territory*, which, says the South, "we helped to acquire by our blood and treasure—towards which we contributed as you did. If you had a gallant regiment in the field in Mexico, had we not the Palmetto and other regiments, which came back—such of them as survived—covered with glory?"

This has been the great subject that has recently divided our political parties—the Republican party, so-called, proclaiming with great earnestness and great decency its sincere conviction that it was a moral and political right to prevent slavery from being carried into new territory, and insisting that the slave-owner, if he went there with his slaves, must bring them to a state of freedom.

There is another party of intelligent and upright men, claiming that the South has the same right to go into the Territories with their slaves as the North has to go with their implements of agriculture; and these irreconcilable differences of opinion are only to be settled at the polls, by determining the question which shall have sway either in the executive councils or in the legislation of the Government. A grand subject of debate, for some time, was the endeavor to acquire Texas; and I need not tell you that the great reason why the acquisition of Texas was opposed by the Whig party was, that they thought it might induce to the extension of slavery. When MR. CHOATE made his great speech against it in New York, he confessed that that was the point, and said: "You may be told that this is a new garden of the Hesperides; but do not receive any of its fruits: touch not, taste not, handle not, for in the hour that you eat thereof you shall surely die."

Next, gentlemen, is *the nullification of the Fugitive-Slave Law by several of the States of New England*, which say: "True it is that the Constitution of the United States declares that the fugitive shall be delivered up to his master; true it is that Congress has made provision for his restoration; true it is that the Supreme Court of the United States has declared that he must be given up; but we say—we, a sovereign State—that if any officer of our Government lends any aid or sanction for such purpose he shall be guilty of a crime. If you want any slave delivered to his master, you must do it exclusively by the authority of the Federal Government, by its power and officers." And because, in the city of Boston, MR. LORING, a virtuous citizen, a respectable lawyer, performed, in his official capacity, an official act toward the restoration of a slave to his master, he was removed from his judicial station by the Executive of Massachusetts.

The District Attorney: (To Mr. Evarts) He was not removed for that reason.

Mr. Brady: The District Attorney says he was not removed for that reason. Well, he was removed just about that time. (Laughter.) It was a remarkable coincidence; it was like the caution given to the elder Weller, when he was transferring a number of voters to the Eatonsville election, not to upset them in a certain ditch, and, as he said, by a very extraordinary coincidence, he got them into that very place.

But, gentlemen, this is a solemn subject, and is not to be dealt with lightly. And here it is that I will refer to the great speech of Mr. Webster, in the Senate of the United States, on the *7th of March, 1850*—to be found in the fifth volume of his works, *page* 353. Mr. Webster was a great man, gentlemen, like John Marshall, and he could stand that test of a great man—to be looked at closely. Our country produces an abundance of so-called great men. The very paving-stones are prolific with them. Every village, and hamlet, and blind alley has one, at least. And when we catch a foreigner, just arrived, we first ask him what he thinks of our country, and then, pointing to some person, say, "He is one of the most remarkable men in the country;" until, finally, the foreigner begins to conclude that we are all remarkable men; that, like children, we are all prodigies until we grow up, when we give up the business of being prodigies very soon, as most of us have had occasion to illustrate.

Mr. Webster, I say, was a great man, because he could stand the test of being looked at very near, and he grew greater all the time. There is no incident in my life of which I cherish a more pleasant or more vivid recollection than being once in a small room, with some other counsel, associated with Mr. Webster, about the time he made his last professional effort, when, in a moment of melancholy, one night about twelve o'clock, he came up, and, sitting down on the corner of a very old-fashioned bedstead, put his arm around the post, and proceeded to enlighten and fascinate us with a familiar, and sometimes playful, account of his early life; his first arguments in the Supreme Court of the United States; and the course, in its inner developments, of that life which, in its public features, has been so interesting to the country, and is to be always so interesting to mankind.

"Mr. President," said he, "in the excited times in which we live there is found to exist a state of crimination and recrimination between the North and South. There are lists of grievances produced by each, and those grievances, real or supposed, alienate the minds of one portion of the country from the other, exasperate the feelings, and subdue the sense of fraternal affection, patriotic love, and mutual regard. I shall bestow a little attention, sir, upon these various grievances existing on the one side and on the other. I begin with *complaints of the South*. I will not answer further than I have the general statements of the honorable Senator from South Carolina, that the North has prospered at the expense of the South, in consequence of the manner of administering this Government, in the collecting of its revenues, and so forth. These are disputed topics, and I have no inclination to enter into them. But I will allude to other complaints of the South, and *especially to one which has, in my opinion, just foundation*; and that is, that there has been found at the North, among individuals and among legislators, a disinclination to perform fully their constitutional duties in regard to the return of persons bound to service who have escaped into the Free States. In that respect the South, in my judgment, is right, and the North is wrong. Every member of any Northern Legislature is bound by oath, like every other officer in the country, to support the Constitution of the United States; and the article of the Constitution (Art. iv., sec. 2, subd. 2) which says to these States that they shall deliver up fugitives from service, is as binding in honor and conscience as any other article. No man fulfills his duty in any Legislature who sets himself to find excuses, evasions, escapes, from this constitutional obligation. I have always thought that the Constitution addressed itself to the Legislatures of the States, or to the States themselves. It says that those persons escaping to other States 'shall be delivered up;' and I confess I have always been of the opinion that it was an injunction upon the States themselves. When it is said that a person escaping into another State, and coming, therefore, within the jurisdiction of that State, shall be delivered up, it seems to me the import of the clause is, that the State itself, in obedience to the Constitution, shall cause him to be delivered up. That is my judgment. I have always entertained that opinion, and I entertain it now. But when the subject, some years ago, was before the Supreme Court of the United States, the majority of the Judges held that the power to cause fugitives from service to be delivered up was a power to be exercised under the authority of this Government. I do not know, on the whole, that it may not have been a fortunate decision. My habit is to respect the result of judicial deliberations and the solemnity of judicial decisions. As it now stands, the business of seeing that these fugitives are delivered up resides in the power of Congress and the national judicature; and my friend at the head of the Judiciary Committee (Mr. Mason) has a bill on the subject now before the Senate, which, with some amendments to it, I propose to support, with all its provisions, to the fullest extent. And I desire to call the attention of all sober-minded men at the North, of all conscientious men, of all men who are not carried away by some fanatical idea or some false impression, to their constitutional obligations. I put it to all the sober and sound minds at the North, as a question of morals and a question of conscience: What right have they, in their legislative capacity or any other capacity, to endeavor to get around this Constitution, or to embarrass the free exercise of the rights secured by the Constitution to the persons whose slaves escape from them? None at all—none at all. Neither in the forum of conscience, nor before the face of this Constitution, are they, in my opinion, justified in such an attempt. Of course, it is a matter for their consideration. They, probably, in the excitement of the times, have not stopped to consider of this. They followed what seemed to be the current of thought and of motives, as the occasion arose; and they have neglected to investigate fully the real question, and to consider their constitutional obligations; which I am sure, if they did consider, they would fulfill with alacrity. I repeat, therefore, sir, that here is a well-founded ground of complaint against the North, which ought to be removed; which it is now in the power of the different departments of this Government to remove; which calls for the enactment of proper laws authorizing the judicature of this Government in the several States to do all that is necessary for the recapture of fugitive slaves, and for their restoration to those who claim them. Wherever I go, and whenever I speak on the subject,—and when I speak here I desire to speak to the whole North,—I say that the South has been injured in this respect, and has a right to complain; and the North has been too careless of what I think the Constitution peremptorily and emphatically enjoins upon her as a duty."

Now, gentlemen, this may not accord with the sentiments of some of you; but what right have you—if you should differ entirely with Mr. Webster—if you should believe that there is a great law of our Maker, a higher law than any created on earth, which requires you to refuse obedience to that Fugitive-Slave Law, and makes it a high duty to resist its execution—what right, I say, have you to *force* that opinion upon me? What right have you to require that I shall yield an allegiance to all parts of the Constitution which *you* approve, while *you* refuse it allegiance whenever you please?

They have assigned, as another cause, the notorious fact of *the establishment of what is known as "the Underground Railroad," aiding in the escape and running off of slaves*, and the clandestine removal of property which belongs to the people of the South. They assign, as another, the *rescue of persons claimed as fugitive slaves*, as in the case of the *Jerry rescue*, in or near Syracuse. Passing once through that city, I saw a placard announcing a grand demonstration to come off in honor of that achievement—the forcible rescue of a man from the hands of the Government who was claimed under the provisions of the Constitution and an act of Congress which the Federal Courts had declared to be constitutional!

They refer, also, to the *Creole case, in which, according to the Southern view of the subject, it was virtually and practically decided that no protection was to be afforded to slaves, as property of Southern men, on the high seas*. That is their view of it, and it has been expressed by able men with a great deal of force.

They also refer to the *John Brown raid*, which we have not forgotten—to the invasion of Virginia by that man, who furnished the negroes with implements of slaughter. With the results of that outrage you are all familiar.

They refer to *the general assault on the institution of slavery* which many men at the North have felt it on their conscience to make, including such distinguished orators as LLOYD GARRISON, GERRIT SMITH, the fascinating and silver-tongued PHILLIPS—to whom I have listened with pleasure, much as I detested his sentiments—and THEODORE PARKER, the greatest of them all.

They refer to the declarations of cultivated men at the North, that there were no means to which men might not resort to extirpate slavery; and who, when against them were cited certain passages of Scripture that were supposed to sanction the institution of slavery, fell back on the position that our Constitution was *an "infidel Constitution,"* and that even the Bible was not to be regarded as any authority for such a monstrous error as that.

They refer to *the declaration of Mr. Lincoln,* in one of his addresses to the public, *that Government could not endure half slave and half free.*

But, gentlemen, it was not strange to the American people to know that there was danger of such a secession as has occurred. Some years ago it would have been esteemed the most impossible thing in the world. It has come to happen in your time and mine. It has been predicted. I know a very remarkable instance in which that prediction was stated so clearly that the author of it would seem to have been invested with the spirit and power of prophecy. We cherished the abiding hope that this would not occur; but we now see that the causes moving toward it were irresistible, and that it has become an event of history.

Now, if these seceded States, on any reasoning, good or bad, on sufficient cause, or on a belief that they had sufficient cause, determined that it was not their interest to remain in the Union, they only subscribed to those doctrines promulgated by the Hartford Convention, and agreed with Blackstone, and with all the writers on civil law, that a state of things having happened in which they could have no redress, except by their own act, what course were they to adopt? It is not for you or for me to say, at this time, whether they were right or wrong in their opinions or reasons. I ask you, what course were they to adopt? and what has been the argument heretofore? Why, the argument that, when such a collision of interest took place—when the States supposed that the General Government was trespassing on them and usurping powers, making war upon their institutions, oppressing them, or failing to accomplish the ends for which the Government was established— they should appeal to the Supreme Court of the United States as common arbiter, and that its decision should be final. My friend, Mr. Larocque, has called attention to cases that might happen, of collision between executives of States and of the United States, which could not possibly be submitted to the decision of the Supreme Court of the United States, and I shall not mar his argument or his examples by repeating them or saying anything in addition.

But, suppose that the next Congress should pass a law providing that the State of New York should pay all the expenses of this war for ten years to come, if it last so long; and that every boy of eighteen years, in the State of New York, should be mustered into the service, and coerced to march to Washington within ten days; and that no man in the State of New York should be permitted to go into another State without permission from the Executive; or should do anything of a similar character,—what course would the State of New York have under such circumstances? What course, but disobedience to the law, or insurrection, or revolution? Will my learned friends say that, in a case like that, you could appeal to the arbitrament of the Supreme Court of the United States? Is that so? Has the Supreme Court of the United States, under such circumstances, any way of redressing this wrong? But, suppose I concede that it has: what said the Republican party in reference to that Court? I instance that party, because it has the administration of the General Government.

I remember distinctly that MR. CHASE, now one of the Cabinet officers, in a public speech, shortly before the Presidential election, and MR. WADE, of Ohio, a Senator of the United States—both able men, grave men, honorable men—insisted, before the people, that the Supreme Court of the United States was a mere organization of a certain number of respectable gentlemen, whose opinions were entirely conclusive, no doubt, as between parties litigant, but had no control over the political sentiments, rights, or actions of the people; that their adjudications would be a rule and a precedent in future cases of just the same character; but, beyond that, should have no efficacy whatever.

Gentlemen, I will tell you what, in confirmation of these views, Mr. Lincoln says. In the Message that has been read to you he states exactly the same thing, with the addition that, if we were to submit to the Supreme Court of the United States to decide for us what is right in our Government, and what principles should be maintained, and what course the Administration should adopt, we would be surrendering to the Supreme Court the political power of the nation, and would become a species of serfs and slaves.

When *nullification* reared its head within our territory, and the people of South Carolina claimed that an Act of the General Government was an aggression upon them, against which they had a right to make physical resistance, if necessary, the parties of this country were divided into Whigs and Democrats. They were two formidable parties. There had not then grown up any of these little schismatic organizations, which are, in these latter days, numerous as the eddies on the biggest stream. They were not the days for certain clubs of professional politicians, with very imperfect wardrobes and more imperfect consciences, who sit in judgment on the qualifications of judicial officers, and measure their fitness for office by their capacity to pay money to strikers.

"Now," said that great party claiming to be conservative, "South Carolina has no right to resist. If she has suffered any wrong—if the General Government has attempted any aggression on her—let her submit the whole matter to the Supreme Court of the United States, and let its arbitration be final." Yes; and so the cry continued, till it was supposed that the Supreme Court of the United States was said to have decided that the owner of slave property might carry it into the Territories. Then the note was changed. Instantly the doctrine was reversed, and the Supreme Court was no longer the great, solemn, majestic, and omnipotent arbiter to dispose of this question. Then that Court became "a convention of very respectable gentlemen," who took their seats with black robes, and who were very competent to decide the right of a controversy between John Doe and Richard Roe, but must not lay their hands on politics. Why, they talk about the Earl of Warwick being a King-maker; but your man who seats himself on the head of a whisky barrel, in a corner grocery store, is a greater King-maker than ever Warwick was; and such a man as that, in his prerogatives, is not to be displaced by the Supreme Court of the United States! He may get up a town meeting, at which it will be declared that the doctrine laid down by the Supreme Court of the United States is all preposterous and absurd, and that the people are not going to submit to that tribunal.

There is no recognition, therefore, by this Administration, of the idea that the Supreme Court of the United States is capable of affording any relief in such case as that which has led to the action of the seceded States. And so, that argument being out of the way, I ask you, I ask the learned Court, and I ask our opponents, whether, under the law of nations, as expounded, there was any other course left except that which the seceding States have adopted, assuming that any action whatever was to be taken?

Adjourned till Tuesday, 29th October, at 11 o'clock A.M.

SIXTH DAY.

Tuesday, Oct. 29th, 1861.

Mr. Brady resumed his address, and said:

In the same general line of discussion which I adopted yesterday, I will refer you to a striking passage from a distinguished gentleman, and, when I have read the extract, will state from whom it emanated:

"Any people anywhere, being *inclined* and having the *power*, have a *right* to rise up and *shake off the existing Government*, and *form a new one that suits them better.* This is a most valuable, a most sacred right—a right which, we hope and believe, is to liberate the world. Nor is this right confined to cases in which *the whole people* of an existing Government may choose to exercise it. *Any portion of such people* that *can*, MAY REVOLUTIONIZE and make their *own* of *so much of the territory as they inhabit.* More than this: a *majority* of any portion of such people may revolutionize—putting down a *minority* intermingled with or near about them who may oppose their movements. IT IS A QUALITY OF REVOLUTIONS NOT TO GO BY OLD LINES OR OLD LAWS, BUT TO BREAK UP BOTH AND MAKE NEW ONES."—Appendix Con. Globe, 1st Session 35th Congress, p. 94.

Would you suppose, gentlemen, that it was an ardent South Carolina secessionist who declared that any people may revolutionize and hold mastery of any territory which they occupy? Would you suppose that was from Jefferson Davis, in the Senate of the United States? No, gentlemen; it is from Abraham Lincoln, the President of the United States, when he was a member of Congress, and was delivered on the 12th of January, 1848.

Now, gentlemen, I do not think that an intelligent gentleman born in South Carolina, Kentucky, or Virginia, and educated by his parents in a certain political faith, has not as much right to adhere to it as he has to the religious faith in which he is brought up; and if he should happen to say all that is substantially claimed by these seceding States, he would be sustained by authority quoted here, and have the express sanction of the distinguished and excellent gentleman now at the head of this nation.

Let me now cite to you *Wheaton's International Law, page* 30, in which he says, that "*sovereignty* is acquired by a State, *either* at the *origin* of the civil society of which it is composed, *or* when it *separates itself* from the community of which it previously formed a part, and on which it was dependent." Then he says, that "CIVIL WAR *between the members of the same society is, by the general usages of nations, such a war as entitles both the contending parties to all the rights of war as against each other, and as against neutral nations."*

This, if your honors please, seems to me an answer to the doctrine put forward in this case, that the Judges are to treat this question in reference to the seceding States as it has been viewed by the executive and legislative branches of the Government. If it be true that when a state of civil war exists, as stated by Wheaton, both the contending parties have all the rights of war as against each other, as well as against neutral nations, then it follows very clearly that the seceding States, as well as our own, have all the rights of war; and there is no such rule as that they must have those rights determined only by the executive or legislative branches of the Government, or by both.

And here, gentlemen, let us refer to the matter of blockade, which I take to be the highest evidence of a distinct recognition, by the General Government, of a state of war as between the United and the Confederate States. I see no escape from that conclusion. It is true that a learned Judge in New England, an eminent and pure man, has determined, as we see from the newspapers, that in his judgment it is not a blockade which exists, but merely the exercise by the General Government of its authority over commerce and territory in a state of insurrection—that it is a mere police or municipal regulation. Well, gentlemen, that is not the view taken by the Judges elsewhere. Certainly it is not adopted in this District, where prize cases have arisen, instituted by the Government, which calls this a blockade; and I undertake to say that, in the history of the human race, that word, blockade, never was applied except in a state of war; and the exercise of that power never can occur except in a state of war, because, as the writers inform us, blockade is the right of a belligerent *affecting a neutral, and* ONLY ALLOWABLE IN A STATE OF WAR. Why is it that France and England and all the other countries of the world do not attempt to send their vessels to any of the ports in guard of which we place armed vessels?

A word more about piracy: A pirate is an offender against the law of nations. He is called in the Latin, and by the jurists, the enemy of the human race. Any nation can lay hold of him on the high seas, take him to its country, and punish him. Now, if a ship of war—British, French, Russian, or of any other nation—should meet with a piratical craft, she would capture and condemn it in the courts of her country, and the crew would suffer the punishment of pirates. No one will dispute that proposition. But if such a ship of war had met with the privateer Savannah, even in the very act of capturing the Joseph, would she have captured the Savannah, or attempted to arrest her crew as pirates? If not, does it not follow, as a necessary consequence, that the "Savannah" was not engaged in piratical business? and does it not involve a palpable absurdity to say, that a vessel on the high seas, cruising under a privateer's commission, can be treated as a pirate by the power with which it is at war, and yet be declared not a pirate by all the other powers of the earth? This must be so, if there is anything in the idea that piracy is an offence against the law of nations.

There is not a case in our books where any man, under a commission emanating from any authority or person, was ever treated as a pirate, and so condemned, unless the *actual* intent to steal was proved. In the case of *Aurey* such was the fact, as in many other cases which have been cited. And so it seems that if the Confederate States were either an actual Government, established in virtue of the principles of right to which I have referred, or if a Government *de facto*, as distinguished from one having that right, or if these men believed that the commission emanated from either kind of Government was—lawfully issued—we claim that it is impossible in law, and would be wrong in morals, and unjust in all its consequences, to hold them as pirates, or to treat them otherwise than as prisoners of war. And, gentlemen, I am sorry to say, or rather I am glad to say, that if they should be acquitted of the crime of piracy, they would yet remain as prisoners of war. The worst thing to do with them is to hang them. By preserving their lives we have just their number to exchange for prisoners taken by the enemy.

You, gentlemen, will do your duty under the law, whatever be the consequences. If you have no doubt that these men have committed piracy, they should be convicted of piracy. No threat of retaliation from any quarter should or will influence right-minded men in the disposition to be made of cases where they have to give a verdict according to their conscience, the evidence, and the law of the land.

But the fact of retaliation, as a danger that may ensue from treating as pirates men engaged in war, is referred to by VATTEL in his treatise on the laws of nations. It is one of the considerations which enjoin on Courts and Governments the duty of seeing that, when people are prosecuting civil war, they shall enjoy the humanities of war.

I will now consider this case under the ninth section of the Act of 1790, which is as follows:

"If any *citizen* shall commit any piracy or robbery aforesaid, or *any act of hostility* against the United States, *or any of the citizens thereof*, on the high seas, under color of any commission from *any foreign Prince or State*, or on *pretence* of authority *from any person*, such offender shall, notwithstanding the pretence of any such authority, be deemed, adjudged, and taken to be a pirate, felon, and robber, and, on being thereof convicted, shall suffer death."

Now, in the first place, we say, as was before urged, that statute has no bearing whatever on the case of the eight foreigners, and you are to disregard them entirely in passing upon all the questions which this Act may raise; and we say that it has no bearing on the four Americans before you, even if it be a valid Act and applicable to a case of this character, because, at the time of the acts charged, they were *citizens of another Government, owing it allegiance, receiving its protection, engaged in its service, and bound to perform such service.* We have been told that allegiance and protection are reciprocal. The people of the Southern States would be placed in a very extraordinary condition if the arguments of my learned opponent are to prevail. Look at the citizens of Charleston. There are men in that city who love the Union, among whom is MR. PETTIGREW, an able lawyer, a patriot, and a man of great virtue, talents, and distinction. If those loyal people wanted to leave Charleston and come North, they could not do it. If they felt inclined to utter, at this moment, their sentiments in favor of reunion of the States, it would be an act of folly and danger. They are living in A STATE, under its government and jurisdiction, and bound to perform their duties as citizens. Can they refuse? They may be ordered into the service of the government—sent to sea—enlisted as soldiers. They cannot refuse to fight. If they do, they make themselves amenable to their own Judges. I refer to *1st Hawkins, Pl. Crown*, 87, 89, where it is said:

"*There is a* NECESSITY *that the realm should have a King, by whom and in whose name the laws shall be administered; and the King* IN POSSESSION, *being the only person who either doth or can administer those laws*, MUST BE THE ONLY PERSON *who has a right to that obedience which is due to him who administers those laws; and since, by virtue thereof, he secures us the safety of our lives, liberties, and properties, and all the advantages of Government, he may* JUSTLY CLAIM RETURNS OF DUTY, ALLEGIANCE, AND SUBJECTION."

And BLACKSTONE is equally explicit (*4 Blackstone's Comm.*, 78):

"When, therefore, an USURPER is *in possession*, the subject is *excused* and *justified in obeying and giving him assistance*; OTHERWISE, UNDER AN USURPATION, NO MAN *could* BE SAFE, *if the lawful Prince had a right to hang him for obedience to the power in being, as the* USURPER WOULD CERTAINLY DO FOR DISOBEDIENCE."

3d Inst. (Coke) 7, is to the same point:

"The stat. 11 Henry VII., ch. 1, is declaratory of the law on this subject; and the year books, 4 Edw. IV., 1, 9 Edw. IV., 1, 2, show that it was always the English law."

Our statute, or rather constitutional definition, of *treason*, is a transcript of the English statute of treason; and it is hardly necessary to cite *2 Story on the Constitution, sec. 1799*, to the point that our Courts will construe the Constitution as the English law is construed by the English Courts. And here we observe a marked difference between a revolt by the subjects of a single consolidated Government which is a unit, and the action of one or more States in a Confederacy, or of the people dwelling within them, when such States resolve, as States, to recognize no sovereignty or Government within their territory except that established under their own Constitution.

But I insist upon it that *Congress had no power to pass this 9th section of the Act of 1790*; that the construction put upon it by our opponents is entirely unwarranted; and that it cannot be applied to a case like this. Your honors are aware that in *The case of Smith, 5 Wheaton*, Mr. Webster took the ground that the law was not constitutional, because it did not define piracy otherwise than by referring to the law of nations. The authority given to Congress on that subject is to define and punish piracy and other offences against the law of nations. "To define and punish piracy" is all of the phrase with which I have to deal. Now, you understand, gentlemen, that there is no common-law jurisdiction of offences residing in the United States Courts. They can punish no crime except by statute. Congress had fully defined piracy and robbery in the *eighth* section of the Act of 1790; and, having done so, what power or authority was there in Congress to go on and say that something else should be called piracy, when the definition of it was complete? Let me refer your honors again to the language of the law, which furnishes a strong argument on this subject: "If any citizen shall commit any piracy or robbery *aforesaid*, or any act of hostility against the United States," &c. Does not that clearly recognize and admit that piracy has been defined? and can it be pretended that Congress, under pretence of defining piracy, can provide that a common assault and battery on the high sea shall be piracy? Is there no limitation to that grant? We claim that its terms are just as much a *restriction* as a *delegation* of power. It defines as clearly the limits which the Government shall not transcend, as it does the area which Congress may occupy. You may "define piracy and punish it:" does this mean that you can call anything piracy, whether it be so or not? Suppose Congress passed an Act providing that, if any man *on land* should, during a state of war, attempt to make reprisals on another, it should be piracy, punishable with death: would that be a legitimate exercise of the authority vested in Congress? We claim that it would not, and that it would be a manifest usurpation against the true meaning, spirit, and proper effect of the Constitution.

Again, it has been argued to your honors, and we insist, that *this statute, if it be operative,* only *relates to the case of a person taking a commission from a* FOREIGN *Government or State.* To say that an act of hostility committed by authority of any *person* whatever—using the word "person" to mean a human being—against another, on the high seas, would be piracy, and punishable by death, is a monstrous construction of this Act; and if I understood brother Evarts, in the course of the discussion that took place between him and myself, he conceded that the case which I suggested, of throwing a belaying-pin, by order of the Captain of one vessel, at the Captain of another, on the high seas, *although an act of hostility by one citizen against another,* under pretence of authority from a person, would not come within the law; yet this assault would be within the *very letter* of the Act. Read that law just as it is, and say, after the words "Prince" and "State" have been used, what other term is necessary or apposite. Why, no other, except as in the case of Aurey, an *individual* fitting out an expedition against a foreign Government, and undertaking to grant commissions; or as in the case of *James II.,* who, as shown by Mr. Lord, was an exile in a foreign land, having no territory, no Government, and no subjects; and he was treated in the English Act—from which ours is taken—as a *mere person,* not to be denominated King. I do not mean to concede that the case of *Miranda,* who fitted out the expedition against Spain, assisted by some of our citizens, and granted commissions to privateers, would be a case within the statute of 1790; but if it would, it will not subserve the purposes of the prosecution at all, or be injurious to us. The word "person," in this connection, means a person standing in the same relation to another as a Prince or a State. Gentlemen, that this was never intended to apply between so many States as remained in the Union and those that went out, is a proposition about which Mr. Lord has been heard, and I see no answer to his argument.

Now, there is a dilemma here. If the gentlemen insist that, in the construction I have given, we are right, and that Mr. Jefferson Davis or the Confederate States, in the giving of this commission or authority, are to be regarded as a power or person within my definition, then it is as a foreign power; in which case Capt. Baker is the subject or citizen of that power, and not a citizen of the United States, and not within the Act of 1790. And if the Confederate States is *not* a foreign power, within the construction and meaning of the Act of 1790, then there is no violation of that statute by Capt. Baker, or any one associated with him, if it be true, as I contend, that the pretence of authority must be of one from a foreign source. If they make out that the Confederate States is a foreign power, it is because it is a Government in existence; and if it be a Government in existence, then its commission must be recognized by the law of nations.

Now, I certainly understood, from the opening by the learned District Attorney, that the prosecution did not rely much on the piracy branch of this case; they did not abandon it; they have never said they would not press a conviction upon it. But the strong effort is made to convict under the ninth section of the Act of 1790, saying to you of the Jury, "All you have to find is, that Baker and three of his associates were citizens of the United States; that they were on the high seas; and that, being there, they committed an act of hostility against another citizen of the United States, under pretence of authority from Jefferson Davis; and, then, they are pirates." I think it would have been a little more magnanimous in the Government not to attempt any scheme of this kind. I think, if it be possible to drag these men, manacled, within the construction of a statute which exposes their lives to danger, it is yet not the right way to deal with them. When they were captured they were entitled to be treated either as prisoners of war, or as traitors to the Government. Why were they not indicted for treason?

Now, my learned friend said that this indictment was drawn with the utmost possible care and circumspection, when he spoke of the averment that this act of the defendants was done under pretence of the authority of "*one Jefferson Davis.*" The pleader did not wish to admit, by the language of the indictment, that it was under pretence of any authority from any Government or Confederate States. He wanted to regard it as the act of a mere individual, who, although he claimed to represent so-called States, was, after all, merely a person signing a paper on his own account, and for which he was to take the exclusive responsibility.

I will refer your honors to *Blackstone, 4 vol., p.* 72, where he interprets this statute of *11 and 12 William III., chap.* 4, to relate to acts done under color of a commission from a *foreign power*, and it was never supposed to have meant anything else. In 1819, Great Britain passed a law making it a crime for British subjects to be connected in any way with the sending out of vessels to cruise against a power at peace with England. By the *18th George II., chap.* 30, it is made piracy, in time of war, for English subjects to commit hostilities of any kind against fellow subjects. How did that act become necessary in the legislation of England, if the previous law had already provided for the same thing? That, certainly, is a question of some importance in this case. We have statutes that punish citizens of the United States, under certain circumstances when they are engaged in privateering; and there have been trials and convictions under these statutes, as your honors will find by referring to *Wharton's State Trials.*

We contend, therefore, that the ninth section of the Act of 1790, as construed by our opponents, would be unconstitutional; that it only applies, if valid, to acts done under authority of a foreign power or person; that if Jefferson Davis was, or represented, such foreign power, then the defendants were subjects of that power, not citizens of the United States, and not within the Act; if he were not or did not represent a foreign power, the Act does not apply to the case; and so, in every view of the subject, there is no right to convict any of these men under this Act.

I will now cite some authorities on the question of *variance* made by my friend, Mr. Lord, in describing this commission as a pretence of authority from one Jefferson Davis. Certainly, in law, that commission is the act and authority of the Confederate States. There can be no dispute about that.

I refer my learned opponents to *Wharton's Criminal Treatise, at pps. 78, 91, 93, 94 and 96*, for these two propositions: In the first place, that, where a new offence is created by statute, the utmost particularity is required, when drawing the indictment, to set forth all the statutory elements of the offence; and, in the second place, what is thus averred must be proved strictly as laid. Well, it may seem to you, gentlemen, rather a technical and immaterial question, whether this was set out as a pretence of authority from one Jefferson Davis, or from the Confederate States,—and it is. But, nevertheless, it is a legal technicality; and these prisoners, if it be well founded, have a right to the benefit of it. It is very little that I have to read from this book, for the propositions are pointedly stated:

Page 91. "It is a general rule that, in regard to offences created by statutes, it is necessary that the defendant be brought within all the material words of the statute; and nothing can be taken by intendment."

Page 93. "Defects in the description of a statutory offence will not be aided by a verdict, nor will the conclusion *contra formam statutis* cure it."

Page 94. "An indictment under the Stat. 5th Elizabeth, which makes it high treason to clip round or file any of the coin of the realm for wicked lucre or gain sake,—it was necessary to charge the offence as being committed for wicked lucre or gain sake, otherwise the indictment was bad. In another case, an indictment on that part of the black act which made it felony willfully or maliciously to shoot at a person in a dwelling-house was held to be bad, because it charged the offence to have been done '*unlawfully and maliciously*,' without the word '*willfully*.'"

That is technical enough, I admit, but it emanates from high authority.

[Mr. Brady read other passages from Wharton, and said]:

And, now, what relates more particularly to the matter in hand, is the case of *The United States* vs. *Hardiman, 13 Peters*, 176. In that case the defendant was indicted for receiving a fifty-dollar treasury note, knowing it to have been stolen out of the mail of the United States. The indictment was under the 45th section of the Post-Office Law. The thing stolen was described as a fifty-dollar *treasury note, bearing interest at one per cent.*; and it turned out to be a treasury note which, although of fifty-dollars' denomination, bore interest at the rate of *one mill per cent.*; and the Court held the variance to be fatal. Now, we claim that to describe the commission as emanating from one Jefferson Davis, when in fact it emanated from the Confederate States, is such a variance as is here referred to; and, on that ground, the indictment is not sustained.

The argument is made here, that, no matter what publicists may say,—no matter what Courts of other countries may declare as international law, about the organization of government or the creation of powers *de jure* or *de facto*,— this Court has nothing to do with the debate; that your honors have simply to inquire whether Mr. Lincoln, the President, has said, or whether Congress has said, a certain thing, and the matter proceeds no further; that the citizen is not entitled to have a trial, in a Court of Justice, on the question whether, being in a state of revolt, a civil war does in fact exist; and that the right of trial by Jury does not, as to such a question, exist at all.

It is utterly absurd to have you here, gentlemen, if all that is necessary to be shown against these men is the proclamation by the Executive, and an Act of Congress calling them rebels and pirates. Is there any trial by Jury under such circumstances? The form of it may exist, but not the substance. It is a mockery. No, your honors; this question, as to the *status* of the Confederate States, is a judicial question, when it arises in a Court of Justice. It is a juridical question. It is one of which Courts may take cognizance—must take cognizance—in view of and with the aid of that international law which is part of the common law, part of the birthright of all our citizens, and to the benefit and immunities as well as responsibilities of which they are subject and may make claim.

Otherwise it would lead to this most extraordinary consequence, that, whenever any portion of a State or any State of a Confederacy, either here or elsewhere, revolts, and attempts to withdraw itself from the old Government, the old Government shall be the only judge on earth to determine whether the seceders, or the revolutionists, or the rebels, shall be treated as pirates or robbers.

Would it not be very strange if our nation should extend to those who revolt in any other country, when they have attained a certain formidable position before the world, the rights and humanities of civil war; and that, when any of our own people, under the claim of right and justice, however ill-founded, unfortunate, or otherwise, put themselves in an attitude of hostility to the Government, they are to be treated as outlaws and enemies to the human race, having no rights whatever incident to humanity and growing out of benign jurisprudence?

Then, apart from all that has been said, *if the United States made war upon the South, as it certainly did by the act of the President, it is one of the propositions which these men may insist upon, that the States had a right to defend themselves, to make reprisals, to issue letters of marque, and that they had all the other rights of warfare.* On this point, Mr. Larocque has given copious and apposite arguments and citations. The Constitution itself, when it comes to prohibit a State from making war and granting letters of marque, distinctly recognizes that privateers are not illegal. It has limited the prohibition against granting letters of marque, &c., by saying that a State may do so in the case of invasion, and when the danger is imminent.

Now, what are the facts before us here which raise this as a question in the case? There was no declaration of war by our Government, and none by the South; but at a certain time there was a firing on an unarmed vessel entering Charleston harbor—the "Star of the West." General Anderson, who was in command of Fort Sumter—whether acting under the authority of the Government, or not, does not very clearly appear in the case—sent a communication to Governor Pickens, to the effect that, if unarmed vessels were to be fired upon, he wished to be informed of the fact, saying, "You have not yet declared war against the United States;" and that, if the offence were repeated, he should open his batteries on Charleston.

That is the substance of it. Mr. Pickens retorted, saying, substantially, that they would maintain their positions. The next thing in order is the proclamation by the President, for the organization of the army, for the purpose, as he said, of retaking our forts. When, therefore, that condition of things had arrived, war was begun by the United States upon the South.

You may say it was not a war. You may say it was the employment of means to put down an insurrection. I care not for the mere use of language. It was, in effect and substance, a war against those States which claimed the authority to hold territory for themselves, under a separate and independent Government; and that would give them the right to oppose force by force, unless, indeed, the whole thing was a tumultuous act—a mere act of treason—and so to be regarded in all aspects of the case.

There is a principle applicable to this whole case, referred to by MR. DUKES, in his argument—the doctrine of *respondeat superior*, of which he gave some instances. These men may go wholly free by the law of nations, and yet the State which, in the name of Jefferson Davis or the Confederate States, issued this commission, would be responsible to the General Government for the consequences. We had a memorable instance of this in this State, some years since. You will remember that a man, named MCLEOD, was charged with coming across the lines from Canada and setting fire to an American steamer. He was tried, and acquitted on the ground—not very complimentary to him—that he did not do any such thing, although he had boasted of it. It was rather humiliating to be absolved of crime on the ground that the accused was a liar; yet still that is the history of the case. Now, there was a diplomatic correspondence in reference to this incident, as some of you well remember. Great Britain insisted that Mr. McLeod must not be tried at all; that the American Government had no authority to take cognizance of the act; and that we must look to Great Britain for redress. Well, gentlemen, I am sorry to say that our Government has very often acted like the Government of England. Each of us has been quite willing, occasionally, to swoop down on an inferior power, as the vulture on its prey; but, whenever there was a possibility of conflict with a power equal to either, a great deal of caution and reserve has been evinced. We have been for years—almost from the foundation of our Government—truckling to British ideas, British principles, British feelings, and British apprehensions, in a manner which has not done us any honor; and we see to-day what reward we are enjoying for it. There has not been a public speaker in England who has ever designated us, for a long period, by any other name than that of the Anglo-Saxon race— a designation which includes but one element of even the race which exists in the British Islands, omitting the gentle, noble, and effective traits imported into it by the Normans, and excluding those countrymen of my ancestors who do not like to be outside when there is anything good going on within. What said our Government to that? I understand that they distinctly admitted that McLeod was not amenable to our jurisdiction; but the State of New York held on, in virtue of its jurisdiction and sovereignty, and Mr. McLeod had to be tried, and was tried and acquitted. There the principle of *respondeat superior* was acknowledged by our Government; and I believe that is the policy upon which it has acted on every occasion when the case arose.

Gentlemen, I will detain you but a few moments longer. I have endeavored to show, in the first place, that these men cannot be convicted of piracy, because they had not the intent to steal, essential to the commission of that offence, and that you are the judges whether that intent did or did not exist. If it did not, then the accused men are entitled to acquittal on that ground. If the Act of 1790 be constitutional, and if it can be construed to extend to a case like this, then eight of the prisoners are to be discharged—being foreigners, not naturalized; and the other four, also—having acted under a commission issued in good faith by a Government which claimed to have existence, acted upon in good faith by themselves, and with the belief that they were not committing any lawless act of aggression. In this connection I hold it to be immaterial whether the Confederate Government was one of right, established on sufficient authority according to the law of nations, and to be recognized as such, or whether it was merely a Government in fact. We claim, beyond all that, and apart from the question of Government in law or Government in fact, that there exists a state of civil war; which entitles these defendants to be treated in every other manner than as pirates; which may have rendered them amenable to the danger of being regarded as prisoners of war, but which has made it impossible for them to be ever dealt with as felons. I am sorry that it has become necessary in this discussion to open subjects for debate, any inquiry about which, at this particular juncture in our history, is not likely to be attended with any great advantage. But, like my brethren for the defence, I have endeavored to state freely, fearlessly, frankly and correctly, the positions on which the defendants have a right to rely before the Court and before you. It would have been much more acceptable to my feelings, as a citizen, if we had been spared the performance of any such duty. But, gentlemen, it is not our fault. The advocate is of very little use in the days of prosperity and peace, in the periods of repose, in protecting your property, or aiding you to recover your rights of a civil nature. It is only when public opinion, or the strong power of Government, the formidable array of influence, the force of a nation, or the fury of a multitude, is directed against you, that the advocate is of any use. Many years ago, while we were yet Colonies of Great Britain, there occurred on this island what is known as the famous negro insurrection,—the result of an idle story, told by a worthless person, and yet leading to such an inflammation of the public mind that all the lawyers who then practiced at the bar of New York (and it is the greatest stigma on our profession of which the world can furnish an example) refused to defend the accused parties. One of them was a poor priest, of, I believe, foreign origin. The consequence was, that numerous convictions took place, and a great many executions. And yet all mankind is perfectly satisfied that there never was a more unfounded rumor—never a more idle tale—and that judicial murders were never perpetrated on the face of the earth more intolerable, more inexcusable, more without palliation. How different was it in Boston, at the time of what was called the massacre of Massachusetts subjects by British forces! The soldiers, on being indicted, sought for counsel; and they found two men, of great eminence in the profession, to act for them. One of them was Mr. Adams, and the other Mr. Quincy. The father of Mr. Quincy addressed a letter, imploring him, on his allegiance as a son, and from affection and duty toward him, not to undertake the defence of these men. The son wrote back a response, recognizing, as he truly felt, all the filial affection which he owed to that honored parent, but, at the same time, taking the high and appropriate ground that he must discharge his duty as an advocate, according to the rules of his profession and the obligation of his official oath, whatever might be the result of his course.

The struggles, in the history of the world, to have, in criminal trials, an honest judiciary, a fearless jury, and a faithful advocate, disclose a great deal of wrong and suffering inflicted on advocates silenced by force, trembling at the bar where they ought to be utterly immovable in the discharge of their duty—on juries fined, and imprisoned, and kept lying in dungeons for years, because they dared, in State prosecutions, to find verdicts against the direction of the Court. The provisions of our own Constitution, which secure to men trial by jury and all the rights incident to that sacred and invaluable privilege, are the history of wrong against which those provisions are intended to guard in the future. This trial, gentlemen, furnishes a brilliant illustration of the beneficial results of all this care. Nothing could be fairer than the trial which these prisoners have had; nothing more admirable than the attention which you have given to every proceeding in this case. I know all the gentlemen on that Jury well enough to be perfectly certain that whatever verdict they render will be given without fear or favor, on the law of the land, as they shall be informed it does exist, on a calm and patient review of the testimony, with a due sympathy for the accused, and yet with a proper respect for the Government, so that the law shall be satisfied and individual right protected. But, gentlemen, I do believe most sincerely that, unless we have deceived ourselves in regard to the law of the land, I have a right to invoke your protection for these men. The bodily presence, if it could be secured, of those who have been here in spirit by their language, attending on this debate and hovering about these men to furnish them protection—Lee, and Hamilton, and Adams, and Washington, and Jefferson, all whose spirits enter into the principles for which we contend—would plead in their behalf. I do wish that it were within the power of men, invoking the great Ruler of the Universe, to bid these doors open and to let the Revolutionary Sages to whom I have referred, and a Sumter, a Moultrie, a Marion, a Greene, a Putnam, and the other distinguished men who fought for our privileges and rights in the days of old, march in here and look at this trial. There is not a man of them who would not say to you that you should remember, in regard to each of these prisoners, as if you were his father, the history of Abraham when he went to sacrifice his son Isaac on the mount—the spirit of American liberty, the principles of American jurisprudence, and the dictates of humanity, constituting themselves another Angel of the Lord, and saying to you, when the immolation was threatened, "Lay not your hand upon him." (Manifestations of applause in Court.)

ARGUMENT OF WILLIAM M. EVARTS, ESQ., FOR THE PROSECUTION.

May it please your Honors, and Gentlemen of the Jury:

A trial in a Court of Justice is a trial of many things besides the prisoners at the bar. It is a trial of the strength of the laws, of the power of the Government, of the duty of the citizen, of the fidelity to conscience and the intelligence of the Jury. It is a trial of those great principles of faith, of duty, of law, of civil society, that distinguish the condition of civilization from that of barbarism. I know no better instance of the distinction between a civilized, instructed, Christian people, and a rude and barbarous nation, than that which is shown in the assertions of right where might and violence and the rage of passion in physical contest determine everything, and this last sober, discreet, patient, intelligent, authorized, faithful, scrupulous, conscientious investigation, under the lights of all that intelligence with which God has favored any of us; under that instruction which belongs to the learned and accredited expounders of the law of an established free Government; under the aid of, and yet not misled by, the genius or eloquence of advocates on either side.

But, after all, the controlling dominion of duty to the men before you in the persons of the prisoners, to the whole community around you, and to the great nation for which you now discharge here a vital function for its permanence and its safety,—your duty to the laws and the Government of your country (which, giving its protection, requires your allegiance, and finds its last and final resting-place, both here and in England, in the verdicts of Juries),—your duty to yourselves,—requires you to recognize yourselves not only as members of civil society, but as children of the "Father of an Infinite Majesty," and amenable to His last judgment for your acts. Can any of us, then, fail to feel, even more fully than we can express, that sympathies, affections, passions, sentiments, prejudices, hopes, fears, feelings and responsibilities of others than ourselves are banished at once and forever, as we enter the threshold of such an inquiry as this, and never return to us until we have passed from this sacred precinct, and, with our hands on our breasts and our eyes on the ground, can humbly hope that we have done our duty and our whole duty?

Something was said to you, gentlemen of the Jury, of the unwonted circumstances of the prosecution, by the learned counsel who, many days ago, and with an impressiveness that has not yet passed away from your memory, opened on behalf of the prisoners the course of this defence.

He has said to you that the number of those whose fate, for life or for death, hangs on your verdict, is equal to your own—hinting a ready suggestion that that divided responsibility by which twelve men may sometimes shelter themselves, in weighing in the balance the life of a single man, is not yours. Gentlemen, let us understand how much of force and effect there is in the suggestion, and how truly and to what extent the responsibility of a Jury may be said to include this issue of life and death. In the first place, as Jurymen, you have no share or responsibility in the wisdom or the justice of those laws which you are called upon to administer. If there be defects in them—if they have something of that force and severity which is necessary for the maintenance of Government and the protection of peace and property, and of life on the high seas—you have had no share in their enactment, and have no charge, at your hands, of their enforcement. In the next place, you have no responsibility of any kind in regard to the discretion of the representatives of this Government in the course which they choose to take, as to whether they will prosecute or leave unprosecuted. You do not, within the limits of the inquiry presented to you, dispose of the question, why others have not been presented to you; nor may that which has been done in a case not before you, serve as a guide for the subject submitted to your consideration. So, too, you have no responsibility of any kind concerning the course or views of the law which this tribunal may give for your guidance. The Court does not make the law, but Congress does. The Court declares the law as enacted by the Government, and the Jury find the facts—giving every scrutiny, every patient investigation, every favor for life, and every reasonable doubt as to the facts, to the prisoners. Having disposed of that duty, as sober, intelligent and faithful men, graduating your attention only by the gravity of the inquiry, you have no further responsibility. But I need not say to you, gentlemen, that if any civilized Government is to have control of the subject of piracy—if pirates are to be brought within the jurisdiction of the criminal law—the very nature of the crime involves the fact that its successful prosecution necessarily requires that considerable numbers shall be engaged in it. I am quite certain that, if my learned friends had found in the circumstances of this case nothing which removed it out of the category of the heinous crime of private plunder at sea, exposing property and life, and breaking up commerce, they would have found nothing in the fact that a ship's crew was brought in for trial, and that the number of that crew amounted to twelve men, that should be pressed to the disturbance of your serene judgment, in any disposition of the case. Now, gentlemen, let us look a little into the nature of the crime, and into the condition of the law.

The penalty of the crime of piracy or robbery at sea stands on our statute books heavier than the penalty assigned for a similar crime committed on land—which is, in fact, similar, so far as concerns its being an act of depredation. It may be said, and it is often argued, that, when the guilt of two offences is equal, society transcends its right and duty when it draws a distinction in its punishments; and it may be said, as has been fully argued to you—at least, by implication, in the course of this case—that the whole duty and the whole responsibility of civil Governments, in the administration of criminal law and the punishment of crime, has to do with retributive vengeance, as it were, on the moral guilt of the prisoner. Now, gentlemen, I need not say to you, who are experienced at least in the common inquiries concerning Governments and their duties, that, as a mere naked and separate consideration for punishing moral guilt, Government leaves, or should leave, vengeance where it belongs—to Him who searches the heart and punishes according to its secret intents—drawing no distinction between the wicked purpose which fully plans, and the final act which executes that purpose. The great, the main duty—the great, the main right—of civil society, in the exercise of its dominion over the liberties, lives, and property of its subjects, is the good of the public, in the prevention, the check, the discouragement, the suppression of crime. And I am sure that there is scarcely one of us who, if guilt, if fault, if vice could be left to the punishment of conscience and the responsibility of the last and great assize, without prejudice to society, without injury to the good of others, without, indeed, being a danger and a destruction to all the peace, the happiness, and the safety of communities, would not readily lay aside all his share in the vindictive punishments of guilty men. But society, framed in the form and for the purposes of Government, finds, alas! that this tribunal of conscience, and this last and future accountability of another world, is inadequate to its protection against wickedness and crime in this.

You will find, therefore, in all, even the most enlightened and most humane codes of laws, that some necessary attention is paid to the predominant interest which society has in preventing crime. The very great difficulty of detecting it, the circumstances of secrecy, and the chances of escape on the part of the criminal, are considerations which enter into the distribution of its penalties. You will find, in a highly commercial community, like that of England, and to some extent—although, I am glad to say, with much less severity—in our own, which is also a highly commercial community, that frauds against property, frauds against trade, frauds in the nature of counterfeiting and forgery, and all those peaceful and not violent but yet pernicious interferences with the health and necessary activity of our every-day life, require the infliction of severe penalties for what, when you take up the particular elements of the crime, seems to have but little of the force, and but little of the depth of a serious moral delinquency.

The severity of the penalties for passing counterfeit money are inflicted upon the poor and ignorant who, in so small a matter as a coin of slight value, knowingly and intelligently, under even the strongest impulses of poverty, are engaged in the offence. Now, therefore, when commercial nations have been brought to the consideration of what their enactments on the subject of piracy shall be, they have taken into account that the very offence itself requires that its commission should be outside of the active and efficient protection of civil society—that the commission of the crime involves, on the part of the criminals, a fixed, deliberate determination and preparation—and that the circumstances under which the victims, either in respect of their property or of their lives, are exposed to these aggressions, are such as to make it a part of the probable course of the crime, that the most serious evils and the deepest wounds may be inflicted. Now, when a crime, not condemned in ethics or humanity, and which the positive enactments of the law have made highly penal, yet contains within itself circumstances that appeal very strongly to whatever authority or magistrate has rightful control of the subject for a special exemption, and special remission, and special concession from the penalty of the law, where and upon what principles does a wise and just, a humane and benignant Government, dispose of that question? I agree that, if crimes which the good of society requires to be subjected to harsh penalties, must stand, always and irrevocably; upon the mere behest of judicial sentence, there would be found an oppression and a cruelty in some respects, that a community having a conscientious adherence to right and humanity would scarcely tolerate. Where, then, does it wisely bestow all the responsibility, and give all the power that belongs to this adjustment, according to the particular circumstances of the moral and personal guilt, which must be necessary, and is always conceded? Why, confessedly, to the pardoning power, alluded to on one side or the other—though chiefly on the part of the prisoners' counsel—in the course of this trial. Now, you will perceive, at once, what the difference is between a Court, or a Jury, or a public prosecuting officer, yielding to particular circumstances of actual or of general qualification of a crime charged,—so that the law shall be thwarted, and the certainty and directness of judicial trial and sentence be made the sport of sympathy, or of casual or personal influences,—and placing the pardoning power where it shall be governed by the particular circumstances of each case, so that its exercise shall have no influence in breaking down the authority of law, or in disturbing the certainty, directness, and completeness of judicial rules. For, it is the very nature of a pardon,—committed to the Chief Magistrate of the Federal Union in cases of which this Court has jurisdiction, and to the Chief Magistrate of every State in the Union in cases of which the State tribunals take cognizance,—that it is a recognition of the law, and of the sentence of the law, and leaves the laws undisturbed, the rules for the guidance of men unaffected, the power and strength of the Government unweakened, the force of the judiciary unparalyzed, and yet disposes of each case in a way that is just, or, if not just, is humane and clement, where the pardon is exercised.

Now, gentlemen, I shall say nothing more on the subject of pardon. It is a thing with which I have nothing to do—with which this learned Court has nothing to do—with which you, as Jurymen, have nothing to do—beyond the fact that this beneficent Government of ours has not omitted from its arrangement, in the administration of its penal laws, this divine attribute of mercy.

Now, there being the crime of piracy or robbery on the high seas, which the interests of society, the protection of property and of life, the maintenance of commerce, oblige every State and every nation, like ours, to condemn—what are the circumstances, what are the acts, that, in view of the law, amount to piracy? You will understand me that, for the present, I entirely exclude from your consideration any of the particular circumstances which are supposed to give to the actual crime perpetrated a public character, lifting it out of the penal law that you administer, and out of the region of private crime, into a field of quite different considerations. They are, undoubtedly, that the act done shall be with intent of depriving the person who is in possession of property, as its owner, or as the representative of that owner, of that property. That is what is meant by the Latin phrase, with which you are quite as familiar now, at least, as I, *animo furandi*—with the intention of despoiling the owner of that which belongs to him. And, to make up the crime of robbery on land, in distinction from larceny or theft, as we generally call it, (though theft, perhaps, includes all the variety of crime by which the property of another is taken against his will,) robbery includes, and *piracy*, being robbery at sea, includes, the idea that it is done with the application, or the threat, or the presence of force. There must be actual violence, or the presence and exhibition of power and intent to use violence, which produces the surrender and delivery of the property. Such are the ingredients of robbery and piracy. And, gentlemen, these two ingredients are all; and you must rob one or the other of them of this, their poison, or the crime is completely proved, when the fact of the spoliation, with these ingredients, shall have been proved. The use that the robber or the pirate intends to make of the property, or the justification which he thinks he has by way of retaliation, by way of injury, by way of provocation, by way of any other occasion or motive that seems justifiable to his own conscience and his own obedience to any form whatever of the higher law, has nothing to do with the completeness of the crime, unless it come to what has been adverted to by the learned counsel, and displayed before you in citations from the law-books—to an honest, however much it may be a mistaken and baseless, idea that the property is really the property of the accused robber, of which he is repossessing himself from the party against whom he makes the aggression.

Now, unless, in the case proved of piracy, or robbery on land, there be some foundation for the suggestion that the willful and intentional act of depriving a party of his property rests upon a claim of the robber, or the pirate, that it is his own property (however baseless may be the claim), you cannot avoid, you cannot defeat, the criminality of the act of robbery, within the intention of the law, by showing that the robber or the pirate had, in the protection of his own conscience, and in the government of his own conduct, certain opinions or views that made it right for him to execute that purpose. Thus, for instance, take a case of morals: A certain sect of political philosophers have this proposition as a basis of all their reasoning on the subject of property,—that is, that property, the notion of separate property in anything, as belonging to anybody, is theft; that the very notion that I can own anything, whatever it may be, and exclude other people from the enjoyment of it, is a theft made by me, a wrongful appropriation, when all the good things in this world, in the intention of Providence, were designed for the equal enjoyment of all the human race. Well, now, a person possessed of that notion of political economy and of the moral rights and duties of men, might seek to avail himself of property owned and enjoyed by another, on the theory that the person in possession of it was the original thief, and that he was entitled to share it. I need not say to you that all these ideas and considerations have nothing whatever to do with the consideration of the moral intent with which a person is despoiled of his property.

Now, with regard to force, I do not understand that my learned friends really make any question, seriously, upon the general principle of what force is, or upon the facts of this case, that this seizure of the Joseph by the Savannah had enough of force,—the threat, the presence, and exhibition of power,—and of the intent to use it, to make the capture one of force, if the other considerations which are relied upon do not lift it out of that catalogue of crime.

It is true that the learned counsel who last addressed you seemed to intimate, in some of his remarks, near the close of his very able and eloquent and interesting address, that there was not any force about it, that the master of the Joseph was not threatened, that there was no evidence that the cannon was even loaded, and that it never had been fired off. Well, gentlemen, the very illustration which he used of what would be a complete robbery on land,—the aggressor possessing a pistol, and asking, in the politest manner, for your money,—relieves me from arguing that you must fire either a cannon or a pistol, before you have evidence of force. If our rights stand on that proposition, that when a pistol is presented at our breast, and we surrender our money, we must wait for the pistol to be fired before the crime is completed, you will see that the terrors of the crime of robbery do not go very far towards protecting property or person, which is the object of it.

When, gentlemen, the Government, within a statute which, in the judgment of the Court, shall be pronounced as being lawfully enacted under the Constitution of the United States, has completed the proof of the circumstances of the crime charged, it is entitled at your hands to a conviction of the accused, unless, by proof adduced on his part, he shall so shake the consistency and completeness of the proof on the part of the Government, or shall introduce such questions of uncertainty and doubt, that the facts shall be disturbed in your mind, or unless he shall show himself in some predicament of protection or right under the law,—(and, by "under the law," I mean, under the law of the land where the crime is punishable, and where the trial and the sentence are lawfully attributed to be,)—or unless he shall introduce some new facts which, conceding the truthfulness and the sufficiency of the case made by the Government, shall still interpose a protection, in some form, against the application of the penalty of the law. I take it that I need not say to you that this protection or qualification of the character of the crime must be by the law of the land; and, whether it comes to be the law of the land by its enactment in the statutes of the United States, or by the adoption and incorporation into the law of the land of the principles of the law of nations, is a point quite immaterial to you. You are not judges of what the statutes of the United States are, except so far as their interpretation may rightfully become a subject of inquiry by the Jury, in the sense of whether the crime is within the intent of the Act, in the circumstances proved. You are not judges of what the law of nations is, in the first place; nor are you judges of how much of the law of nations has been adopted or incorporated into the system of our Government and our laws, by the authority of its Congress or of its Courts.

Whether, as I say to you, there is a defence, or protection, or qualification of the acts and transactions which, in their naked nature, and in their natural construction, are violent interferences with the rights of property, against the statute, and the protection of property intended by the statute,—whether the circumstances do change the liability or responsibility of the criminal, by the introduction of a legal defence under the law of nations, or under the law of the land in any other form, is a question undoubtedly for the Court,—leaving to you always complete control over the questions of fact that enter into the subject. So that the suggestion, also dropped by my learned friend, at the close of his remarks, that any such arrangement would make the Jury mere puppets, and give them nothing to do, finds no place. It would not exclude from your consideration any matters of fact which go to make up the particular condition of public affairs or of the public relations of the community towards each other, in these collisions which disturb the land, provided the Court shall hold and say that, on such a state of facts existing, or being believed by you, there is introduced a legal qualification or protection against the crime charged. But, if it should be held that all these facts and circumstances, to the extent and with the effect that is claimed for them by the learned counsel as matter of fact, yet, as matter of law, leave the crime where it originally stood, being of their own nature such as the principles of law do not permit to be interposed as a protection and a shield, why, then you take your law on the subject in the same way as you do on every other subject, from the instructions of the learned and responsible Bench, whose errors, if committed, can be corrected; while your confusion between your province and the province of the Court would, both in this case, and in other cases, and sometimes to the prejudice of the prisoner, and against his life and safety, when prejudices ran that way, confound all distinctions; and, in deserting your duty, to usurp that of another portion of the Court, you would have done what you could, not to uphold, but to overthrow the laws of your country and the administration of justice according to law, upon which the safety of all of us, at all times, in all circumstances, depends.

Now, gentlemen, let me ask your attention, very briefly, to the condition of the proof in this case, from the immediate consideration of which we have been very much withdrawn by the larger and looser considerations, as I must think them, which have occupied most of the attention of the counsel, and been made most interesting, undoubtedly, and attractive to you. These twelve men now on trial—four of them citizens of the United States, and eight of them foreigners by birth and not naturalized—formed part of the crew of a vessel, originally a pilot-boat, called the Savannah. That crew consisted of twenty men, and one of them has given the circumstances of the preparation for the voyage, of the embarkation upon the vessel, of her weighing anchor from the port of Charleston and making her course out to sea without any port of destination, and without any other purpose than to make seizures of vessels belonging to the loyal States of the Union and its citizens. He has shown you that all who went on board, all who are here on trial, had a complete knowledge of, and gave their ready and voluntary assent to and enlistment in this service; and that the service had no trait of compulsion, or of organized employment under the authority of Government, in any act or signature of any one of the crew, as far as he knew, leaving out, of course, what I do not intend to dispute, and what you will not understand me as disregarding—the effect that may be gained from the notorious facts and the documents that attended the enterprise. He has shown you that, going to sea with that purpose, without any crew list, without any contract of wages, they descried, early in the morning after they adventured from the port, and at a point about sixty miles to sea, this bark, and ran down to her; and that, while running down to her, they sailed under the flag of the United States, and, hailing the brig, when within hailing distance, required the master of it to come on board with his papers. Upon the inquiry of the master, by what authority they made that demand on him, the stars and stripes being then floating at the masthead of the Savannah, Captain Baker informed him that it was in the name and by the authority of the Confederate States of America, at the same time hauling down the American flag and running up the flag of the Confederacy. Whatever followed after this, gentlemen, except so far as to complete the possession of the captured vessel, by putting a prize crew on board of it, (so called,) sending it into Charleston, and there lodging in jail the seamen or ship's company of the Joseph that accompanied it, and procuring a sale of the vessel—anything beyond that (and this only to show the completeness of the capture, and the maintenance of the design to absolutely deprive the owners of the vessel and cargo of their property) seems to be quite immaterial. Now, when we add to this the testimony of Mr. Meyer, the master of the captured vessel, who gives the same general view of the circumstances under which his vessel was overhauled and seized by the Savannah, as well as the observations and the influences which operated upon his mind while the chase was going on, we have the completeness of the crime,—not forgetting the important yet undisputed circumstances of the ownership of the vessel, and of the nature of the voyage in which she was engaged. You will observe that this vessel, owned by, and, we may suppose, judging from the position of the witnesses examined before you, constituting a good part of the property of, our fellow-countrymen in the State of Maine, sailed on the 28th day of April, from Philadelphia, bound on a voyage to Cardenas, in Cuba, with a charter party out and back, under which she was to bring in a cargo of sugar and molasses. You will have noticed, comparing this date with some of the public transactions given in evidence, that it was after both the proclamation of Mr. Davis, inviting hostile aggressions against the commerce of the United States, on the part of whosoever should come to take commissions from him; and after the proclamation of the President of the United States, made to the people of the United States and all under its peace and protection, that if, under this invitation of Mr. Davis, anybody should assume authority to make aggressions, on the high seas, upon the private property of American citizens, they should be punished as pirates. This vessel, therefore, sailed on her voyage under the protection of the laws of the United States, and under this statement of its Government, that the general laws which protected property and seamen on the high seas against the crime of piracy were in force, and would be enforced by the Government of the United States, wherever it held power, against any aggressions that should assume to be made under the protection of the proclamation of Mr. Davis. While returning, under the protection of this flag and of this Government, she meets with hostile aggression at the hands of an armed vessel, which has nothing to distinguish it from the ordinary condition of piracy, except this very predicament provided against by the proclamation of the President, and under the protection of which the vessel had sailed, to wit, the supposed authority of Jefferson Davis; which should not, and cannot, and will not, as I suppose, protect that act from the guilt and the punishment of piracy.

Now, you will have observed, gentlemen, in all this, that whatever may be the circumstances or the propositions of law connected with this case, that may change or qualify the acts and conduct of Mr. Baker, so far as the owners of this vessel and the owners of this cargo are concerned, there has been as absolute, as complete, as final and as perfect a deprivation of their property, as if there had been no commission—no public or other considerations that should expose them to having the act done with impunity. You will discover, then, that, so far as the duty of protection from this Government to its citizens and their property—so far as the duty of maintaining its laws and enforcing them upon the high seas—is concerned, there is nothing pretended—there is nothing, certainly, proved—that has excused or can excuse this Government, in its Executive Departments, in its Judicial Departments, in the declaration of law from the Court, or in the finding of facts by the Jury, from its duty towards its citizens and their property. And, while you have been led to look at all the qualifying circumstances that should attend your judgment concerning the act and the fact on the part of these prisoners, I ask your ready assent to the proposition, that you should look at the case of these sufferers, the victims of those men, whose property has been ventured upon the high seas in reliance on its safety against aggression, from whatever source, under the exercise of the authority of the Government to repel and to punish such crimes.

Before I go into any of the considerations which are to affect the relations of these prisoners to this alleged crime, and to this trial for such alleged crime, let us see what there are in the private circumstances particular to themselves, and their engagement in this course of proceeding, that is particularly suited to attract your favor or indulgence. Now, these men had not, any of them, been under the least compulsion, or the least personal or particular duty of any kind, to engage in this enterprise. Who are they? Four of them are citizens of the United States. Mr. Baker is, by birth, a citizen of the State of Pennsylvania; two are citizens, by birth, of the State of South Carolina, and one of North Carolina. The eight men, foreigners, are, three of Irish origin, two of Scotch, one a German, one a native of Manilla, in the East Indies, and one of Canton, in China. Now, you will observe that no conscription, no enlistment, no inducement, no authority of any public kind has been shown, or is suggested, as having influenced any of them in this enterprise. My learned friend has thought it was quite absurd to impute to this Chinaman and this Manillaman a knowledge of our laws. Is it not quite as absurd to throw over them the protection of patriotism—the protection of indoctrination in the counsels and ethics of Calhoun—to give them the benefit of a departure from moral and natural obligations to respect the property of others, on the theory that they must surrender their own rectitude—their own sense of right—to an overwhelming duty to assist a suffering people in gaining their liberty? What I have said of them applies equally to these Irishmen, this German, and these Scotchmen—as good men, if you please, in every respect, as the same kind of men born in this country. I draw no such national distinctions; but I ask what there is, in the sober, sensible, practical consideration of the motives and purposes with which these men entered into this enterprise to despoil the commerce of the United States, and make poor men of the owners of that vessel, that should give them immunity from the laws of property and the laws of the land, or form any part in the struggles of a brave and oppressed people, (as we will consider them, for the purpose of the argument), against a tyrannical and bloodthirsty Government?

No! no! Let their own language indicate the degree and the dignity of the superior motives that entered into their adoption of this enterprise: "We thought we had a right to do it, and we did it." Was there the glow of patriotism—was there the self-sacrificing devotion to work in the cause of an oppressed people, in this? No! And the only determination that these men knew or looked at, was the lawfulness of the enterprise, in respect of the sanctions and punishments of the law. They, undoubtedly, had not any purpose or any thought of running into a collision with the comprehensive power and the all-punishing condemnation of the statutes of the United States, whether they knew what the statutes were or not; but they did take advantage of the occasion and opportunity to share the profits of a privateering enterprise against the commerce of the United States; and they were unquestionably acquainted, either by original inspection or by having a favorable report made to them with the fundamental provision in regard to this system of privateering, so called. They knew that the entire profits of the transaction would be distributed among those who were engaged in it. Now, I am not making any particular or special condemnation of these men, (in thus readily, without compulsion, and without the influence of any superior motives, however mistaken, of patriotism,) beyond what the general principles of public law, and general opinion, founded on the experience of privateering, have shown to be the reckless and greedy character of those who enter upon private war, under the protection of any, however recent, flag. Every body knows it—every body understands it—every body recognizes the fact that, if privateers, who go in under the hope of gain, and for the purposes of spoliation, are not corrupt and depraved at the outset, they expose themselves to influences, and are ready to expose themselves to influences, which will make them as dangerous, almost, to commerce, and as dangerous to life, as if the purpose and the principle of privateering did not distinguish them from pirates. And, to show that, in this law of ours, there is nothing that is forced in its application to privateers—that there is nothing against the principles of humanity or common sense in the nation's undertaking to say, We will not recognize any of those high moral motives, any of this superior dignity, about privateers; we understand the whole subject, and we know them to be, in substance and effect, dangerous to the rights of peaceful citizens, in their lives and their property,—reference need only be had to the action of civilized Governments, and to that of our Government as much as any, in undertaking to brush away these distinctions, wherever it had the power—that is my proposition—wherever it had the power to do so. And I ask your Honors' attention to the provision on this subject, in the first treaties which our Government—then scarcely having a place among the nations of the earth—introduced upon this very question of piracy and privateers. I refer to the twenty-first article of the Treaty of Commerce with France, concluded on the 6th of February, 1778, on page 24 of the eighth volume of the Statutes at Large. This is a commercial arrangement, entered into by this infant Government, before its recognition by the Throne of Great Britain, with its ally, the most Christian Monarch of France:

"No subjects of the Most Christian King shall apply for or take any commission or letters of marque, for arming any ship or ships to act as privateers against the said United States, or any of them, or against the subjects, people or inhabitants of the said United States, or any of them, or against the property of any of the inhabitants of any of them, from any Prince or State with which the said United States shall be at war; nor shall any citizen, subject or inhabitant of the said United States, or any of them, apply for or take any commission or letters of marque for arming any ship or ships, to act as privateers against the subjects of the Most Christian King, or any of them, or the property of any of them, from any Prince or State with which the said King shall be at war; and if any person of either nation shall take such commissions or letters of marque, he shall be punished as a pirate."

Now, we have had a great deal of argument here to show that, under the law of nations,—under the law that must control and regulate the international relations of independent powers—it is a gross and violent subversion of the natural, inherent principles of justice, and a confusion between crime and innocence, to say to men who, under the license of war, take commissions from other powers, that they shall be hanged as pirates. And yet, in the first convention which we, as an infant nation, formed with any civilized power, attending in date the Treaty of Alliance which made France our friend, our advocate, our helper, in the war of the Revolution, his Most Christian Majesty, the King of France, standing second to no nation in civilization, signalized this holy alliance of friendship in behalf of justice, and humanity, and liberty, by engaging that, whatever the law of nations might be, whatever the speciousness of publicists might be, his subjects, amenable to the law, should never set up the pretence of a commission of privateering against the penalties of piracy. Nor had this treaty of commerce which I have referred to, anything of the nature of a temporary or warlike arrangement between the parties, pending the contest with Great Britain. It was a treaty independent of the Treaty of Alliance which engaged them as allies, offensive and defensive, in the prosecution of that war. Nor is this an isolated case of the morality and policy of this Government on the subject of piracy. By reference to the 19th Article of the Treaty between the Netherlands and the United States, concluded in 1782, at p. 44 of the same volume, your honors will find the same provision. After the same stipulation, excluding the acceptance of commissions from any power, to the citizens or subjects of the contracting parties, there is the same provision: "And if any person of either nation shall take such commissions or letters of marque, he shall be punished as a pirate."

Now, our Government has never departed from its purpose and its policy, to meliorate the law of nations, so as to extirpate this business of private war on the ocean. It is entirely true that, in its subsequent negotiations with the great powers of Christendom, it has directed its purpose to the more thorough and complete subversion and annihilation of the whole abominable exception, which is allowed on the high seas, from the general melioration of the laws of war, that does not tolerate aggressions of violence, and murder, and rapine, and plunder, except by the recognized forces contending in the field. It has attempted to secure not only the exclusion of private armed vessels from privateering, but the exclusion of aggressions on the part of public armed vessels of belligerents on private property of all kinds upon the ocean. And no trace of any repugnance or resistance on the part of our Government to aid and co-operate in that general melioration in the laws of war, in respect to property on the ocean, can be charged or proved. In pursuance of that purpose, as well as in conformity with a rightful maintenance of its particular predicament in naval war,—to wit., a larger commerce than most other nations, and a smaller navy,—it has taken logically, and diplomatically, and honestly, the position: I will not yield to these false pretences of humanity and melioration which will only deprive us of privateers, and leave our commerce exposed to your immense navies. If you are honest about it, as we are, and opposed to private war, why, condemn and repress private war in respect to the private character of the property attacked, as well as private war in respect to the vessels that make the aggressions.

Nor, gentlemen, do I hesitate to say that, whatever we may readily concede to an honest difference of opinion and feeling, in respect to great national contests, where men, with patriotic purposes, raise the standard of war against the Government, and, on the other hand, uphold the old standard to suppress the violence of war lifted against it, we do not, we cannot, as honest and sensible men, look with favor upon an indiscriminate collection from the looser portions of society, that rush on board a marauding vessel, the whole proceeds and results of whose aggressions are to fill their own pockets. And, when my learned friends seek to go down into the interior conscience and the secret motives of conduct, I ask you whether, if this had been a service in which life was to be risked, and all the energies of the man were to be devoted to the public service, for the glory and the interests of the country, and the poor food, poor clothing and poor pay of enlisted troops, you would have found precisely such a rush to that service?

Now, I am not seeking, by these considerations, to disturb in the least the legal protections, if there be any, in any form, which it is urged have sprung out of the character of privateering which this vessel had assumed, and these men, as part of its crew, had been incorporated in. If legal, let it be so; but do not confound patriotism, which sacrifices fortune and life for the love of country, with the motives of these men, who seek privateering because they are out of employment. Far be it from me to deny that the feeling of lawful right, the feeling that statutory law is not violated, if it draw the line between doing and not doing a thing, is on the whole a meritorious consideration and a trait that should be approved. But I do object to having the range of these men's characters and motives exalted, from the low position in which their acts and conduct place them, into the high purity of the patriot and the martyr. We are trying, not the system of privateering—we are trying the privateers, as they are called; and, when they fail of legal protection, they cannot cover themselves with this robe of righteousness in motive and purpose.

Now, how much was there of violence in the meditated course, or in the actual aggression? Why, the vessel is named in the commission as having a crew of thirty. In fact, she had twenty. Four men was a sufficient crew for a mercantile voyage. She had an eighteen pounder, a great gun that must have reached half way across the deck, resting on a pivot in the middle, capable of being brought around to any quarter, for attack. At the time this honest master and trader of the Joseph descried the condition of the vessel, he was struck with this ugly thing amidships, as he called it—to wit, this eighteen pound cannon, and was afraid it was a customer probably aggressive—a robber. But he was encouraged by what? Although he saw this was a pilot boat, and not likely, with good intent, to be out so far at sea, what was this honest sailor encouraged by? The flag of the United States was flying at her mast! But, when hailed—still under that view as to the aspect presented by the marauding vessel—he is told to come on board, and asks by what authority—instead of what would have been the glad and reassuring announcement—the power of the American flag—the Confederate States were announced as the marauding authority, and the flag of his country is hauled down, and its ensign replaced by this threat to commerce. Now, when this gun, as he says, was pointed at him, and this hostile power was asserted, my learned friends, I submit to you, cannot, consistently with the general fairness with which they have pursued this argument, put the matter before you as failing in any of the completeness of proof concerning force. For, when we were proposing to show that these prisoners all the while, in their plans, had the purpose of force, if force was necessary, and that, in the act of collision with the capturing vessel, that force occurred, we were stopped, upon the ground that it was unnecessary to occupy the attention of the Court and the Jury with anything that was to qualify this vessel's violent character, by reason of the admission that, if it was not protected by the commission, or the circumstances of a public character of whatever kind and degree—about which I admit there was no restriction of any kind,—if it stood upon the mere fact that the vessel was taken from its owners by the Savannah, in the way that was testified,—it would not be claimed to be wanting in any of the quality of complete spoliation, or in any of the quality of force. Now, that defence, we may say, must not be recurred to, to protect, in your minds, these men from the penalty which the law has imposed upon the commission of piracy. It cannot be pretended that there was any defect in the purpose of despoiling the original owners, nor that there is any deficiency in the exhibition of force, to make it piracy; and you will perceive, gentlemen, that although my learned friends successively, Mr. Dukes, Mr. Sullivan, and Mr. Brady, have, with the skill and the purpose of advocates, taken occasion, at frequent recurring points, to get you back to the want of a motive and intent or purpose of the guiltiness of robbing, yet, after all, it comes to this—that the inconsistency of the motive and intent, or the guiltiness of robbing, with the lawfulness, under the law of nations, of privateering, is the only ground or reason why the crime is deficiently proved.

I do not know that I need say anything to you about privateering, further than to present somewhat distinctly what the qualifications, what the conditions, and what the purposes, of privateering are. In the first place, privateering is a part of war, or is a part of the preliminary hostile aggressions which are in the nature of a forcible collision between sovereign powers. Now what is the law of nations on this subject—and how does there come to be a law of nations—and what is its character, what are its sanctions, and who are parties to it? We all know what laws are when they proceed from a Government, and operate upon its citizens and its subjects. Law then comes with authority, by right, and so as to compel obedience; and laws are always framed with the intent that there shall be no opportunity of violent or forcible resistance to them, or of violent or forcible settlement of controversies under them, but that the power shall be submitted to, and the inquiry as to right proceed regularly and soberly, under the civil and criminal tribunals. But, when we come to nations, although they have relations towards each other, although they have duties towards each other, although they have rights towards each other, and although, in becoming nations, they nevertheless are all made up of human beings, under the general laws of human duty, as given by the common lawgiver, God, yet there is no real superior that can impose law over them, or enforce it against them. And it is only because of that, that war, the scourge of the human race—and it is the great vice and defect of our social condition, that it cannot be avoided—comes in, as the only arbiter between powers that have no common superior. I am sure that the little time I shall spend upon this topic will be serviceable; as, also, in some more particular considerations, as to what is called a state of war, and as to the conditions which give and create a war between the different portions of our unhappy country and its divided population. So, then, nations have no common superior whom they recognize under this law, which they have made for themselves in the interest of civilization and humanity, and which is a law of natural right and natural duty, so far as it can be applied to the relations which nations hold to one another. They recognize the fact that one nation is just as good, as matter of right, of another; that whether it be the great Powers of Russia, as England, of France, of the United States of America, or of Brazil, or whether it be one of the feeble and inferior Powers, in the lowest grade,—as, one of the separate Italian Kingdoms, or the little Republic of San Marino, whose territories are embraced within the circuit of a few leagues, or one of the South American States, scarcely known as a Power in the affairs of men,—yet, under the proposition that the States are equal in the family of nations, they have a right to judge of their quarrels, and, finding occasions for quarrel, have a right to assert them, as matter of force, in the form of war. And all the other nations, however much their commerce may be disturbed and injured, are obliged to concede certain rights that are called the rights of war. We all understand what the rights of war are on the part of two people fighting against each other. A general right is to do each other as much injury as they can; and they are very apt to avail themselves of that right. There are certain meliorations against cruelty, which, if a nation should transgress, probably other nations might feel called upon to suppress. But, as a general thing, while two nations are fighting, other nations stand by, and do not intervene. But the way other nations come to have any interest, and to have anything to say whether there is war between sovereign powers, grows out of certain rights of war which the law of nations gives to the contending parties, against neutrals. For instance: Suppose Spain and Mexico were at war. Well, you would say, what is that to us? It is this to us. On the high seas, a naval vessel of either power has a right, in pursuit of its designs against the enemy, to interrupt the commerce of other nations to a certain extent. It has a right of visitation and of search of vessels that apparently carry our flag. Why? In order to see whether the vessel be really our vessel, or whether our flag covers the vessel of its enemy, or the property of its enemy. It has also a right to push its inquiries farther, and if it finds it to be a vessel of the United States of America, to see whether we are carrying what are called contraband of war into the ports of its enemy; and, if so, to confiscate it and her. Each of the powers has a right to blockade the ports of the other, and thus to break up the trade and pursuits of the people of other nations—and that without any quarrel with the other people. And so you see, by the law of nations, this state of war, which might, at first, seem to be only a quarrel between the two contending parties, really becomes, collaterally, and, in some cases, to a most important extent, a matter of interest to other nations of the globe. But however much we suffer—however much we are embarrassed (as, for example, in the extreme injury to British commerce and British interests now inflicted in this country—the blockade keeping out their shipping, and preventing shipments of cotton to carry on their industry)—we must submit, as the English people submit, in the view their Government has chosen to take of these transactions.

Now, gentlemen, this being the law of nations, you will perceive that, as there is no human earthly superior, so there are no Courts that can lay down the law, as our Courts do for our people, or as the Courts of England do for their people. There are no Courts that can lay down the law of nations, so as to bind the people of another country, except so far as the Courts of that country, recognizing the sound principles of morality, humanity and justice obtaining in the government and conduct of nations towards each other, adopt them in their own Courts. So, when my learned friends speak of the law of nations as being the law that is in force here, and that may protect these prisoners in this case against the laws of the United States of America, why, they speak in the sense of lawyers, or else in a sense that will confuse your minds, that is to say, that the law of nations, as the Court will expound and explain it, has or has not a certain effect upon what would be otherwise the plain behests of the statute law.

Now, it is a part of the law of nations, except so far as between themselves they shall modify it by treaty—(two instances of which I have read in the diplomacy of our own country, and a most extensive instance of which is to be found in the recent treaty of Paris, whereby the law of nations, in respect to privateering, has been so far modified as to exclude privateering as one of the means of war)—outside of particular arrangements made by civilized nations, it was a part of the original law of war prevailing among nations, that any nation engaged in war might fit out privateers in aid of its belligerent or warlike purposes or movements. No difficulty arose about this when war sprang up between two nations that stood before the world in their accredited and acknowledged independence. If England and France went to war, or if England and the United States, as in 1812, went to war, this right of fitting out privateers would obtain and be recognized. But, there arises, in the affairs of nations, a condition much more obscure and uncertain than this open war between established powers, and that is, when dissension arises in the same original nation—when it proceeds from discontent, sedition, private or local rebellion, into the inflammation of great military aggression; and when the parties assume, at least, (assume, I say), to be rightfully entitled to the position of Powers, under the law of nations, warring against one another. The South American States, in their controversy which separated them from the parent country, and these States, when they were Colonies of Great Britain, presented instances of these domestic dissensions between the different parts of the same Government, and the rights of war were claimed. Now, what is the duty of other nations in respect to that? Why, their duty and right is this—that they may either accord to these struggling, rebellious, revolted populations the rights of war, so far as to recognize them as belligerents, or not; but, whether they will do so, or not, is a question for their Governments, and not for their Courts, sitting under and by authority of their Governments. For instance, you can readily see that the great nations of the earth, under the influences upon their commerce and their peace which I have mentioned, may very well refuse to tolerate the quarrel as being entitled to the dignity of war. They may say—No, no; we do not see any occasion for this war, or any justice or benefit that is to be promoted by it; we do not see the strength or power that is likely to make it successful; and we will not allow a mere attempt or effort to throw us into the condition of submitting to the disturbance of the peace, or the disturbance of the commerce of the world. Or, they may say—We recognize this right of incipient war to raise itself and fairly contend against its previous sovereign— not necessarily from any sympathy, or taking sides in it, but it is none of our affair; and the principles of the controversy do not prevent us from giving to them this recognition of their supposed rights. Now, when they have done that, they may carry their recognition of right and power as far as they please, and stop where they please. They may say—We will tolerate the aggression by public armed vessels on the seas, and our vessels shall yield the right of visitation and search to them. They may say—We will extend it so far as to include the right of private armed vessels, and the rights of war may attend them; or they may refuse to take this last step, and say—We will not tolerate the business of privateering in this quarrel. And, whatever they do or say on that subject, their Courts of all kinds will follow.

Apply this to the particular trouble in our national affairs that is now progressing to settle the fate of this country. France and England have taken a certain position on this subject. I do not know whether I accurately state it (and I state it only for the purpose of illustration, and it is not material), but, as I understand it, they give a certain degree of belligerent right, so that they would not regard the privateers on the part of the Southern rebellion as being pirates, but they do not accord succor or hospitality in their ports to such privateers. Well, now, suppose that one of these privateers intrudes into their ports and their hospitalities, and claims certain rights. Why, the question, if it comes up before a Court in Liverpool or London, will be—Is the right within the credit and recognition which our Government has given? And only that. So, too, our Government took the position in regard to the revolting States of South America, that it would recognize them as belligerents, and that it would not hang, as pirates, privateers holding commissions from their authority. But, when other questions came up, as to whether a particular authority from this or that self-styled power should be recognized, our Government frowned upon it, and would not recognize it. With regard to Captain Aury, who styled himself Generalissimo of the Floridas, or something of that kind, when Florida was a Spanish province, our Courts said—We do not know anything about this—his commissions are good for nothing here—our Government has not recognized any such contest or incipient nationality as this. So, too, in another case, where there was an apparent commission from one struggling power, the Court say—Our Government does not recognize that power, and we do not, in giving any rights of war to it; but, the Court say, it appears in the proof that this vessel claims to have had a commission from Buenos Ayres, another contending power; if so, that is a power which our Government recognizes; and the case must go down for further proof on that point.

I confess that, if the views of my learned friends are to prevail, in determining questions of crime and responsibility under the laws and before the Court, and are to be accepted and administered, I do not see that there is any Government at all. For you have every stage of Government: first, Government of right; next, a Government in fact; next, a Government trying to make itself a fact; and, next, a Government which the culprit thinks ought to be a fact. Well, if there are all these stages of Government, and all these authorities and protections, which may attend the acts of people all over the world, I do not see but every Court and every Jury must, finally, resolve itself into the great duty of searching the hearts of men, and putting its sanctions upon pure or guilty secret motives, or notions, or interpretations of right and wrong—a task to which you, gentlemen of the Jury, I take it, feel scarcely adequate.

Now, gentlemen, I have perhaps wearied you a little upon this subject; because it is from some confusion in these ideas,—first, of what the law of nations permits a Government to do, and how it intrudes upon and qualifies the laws of that Government; and, second, upon what the rights are that grow out of civil dissensions, as towards neutral powers,—that some difficulty and obscurity are introduced into this case.

If the Court please, I maintain these propositions, in conformity with the views I have heretofore presented—first, that the law of the land is to determine whether this crime of piracy has been committed, subject only to the province of the Jury in passing upon the facts attending the actual perpetration of the offence; and, second, upon all the questions invoked to qualify, from the public relations of the hostile or contending parties in this controversy, the attitude that this Government holds towards these contending parties, is the attitude that this Court, deriving its authority from this Government, must necessarily hold towards them.

I have argued this matter of the choice and freedom of a Government to say how it will regard these civil dissensions going on in a foreign nation, as if it had some application to this controversy, in which we are the nation, and this Court is the Court of this nation.

But, gentlemen, the moment I have stated that, you will see that there is not the least pretence that there is any dispensing power in the Court, or that there has been any dispensing power exercised by our Government, or that there has been any pardon, or any amnesty, or any proclamation, saving from the results of crime against our laws, any person engaged in these hostilities, who at any time has owed allegiance and obedience to the Government of the United States. Therefore, here we stand, really extricated from all the confusion, and from all the wideness of controversy and of comment that attends these remote considerations of this case, that have been pressed upon your attention as if they were the case itself, on the part of our learned friend.

Now, if the Court please, I shall bestow some particular consideration upon the statute, but I shall think it necessary to add very little to the remarks I have heretofore made to the Court. The 8th section of the statute has been characterized by the learned counsel, and, certainly, with sufficient accuracy, for any purposes of this trial, as limited to the offence of piracy as governed by the law of nations. I do not know that any harm comes from that description, if we do not confuse it with the suggestion that the authority of this Government over the crime is limited to the construction of the law of nations which is expressed in that section of the statute. At all events, as they concede, I believe, that the 8th section is within the constitutional right and power of Congress, under the special clause giving them authority to define and punish piracy, under the law of nations, there is no room for controversy here on the point. When we come to the 9th section, we have two different and quite inconsistent views presented by the different counsel. One of the counsel (I think, Mr. Dukes) insists that the 9th section does not create any additional crime beyond that of piracy as defined in the 8th section, but only robs that crime of piracy of any apparent protection from a commission or authority from any State. But, my friend Mr. Brady contends (and, I confess, according to my notion of the law, with more soundness) that there is an additional crime, which would not be embraced, necessarily, in the crime of piracy or robbery on the high seas—which is the whole purview of the 8th section, and which is in terms repeated in the 9th—and that the additional words, "or any act of hostility against the United States, or any citizens thereof," create a punishable offence, although it may fall short of the completed crime of piracy and robbery, as defined. Now, I concede to my learned friend that the particular case he put of a quarrel between two ships' crews on the high seas, and of an attack by one of the crew of one upon one of the crew of the other with a belaying pin, would not, in my judgment, as an indictable, punishable offence, fall within the 9th section. But, whether I am right or wrong about it, it does not impede the argument of the Government, that there are crimes which are in the nature of and up to the completeness of hostile attacks upon vessels or citizens of the United States which would not be piracy, but yet are punishable under the 9th section.

Now, agreeing, thus far, that there is an added offence to the crime of piracy in the 9th section, I am obliged to meet his next proposition, that such additional offence is beyond the constitutional power of Congress, because it is an offence which does not come up to the crime of piracy, and, therefore, exceeds the grant of authority under the particular section of the Constitution which gives to Congress power over the definition and punishment of piracy under the law of nations.

Now, if the Court please, the argument is a very simple one. This 9th section does not profess to carry the power of this Government where alone the principles of the law of nations would justify; that is, to operate upon all the world, so far as the subjects of it—that is, the persons included in its sanctions—are concerned, or so far as the property protected by it is concerned. It is limited to citizens, and limited to hostilities against citizens of the United States, or their property at sea. Now, the authority in respect to this comes to Congress under the provision of the Constitution which gives the regulation of commerce and its control, in regard to which I need not be more particular to your Honors, because there are statutes of every-day enforcement, and under the highest penalty, too, of the law, such as revolt, mutiny, &c., which have nothing to do with the national considerations of the law of piracy, and nothing to do with the clause of the Constitution which gives to Congress power over the crime of piracy, but rest in the power reposed in Congress to protect the commerce of the United States. So, this is wholly within the general competency of Congress to govern citizens of the United States on the high seas, and to protect the property of citizens on the high seas, although there is no common law of general jurisdiction of Congress on the subject of crimes.

Now, upon this subject there is but one other criticism, and that is—that although the statute is framed with the intent, and its language covers the purpose, of prohibiting any defence or protection being set up under an assumed or supposed authority from any foreign Government, State, or Prince, or from any person, yet the particular authority which is averred in the indictment and produced in proof, if you take it in the sense that we give to it, is not within the purview of the statute, and, if you take it in any other sense, is not proved; and that thus a variance arises between the indictment and the proof, because the proof goes so far as to remove from under the statute the four defendants who would otherwise be amenable as citizens, by making the Government foreign, and making them foreign citizens. Now, to take up one branch of this at a time, I do not care at all whether the Government of the United States, when they passed this law, anticipated that there ever would be an occurrence which would give shape to such a commission as this, from either a person or an authority that emanated from what was or ever had been a part or a citizen of the United States. If these new occurrences here have produced new relations—(and that is the entire argument of my learned friends, for, if they have produced no new relations, what have we to do with any of these discussions?)—if they have produced new relations, perfect or imperfect, effectual or ineffectual, to this or that extent, why then, if these new relations and attitude have brought this matter within the purview of a statute of the United States which was framed to meet all relations that might arise at any time, they come within its predicament, and the argument seems to me to amount to nothing. It will not be pretended that the 9th section of this statute can only be enforced as to Powers in existence at the time it was passed. Whenever a new Power or new authority is set forth as a protection to the crime of piracy, the 9th section of the statute says: "Well, we do not know or care anything about what the law of nations says about your protection, or your authority—we say that no citizen of the United States, depredating against our commerce, shall set up any authority to meet the justice of our criminal law." Well, now, that the statute has said; and we have averred and proved the commission such as it is. It is either the commission of a foreign Prince, or State, or it is an authority from some person. We do not recognize it as from a foreign State or Prince. Indeed, Mr. Davis does not call himself a Prince, and we do not recognize the Confederate States as a nation or State, in any relation. Therefore, if we would prove this authority under our law, we must aver it as it is, coming from an individual who was once a citizen of the United States, and still is, as the law decides, a citizen of the United States. Whatever port or pretension of authority he assumes, and whatever real fact and substance there may be to his power, it is, in the eye of the law, nothing. It is not provable, and it is not proved.

Now, as to the right of Congress to include the additional crime, under the authority given to it to punish piracy according to the law of nations, my learned friend contends that this statute is limited by that authority, and is, as respects anybody within its purview, unconstitutional, and that, although a particular act may be within the description of the statute, so far as regards hostility, it is not piracy. On that subject I refer your Honors to a very brief proposition contained in the case of *The United States* v. *Pirates (5 Wheaton, 202)*:

"And if the laws of the United States declare those acts of piracy in a citizen, when committed on a citizen, which would be only belligerent acts when committed on others, there can be no reason why such laws should not be enforced. For this purpose the 9th section of the Act of 1790 appears to have been passed. And it would be difficult to induce this Court to render null the provisions of that clause, by deciding either that one who takes a commission under a foreign power, can no longer be deemed a citizen, or that all acts committed under such a commission, must be adjudged belligerent, and not piratical acts."

I would also refer to the case of *The Invincible*, to which my learned friend called the attention of the Court, in the opinion of the late Attorney-General, Mr. Butler. It is to be found in the 3d volume of the *Opinions of the Attorney-Generals*, page 120. My learned friend cited this case in reference to the proposition that persons holding a commission (as I understood him) should not be treated as pirates, under the law of nations, by reason of any particular views or opinions of our Government. I refer to that part of the opinion where he says: "A Texan armed schooner cannot be treated as a pirate under the Act of April 30th, 1790, for capturing an American merchantman, on the alleged ground that she was laden with provisions, stores, and munitions of war for the use of the army of Mexico, with the Government of which Texas, at the time, was in a state of revolt and civil war."

Now, undoubtedly, Mr. Butler does here hold that, by the law of nations, in a controversy between revolting Colonies and the parent State, where our Government recognizes a state of war as existing, a privateer cannot be treated as a pirate. But we will come to the opinion of the Attorney-General on the other proposition we contend for—that is, in support of the 9th section of the statute, as far as it would have exposed citizens of the United States to the penalty of piracy:

"In answer to this question, I have the honor to state that, in my opinion, the capture of the American ship *Pocket* can in no view of it be deemed an act of piracy, *unless it shall appear that the principal actors in the capture were citizens of the United States*. The ninth section of the Crimes Act of 30th April, 1790, declares 'that if any citizen shall commit any piracy or robbery, or any act of hostility against the United States, or any citizen thereof, upon the high seas, under color of any commission from any foreign Prince, or State, or on pretence of authority from any person, such offender shall, notwithstanding the pretence of any such authority, be deemed, adjudged and taken to be a pirate, felon and robber, and on being thereof convicted, shall suffer death.' This provision is yet in force, and *should it be found that any of those who participated in the capture of the Pocket are American citizens, the flag and commission of the Government of Texas would not protect them from the charge of piracy*."

It will be seen here, that the condition of belligerents will not protect our citizens from aggressions against our commerce; and there is no place for my learned friends to put this authority, and this assumed belligerent power and right, on any footing that must not make it, either actually or in pretence, at least, proceed from a separate contending power. And, if they say, (as, in one of their points substantially is said,) that the 9th section cannot apply, because the alleged authority is not from a foreign State, or a foreign personage, but from a personage of our own country,—why, then, we are thrown back at once to the 8th section entirely, and there is either no pretence of authority at all, and it is just like arguing that the pirate accused was authorized by the merchant owner of a vessel in South street, to commit piracy, or we are put in the position, which is unquestionably the true one, that the 9th section was intended to cover all possible although unimagined forms in which the justice of the country could be attempted to be impeded under the claim of authority.

Now, gentlemen, if the Court please, I come to a consideration of the political theories or views on which these prisoners are sought to be protected against the penalties of this law. In that argument, as in my argument, it must be assumed that these penalties, but for those protections, would be visited upon them; for we are not to be drawn hither and thither by this inquiry, and to have it said, at one time, that the crime itself, in its own nature, is not proved, and, at another time, that, if it be proved, these are defences. I have said all I need to say, and all I should say, about the crime itself. The law of the case on that point will be given to you by the Court, and, if it should be, as I suppose it must, in accordance with that laid down by the Court in the Circuit of Pennsylvania, then, as my learned friend Mr. Brady has said of that, that he could not see how the Jury could find any verdict but guilty, it necessarily follows, if that is a sound view of the law, that you cannot find any other verdict but guilty. I proceed, therefore, to consider these other defences which grow out of the particular circumstances of the piracy.

Now, there are, as I suggested, three views in which this subject of the license, or authority, or protection against our criminal laws in favor of these prisoners, is urged, from their connection with particular occurrences disclosed in the evidence. One is, that they are privateers; but I have shown you that, to be privateers, their commission must come from an independent nation, or from an incipient nation, which our Government recognizes as such. Therefore, they fail entirely to occupy that explicit and clear position, under the law of the land, and the law of nations. But, as they say, they are privateers either of a nation or a Power that exists, as the phrase is, *de jure*,— that has a right, the same as we, or England, or France,—or of a Power that has had sufficient force and strength to establish itself, as matter of fact.

Without considering the question of right, as recognized under the system of nations, they contend, and with a great deal of force and earnestness, in the impression of their views upon the Jury, and great skill and discretion in handling the matter,—they contend that there is a state of civil war in this country, and that a state of civil war gives to all nations engaged in it, against the Government with which they are warring, rights of impunity, of protection, of respect, of regard, of courtesy, which belong to the laws of war; and that, without caring to say whether they are a Government, or ever will be a Government, so long as they fight, they cannot be punished.

That is the proposition,—there is nothing else to it. They come down from the region of *de jure* Government and *de facto* Government, and have nothing to prove but the rage of war on the part of rebels, in force enough to be called war. Then they say that, by their own act, they are liberated from the laws, and from their duty to the laws, which would otherwise, they admit, have sway over them, and against which they have not as yet prevailed. That is the proposition.

Another proposition, on which they put themselves, is that whatever may be the law, and whatever the extent of the facts, if any of these persons believed that there was a state of war, rightful to be recognized, and believed, in good faith, that they were fighting against the United States Government, they had a right to seize the property of United States' citizens; and that, if they believed that they constituted part of a force co-operating, in any form or effect, with the military power which has risen up against the United States of America, then, so long as they had that opinion, they, by their own act, and their own construction of their own act, impose the law upon this Government, and upon this Bench, and upon this Jury, and compel you to say to them that if, in taking, in a manner which would have been robbery, this vessel, the Joseph, they were also fighting against the United States of America, they have not committed the crime of piracy.

Now, if the Court please, and gentlemen of the Jury, let us, before we explore and dissect these propositions,—before we discover how utterly subversive they are of any notions of Government, of fixity in the interpretation of the law, or certainty in the enforcement of it,—let us see what you will fairly consider as being proved, as matter of fact, concerning the condition of affairs in this country. Let us see what legal discrimination or description of this state of things is likely to be significant and instructive, in determining the power and authority of the Government, and the responsibility of these defendants. They began with an Ordinance of South Carolina, passed on the 20th of December of last year, which, in form and substance, simply annulled the Ordinance of that State with which, as they say, they ratified or accepted the Constitution of the United States. They then went on with similar proceedings on the part of the States of Georgia, Alabama, Mississippi, and

Florida, showing the establishment and adoption of a Provisional Constitution, by which they constituted and called themselves the Confederate States of America. They proved, then, the organization of the Government, the election of Mr. Davis and Mr. Stephens as President and Vice-President, and the appointment of Secretaries of War, and of the Navy, and other portions of the civil establishment. They proved, then, the occurrences at Fort Sumter, and gave particular evidence of the original acts at Charleston—the firing on the Star of the West, and the correspondence which then took place between Major Anderson and the Governor of South Carolina. They then went on to prove the evacuation of Fort Moultrie; the storming of Fort Sumter; the Proclamation of the President of the United States, of the 15th of April, calling for 75,000 troops; Mr. Davis' Proclamation, of the 17th of April, inviting privateers; and then the President's Proclamation, of the 19th of April, denouncing the punishment of piracy against privateers, and putting under blockade the coasts of the revolted States. The laws about privateering passed by what is called the Confederate Government, have, also, been read to you; and this seems to complete the documentary, and constitutional, and statutory proceedings in that disaffected portion of the country. But what do the prisoners prove further? That an actual military conflict and collision commenced, has proceeded, and is now raging in this country, wherein we find, not one section of the country engaged in a military contest with another section of the country—not two contending factions, in the phrase of Vattel, dividing the nation for the sake of national power—but the Government of the United States, still standing, without the diminution of one tittle of its power and dignity—without the displacement or disturbance of a single function of its executive, of its legislative, of its judicial establishments—without the disturbance or the defection of its army or its navy—without any displacement in or among the nations of the world—without any retreat, on its part, or any repulsion, on the part of any force whatever, from its general control over the affairs of the nation, over all its relations to foreign States, over the high seas, and over every part of the United States themselves, in their whole length and breadth, except just so far as military occupation and military contest have controlled the peaceful maintenance of the authority and laws of the Government.

Now, this may be conceded for all sides of the controversy. I do not claim any more than these proofs show, and what we all know to be true; and I am but fair in conceding that they do show all the proportions and extent which make up a contest by the forces of the nation, as a nation, against an armed array, with all the form and circumstances, and with a number and strength, which make up military aggression and military attack on the part of these revolting or disaffected communities, or people.

Now, some observations have been made, at various stages of this argument, of the course the Government has taken in its declaration of a blockade, and in its seizure of prizes by its armed vessels, and its bringing them before the Prize Courts; and my learned friend, Mr. Brady, has done me the favor to allude to some particular occasion on which I, on behalf of the Government, in the Admiralty Court, have contended for certain principles, which would lead to the judicial confiscation of prizes, under the law of the land, or under the law of nations adopted and enforced as part of the law of the land. Well, now, gentlemen, I understand and agree that, for certain purposes, there is a condition of war which forces itself on the attention and the duty of Governments, and calls on them to exert the power and force of war for their protection and maintenance. And I have had occasion to contend—and the learned Courts have decided—that this nation, undertaking to suppress an armed military rebellion, which arrays itself, by land and by sea, in the forms of naval and military attack, has a right to exert—under the necessary principles which control and require the action of a nation for its own preservation, in these circumstances of danger and of peril—not only the usual magisterial force of the country—not only the usual criminal laws— not only such civil posses or aids to the officers of the law as may be obtained for their assistance—but to take the army and the navy, the strength and the manhood of the nation, which it can rally around it, and in every form, and by every authority, human and divine, suppress and reduce a revolt, a rebellion, a treason, that seeks to overthrow this Government in, at least, a large portion of its territory, and among a large portion of its people. In doing so, it may resort—as it has resorted—to the method of a warlike blockade, which, by mere force of naval obstruction, closes the harbors of the disaffected portion of the country against all commerce. Having done that, it has a right, in its Admiralty Courts, to adjudicate upon and condemn as prizes, under the laws of blockade, all vessels that shall seek to violate the blockade. Nor, gentlemen, have I ever denied—nor shall I here deny—that, when the proportions of a civil dissension, or controversy, come to the port and dignity of war, good sense and common intelligence require the Government to recognize it as a question of fact, according to the actual circumstances of the case, and to act accordingly. I, therefore, have no difficulty in conceding that, outside of any question of law and right— outside of any question as to whether there is a Government down there, whether nominal or real, or that can be described as having any consistency of any kind, under our law and our Government—there is prevailing in this country a controversy, which is carried on by the methods, and which has the proportions and extent, of what we call war.

War, gentlemen, as distinguished from peace, is so distinguished by this proposition—that it is a condition in which force on one side and force on the other are the means used in the actual prosecution of the controversy.

Now, gentlemen, if the Court please, I believe that that is all that can be claimed, and all that has been claimed, on behalf of these prisoners, in regard to the actual facts, and the condition of things in this country. And I admit that, if this Government of ours were not a party to this controversy,—if it looked on it from the outside, as England and France have done,—our Government would have had the full right to treat these contending parties, in its Courts and before its laws, as belligerents, engaged in hostilities, as it would have had an equal right to take the opposite course. Which course it would have taken, I neither know, nor should you require to know.

But, I answer to the whole of this, if the Court please, that it is a war in which the Government recognizes no right whatever on the part of the persons with whom it is contending; and that, in the eye of the law, as well as in the eye of reason and sound political morality, every person who has, from the beginning of the first act of levying war against the United States until now, taken part in this war, actively and effectively, in any form—who has adhered to the rebels—who has given aid, information, or help of any kind, wherever he lives, whether he sends it from New Hampshire or New York, from Wisconsin or from Baltimore—whether he be found within or without the armed lines—is, in his own overt actions, or open espousal of the side of this warring power, against the Government of the United States, a traitor and a rebel. I do not know that there is any proposition whatever, of law, or any authority whatever, that has been adduced by my learned friends, in which they will claim, as matter of law, that they are not *rebels*. I invited the attention of my learned friends, as I purposed to call that of the Court, to the fact, that the difficulty about all this business was, that the plea of authority or of war, which these prisoners interposed against the crime of piracy, was nothing but a plea of their implication in treason. I would like to hear a sober and solemn proposition from any lawyer, that a Government, as matter of law, and a Court, as matter of law, cannot proceed on an infraction of a law against violence either to person or property, instead of proceeding on an indictment for treason. The facts proved must, of course, maintain the personal crime; and there are many degrees of treason, or facts of treason, which do not include violent crime. But, to say that a person who has acted as a rebel cannot be indicted as an assassin, or that a man who has acted, on the high seas, as a pirate, if our statutes so pronounce him, cannot be indicted, tried and convicted as a pirate, because he could plead, as the shield of his piracy, that he committed it as part of his treason, is, to my apprehension, entirely new, and inconsistent with the first principles of justice.

Now, this very statute of piracy is really a general Crimes Act. The first section is:

"If any person or persons owing allegiance to the United States of America shall levy war against them, or shall adhere to their enemies, giving them aid and comfort within the United States, or elsewhere, and shall be thereof convicted," "such person or persons shall be adjudged guilty of treason against the United States, and shall suffer death."

Now, you will observe that treason is not a defence against piracy; nor is good faith in treason a defence against treason, or a defence against piracy. What would be the posture of these prisoners, if, instead of being indicted for piracy, they were indicted for treason? Should we then hear anything about this notion that there was a war raging, and that they were a party engaged in the war? Why, that is the very definition of treason. Against whom is the war? Against the United States of America. Did you owe allegiance to the United States of America? Yes, the citizens did; and I need not say to you, gentlemen, that those residents who are not citizens owe allegiance. There is no dispute about that. Those foreigners who are living here unnaturalized are just as much guilty of treason, if they act treasonably against the Government, as any of our own citizens can be. That is the law of England, the law of treason, the necessary law of civilized communities. If we are hospitable, if we make no distinction, as we do not, in this country, between citizens, and foreigners resident here and protected by our laws, it is very clear we cannot make any distinction when we come to the question of who are faithful to the laws. So, therefore, if they were indicted for treason, what would become of all this defence? It would be simply a confession in open Court that they were guilty of treason. Well, then, if they fell back on the proposition,—"We thought, in our consciences and judgments, that either these States had a right to secede, or that they had a right to carry on a revolution; that they were oppressed, and were entitled to assert themselves against an oppressive Government, and we, in good faith, and with a fair expectation of success, entered into it,"—what would become of them? The answer would be, "Good faith in your attempt to overthrow the Government, does not excuse you from responsibility for the crime of attempting it." Our statute is made for the purpose of protecting our Government against efforts made, in good faith or in bad faith, for its overthrow.

And now, in this connection, gentlemen, as your attention, as well as that of the Court, has been repeatedly called to it, let me advert again to the citation from that enlightened public writer, Vattel, who has done as much, perhaps, as our learned friends have suggested, to place on a sure foundation the amelioration of the law of nations in time of war, and their intercourse in time of peace, as any writer and thinker whom our race has produced. You remember, that he asks—How shall it be, when two contending factions divide a State, in all the forms and extent of civil war—what shall be the right and what the duty of a sovereign in this regard? Shall he put himself on the pride of a king, or on the flattery of a courtier, and say, I am still monarch, and will enforce against every one of this multitude engaged in this rebellion the strict penalties of my laws? Vattel reasons, and reasons very properly: You must submit to the principles of humanity and of justice; you must govern your conduct by them, and not proceed to an extermination of your subjects because they have revolted, whether with or without cause. You must not enforce the sanctions of your Government, or maintain its authority, on methods which would produce a destruction of your people. And you must not further, by insisting, under the enforced circumstances which surround you, on the extreme and logical right of a king, furnish occasion for the contending rebels, who have their moments of success and power, as well as you, to retaliate on your loyal people, victims of their struggle on your behalf, and thrown into the power of your rebellious subjects,—to retaliate, I say, on them the same extreme penalties, without right, without law, but by mere power, which you have exerted under your claim of right.

And now, gentlemen of the Jury, as the Court very well understands, this general reasoning, which should govern the conduct of a Sovereign, or of a Government, against a mere local insurrection, does not touch the question as to whether the law of the nation in which the Sovereign presides, and in violation of which the crime of the rebels has been perpetrated, shall be enforced. There has been, certainly, in modern times, no occasion when a Sovereign has not drawn, in his discretion, and under the influence of these principles of humanity and justice, this distinction, and has not interposed the shield of his own mercy between the offences of misled and misguided masses of his people and offended laws. We know the difference between law and its condemnation, and mercy and its saving grace; and we know that every Government exercises its discretion. And, I should like to know why these learned counsel, who are seeking to interpose, as a legal defence on the part of a criminal, the principles of policy and mercy which should guide the Government, are disposed to insist that this Government, in its prosecutions and its trials, has shown a disposition to absolve great masses of criminals from the penalties of its laws. I should like to know, when my learned friend Mr. Brady, near the close of his remarks, suggested that there had been no trial for treason, whether this Government, from the first steps in the outbreak, down to the final and extensive rage of the war, has not foreborne to take satisfaction for the wrongs committed against it, and has not been disposed to carry on and sustain the strength of the Government, without bloody sacrifices for its maintenance, and for the offended justice of the land. But it is certainly very strange if, when a Government influenced by those principles of humanity of which Vattel speaks, and which my learned friends so much insist upon, has foreborne, except in signal instances, or, if you please, in single instances that are not signal, to assert the standard of the law's authority and of the Government's right,—that it may be seen that the sword of justice, although kept sheathed for the most part, has yet not rusted in its scabbard, and that the Government is not faithless to itself, or to its laws, its powers, or its duties, in these particular prosecutions that have been carried, one to its conclusion, in Philadelphia, and the other to this stage of its progress, here,—it is strange, indeed, that the appeal is to be thrust upon it—"Do not include the masses of the misguided men!" and, when it yields so mercifully to that appeal, and says—"I will limit myself to the least maintenance and assertion of a right," that the answer is to come back: "Why, how execrable—how abominable, to make distinctions of that kind!"

But, gentlemen, the mercy of the Government, as I have said to you, remains after conviction, as well as in its determination not to press numerous trials for treason; but it is an attribute, both in forbearing to try and in forbearing to execute, which is safely left where the precedents that are to shape the authority of law cannot be urged against its exercise. Now, I look upon the conduct and duty of the Government on somewhat larger considerations than have been pressed before you here. The Government, it is said, does not desire the conviction of these men, or, at least, should not desire it. The Government does not desire the blood of any of its misguided people. The Government—the prosecution—should have no passion, no animosities, in this or in any other case; and our learned friends have done us the favor to say that the case is presented to you as the law should require it to be; that you, and all, are unaffected and unimpeded in your judgment; and that, with a full hearing of what could be said on the part of these criminals, you have the case candidly and openly before you.

Now, gentlemen, the Government, although having a large measure of discretion, has no right, in a country where the Government is one wholly of law, to repeal the criminal law, and no right to leave it without presenting it to the observation, the understanding, and the recognition of all its citizens, whether in rebellion or not, in its majesty, in its might, and in its impartiality. The Government has behind it the people, and it has behind it all the great forces which are breathing on our agitated society, all the strong passions, all the deep emotions, all the powerful convictions, which impress the loyal people of this country as to the outrage, as to the wickedness, as to the perils of this great rebellion. Do you not recollect how, when the proclamation of Mr. Davis invited marauders to prey upon our commerce, from whatever quarter and from whatever motives—(patriotism and duty not being requisite before they would be received)—the cry of the wounded sensibilities of a great commercial people burst upon this whole scene of conflict? What was there that as a nation we had more to be proud of, more to be glad for in our history, than our flag? To think that in an early stage of what was claimed to be first a constitutional, and then a peaceful, and then a deliberate political agitation and maintenance of right, this last extreme act, the arming of private persons against private property on the sea, was appealed to before even a force was drawn on the field on behalf of the United States of America! The proclamation of the President was but two days old when privateers were invited to rush to the standard. The indignation of the community, the sense of outrage and hatred was so severe and so strong, that at that time, if the sentiment of the people had been consulted, it would have found a true expression in what was asserted in the newspapers, in public speeches, in private conversations—that the duty of every merchantman and of every armed vessel of the country, which arrested any of these so-called privateers, under this new commission, without a nation and without authority, was, to treat them as pirates caught in the act, and execute them at the yard-arm by a summary justice.

Well, I need not say to you, gentlemen, that I am sure you and I and all of us would have had occasion to regret, in every sense, as wrong, as violent, as unnecessary, and, therefore, as wholly unjustifiable, on the part of a powerful nation like ourselves, any such rash execution of the penalties of the law of nations, and of the law of the land, while our Government had power on the sea, had authority on the land, had Courts and laws and juries under its authority to inquire and look into the transaction.

The public passions on this subject being all cool at this time, after an interval of four months or more from the arrest, we are here trying this case. Yet my learned friends can find complaint against the mercy of the Government and its justice, that it brings any prosecution; and great complaint is made before you, without the least ground or cause, as it seems to me, that the prosecution is pressed in a time of war, when the sentiments of the community are supposed to be inflamed.

Well, gentlemen, what is the duty of Government, when it has brought in prisoners arrested on the high seas, but to deliver them promptly to the civil authorities, as was done in this case—and then, in the language of the Constitution, which secures the right to them, to give them a speedy and impartial trial? That it is impartial, they all confess. How speedy is it? They say, they regret that it proceeds in time of war. Surely, our learned friends do not wish to be understood as having had denied to them in this Court any application which they have made for postponement. The promptness of the judicial and prosecuting authorities here had produced this indictment in the month of June, I believe, the very month in which the prisoners were arrested, or certainly early in July; and then the Government was ready to proceed with the trial, so far as I am advised. But, at any rate, an application—a very proper and necessary application—was made by our learned friends, that the trial should be postponed till, I believe, the very day on which it was brought on. That application was not objected to, was acquiesced in, and the time was fixed, and no further suggestion was made that the prisoners desired further delay; and, if the Government had undertaken to ask for further delay, on the ground of being unprepared, there was no fact to sustain any such application. If it was the wish of the prisoners, or for their convenience, that there should be further delay, it was for them to suggest it. But, being entitled by the Constitution to a speedy as well as an impartial trial, and the day being fixed by themselves on which they would be ready, and they being considered ready, and no difficulty or embarrassment in the way of proof having been suggested on the part of the Government, it seems to me very strange that this regret should be expressed, unless it should take that form of regret which all of us participate in, that the war is not over. That, I agree, is a subject of regret. But how there has ever been any pressure, or any—the least—exercise of authority adverse to their wishes in this matter, it is very difficult for me to understand.

Now, gentlemen, I approach a part of this discussion which I confess I would gladly decline. I have not the least objection—no one, I am sure, can feel the least objection—to the privilege or supposed duty of counsel, who are defending prisoners on a grave charge,—certainly not in a case which includes, as a possible result, the penalty of their client's lives,—to go into all the inquiries, discussions and arguments, however extensive, varied, or remote, that can affect the judgment of the Jury, properly or fairly, or that can rightly be invoked. But, I confess that, looking at the very interesting, able, extensive and numerous arguments, theories and illustrations, that have been presented in succession by, I think, in one form or another, seven counsel for these prisoners, as the introduction into a judicial forum, and before a Jury, of inquiries concerning the theories of Government, the course of politics, the occasion of strife on one side or the other, within the region of politics and the region of peace, in any portion of the great communities that composed this powerful nation—in that point of view, I aver, they seem to me very little inviting and instructive, as they certainly are extremely unusual in forensic discussions. Certainly, gentlemen of the Jury, we must conceive some starting point somewhere in the stability of human affairs, as they are entrusted to the control and defence of human Governments. But, in the very persistent and resolute views of the learned counsel upon this point—first on the right of secession as constitutional; second, if not constitutional, as being supposed by somebody to be constitutional; third, on the right of revolution as existing on the part of a people oppressed, or deeming themselves oppressed, to try their strength in the overthrow of the subsisting Government; fourth, on the right to press the discontents inside of civil war; and then finally and at last, that whoever thinks the Government oppresses him, or thinks that a better Government would suit his case, has not only the right to try the venture, but that, unsuccessful, or at any stage of the effort, his right becomes so complete that the Government must and should surrender at once and to every attempt—I see only what is equivalent to a subversion of Government, and to saying that the right of revolution, in substance and in fact, involves the right of Government in the first place, and its duty in the second place, to surrender to the revolutionist, and to treat him as having overthrown it in point of law, and in contemplation of its duty. That is a proposition which I cannot understand.

Nevertheless, gentlemen, these subjects have been so extensively opened, and in so many points attacks have been made upon what seems to me not only the very vital structure and necessary support of this, our Government, but the very necessary and indispensable support of any Government whatever, and we have been so distinctly challenged, both on the ground of an absolute right to overthrow this Government, whenever any State thinks fit—and, next, upon the clear right, on general principles of human equity, of each State to raise itself against any Government with which it is dissatisfied—and upon the general right of conscience—as well as on the complete support by what has been assumed to have been the parallel case, on all those principles, of the conduct of the Colonies which became the United States of America and established our Government—that I shall find it necessary, in the discharge of my duty, to say something, however briefly, on that subject. Now, gentlemen, these are novel discussions in a Court of Justice, within the United States of America. We have talked about the oppressions of other nations, and rejoiced in our exemption from all of them, under the free, and benignant, and powerful Government which was, by the favor of Providence, established by the wisdom, and courage, and virtue of our ancestors. We had, for more than two generations, reposed under the shadow of our all-protecting Government, with the same conscious security as under the firmament of the heavens. We knew, to be sure, that for all that made life hopeful and valuable—for all that made life possible—we depended upon the all-protecting power, and the continued favor of Divine Providence. We knew, just as well, that, without civil society, without equal and benignant laws, without the administration of justice, without the maintenance of commerce, without a suitable Government, without a powerful nationality, all the motives and springs of human exertion and labor would be dried up at their source. But we felt no more secure in the Divine promise that "summer and winter, seed-time and harvest," should not cease, than we did in the permanent endurance of that great fabric established by the wisdom and the courage of a renowned ancestry, to be the habitation of liberty and justice for us and our children to every generation. We felt no solicitude whatever that this great structure of our constituted liberties should pass away as a scroll, or its firm power crumble in the dust. But, by the actual circumstances of our situation,—and, if not by them, certainly by the destructive theories which are presented for your consideration,—it becomes necessary for us, as citizens, and, in the judgment at least of the learned counsel, for these prisoners, for you, and for this learned Court, in the conduct of this trial, and in the disposition of the issue of "guilty" or "not guilty" as to these prisoners, to pay some attention to these considerations. If, in the order of this discussion, gentlemen, I should not seem to follow in any degree, or even to include by name, many of the propositions, of the distinctions, and of the arguments which our learned friends have pressed against the whole solidity, the whole character, the whole permanence, the whole strength of our Government, I yet think you will find that I have included the principal ideas they have advanced, and have commented upon the views that seem to us—at least so far as we think them to be at all connected with this case—suitable to be considered.

Now, gentlemen, let us start with this business where our friends, in their argument, where many of the philosophers, and partisans, and statesmen of the Southern people, have found many of their grounds of support. Let us start with this very subject of the American Revolution, with the condition that we were in, and with the place that we found ourselves raised to, among the nations of the earth, as the result of that great transaction in the affairs of men. What were we before the Revolution commenced? Was any one of the original thirteen States out of which our nation was made, and which, previous to the Revolution, were Colonies of Great Britain—was any one of them an independent nation at the time they all slumbered under the protection of the British Crown? Why, not only had they not the least pretension to be a nation, any of them, but they had scarcely the position of a thoroughly incorporated part of the great nation of England. Now, how did they stand towards the British power, and under what motives of dignity, and importance, and necessity did they undertake their severance from the parent country? With all their history of colonization, the settlement of their different charters, and the changes they went through, I will not detain you. For general purposes, we all know enough, and I, certainly not more than the rest of you. This, however, was their condition. The population were all subjects of the British Crown; and they all had forms of local Government which they had derived from the British Crown; and they claimed and possessed, as I suppose, all the civil and political rights of Englishmen. They were not subject to any despotic power, but claimed and possessed that right to a share in the Government, which was the privilege of Englishmen, and under which they protected themselves against the encroachment of the Crown. But, in England, as you know, the monarch was attended by his Houses of Parliament, and all the power of the Government was controlled by the people, through their representatives in the House of Commons. And how? Why, because, although the King had prerogatives, executive authority, a vast degree of pomp and wealth, and of strength, yet the people, represented in the House of Commons, by controlling the question of taxation, held all the wealth of the kingdom—the power of the purse, as it was described—and without supplies, without money for the army, for the navy, for all the purposes of Government, what authority, actual and effective, had the Crown of England? These were the rights of Englishmen; these made them a free people, not subject to despotic power. They cherished it and loved it. Now, what relation did these Colonies, becoming off-shoots from the great fabric of the national frame of England, bring with them, and assert, and enjoy here? Why, the king was their king, just as he was the king of the people whom they left in England, but they had their legislatures here, which made their laws for them in Massachusetts, in Connecticut, in Virginia, in South Carolina, and in the rest of these provinces; and among those laws, in the power of law-making, they had asserted, and possessed, and enjoyed the right of laying taxes for the expenses and charges of their Government. They formed no part of the Parliament of England, but, as the subjects of England within the four seas were obedient to the king, and were represented in the Parliament that made laws for them, the Colonies of America were subject to the king, but had local legislatures, to pass laws, raise and levy taxes, and graduate the expenses and contributions which they would bear.

Now, gentlemen, it is quite true that the local legislatures were subject to the revision, as to their statutes, to a certain extent, of the sovereign power of England. The king had the veto power—as he had the veto power over Acts of Parliament—the power of revision—and other powers, as may have been the casual outgrowth of the forms of different charters. In an evil hour—as these Colonies, from being poor, despised, and feeble communities, gained a strength and numbers that attracted the attention of the Crown of England, as important and productive communities, capable of being taxed—the Government undertook to assert, as the principle of the Constitution of England, that the king and Parliament, sitting in London, could tax as they pleased, when they pleased, and in the form, and on the subjects, and to the amount, they pleased, the free people of these Colonies. Now, you will understand, there was not an incidental, a casual, a limited subject of controversy, of right, of danger, but there was an attack upon the first principles of English liberty, which prevented the English people from being the subjects of a despot, and an attempt to make us subject to a despotic Government, in which we took no share, and in which we had no control of the power of the purse. What matter did it make to us that, instead of there being a despotic authority, in which we had no share or representation of vote or voice, exercised by the king alone, it was exercised by the king and Parliament? They were both of them powers of Government that were away from us, and in which we had no share; and we, then, forewarned by the voices of the great statesmen whose sentiments have been read to you, saw in time that, whatever might be said or thought of the particular exercise of authority, the proposition was that we were not entitled to the privilege and freedom of Englishmen, but that the power was confined to those who resided within the four seas—within the islands that made up that Kingdom—and that we were provinces which their King and their Parliament governed. Therefore, you may call it a question of taxation, and my friend may call it "a question of three pence a pound on tea;" but it was the proposition that the power of the purse, in this country, resided in England. We had not been accustomed to it. We did not believe in it. And our first revolutionary act was to fight for our rights as Englishmen (subject to the King, whose power we admitted), and to assert the rights of our local legislature in the overthrow of this usurpation of Parliament. Now, of the course which we took before we resorted to the violence and vehemence of war, I shall have hereafter occasion to present you, very briefly and conclusively, a condensed recital; but this notion, that we here claimed any right to rise up against a Government that was in accordance with our rights, and was such as we had made it, and as we enjoyed it, equally with all others over whom it was exercised—which lies at the bottom of the revolt in this country—had not the least place, or the opportunity of a place, in our relations with England. We expected and desired, as the correspondence of Washington shows—as some of the observations of Hamilton, I think, read in your presence by the learned counsel, show—as the records of history show—we expected to establish security for ourselves under the British Crown, and as a part of the British Empire, and to maintain the right of Englishmen, to wit, the right of legislation and taxation where we were represented. But the parent Government, against the voice and counsels of such statesmen as Burke, and the warnings of such powerful champions of liberty as Chatham, undertook to insist, upon the extreme logic of their Constitution, that we were British subjects, and that the king and Parliament governed all British subjects; and they had a theory, I believe, that we were represented in Parliament, as one English jurist put it, in the fact that all the grants in all the Colonies were, under the force of English law, "to have and to hold, as the Manor of East Greenwich," and that, as the Manor of East Greenwich was represented in Parliament, all this people were represented. But this did not suit our notions. The lawyers of this country, the Judges of this country, and many of the lawyers of England, as mere matter of strict legal right, held that the American view of the Constitution of England, and of the rights of Englishmen who enjoy it, was the true one. But, at any rate, it was not upon an irritation about public sentiment; nor was it upon the pressure of public taxes; nor because we did not constitute a majority of Parliament; nor anything of that kind; but it was on clear criteria of whether we were slaves, as Hamilton presents it, or part of the free people of a Government. We, therefore, by degrees, and somewhat unconscious, perhaps, of our own enlightened progress, but yet wisely, fortunately, prosperously, determined upon our independence, as the necessary means of securing those rights which were denied to us under the Constitution of our country.

Now, there was not the least pretence of the right of a people to overthrow a Government because they so desire—which seems to be the proposition here—because they think they do not like it—and because there are some points or difficulties in its working they would like to have adjusted. No; it was on the mere proposition that the working of the administration in England was converting us into subjects, not of the Crown, with the rights of Englishmen, but subjects of the despotic power of Parliament and the king of England. Now, how did we go to work, and what was the result of that Revolution? In the first place, did we ever become *thirteen* nations? Was Massachusetts a nation? Was South Carolina a nation? Did either of them ever declare its independence, or ever engage in a war, by itself and of itself, against England, to accomplish its independence? No, never; the first and preliminary step before independence was union. The circumstances of the Colonies, we may well believe, made it absolutely necessary that they should settle beforehand the question of whether they could combine themselves into one effectual, national force, to contend with England, before they undertook to fight her. It was pretty plain that Massachusetts could not conquer England, or its own independence, and that Virginia could not do so, and that the New England States alone could not do it, and that the Southern States alone could not do it. It was quite plain that New York, Pennsylvania and New Jersey, alone, could not do it; and, therefore, in the very womb, as it were, and preceding our birth as a nation, we were articulated together into the frame of one people, one community, one nationality. Now, however imperfectly, and however clumsily, and however unsuitably we were first connected, and however necessary and serious the changes which substituted for that inchoate shape of nationality the complete, firm, noble and perfect structure which made us one people as the United States of America, yet you will find, in all the documents, and in all the history, that there was a United States of America, in some form represented, before there was anything like a separation, on the part of any of the Colonies, from the parent country, except in these discontents, and these efforts at an assertion of our liberties, which had a local origin.

The great part of the argument of my learned friend rests upon the fact that these States were nations, each one of them, once upon a time; and that, having made themselves this Government, they have remained nations, in it and under it, ever since, subject only to the Confederate authority, in the terms of a certain instrument called a compact, and with the reserved right of nationality ready, at all times, to spring forth and manifest itself in complete separation of any one of the States from the rest. And I find, strangely enough, in the argument as well of the promoters of these political movements at the South as in the voice of my learned friends who have commented on this subject, a reference to the early diplomacy of the United States, as indicative of the fact that they were separate and independent communities—regarded as such by the contracting Powers into connection with whom they were brought by their treaties and conventions, and, more particularly, in the definitive treaty whereby their independence was recognized by Great Britain. Now, if the Court please, both upon the point (if it can be called a point, connected with your judicial inquiry) that these Colonies were formed into a Union before they secured their national independence, and that there was no moment of time wherein they were not included, either as united Colonies, under the parental protection of Great Britain, or as united in a struggling Provisional Government, or in the perfect Government of the Confederation, and, finally, under the present Constitution—I apprehend there can be no doubt that our diplomacy, commencing, in 1778, with the Treaty of Alliance with France, contains the same enumeration of States that is so much relied upon by the reasoners for independent nationality on the part of all the States. In the preamble to that Treaty, found at page 6 of the 8th volume of the Statutes at Large, the language was: "The Most Christian King and the United States of North America, to wit, New Hampshire, &c., having this day concluded," &c. The United States are here treated as a strictly single power, with whom his Most Christian Majesty comes into league; and the credentials or ratifications pursued the same form. The Treaty of Commerce with the same nation, made at the same time, follows the same idea; and the Treaty with the Netherlands, made in 1782, contains the same enumeration of the States, and speaks of each of the contracting parties as being "countries." The Convention with the Netherlands, on page 50 of the same volume, and which was a part of the same diplomatic arrangement, and made at the same time, speaks, in Article 1, of the vessels of the "two nations." Now, the only argument of my learned friends, on the two treaties with Great Britain, of November, 1782, and September, 1783, is, that they are an agreement between England and the thirteen nations; and it is founded upon the fact, that the United States of America, after being described as such, are enumerated under a "viz." as being so many provinces. Now, the 5th and 6th articles of that Convention of 1782 with the Netherlands speak of "the vessels of war and privateers of one and of the other of the two nations." So that, pending the Revolution, we certainly, in the only acts of nationality that were possible for a contending power, set ourselves forth as only one nation, and were so recognized. And the same views are derivable from the language of the Provisional Treaty with Great Britain of November, 1782, and of the Definitive Treaty of Peace with Great Britain of September, 1783, which

Treaties are to be found at pages 54 and 80 of the same 8th volume. The Preamble to the latter Treaty recites:

"It having pleased the Divine Providence to dispose the hearts of the most serene and most potent Prince George the Third, &c., and of the United States of America to forget all past misunderstandings and differences that have unhappily interrupted the good correspondence and friendship, which they mutually wish to restore; and to establish such a beneficial and satisfactory intercourse *between the two countries*, &c.'"

And then comes the 1st article, which is identical in language with the Treaty with the Netherlands, of 1782:

"His Britannic Majesty acknowledges the said United States, viz., New Hampshire, &c., to be free, sovereign and independent States."

The United States had previously, in the Treaty, been spoken of as one country, and the language I have just quoted is only a statement of the provinces of which they were composed; for, we all know, as matter of history, that there were other British provinces that might have joined in this Revolution, and might, perhaps, have been included in the settlement of peace; and this rendered it suitable and necessary that the provinces whose independence was acknowledged should be specifically described. But, in the 2d article, so far from the separateness of the nationalities with which the convention was made being at all recognized, that important article, which is the one of boundaries, goes on to bound the entire nation as one undivided and integral territory, without the least attention to the divisions between them. It may be very well to say that England was only concerned to have one continuous boundary, coterminous to her own possessions, described, and that that was the object of the geographical bounding; but the entire Western, Eastern, and Southern boundaries are gone through as those of one integral nation. The 3d article speaks, again, of securing certain rights to the citizens or inhabitants of "both countries." Now, that "country" and "nation," in the language of diplomacy, are descriptive, not of territory, in either case, but of the nationality, admits of no discussion; and yet, I believe that the most substantial of all the citations and of all the propositions from the documentary evidence of the Revolution, which seeks to make out the fact that we came into being as thirteen nations, grows out of this British Treaty, which, in its preamble, takes notice of but one country, called the United States of America, and, then, in recognition of the United States of

America, names the States under a "viz."—they being included in the single collective nation before mentioned as the United States.

Now, gentlemen, after the Revolution had completed our independence, how were we left as respects our rights, our interests, our hopes, and our prospects on this very subject of nationality? Why, we were left in this condition—that we always had been accustomed to a parent or general Government, and to a local subordinate administration of our domestic affairs within the limits of our particular provinces. Under the good fortune, as well as the great wisdom which saw that this arrangement—a new one— quite a new one in the affairs of men—now that we were completely independent, and capable of being masters of our whole Government, both local and general, admitted of none of those discontents and dangers which belonged to our being subject collectively to the dominion of a remote power beyond the seas—under the good fortune and great wisdom of that opportunity, we undertook and determined to establish, and had already established provisionally, a complete Government, which we supposed would answer the purpose of having a general representation and protection of ourselves toward the world at large, and yet would limit the local power and authority, consistently with good and free Government, as respected populations homeogeneous, and acquainted with each other, and with their own wants and the methods of supplying them.

The Articles of Confederation, framed during the Revolution, ratified at different times during its progress, and at its close, was a Government under which we subsisted—for how long? Until 1787—but four years from the time that we had an independent nationality—we were satisfied with the imperfect Union that our provisional Government had originated, and that we had shaped into somewhat more consistency under the Articles of Confederation. Why did we not stay under that? We were a feeble community. We had but little population, but little wealth. We had but few of the occasions of discontent that belong to great, and wealthy, and populous States. But the fault, the difficulty, was, that there were, in that Confederation, too many features which our learned friends, their clients here, and theoretical teachers of theirs elsewhere, contend, make the distinctive character of the American Constitution, as finally developed and established. The difficulty was that, although we were apparently and intentionally a nation, as respected the rest of the world, and for all the purposes of common interest and common protection and common development, yet this element of separate independency, and these views that the Government thus framed operated, not as a Government over individuals, but as a Government over local communities in an organized form, made its working imperfect, impossible, and the necessary occasion of dissension, and weakness, and hostility, and left it without the least power, except by continued force and war, to maintain nationality.

Now, it was not because we were sovereigns, all of us, because we had departed from sovereignty. There was not the least right in any State to send an ambassador, or make a treaty, or have anything signed; but the vice was, that the General Government had no power or authority, directly, on the citizens of the States, but had to send its mandates for contributions to the common treasury, and its requirements for quotas for the common army and the common navy, directly to the States. Now, I tarry no longer on this than to say, that the brief experience of four years showed that it was an impossible proposition for a Government, that there should be in it even these imperfect, clipped and crippled independencies, that were made out of the original provinces and called States. In 1787, the great Convention had its origin, and in 1789 the adoption of the Constitution made something that was supposed to be, and entitled to be, and our citizens required to be, as completely different, on this question of double sovereignty, and divided allegiance, and equal right of the nation to require and of a State to refuse, as was possible. If, indeed, instead of the Confederation having changed itself from an imperfect connection of States limited and reduced in sovereignty, into a Government where the nation is the coequal and co-ordinate power (as our friends express it) of every State in it, why surely our brief experience of weakness and disorder, and of contempt, such as was visited upon us by the various nations with whom we had made treaties, that we could not fulfil them, found, in the practical wisdom of the intelligent American people, but a very imperfect and unsatisfactory solution, if the theories of the learned counsel are correct, that these United States are, on the one part, a power, and on the other part, thirty-four different powers, all sovereign, and the two having complete rights of sovereignty, and dividing the allegiance of our citizens in every part of our territory.

Now, the language of the Constitution is familiar to all of you. That it embodies the principle of a General Government acting upon all the States, and upon you, and upon me, and upon every one in the United States; that it has its own established Courts—its own mandate by which jurors are brought together—its own laws upon all the subjects that are attributed to its authority; that there is an establishment known as the Supreme Court, which, with the appropriate inferior establishments, controls and finally disposes of every question of law, and right, and political power, and political duty; and that this adjusted system of one nation with distributed local power, is, in its working, adequate to all the varied occasions which human life develops—we all know. We have lived under it, we have prospered under it, we have been made a great nation, an united people, free, happy, and powerful.

Now, gentlemen, it is said—and several points in our history have been appealed to, as well as the disturbances that have torn our country for the last year—that this complete and independent sovereignty of the States has been recognized. Now, there have been several occasions on which this subject has come up. The first was under the administration of the first successor of General Washington—John Adams,—when the famous Virginia and Kentucky resolutions had their origin. About these one of my learned friends gave you a very extensive discussion, and another frankly admitted that he could not understand the doctrine of the co-ordinate, equal sovereignty of two powers within the same State. On the subject of these Virginia resolutions, and on the question of whether they were the recognized doctrines of this Government, I ask your attention to but one consideration of the most conclusive character, and to be disposed of in the briefest possible space. The proposition of the Virginia resolutions was, that the States who are parties to the compact have the right and are in duty bound to interpose to arrest the progress of the evil (that is, when unconstitutional laws are passed), and to maintain, within their respective limits, the authority, rights, and liberties pertaining to them. That is to say, that where any law is passed by the Congress of the United States, which the State of Virginia, in its wise and independent judgment, pronounces to be in excess of the constitutional power, it is its right and duty to interpose. How? By secession? No. By rebellion? No. But by protecting and maintaining, within its territory, the authority, rights, and liberties pertaining to it. Now, these resolutions grew out of what? Certain laws, one called the "Alien" and the other the "Sedition" law, rendered necessary by the disturbances communicated by the French revolution to this country, and which necessarily came within the doctrine of my friend, Mr. Larocque, that there is not the least right of secession when the laws are capable of being the subject of judicial investigation. Well, those laws were capable of being the subject of judicial investigation, and the resolutions did not claim the right of secession, but of nullification. My learned friend says that the doctrine of "secession" has no ground.

But what was the fate of the "Virginia resolutions"? For Virginia did not pretend that she had all the wisdom, and virtue, and patriotism of the country within her borders. She sent these resolutions to every State in the Union, and desired the opinion of their legislatures and their governors on the subject. Kentucky passed similar resolutions; and Kentucky, you will notice, had just been made a State, in 1793—an off-shoot from Virginia; and, as the gentleman has told you, Mr. Madison wrote the resolutions of Virginia, and Mr. Jefferson those of Kentucky. So that there was not any great independent support, in either State, for the views, thus identical, and thus promulgated by these two Virginians. Their great patriotism, and wisdom, and intelligence, are a part of the inheritance we are all proud of. But, when the appeal was sent for concurrence to New York, South Carolina, Georgia, Massachusetts, and the New England States, what was the result? Why, Kentucky, in 1799, regrets that, of all the States, none, except Virginia, acquiesced in the doctrines; and the answers of every one of the States that made response are contained in the record which also contains the Virginia and Kentucky resolutions. And that doctrine there exploded, and exploded forever, until its recurrence in the shape of nullification, in South Carolina, as part of the doctrines of this Constitution.

We had another pressure on the subject of local dissatisfaction, in 1812; and then the seat of discontent and heresy was New England. I do not contend, and never did contend, in any views I have taken of the history of affairs in this country, that the people of any portion of it have a right to set themselves in judgment as superiors over the people of any other portion. I never have had any doubt that, just as circumstances press on the interests of one community or another, just so are they likely to carry their theoretical opinions on the questions of the power of their Government and of their own rights, and just so to express themselves. So long as they confine themselves to resolutions and politics, to the hustings and to the elections, nobody cares very much what their political theories are. But my learned friend Mr. Brady has taken the greatest satisfaction in showing, that this notion of the co-ordinate authority of the States with the nation, found its expression and adoption, during the war of 1812, in some of the States of New England. Well, gentlemen, I believe that all sober and sensible people agree that, whether or not the New England States carried their heresies to the extent of justifying the nullification of a law, or the revocation of their assent to the Confederacy, and their withdrawal from the common Government, the doctrines there maintained were not suitable for the strength and the harmony, for the unity and the permanency, of the American Government. I believe that the condemnation of those principles that followed, from South Carolina, from Virginia, from New York, and from other parts of the country, and the resistance which a large, and important, and intelligent, and influential portion of their own local community manifested, exterminated those heresies forever from the New England mind.

Next, we come to 1832, and then, under the special instruction and authority of a great Southern statesman, (Mr. Calhoun,) whose acuteness and power of reasoning have certainly been scarcely, if at all, surpassed by any of our great men, the State of South Carolina undertook, not to secede, but to nullify; and yet Mr. Larocque says, that this pet doctrine of Mr. Calhoun,—nullification, and nothing else,—is the absurdest thing ever presented in this country; and we are fortunate, I suppose, in not having wrecked our Union upon that doctrine.

Now we come, next, to the doctrine of secession. Nullification, rejected in 1798 by all the States, except Virginia and Kentucky, and never revived by them,—nullification, rejected by the sober sense of the American People,—nullification was put down by the strong will of Jackson, in 1832,—having no place to disturb the strength and hopes and future of this country. And what do we find is the proposition now put forward, as matter of law, to your Honors, to relieve armed and open war from the penalties of treason, and from the condemnation of a lesser crime? What is it, as unfolded here by the learned advocate (Mr. Larocque), with all his acuteness, but so manifest an absurdity that its recognition by a lawyer, or an intelligent Jury, seems almost impossible? It is this: This Union has its power, its authority, its laws. It acts directly upon all the individuals inside of every State, and they owe it allegiance as their Government. It is a Government which is limited, in the exercise of its power, to certain general and common objects, not interfering with the domestic affairs of any community. Within that same State there is a State government, framed into this General Government, to be certainly a part of it in its territories, a part of it in its population, a part of it in every organization, and every department of its Government. The whole body of its administration of law, the Legislature and the Executive, are bound, by a particular oath, to sustain the Constitution of the United States. But, although it is true that the State Government has authority only where the United States Government has not, and that the United States have authority only where the State has not; and although there is a written Constitution, which says what the line of separation is; and although there is a Supreme Court, which, when they come into collision, has authority to determine between them, and no case whatever, affecting the right or the conduct of any individual man, can be subtracted from its decision; yet, when there comes a difference between the State and the General Government, the State has the moral right, and political right, to insist upon its view, and to maintain it by force of arms, and the General Government has the right to insist upon its view, and to maintain it by force of arms. And then we have this poor predicament for every citizen of that unlucky State,—that he is bound by allegiance, and under the penalty of treason, to follow each and both of these powers. And as, should he follow the State, the United States, if it be treason, would hang him, and, if he should follow the United States, the State, if it be treason, would hang him, this peculiar and whimsical result is produced,—that when the United States undertake to hang him for treason his answer is—"Why, if I had not done as I did, the State would have hanged me for treason, and, surely, I cannot be compelled to be hanged one way or the other—so, I must be protected from hanging, as to both!" Well, *that*, I admit, is a sensible way to get out of the difficulty, for the man and for the argument, if you can do it. But, it is a peculiar result, to start with two sovereigns, each of which has a right over the citizen, and to end with the citizen's right to choose which he shall serve, and to throw it in the face of offended majesty and justice—"Why, your statute of treason is repealed as against me, because the State, of which I am a subject, has counseled a particular course of conduct!"

Now, gentlemen, my learned friend qualifies even this theory—which probably must fall within the condemnation of the perhaps somewhat harsh and rough suggestion of Mr. Justice Grier, of a "political platitude"—by the suggestion that it only applies to questions where the united States cannot settle the controversy. And when my learned friend is looking around for an instance or an occasion that is likely to arise in human affairs, and in this nation, and in this time of ours, he is obliged to resort to the most extraordinary and extravagant proposition by way of illustration, and one that has, in itself, so many of the ingredients of remoteness and impossibility, that you can hardly think a Government deficient in not having provided for it. He says, first—suppose we have a President, who is a Massachusetts man. Well, that is not very likely in the course of politics at present. And then, suppose that he is a bad man,—which, probably, my learned friends would think not as unlikely as I should wish it to be. And, then, suppose he should undertake to build up Boston, in its commerce, at the expense of New York; and should put a blockading squadron outside New York, by mere force of caprice and tyranny, without any law, and without any provision for the payment of the men of the Navy, or any commission or authority to any of them under which they could find they were protected for what they should do, in actually and effectually blockading our port. My learned friend acknowledges that this is a pretty violent sort of suggestion, and that no man in his senses would pretend to do such a thing, however bad he was, unless he could find a reasonable sort of pretext for it. Therefore he would, wisely and craftily, pretend that he had private advices that England was going to bombard New York. Now that is the practical case created by my learned friend's ingenuity and reflection, as a contingency in which this contest by war between New York and the United States of America would be the only practical and sensible mode of protecting our commerce, and keeping you and me in the enjoyment of our rights as citizens of the State of New York. Well, to begin with, if we had a fleet off New York harbor, what is there that would require vessels to go to Boston instead of to Philadelphia, Baltimore, and other places that are open? In the second place, how long could we be at war, and how great an army could we raise in New York, to put in the field against the Federal Government, before this pretence of private advices that England was going to bombard New York, would pass away, and the naked deformity of this bad Massachusetts President be exposed? Why, gentlemen, it is too true to need suggestion, that the wisdom which made this a Government over all individual citizens, and made every case of right and interest that touches the pocket and person of any man in it a question of judicial settlement, made it a Government which requires for the solution of none of the controversies within it, a resort to the last appeal—to battle, and the right of kings.

(Adjourned to 11 o'clock to-morrow.)

SEVENTH DAY.

Wednesday, October 30, 1861.

The Court met at 11 o'clock A.M., when *Mr. Evarts* resumed his argument.

Gentlemen of the Jury: In resuming the course of my remarks, already necessarily drawn to a very considerable length, I must recall to your attention the point that I had reached when the Court adjourned. I was speaking of this right of secession, as inconsistent with the frame, the purpose, and the occasion upon which the General Government was formed; and of the illustration invented by my learned friend, and so improbable in its circumstances, of the position of the United States and one of the States of the Union, that could bring into play and justify this resort to armed opposition. I had said what I had to say, for the most part, as to the absurdity and improbability of the case supposed, and the inadequacy, the worthlessness, the chimerical nature of the remedy proposed. Now, you will observe that, in the case supposed, the blockade of New York was to be without law, without authority, upon the mere capricious pretence of the President—a pretence so absurd that it could not stand the inspection of the people for a moment. What is the use of a pretence unless it is a cover for the act which it is intended to cloak? In such a case, the only proper, peaceful course would be to raise the question, which might be raised judicially, by attempting, in a peaceful manner, to pass the blockade, and throw the consequences upon the subordinate officers who attempted to execute the mere usurpation of the President, and, following the declaration of the Divine writings, that "wisdom is better than weapons of war," wait until the question could be disposed of under the Constitution of the United States. For you will observe that, in the case supposed, there is no threat to the integrity, no threat to the authority, no threat to the existence of the State Government, or its Constitution; but an impeding of the trade or interests of the people of this city, and of the residents of all parts of the country interested in the commerce of New York. That port is not the port of New York alone. It is the port of the United States of America, and all the communities in the Western country, who derive their supplies of foreign commodities through our internal navigation, when commerce has introduced them into this port, are just as much affected—just as much injured and oppressed—by this blockade of our great port and emporium, as are the people of the State of New York. So that, so far from its being a collision between the Government of the State of New York and the Government of the United States, it is a violent oppression, by usurpation—exposing to the highest penalties of the law the magistrate who has attempted it—exercised upon the people of the United States wherever residing, in the far West, in the surrounding States, in the whole country, who are interested

- 363 -

in the maintenance of the commerce of this port. I need not say that the action of our institutions provides a ready solution for this difficulty. Two or three weeks must bring to the notice of every one the frivolity of the pretence of the Executive, that there was a threat of armed attack by a foreign nation. But if two or three weeks should bring the evidence that this was not an idle fear, and that, by information conveyed to the Government, this threat was substantial, and was followed by its attempted execution,—why, then, how absurd the proposition that, under the opinion of the State of New York, that this was but an idle pretext, for purposes of oppression, the State should fly into arms against the power exercised to protect the city from foreign attack! The working of our affairs, which brings around the session of Congress at a time fixed by law—not at all determinable by the will of the President—exposes him to the grand inquest of the people, which sits upon his crime, and, by his presentation and trial before the great Court of Impeachment, in the course of one week—nay, in scarcely more than one day after its coming into session—both stamps this act as an usurpation, and dispossesses the magistrate who has violated the Constitution. And yet, rather than wait for this assertion of the power of the Constitution peacefully to depose the usurping magistrate, my friend must resort to this violent intervention of armed collision, that would keep us—in theory, at least— constantly maintaining our rights by the mere method of force, and would make of this Government—at the same time that they eulogize the founders of it, as the best and wisest of men—but an organization of armed hostilities, and its framers only the architects of an ever-impending ruin!

My learned friend, Mr. Brady, has asked my attention to the solution of a case wherein he thinks the State Government might be called upon to protect the rights of its citizens against the operation of an Act of Congress, by proposing this question: Suppose Congress should require that all the expenses of this great war, as we call it, should be paid by the State of New York,—what should we do in that case? Nothing but hostilities are a solution for that case, it is suggested. Now, I would freely say to my learned friend, Mr. Brady, that if the General Government, by its law, should impose the whole taxation of the war upon the State of New York, I should advise the State of New York, or any citizen in it, not to pay the taxes. That is the end of the matter. And I would like to know if there is any warlike process by which the General Government of the United States exacts its tribute of taxation, that could impose the whole amount on New York? As the process of taxation goes on, it is distributed through different channels, and presents itself as an actual and effective process, from the tax-gatherer to the tax-payer: "Give me so many dollars." And the tax-payer says: "There is no law for it, and I will not do it." Then the process of collection raises for consideration this inquiry—whether the tax is according to law, and according to the constitutional law of the United States of America. And this tribunal, formed to decide such questions—formed to settle principles in single cases, that shall protect against hostilities these great communities—disposes of the question. If the law is constitutional, then the tax is to be paid—if unconstitutional, then the tax is not collectable; and the question is settled. But my learned friends, in their suggestions of what is a possible state of law that may arise in this country, forget the great distinction between our situation under the Federal Government and our situation as Colonies under the authority of the King and Parliament of England. It is the distinction between not being represented and being represented.

Why, my learned friends, in order to get the basis of a possible suggestion of contrariety of duty and of interest between the Government of the United States and the people in these States, must overlook, and do overlook the fact that there is not a functionary in the Federal Government, from the President down to the Houses of Congress, that does not derive his authority from the people, not of one State, not of any number of States, but of all the States. And thus standing, they are guardians and custodians, in their own interests—in their own knowledge of the interests of their own people—in their own knowledge that their place in the protection, power, and authority of the Government of the United States, proceeds by the favor and the approval of the local community in which they reside. So far, therefore, from anything in the arrangement or the working of these political systems being such as to make the Representatives or Senators that compose Congress the masters or the enemies of the local population of the States from which they respectively come, they come there under the authority of the local population which they represent, dependent upon it for their place and continuance, and not on the Federal Government.

Away, then, with the notion, so foreign to our actual, constituted Government, that this Government of the United States of America is a Government that is extended over these States, with an origin, a power, a support independent of them, and that it contains in itself an arrangement, a principle, a composition that can by possibility excite or sustain these hostilities! Why, every act of Congress must govern the whole Union. Every tax must, to be constitutional, be extended over the whole Union, and according to a fixed ratio of distribution between the States, established by the Constitution itself. Now, therefore, when any particular interest, any particular occasion, any supposed necessity, any political motive, suggests a departure, on the part of the General Government, from a necessary adherence to this principle of the Constitution, you will perceive that not only are the Representatives and Senators who come from the State against which this exercise of power is attempted, interested to oppose, in their places in Congress, the violation of the Constitution, but the Representatives and the Senators from every other State, in support of the rights of the local communities in which they reside, have the same interest and the same duty, and may be practically relied upon to exercise the same right, and authority, and opposition, in protection of their communities, against an application of the same principle, or an obedience to the same usurpation, on subsequent occasions, in reference to other questions that may arise. Therefore, my learned friends, when they are talking to you, theoretically or practically, about the opposition that may arise between co-ordinate and independent sovereignties, and would make the glorious Constitution of this Federal Government an instance of misshapen, and disjointed, and impractical inconsistencies, forget that the great basis of both of them rests in the people, and in the same people—equally interested, equally powerful, to restrain and to continue the movements of each, within the separate, constitutional rights of each. Now, unquestionably, in vast communities, with great interests, diverse and various, opinions may vary, and honest sentiments may produce the enactment of laws of Congress, which equally honest sentiments, on the part of local communities, expressed through the action of State legislation, may regard as inconsistent with the Government and the Constitution of the United States, and with the rights of the States. But, for these purposes, for these occasions, an ample and complete theoretical and practical protection of the rights of all is found, in this absolute identity of the interests of the people and of their authority in both the form and the structure of their complex Government, and in the means provided by the Constitution itself for testing every question that touches the right, the interest, the liberty, the property, the freedom of any citizen, in all and any of these communities, before the Supreme Court of the United States. Let us not be drawn into any of these shadowy propositions, that the whole people may be oppressed, and not a single individual in it be deprived of any personal right. Whenever the liberty of the citizen is abridged in respect to any personal right, the counsel concede that the Courts are open to him; and that is the theory, the wisdom, and the practical success of the American Constitution.

Now, gentlemen of the Jury, but one word more on this speculative right of secession. It is founded, if at all, upon the theory, that the States, having been, anterior to the formation of the Constitution, independent sovereignties, are, themselves, the creators, and that the Constitution is the creature proceeding from their power. I have said all I have to say about either the fact, or the result of the fact, if it be one, of the existence of these antecedent, complete national sovereignties on the part of any of the original States. But, will my learned friends tell me how this theory of theirs, in respect to the original thirteen States, has any application to the States, now quite outnumbering the original thirteen, which have, since the Constitution was formed, entered into the Government of this our territory, this our people? Out of thirty-four States, eleven have derived their existence, their permission to exist, their territory, their power to make a Constitution, from the General Government itself, out of whose territory—either acquired originally by the wealth or conquest of the Federal Government, or derived directly or indirectly through the cession or partition or separation of the original Colonies—they have sprung into existence. Of these eleven allied and confederate States, but four came from the stock of the original thirteen, and seven derived their whole power and authority from the permission of the Constitution of the United States, and have sprung into existence, with the breath of their lives breathed into them through the Federal Government. When the State of Louisiana talks of its right to secede by reason of its sovereignty, by reason of its being one of the creators of the Federal Government, and of the Federal Constitution—one of the actors in the principles of the American Revolution, and in the conquest of our liberties from the English power— we may well lift our hands in surprise at the arrogance of such a suggestion. Why, what was Louisiana, in all her territory, at the time of the great transaction of the Federal Revolution, and for a long time afterwards, but a province of Spain, first, and afterwards of France? How did her territory— the land upon which her population and her property rest—come to be a part of our territory, and to give support to a State government, and to State interests? Why, by its acquisition, under the wise policy of Mr. Jefferson, early in this century, upon the opportunity offered, by the necessity or policy of the Emperor Napoleon, for its purchase, by money, as you would buy a ship, or a strip of land to build a fort on. Coming thus to the United States, by its purchase, how did Louisiana come to be set apart, carved out of the immense territory comprehended under the name of Louisiana, but by lines of division and concession of power, proceeding from the Government of the United States? And why did we purchase it? We purchased it preliminarily, not so much to seize the opportunity for excluding from a foothold on this Continent a great foreign Power, which, although its territory here was waste and uninhabited, had the legal right to fill it, and might, in the course of time, fill it, with a population hostile in interests to our own,—not so much for this remote contingency, as to meet the actual and pressing necessity, on the part of the population that was beginning to fill up the left or eastern bank of the Mississippi, from its source to near its mouth, that they should have the mouth of the Mississippi also within their territory, governed by the same laws and under the same Government. And now, forsooth, the money and the policy of the United States having acquired this territory, and conceded the political rights contained in the Constitution of Louisiana, we are to justify the secession of the territory of Louisiana, carrying the mouth of the Mississippi with her, on the theory that she was one of the original sovereignties, and one of the creators of the Constitution of the United States! Well, gentlemen, how are our learned friends to escape from this dilemma? Are they to say that our constituted Government, complex, composed of State and of Federal power, has two sets of State and Federal relations within it, to wit, that which existed between the General Government and the thirteen sovereign, original States, and that which exists between the Federal Government and the other twenty-one States of the Union? Is it to follow, from this severance, that these original Colonies, declaring their independence—South Carolina, North Carolina, Virginia and Georgia—are to draw back to themselves the portions of their original territory that have since, under the authority of the Constitution, been formed into separate communities? Our Constitution was made by and between the States, and the people of the States—not for themselves alone— not limited to existing territory, and arranged State and Provincial Governments—but made as a Government, and made with principles in respect to Government that should admit of its extension by purchase, by conquest, by all the means that could bring accretion to a people in territory and in strength, and that should be, in its principles, a form of Government applicable to and sufficient for the old and the new States, and the old and the new population. I need but refer to the later instances, where, by purchase, we acquired Florida, also one of the seceded States, and where, by our armies, we gained the western coast of the Pacific. Are these the relations into which the power, and blood, and treasure of this Government bring it, in respect to the new communities and new States which, under its protection, and from its conceded power, have derived their very existence? Why, gentlemen, our Government is said, by those who complain of it, or who expose what they regard as its difficulties, to have one element of weakness in it, to wit, the possibility of discord between the State and the Federal authorities. But, if you adopt the principle, that there is one set of rules, one set of rights, between the Federal Government and the original States that formed the Union, and another set of rules between the Federal Government and the new States, I would like to know what becomes of the provision of the Constitution, that the new States may be admitted on the same footing with the old? What becomes of the harmony and accord among the local Governments of this great nation, which we call State Governments, if there be this superiority, in every political sense, on the part of the old States, and this absolute inferiority and subjection on the part of the new?

And now, gentlemen, having done with this doctrine of secession, as utterly inconsistent with the theory of our Government, and utterly unimportant, as a practical right, for any supposable or even imaginable case that may be suggested, I come to consider the question of the right of revolution. I have shown to you upon what principles, and upon what substantial question, between being subjects as slaves, or being participants in the British Government, our Colonies attempted and achieved their independence. As I have said to you, a very brief experience showed that they needed, to meet the exigencies of their situation, the establishment of a Government that should be in accordance with the wishes and spirit of the people, in regard of freedom, and yet should be of such strength, and such unity, as would admit of prosperity being enjoyed under it, and of its name and power being established among the nations of the earth. Now, without going into the theories of Government, and of the rights of the people, and of the rights of the rulers, to any great extent, we all know that there has been every variety of experiment tried, in the course of human affairs, between the great extreme alluded to by my learned friend (Mr. Brady) of the slavery of Egyptians to their king—the extreme instance of an entire population scarcely lifted above the brutes in their absolute subjection to the tyranny of a ruler, so that the life, and the soul, and the sweat, and the blood of a whole generation of men are consumed in the task of building a mausoleum as the grave of a king—and the later efforts of our race, culminating in the happy success of our own form of Government, to establish, on foundations where liberty and law find equal support, the principle of Government, that Government is by, and for, and from all the people—that the rulers, instead of being their masters and their owners, are their agents and their servants— and that the greatest good of the greatest number is the plain, practical and equal rule which, by gift from our Creator, we enjoy.

Now this, you will observe, is a question which readily receives our acceptance. But the great problem in reference to the freedom of a people, in the establishment of their Government, presents itself in this wise: The people, in order to maintain their freedom, must be masters of their Government, so that the Government may not be too strong, in its arrangement of power, to overmaster the people; but yet, the Government must be strong enough to maintain and protect the independence of the nation against the aggressions, the usurpations, and the oppressions of foreign nations. Here you have a difficulty raised at once. You expose either the freedom of the nation, by making the Government too strong for the preservation of individual independence, or you expose its existence, by making it too weak to maintain itself against the passions, interests and power of neighboring nations. If you have a large nation—counting its population by many millions, and the circumference of its territory by thousands of miles—how can you arrange the strength of Government, so that it shall not, in the interests of human passions, grow too strong for the liberties of the people? And if, abandoning in despair that effort and that hope, you circumscribe the limits of your territory, and reduce your population within a narrow range, how can you have a Government and a nation strong enough to maintain itself in the contests of the great family of nations, impelled and urged by interests and passions?

Here is the first peril, which has never been successfully met and disposed of in any of the forms of Government that have been known in the history of mankind, until, at least, our solution of it was attempted, and unless it has succeeded and can maintain itself. But, again, this business of self-government by a people has but one practical and sensible spirit and object. The object of free Government is, that the people, as individuals, may, with security, pursue their own happiness. We do not tolerate the theory that all the people constituting the nation are absorbed into the national growth and life. The reason why we want a free Government is, that we may be happy under it, and pursue our own activities according to our nature and our faculties. But, you will see, at once, that it is of the essence of being able to pursue our own interests under the Government under which we live, that we can do so according to our own notions of what they are, or the notions of those who are intelligently informed of, participate in, and sympathize with, those interests. Therefore, it seems necessary that all of the every-day rights of property, of social arrangements, of marriage, of contracts— everything that makes up the life of a social community—shall be under the control, not of a remote or distant authority, but of one that is limited to, and derives its ideas and principles from, a local community.

Now, how can this be in a large nation—in a nation of thirty millions, distributed over a zone of the earth? How are we to get along in New York, and how are others to get along in South Carolina, and others in New England, in the every-day arrangements that proceed from Government, and affect the prosperity, the freedom, the independence, the satisfaction of the community with the condition in which it lives? How can we get along, if all these minute and every-day arrangements are to proceed from a Government which has to deal with the diverse opinions, the diverse sentiments, the diverse interests, of so extensive a nation? But if, fleeing from this peril, you say that you may reduce your nation, you fall into another difficulty. The advanced civilization of the present day requires, for our commercial activity, for our enjoyment of the comforts and luxuries of life, that the whole globe shall be ransacked, and that the power of the nation which we recognize as our superior shall be able to protect our citizens in their enterprises, in their activities, in their objects, all over the world. How can a little nation, made up of Massachusetts, or made up of South Carolina, have a flag and a power which can protect its commerce in the East Indies and in the Southern Ocean? Again—we find that nations, unless they are separated by wide barriers, necessarily, in the course of human affairs, come into collision; and, as I have shown to you, the only arbitrament for their settlement is war. But war is a scourge—an unmitigated scourge—so long as it lasts, and in itself considered. But for objects which make it meritorious and useful, it is a scourge never to be tolerated. It puts in abeyance all individual rights, interests, and schemes, until the great controversy is settled.

If, then, we are a small nation, surrounded on all sides by other nations, with no natural barriers, with competing interests, with occasions of strife and collision on all sides, how can we escape war, as a necessary result of that miserable situation? But war strengthens the power of Government, weakens the power of the individual, and establishes maxims and creates forces, that go to increase the weight and the power of Government, and to weaken the rights of the people. Then, we see that, to escape war, we must either establish a great nation, which occupies an extent of territory, and has a fund of power sufficient to protect itself against border strifes, and against the ambition, the envy, the hatred of neighbors; or else one which, being small, is exposed to war from abroad to subjugate it, or to the greater peril to its own liberties, of war made by its own Government, thus establishing principles and introducing interests which are inconsistent with liberty.

I have thus ventured, gentlemen, to lay before you some of these general principles, because, in the course of the arguments of my learned friends, as well as in many of the discussions before the public mind, it seems to be considered that the ties, the affections and the interests, which oblige us to the maintenance of this Government of ours, find their support and proper strength and nourishment only in the sentiments of patriotism and duty, because it happens to be our own Government; and that, when the considerations of force or of feeling which bring a people to submit to a surrender of their Government, or to a successful conquest of a part of their territory, or to a wresting of a part of their people from the control of the Government, shall be brought to bear upon us, we shall be, in our loss and our surrender, only suffering what other nations have been called upon to lose and to surrender, and that it will be but a change in the actual condition of the country and its territory. But you will perceive that, by the superior fortune which attended our introduction into the family of nations, and by the great wisdom, forecast, and courage of our ancestors, we avoided, at the outset, all the difficulties between a large territory and a numerous population on the one hand, and a small territory and a reduced population on the other hand, and all those opposing dangers of the Government being either too weak to protect the nation, or too strong, and thus oppressive of the people, by a distribution of powers and authorities, novel in the affairs of men, dependent on experiment, and to receive its final fate as the result of that experiment. We went on this view—that these feeble Colonies had not, each in itself, the life and strength of a nation; and, yet, these feeble Colonies, and their poor and sparse population, were nourished on a love of liberty and self-government. These sentiments had carried them through a successful war against one of the great powers of the earth. They were not to surrender that for which they had been fighting to any scheme, to any theory of a great, consolidated nation, the Government of which should subdue the people and re-introduce the old fashion in human affairs—that the people were made for the rulers, and not the rulers by and for the people. They undertook to meet, they did meet, this difficult dilemma in the constitution of Government, by separating the great fund of power, and reposing it in two distinct organizations. They reserved to the local communities the control of their domestic affairs, and attributed the maintenance and preservation of them to the State governments. They undertook to collect and deposit, under the form of a written Constitution, with the general Government, all those larger and common interests which enter into the conception and practical establishment of a distinct nation among the nations of the earth, and determined that they would have a central power which should be adequate, by drawing its resources from the patriotism, from the duty, from the wealth, from the numbers, of a great nation, to represent them in peace and in war,— a nation that could protect the interests, encourage the activities, and maintain the development of its people, in spite of the opposing interests or the envious or hostile attacks of any nation. They determined that this great Government, thus furnished with this range of authority and this extent of power, should not have anything to do with the every-day institutions, operations and social arrangements of the community into which the vast population and territory of the nation were distributed. They determined that the people of Massachusetts, the people of New York, and the people of South Carolina, each of them, should have their own laws about agriculture, about internal trade, about marriage, about apprenticeship, about slavery, about religion, about schools, about all the every-day pulsations of individual life and happiness, controlled by communities that moved with the same pulsations, obeyed the same instincts, and were animated by the same purposes. And, as this latter class of authority contains in itself the principal means of oppression by a Government, and is the principal point where oppression is to be feared by a people, they had thus robbed the new system of all the dangers which attend the too extensive powers of a Government. They divided the fund of power, to prevent a great concentration and a great consolidation of the army of magistrates and officers of the law and of the Government which would have been combined by a united and consolidated authority, having jurisdiction of all the purposes of Government, of all the interests of citizens, and of the entire population and entire territory in these respects. They thus made a Government, complex in its arrangements, which met those opposing difficulties, inherent in human affairs, that make the distinction between free Governments and oppressive Governments. They preserved the people in their enjoyment and control of all the local matters entering into their every-day life, and yet gave them an establishment, springing from the same interests and controlled by the same people, which has sustained and protected us in our relations to the family of nations on the high seas and in the remote corners of the world.

Now, this is the scheme, and this is the purpose, with which this Government was formed; and you will observe that there is contained in it this separation, and this distribution. And our learned friends, who have argued before you respecting this theory, and this arrangement and practice of the power of a Government, as inconsistent with the interests and the freedom of the people, have substantially said to you that it was a whimsical contrivance, that it was an impossible arrangement of inconsistent principles, and that we must go back to a simple Government composed of one of the States, or of a similar arrangement of territory and people, which would make each of us a weak and contemptible power in the family of nations—or we must go back to the old consolidation of power, such as is represented by the frame of France or England in its Government, or, more distinctly, more absolutely, and more likely to be the case, for so vast a territory and so extensive a population as ours, to the simple notion of Russian Autocracy.

That, then, being the object, and that the character, of our institutions, and this right of secession not being provided for, or imagined, or tolerated in the scheme, let us look at the right of revolution, as justifying an attempt to overthrow the Government; and let us look at the occasions of revolution, which are pretended here, as giving a support, before the world, in the forum of conscience, and in the judgment of mankind, for the exercise of that right.

And first, let me ask you whether, in all the citations from the great men of the Revolution, and in the later stages of our history, any opinion has been cited which has condemned this scheme, as unsuitable and insufficient for the freedom and happiness of the people, if it can be successful? I think not. The whole history of the country is full of records of the approval, of the support, of the admiration, of the reverent language which our people at large, and the great leaders of public opinion—the great statesmen of the country—have spoken of this system of Government. Let me ask your attention to but two encomiums upon it, as represented by that central idea of a great nation, and yet a divided and local administration of popular interests—to wit, one in the first stage of its adoption, before its ratification by the people was complete; and the other, a speech made at the very eve of, if not in the very smoke of, this hostile dissolution of it.

Mr. Pinckney, of South Carolina, who had been one of the delegates from that State in the National Convention, and had co-operated with the Northern statesmen, and with the great men of Virginia, in forming the Government as it was, in urging on the Convention of South Carolina the adoption of the Constitution, and its ratification, said:

"To the Union we will look up as the temple of our freedom,—a temple founded in the affections and supported by the virtue of the people. Here we will pour out our gratitude to the Author of all good, for suffering us to participate in the rights of a people who govern themselves. Is there, at this moment, a nation on the earth which enjoys this right, where the true principles of representation are understood and practised, and where all authority flows from, and returns at stated periods to, the people? I answer, there is not. Can a Government be said to be free where those do not exist? It cannot. On what depends the enjoyment of those rare, inestimable rights? On the firmness and on the power of the Union to protect and defend them."

Had we anything from that great patriot and statesman of this right of secession, or independence of a State, as an important or a useful element in securing these rare, these unheard of, these inestimable privileges of Government, which the Author of all good had suffered the people of South Carolina to participate in? No—they depended "on the firmness and on the power of the Union to protect and defend them." Mr. Pinckney goes on to say:

"To the philosophic mind, how new and awful an instance do the United States at present exhibit to the people of the world! They exhibit, sir, the first instance of a people who, being thus dissatisfied with their Government, unattacked by a foreign force and undisturbed by domestic uneasiness, coolly and deliberately resort to the virtue and good sense of the country for a correction of their public errors."

That is, for the abandonment of the weakness and the danger of the imperfect Confederation, and the adoption of the constitutional and formal establishment of Federal power. Mr. Pinckney goes on to say:

"It must be obvious that, without a superintending Government, it is impossible the liberties of this country can long be secure. Single and unconnected, how weak and contemptible are the largest of our States! how unable to protect themselves from external or domestic insult! how incompetent, to national purposes, would even the present Union be! how liable to intestine war and confusion! how little able to secure the blessings of peace! Let us, therefore, be careful in strengthening the Union. Let us remember we are bounded by vigilant and attentive neighbors"—(and now Europe is within ten days, and they are near neighbors)—"who view with a jealous eye our rights to empire."

Pursuing my design of limiting my citations of the opinions of public men to those who have received honor from, and conferred honor on, that portion of our country and those of our countrymen now engaged in this strife with the General Government, let me ask your attention to a speech delivered by Mr. Stephens, now the Vice-President of the so-called Confederate States, on the very eve of, and protesting against, this effort to dissolve the Union. I read from page 220 and subsequent pages of the documents that have been the subject of reference heretofore:

"The first question that presents itself"—(says Mr. Stephens to the assembled Legislature of Georgia, of which he was not a member, but which, as an eminent and leading public man, he had been invited to address)—"is, shall the people of the South secede from the Union in consequence of the election of Mr. Lincoln to the Presidency of the United States? My countrymen, *I tell you frankly, candidly, and earnestly, that I do not think that they ought.* In my judgment, the election of no man, constitutionally elected to that high office, is sufficient cause for any State to separate from the Union. It ought to stand by and aid still in maintaining the Constitution of the country. To make a point of resistance to the Government—to withdraw from it because a man has been constitutionally elected—puts us in the wrong. We are pledged to maintain the Constitution. Many of us have sworn to support it.

"But it is said Mr. Lincoln's policy and principles are against the Constitution, and that if he carries them out it will be destructive of our rights. Let us not anticipate a threatened evil. If he violates the Constitution, then will come our time to act. Do not let us break it because, forsooth, he may. If he does, that is the time for us to strike. * * * My countrymen, I am not of those who believe this Union has been a curse up to this time. True men—men of integrity—entertain different views from me on this subject. I do not question their right to do so; I would not impugn their motives in so doing. Nor will I undertake to say that this Government of our fathers is perfect. There is nothing perfect in this world, of a human origin. Nothing connected with human nature, from man himself to any of his works. You may select the wisest and best men for your Judges, and yet how many defects are there in the administration of justice? You may select the wisest and best men for your legislators, and yet how many defects are apparent in your laws? And it is so in our Government.

"But that this Government of our fathers, with all its defects, comes nearer the objects of all good Governments than any on the face of the earth, is my settled conviction. Contrast it now with any on the face of the earth." ["England," said Mr. Toombs.] "England, my friend says. Well, that is the next best, I grant; but I think we have improved upon England. Statesmen tried their apprentice hand on the Government of England, and then ours was made. Ours sprung from that, avoiding many of its defects, taking most of the good and leaving out many of its errors, and, from the whole, constructing and building up this model Republic—the best which the history of the world gives any account of.

"Compare, my friends, this Government with that of Spain, Mexico, the South American Republics, Germany, Ireland—are there any sons of that down-trodden nation here to-night?—Prussia, or, if you travel further east, to Turkey or China. Where will you go, following the sun in his circuit round our globe, to find a Government that better protects the liberties of its people, and secures to them the blessings we enjoy? I think that one of the evils that beset us is a surfeit of liberty, an exuberance of the priceless blessings for which we are ungrateful. * * * * *

"When I look around and see our prosperity in every thing—agriculture, commerce, art, science, and every department of education, physical and mental, as well as moral advancement, and our colleges—I think, in the face of such an exhibition, if we can, without the loss of power, or any essential right or interest, remain in the Union, it is our duty to ourselves and to posterity to—let us not too readily yield to this temptation—do so. Our first parents, the great progenitors of the human race, were not without a like temptation when in the garden of Eden. They were led to believe that their condition would be bettered—that their eyes would be opened—and that they would become as gods. They in an evil hour yielded. Instead of becoming gods, they only saw their own nakedness.

"I look upon this country, with our institutions, as the Eden of the world, the paradise of the Universe. It may be that out of it we may become greater and more prosperous, but I am candid and sincere in telling you that I fear if we rashly evince passion, and, without sufficient cause, shall take that step, that instead of becoming greater or more peaceful, prosperous and happy— instead of becoming gods—we will become demons, and, at no distant day, commence cutting one another's throats."

Still speaking of our Government, he says:

"Thus far, it is a noble example, worthy of imitation. The gentleman (Mr. Cobb) the other night said it had proven a failure. A failure in what? In growth? Look at our expanse in national power. Look at our population and increase in all that makes a people great. A failure? Why, we are the admiration of the civilized world, and present the brightest hopes of mankind.

"Some of our public men have failed in their aspirations; that is true, and from that comes a great part of our troubles.

"No, there is no failure of this Government yet. We have made great advancement under the Constitution, and I cannot but hope that we shall advance higher still. Let us be true to our cause."

Now, wherein is it that this Government deserves these encomiums, which come from the intelligent and profound wisdom of statesmen, and gush spontaneously from the unlearned hearts of the masses of the people? Why, it is precisely in this point, of its not being a consolidated Government, and of its not being a narrow, and feeble, and weak community and Government. Indeed, I may be permitted to say that I once heard, from the lips of Mr. Calhoun himself, this recognition, both of the good fortune of this country in possessing such a Government, and of the principal sources to which the gratitude of a nation should attribute that good fortune. I heard him once say, that it was to the wisdom, in the great Convention, of the delegates from the State of Connecticut, and of Judge Patterson, a delegate from the State of New Jersey, that we owed the fact that this Government was what it was, the best Government in the world, a confederated Government, and not what it would have been—and, apparently, would have been but for those statesmen—the worst Government in the world—a consolidated Government. These statesmen, he said, were wiser for the South than the South was for herself.

I need not say to you, gentlemen that, if all this encomium on the great fabric of our Government is brought to naught, and is made nonsense by the proposition that, although thus praised and thus admired, it contains within itself the principle, the right, the duty of being torn to pieces, whenever a fragment of its people shall be discontented and desire its destruction, then all this encomium comes but as sounding brass and a tinkling cymbal; and the glory of our ancestors, Washington, and Madison, and Jefferson, and Adams—the glory of their successors, Webster, and Clay, and Wright, and even Calhoun—for he was no votary of this nonsense of secession—passes away, and their fame grows visibly paler, and the watchful eye of the English monarchy looks on for the bitter fruits to be reaped by us for our own destruction, and as an example to the world—the bitter fruits of the principle of revolution and of the right of self-government which we dared to assert against her perfect control. Pointing to our exhibition of an actual concourse of armies, she will say—"It is in the dragon's teeth, in the right of rebellion against the monarchy of England, that these armed hosts have found their seed and sprung up on your soil."

Now, gentlemen, such is our Government, such is its beneficence, such is its adaptation, and such are its successes. Look at its successes. Not three-quarters of a century have passed away since the adoption of its Constitution, and now it rules over a territory that extends from the Atlantic to the Pacific. It fills the wide belt of the earth's surface that is bounded by the provinces of England on the North, and by the crumbling, and weak, and contemptible Governments or no Governments that shake the frame of Mexico on the South. Have Nature and Providence left us without resources to hold together social unity, notwithstanding the vast expanse of the earth's surface which our population has traversed and possessed? No. Keeping pace with our wants in that regard, the rapid locomotion of steam on the ocean, and on our rivers and lakes, and on the iron roads that bind the country together, and the instantaneous electric communication of thought, which fills with the same facts, and with the same news, and with the same sentiments, at the same moment, a great, enlightened, and intelligent people, have overcome all the resistance and all the dangers which might be attributed to natural obstructions. Even now, while this trial proceeds, San Francisco and New York, Boston and Portland, and the still farther East, communicate together as by a flash of lightning—indeed, it may be said, making an electric flash farther across the earth's surface, and intelligible too, to man, than ever, in the natural phenomena of the heavens, the lightning displayed itself. No—the same Author of all good, to whom Pinckney avowed his gratitude, has been our friend and our protector, and has removed, step by step, every impediment to our expansion which the laws of nature and of space had been supposed to interpose. No, no—neither in the patriotism nor in the wisdom of our fathers was there any defect; nor shall we find, in the disposition and purposes of Divine Providence, as we can see them, any excuse or any aid for the destruction of this magnificent system of empire. No—it is in ourselves, in our own time and in our own generation, in our own failing powers and failing duties, that the crash and ruin of this magnificent fabric, and the blasting of the future hopes of mankind, is to find its cause and its execution.

I have shown you, gentlemen, how, when the usurpations of the British Parliament, striking at the vital point of the independence of this country, had raised for consideration and determination, by a brave and free people, the question of their destiny, our fathers dealt with it. My learned friends, in various forms, have spoken poetically, logically and practically about all that course of proceedings that has been going on in this country, as finding a complete parallelism, support, and justification in the course of the American Revolution; and a passage in the Declaration of Independence has been read to you as calculated to show that, on a mere theoretical opinion of the right of a people to govern themselves, any portion of that people are at liberty, as well against a good Government as against a bad one, to establish a bad

Government as well as overthrow a bad Government—have the right to do as they please, and, I suppose, to force all the rest of the world and all the rest of the nation to just such a fate as their doing as they please may bring with it.

Let us see how this Declaration of Independence, called by the great forensic orator, Mr. Choate, "a passionate and eloquent manifesto," and stigmatized as containing "glittering generalities"—let us see, I say, how sober, how discreet, how cautious it is in the presentation of this right, even of revolution. I read what, both in the newspapers and in political discussions, as well as before you, by the learned counsel, have been presented as the doctrines of the Declaration of Independence, and then I add to it the qualifying propositions, and the practical, stern requisitions, which that instrument appends to these general views:

"To secure these rights, Governments are instituted among men, deriving their just powers from the consent of the governed; that whenever any form of Government becomes destructive of these ends, it is the right of the people to alter or abolish it, and to institute new Government, laying its foundation on such principles, and organizing its powers in such form, as to them shall seem most likely to effect their safety and happiness. Prudence, indeed, will dictate, that Governments long established should not be changed for light and transient causes. And, accordingly, all experience hath shown, that mankind are more disposed to suffer, while evils are sufferable, than to right themselves by abolishing the forms to which they are accustomed. But when a long train of abuses and usurpations, pursuing invariably the same object, evinces a design to reduce them under absolute despotism, it is their right, it is their duty, to throw off such Government, and to provide new guards for their future security. Such has been the patient sufferance of these Colonies; and such is now the necessity which constrains them to alter their former systems of Government. The history of the present King of Great Britain is a history of repeated injuries and usurpations, all having in direct object the establishment of an absolute tyranny over these States. To prove this, let facts be submitted to a candid world."

And it then proceeds to enumerate the facts, in the eloquent language of the Declaration, made familiar to us all by its repeated and reverent recitals on the day which celebrates its adoption. There is not anything of moonshine about any one of them. There is not anything of perhaps, or anticipation of fear, or suspicion. There is not anything of this or that newspaper malediction, of this or that rhetorical disquisition, of this or that theory, or of this or that opprobrium, but a recital of direct governmental acts of Great

Britain, all tending to the purpose of establishing complete despotism over this country. And, then, even that not being deemed sufficient, on the part of our great ancestors, to justify this appeal to the enlightened opinion of the world, and to the God who directs the fate of armies, they say:

"In every stage of these oppressions, we have petitioned for redress, in the most humble terms; our repeated petitions have been answered only by repeated injury. A Prince whose character is thus marked by every act which may define a tyrant, is unfit to be the ruler of a free people.

"Nor have we been wanting in attentions to our British brethren. We have warned them, from time to time, of attempts by their Legislature to extend an unwarrantable jurisdiction over us. We have reminded them of the circumstances of our emigration and settlement here. We have appealed to their native justice and magnanimity, and we have conjured them, by the ties of our common kindred, to disavow these usurpations, which would inevitably interrupt our connection and correspondence. They, too, have been deaf to the voice of justice and of consanguinity."

Now, gentlemen, this doctrine of revolution, which our learned friends rely upon, appeals to our own sense of right and duty. It rests upon facts, and upon the purpose, as indicated by those facts, to deprive our ancestors of the rights of Englishmen, and to subject them to the power of a Government in which they were not represented. Now, whence come the occasions and the grievances urged before you, and of what kind are they? My learned friend, Mr. Brady, has given you a distinct enumeration, under nine heads, of what the occasions are, and what the grievances are. There is not one of them that, in form or substance, proceeded from the Federal Government. There is not a statute, there is not a proclamation, there is not an action, judicial, executive, or legislative, on the part of the Federal Government, that finds a place, either in consummation or in purpose, in this indictment drawn by my friend Mr. Brady against the Government, on behalf of his clients. The letter of South Carolina, on completing the revocation of her adoption of the Constitution, addressed to the States, dwells upon the interest of slavery (as does my learned friend Mr. Brady, in all his propositions), and discloses but two ideas—one, that when any body or set of people cease to be a majority in a Government, they have a right to leave it; and the other, that State action, on the part of some of the Northern States, had been inconsistent with, threatening to, or opprobrious of the institution of slavery in the Southern States.

Let me ask your attention to this proposition of the Southern States, and this catalogue of the learned counsel. As it is only the interest of slavery, social and political (for it is an interest, lawfully existing), that leads to the destruction of our Government and of their Government, let us see what there is in the actual circumstances of this interest, as being able, under the forms of our Constitution, to look out for itself, as well, at least, as any other interest in the country, that can justify them in finding an example or a precedent in the appeal of our fathers to arms to assert their rights by the strong hand, because in the Government of England they had no representation. Did our fathers say that, because they had not a majority in the English Parliament, they had a right to rebel? No! They said they had not a share or vote in the Parliament. That was their proposition.

I now invite you to consider this fundamental view of the right and power of Government, and the right and freedom of the people,—to wit, that every citizen is entitled to be counted and considered as good as every other citizen,—as a natural and abstract right—as the basis of our Government, however other arrangements may have adjusted or regulated that simple and abstract right. Then, let us see whether the arrangement of the Federal Government, in departing from that natural right of one man to be as good as another, and to be counted equal in the representation of his Government, has operated to the prejudice of the interest of slavery. We have not heard anything in this country of any other interest for many a long year,—much to my disgust and discontent. There are other interests,—manufacturing interests, agricultural interests, commercial interests, all sorts of interests,—some of them discordant, if you please. Let us see whether this interest of slavery has a fair chance to be heard, and enjoys its fair share of political power under our Government, or whether, from a denial to it of its fair share, it has some pretext for appealing to force. Why, gentlemen, take the fifteen Slave States, which, under the census of 1850, had six millions of white people—that is, of citizens—and, under the census of 1860, about eight millions, and compare them with the white people of the State of New York, which, under the census of 1850, had three millions, and, under the census of 1860, something like four millions.

Now, here we are,—they as good as we, and we as good as they,—we having our interests, and opinions, and feelings—they their opinions, interests, and feelings,—and let us see how the arrangement of representation, in every part of our Government, is distributed between these interests. Why, with a population just double that of the State of New York, the interest of slavery has *thirty* Senators to vote and to speak for it, and the people of New York have *two* Senators to vote and to speak for them. In the House of Representatives these same Slave States have *ninety* Representatives to speak and to vote for them; and the people of the State of New York have *thirty-three* to vote and to speak for them. And, in the Electoral College, which raises to the chief magistracy the citizen who receives the constitutional vote, these same States have *one hundred and twenty* electoral votes, and the State of New York has *thirty-five*. Why, the three coterminous States—New York, Pennsylvania, and Ohio—have, under either census, as great or a greater population than the fifteen Slave States, and they have but six Senators, against the Slave States' thirty.

Do I mention this in complaint? Not in the least. I only mention it to show you that the vote and the voice of this interest has not been defrauded in the artificial distribution of Federal power. And, if I may be allowed to refer to the other august department of our Federal Government, the Supreme Court of the United States, in which the Presiding Justice has his seat as one of the members of that Court, you will see how the vast population, the vast interests of business, commerce, and what not, that reside in the Free States, as compared with the lesser population, the lesser business, and the lesser demand for the authority or intervention of the judiciary in the Slave States, have been represented for years, by the distribution of the nine Judges of that Court, so that the eighteen millions of white people who compose the population of the Free States have been represented (not in any political sense) by four of these Justices; and the rest of the country, the fifteen Slave States, with their population of six or eight millions, have been represented by five. Now, of this I do not complain. It is law—it is government; and no injustice has been done to the Constitution, nor has it been violated in this arrangement. But, has there been any fraud upon the interest of slavery, in the favor the Federal Government has shown in the marking out of the Judicial Districts, and in the apportionment of the Judges to the different regions of the country, and to the population of those regions? If you look at it as regards the business in the different Circuits, the learned Justice who now presides here, and who holds his place for the Second Circuit, including our State, disposes annually, here and in the other Courts, of more business than, I may perhaps say, all the Circuits that are made up from the Slave States. And, if you look at it as regards the population, there was one Circuit—that which was represented by the learned Mr. Justice McLean, lately deceased—which contained within itself five millions of white, free population; while one other Circuit, represented by another learned Justice, lately deceased—a Circuit composed of Mississippi and Arkansas—contained only 450,000, at the time of the completion of the census of 1850. Who complains of this? Do we? Never. But, when it is said to you that there is a parallelism between the right of revolt, because of lack of representation, in the case of our people and the Parliament of England, and the case of these people and the United States, or any of the forms of its administration of power, remember these things. I produce this in the simple duty of forensic reply to the causes put forward as a justification of this revolt—that is to say that, the Government oppressing them, or the Government closed against them, and they excluded from it, they had a right to resort to the revolution of force.

You, therefore, must adopt the proposition of South Carolina, that, when any interest ceases to be the majority in a Government, it has a right to secede. How long would such a Government last? Why, there never was any interest in this country which imagined that it had a majority. Did the tariff interest have a majority? Did the grain interest have a majority? Did the commercial interest have a majority? Did the States of the West have a majority? Does California gold represent itself by a majority? Why, the very safety of such a Government as this is, that no interest shall or can be a majority; but that the concurring, consenting wisdom drawn out of these conflicting interests shall work out a system of law which will conduce to the general interest.

Now, that I have not done my learned friend, Mr. Brady, any injustice in presenting the catalogue of grievances (not in his own view, but in the view of those who have led in this rebellion), let us see what they are:

"The claim to abolish slavery." Is there any statute of the United States anywhere that has abolished it? Has any Act been introduced into Congress to abolish it? Has the measure had a vote?

"Stoppage of the inter-state slave-trade." I may say the same thing of that.

"No more slavery in the Territories." Where is the Act of Congress, where is the movement of the Federal Government, where the decision of the Supreme Court, that holds that slavery cannot go into a territory? Why, so far as acts go, everything has gone in the way of recognizing the confirmation of the right—the repeal of the Missouri Compromise by Congress, and the decision of the Federal Court, if it go to that extent, as is claimed, in the case of Dred Scott.

"Nullification of the fugitive-slave law." Who passed the fugitive-slave law? Congress. Who have enforced it? The Federal power, by arms, in the city of Boston. Who have enjoined its observation, to Grand Juries and to Juries? The Justices of the Supreme Court of the United States, in their Circuits. Who have held it to be constitutional? The Supreme Court of the United States, and the subordinate Courts of the United States, and every State Court that has passed upon the subject, except it be the State Court of the State of Wisconsin, if I am correctly advised.

"Under-ground railroads, supported by the Government, and paid by them." Are they? Not in the least.

"The case of the Creole"—where, they say, no protection was given to slaves on the high seas. Is there any judicial interpretation to that effect? Nothing but the refusal of Congress to pass a bill, under some circumstances of this or that nature, presented for its consideration; and, because it has refused, it is alleged there is the assertion of some principle that should charge upon this Government the inflamed and particular views generally maintained on slavery by Garrison, Phillips, and Theodore Parker.

The other enormities they clothe in general phrase, and do not particularly specify, except one particular subject—what is known as the "John Brown raid"—in regard to which, as it has been introduced, I shall have occasion to say something in another connection, and, therefore, I will not comment upon it now.

I find, however, I have omitted the last—Mr. Lincoln's doctrine, that it is impossible, theoretically, for slave and free States to co-exist. For many years that was considered to be Mr. Seward's doctrine, but, when Mr. Lincoln became a candidate for the Presidency, it was charged on him, being supported by some brief extracts from former speeches made by him in canvassing his State. I cannot discuss all these matters. They are beneath the gravity of State necessity, and of the question of the right of revolution. They are the opinions, the sentiments, the rhetoric, the folly, the local rage and madness, if you please, in some instances, of particular inflammations, either of sentiment or of action, rising in the bosom of so vast, so impetuous a community as ours. But, suppose the tariff States, suppose the grain States, were to attempt to topple down the Government, and maintain a separate and sectional independence upon their interests, of only the degree and gravity, and resting in the proof of facts like these? Now, for the purpose of the argument, let us suppose all these things to be wrong. My learned friends, who have made so great and so passionate an appeal that individual lives should not be sacrificed for opinion, certainly might listen to a proposition that the life of a great nation should not be destroyed on these questions of the opinions of individual citizens. No—you never can put either the fate of a nation that it must submit, or the right of malcontents to assert their power for its overthrow, upon any such proposition, of the ill-working, or of the irritations that arise, and do not come up to the effect of oppression, in the actual, the formal, and the persistent movement of Government. Never for an instant. For that would be, what Mr. Stephens has so ably presented the folly of doing, to require that a great Government, counting in its population thirty millions of men, should not only be perfect in its design and general form and working, but that it should secure perfect action, perfect opinions, perfect spirit and sentiments from every one of its people—and that, made out of mere imperfect individuals who have nothing but poor human nature for their possession, it should suddenly become so transformed, as to be without a flaw, not only in its administration, but in the conduct of every body under it.

Now, my learned friends, pressed by this difficulty as to the sufficiency of the causes, are driven finally to this—that there is a right of revolution when anybody thinks there is a right of revolution, and that that is the doctrine upon which our Government rests, and upon which the grave, serious action of our forefathers proceeded. And it comes down to the proposition of my learned friend, Mr. Brady, that it all comes to the same thing, the *power* and the *right*. All the argument, most unquestionably, comes to that. But do morals, does reason, does common sense recognize that, because power and right may result in the same consequences, therefore there is no difference in their quality, or in their support, or in their theory? If I am slain by the sword of justice for my crime, or by the dagger of an assassin for my virtue, I am dead, under the stroke of either. But is one as right as the other? An oppressive Government may be overthrown by the uprising of the oppressed, and Lord Camden's maxim may be adhered to, that "when oppression begins, resistance becomes a right;" but a Government, beneficent and free, may be attacked, may be overthrown by tyranny, by enemies, by mere power. The Colonies may be severed from Great Britain, on the principle of the right of the people asserting itself against the tyranny of the parent Government; and Poland may be dismembered by the interested tyranny of Russia and Austria; and each is a revolution and destruction of the Government, and its displacement by another—a dismemberment of the community, and the establishment of a new one under another Government. But, do my learned friends say that they equally come to the test of power as establishing the right? Will my learned friend plant himself, in justification of this dismemberment of a great, free, and prosperous people, upon the example of the dismemberment of Poland, by the introduction of such influences within, and by the co-operation of such influences without, as secured that result? Certainly not. And yet, if he puts it upon the right and the power, as coming to the same thing, it certainly cannot make any difference whether the power proceeds from within or from without. There is no such right. Both the public action of communities and the private action of individuals must be tried, if there is any trial, any scrutiny, any judgment, any determination, upon some principles that are deeper than the question of counting bayonets. When we are referred to the ease of Victor Emannuel overthrowing the throne of the King of Naples, and thus securing the unity of the Italian people under a benign Government, are we to be told that the same principle and the same proposition would have secured acceptance before the forum of civilization, and in the eye of morality, to a successful effort of the tyrant of Naples to overthrow the throne of Victor Emannuel, and include the whole of Italy under his, King Bomba's, tyranny? No one. The quality of the act, the reason, the support, and the method of it, are traits that impress their character on those great public and national transactions as well as upon any other.

There is but one proposition, in reason and morality, beyond those I have stated, which is pressed for the extrication and absolution of these prisoners from the guilt that the law, as we say, impresses upon their action and visits with its punishment. It is said that, however little, as matter of law, these various rights and protections may come to, good faith, or sincere, conscientious conviction on the part of these men as to what they have done, should protect them against the public justice.

Now, we have heard a great deal of the assertion and of the execration of the doctrine of the "higher law," in the discussions of legislation, and in the discussions before the popular mind; but I never yet have heard good faith or sincere opinion pressed, in a Court of Justice, as a bar to the penalty which the law has soberly affixed, in the discreet and deliberate action of the Legislature. And here my learned friend furnishes me, by his reference to the grave instance of injury to the property, and the security, and the authority of the State of Virginia, which he has spoken of as "John Brown's raid," with a ready instance, in which these great principles of public justice, the authority of Government, and the sanctions of human law were met, in the circumstances of the transaction, by a complete, and thorough, and remarkable reliance, for the motive, the support, the stimulus, the solace, against all the penalties which the law had decreed for such a crime, on this interior authority of conscience, and this supremacy of personal duty, according to the convictions of him who acts. The great State of Virginia administered its justice, and it found, as its principal victim, this most remarkable man, in regard to whom it was utterly impossible to impute anything like present or future, near or remote, personal interest or object of any kind—a man in regard to whom Governor Wise, of Virginia, said, in the very presence of the transaction of his trial, that he was the bravest, the sincerest, the truthfulest man that he ever knew. And now, let us look at the question in the light in which our learned friend presents it—that John Brown, as matter of theoretical opinion of what he had a right to do, under the Constitution and laws of his country, was justified, upon the pure basis of conscientious duty to God—and let us see whether, before the tribunals of Virginia, as matter of fact, or matter of law, or right, or duty, any recognition was given to it. No. John Brown was not hung for his theoretical heresies, nor was he hung for the hallucinations of his judgment and the aberration of his wrong moral sense, if you so call it, instead of the interior light of conscience, as he regarded it. He was hung for attacking the sovereignty, the safety, the citizens, the property, and the people of Virginia. And, when my learned friend talks about this question of hanging for political, moral, or social heresy, and that you cannot thus coerce the moral power of the mind, he vainly seeks to beguile your judgment. When Ravaillac takes the life of good King Henry, of France, is it a justification that, in the interests of his faith, holy to him—of the religion he professed—he felt impelled thus to take the life of the monarch? When the assassin takes, at the door of the House of Commons, the life of the Prime Minister, Mr. Percival, because he thinks that the course of measures his administration proposes to carry out is dangerous to the country, and falls a victim to violated laws, I ask, in the name of common sense and common fairness—are these executions to be called hanging for political or religious heresies? No. And shall it ever be said that sincere convictions on these theories of secession and of revolution are entitled to more respect than sincere convictions and opinions on the subject of human rights? Shall it be said that faith in Jefferson Davis is a greater protection from the penalty of the law than faith in God was to John Brown or Francis Ravaillac?

But, gentlemen, it was said that certain isolated acts of some military or civil authority of the United States, or some promulgation of orders, or affirmation of measures by the Government, had recognized the belligerent right, or the right to be considered as a power fighting for independence, of this portion of our countrymen. The flags of truce, and the capitulation at Hatteras Inlet, and the announcement that we would not invade Virginia, but would protect the Capital, are claimed as having recognized this point. Now, gentlemen, this attempts either too much or too little. Is it gravely to be said that, when the Government is pressing its whole power for the restoration of peace and for the suppression of this rebellion, it is recognizing a right to rebel, or has liberated from the penalties of the criminal law such actors in it as it may choose to bring to punishment? Is it to be claimed here that, by reason of these proceedings, the Government has barred itself from taking such other proceedings, under the same circumstances, as it may think fit? Why, certainly not. The Government may, at any time, refuse to continue this amenity of flags of truce. It can, the next time, refuse to receive a capitulation as "prisoners of war," and may, in any future action—as, indeed, in its active measures for the suppression of the rebellion it is doing—affirm its control over every part of the revolted regions of this country. There is nothing in this fact that determines anything for the occasion, but the occasion itself. The idea that the commander of an expedition to Hatteras Inlet has it in his power to commit the Government, so as to empty the prisons, to overthrow the Courts, and to discharge Jurors from their duty, and criminals from the penalties of their crimes, is absurd.

I shall now advert to the opinion of Judge Cadwalader, on the trial in Philadelphia, and to the propositions of the counsel there, on behalf of the prisoners, as containing and including the general views and points urged, in one form or another, and with greater prolixity, at least, if not earnestness and force, by the learned counsel who defend the prisoners here. It will be found that those points cover all these considerations:

First. If the Confederate States of America is a Government, either *de facto* or *de jure*, it had a right to issue letters of marque and reprisal; and if issued before the commission of the alleged offence, that the defendant, acting under the authority of such letters, would be a privateer, and not a pirate, and, as such, is entitled to be acquitted.

Second. That if, at the time of the alleged offence, the Southern Confederacy, by actual occupation, as well as acts of Government, had so far acquired the mastery or control of the particular territory within its limits as to enable it to exercise authority over, and to demand and exact allegiance from, its residents, that then a resident of such Confederacy owes allegiance to the Government under which he lives, or, at least, that by rendering allegiance to such Government, whether on sea or land, he did not thereby become a traitor to the Government of the United States.

Third. That if, at the time of the alleged offence and the issuing of the letters of marque and reprisal upon which the defendant acted, the Courts of the United States were so suspended or closed in the Southern Confederacy, as to be no longer able to administer justice and enforce the law in such Confederacy, that the defendant thereby became so far absolved from his allegiance to the United States as to enable him to take up arms for, and to enter the service of, the Southern Confederacy, either on land or sea, without becoming a traitor to the Government of the United States.

Fourth. That if, at the time of the alleged offence and his entering into the service of the Southern Confederacy, the defendant was so situated as to be unable to obtain either civil or military protection from the United States, whilst at the same time he was compelled to render either military or naval service to the Southern Confederacy, or to leave the country, and, in this event, to have his property sequestrated or confiscated by the laws of the said Confederacy, that such a state of things, if they existed, would amount in law to such duress as entitles the defendant here to an acquittal.

Fifth. That this Court has no jurisdiction of the case, because the prisoner, after his apprehension on the high seas, was first brought into another District, and ought to have been there tried.

And now, gentlemen, even a more remote, unconnected topic, has been introduced into this examination, and discussed and pursued with a good deal of force and feeling, by my learned friend, Mr. Brady; and that is, what this war is for, and what is expected to be accomplished by it. Well, gentlemen, is your verdict to depend upon any question of that kind? Is it to depend either upon the purpose of the Government in waging the war, or upon its success in that purpose? If so, the trial had been better postponed to the end of the war, and then you will find your verdict in the result. What is the meaning of this? Let those who began the war say what the war is for. Is it to overthrow this Government and to dismember its territory? Is it to acquire dominion over as large a portion of what constitutes the possessions of the American people, and over as large a share of its population, as the policy or the military power of the interest that establishes for itself an independent Government, for its own protection, can accomplish? Who are seeking to subjugate, and who is seeking to protect? No subjugation is attempted or desired, in respect of the people of these revolting States, except that subjugation which they themselves made for themselves when they adopted the Constitution of the United States, and thanked God, with Charles Cotesworth Pinckney, that his blessing permitted them to do so,— and, up to this time, with Alexander Stephens, have found it to be a Government that can only be likened, on this terrestrial sphere, to the Eden and Paradise of the nations of men. What is the interest that is seeking to wrest from the authority of that benign Government portions of its territory and authority, but the social and political interest of slavery, about which I make no other reproach or question than this—that it has purposes, and objects, and principles which do not consult the general or equal interests of the population of these revolting States themselves, nor contemplate a form of Government that any Charles Cotesworth Pinckney, now, or any Alexander Stephens, hereafter, can thank God for having been permitted to establish; and that, as Mr. Stephens has said, instead of becoming gods, by bursting from the restraints of this Eden, they will discover their own nakedness, and, instead of finding peace and prosperity, they will come to cutting their own throats.

Now, what is the duty of a Government that finds this assault made by the hands of terror and of force against the judgment and wishes of the discreet, sober, and temperate, at least, to those to whom it owes protection, as they owe allegiance to it? What, but to carry on, by the force of the Government, the actual suppression of the rebellion, so that arms may be laid down, peace may exist, and the law and the Constitution be reinstated, and the great debate of opinion be restored, that has been interrupted by this vehement recourse to arms? What, but to see to it that, instead of the consequences of this revolt being an expulsion, from this Paradise of free Government, of these people whom we ought to keep within it, it shall end in the expulsion of that tempting serpent—be it secession or be it slavery—that would drive them out of it. Government has duties, gentlemen, as well as rights. If our lives and our property are subject to its demands under the penal laws, or for its protection and enforcement as an authority in the world, it carries to every citizen, on the farthest sea, in the humblest schooner, and to the great population of these Southern States in their masses at home, that firm protection which shall secure him against the wicked and the willful assaults, whether it be of a pirate on a distant sea, or of an ambitious and violent tyranny upon land. When this state of peace and repose is accomplished by Conventions, by petitions, by representations against Federal laws, Federal oppressions, or Federal principles of government, the right of the people to be relieved from oppression is presented; and then may the spirit and the action of our fathers be invoked, and their condemnation of the British Parliament come in play, if we do not do what is right and just in liberating an oppressed people. But I need not say to you that the whole active energies of this system of terror and of force in the Southern States have been directed to make impossible precisely the same debate, the same discussion, the same appeal, and the same just and equal attention to the appeal. And you will find this avowed by many of their speakers and by many of their writers—as, when Mr. Toombs interrupts Mr. Stephens in the speech I have quoted from, when urging that the people of Georgia should be consulted, by saying: "I am afraid of Conventions and afraid of the people; I do not want to hear from the cross-roads and the groceries," which are the opportunities of public discussion and influence, it appears, in the State of Georgia. That is exactly what they did not want to hear from; and their rash withdrawal of this great question from such honest, sensible consideration, will finally bring them to a point that the people, interested in the subject, will take it by force; and then, besides their own nakedness, which they have now discovered, the second prophecy of Mr. Stephens, that they will cut their own throats, will come about; and nothing but the powerful yet temperate, the firm yet benign, authority of this Government, compelling peace upon these agitations, will save those communities from social destruction and from internecine strife at home.

Now, having such an object, can it be accomplished? It cannot, unless you try; and it cannot, if every soldier who goes into the field concludes that he will not fire off his gun, for it is uncertain whether it will end the war; or if, on any post of duty that is devolved upon citizens in private life, we desert our Government, and our full duty to the Government. But that it can be done, and that it will be done, and that all this talk and folly about conquering eight millions of people will result in nothing, I find no room to doubt. In the first place, where are your eight millions? Why, there are the fifteen Slave States, and four of them—Maryland, Delaware, Kentucky, and Missouri— are not yet within the Confederacy. So we will subtract three millions, at least, for that part of the concern. Then there are five millions to be conquered; and how are they to be conquered? Why, not by destruction, not by slaughter, not by chains and manacles; but by the impression of the power of the Government, showing that the struggle is vain, that the appeal to arms was an error and a crime, and that, in the region of debate and opinion, and in equal representation in the Government itself, is the remedy for all grievances and evils. Be sure that, whatever may be said or thought of this question of war, these people can be, not subjugated, but compelled to entertain those inquiries by peaceful means; and I am happy to be able to say that the feeble hopes and despairing views which my learned friend, Mr. Brady, has thought it his duty to express before you, as to the hopelessness of any useful result to these hostilities, is not shared by one whom my friend, in the eloquent climax to an oration, placed before us as "starting, in a red shirt, to secure the liberties of Italy." I read his letter:

"CAPRERA, *Sept. 10.*

"*Dear Sir.* I saw Mr. Sandford, and regret to be obliged to announce to you that I shall not be able to go to the United States at present. I do not doubt of the triumph of the cause of the Union, and that shortly; but, if the war should unfortunately continue in your beautiful country, I shall overcome the obstacles which detain me and hasten to the defence of a people who are dear to me.

"G. GARIBALDI."

Garibaldi has had some experience, and knows the difference between efforts to make a people free, and the warlike and apparently successful efforts of tyranny; and he knows that a failure, even temporary, does not necessarily secure to force, and fraud, and violence a permanent success. He knows the difference between restoring a misguided people to a free Government, and putting down the efforts of a people to get up a free Government. He knows those are two different things; and, if the war be not shortly ended, as he thinks it will be, then he deems it right for him, fresh from the glories of securing the liberties of Italy, to assist in maintaining— what? Despotism? No! the liberties of America.

One of the learned counsel, who addressed you in a strain of very effective and persuasive eloquence, charmed us all by the grace of his allusion to a passage in classical history, and recalled your attention to the fact that, when the States of Greece which had warred against Athens, anticipating her downfall beneath the prowess of their arms, met to determine her fate, and when vindictive Thebes and envious Corinth counseled her destruction, the genius of the Athenian Sophocles, by the recital of the chorus of the Electra, disarmed this cruel purpose, by reviving the early glories of united Greece. And the counsel asked that no voice should be given to punish harshly these revolted States, if they should be conquered.

The voice of Sophocles in the chorus of the Electra, and those glorious memories of the early union, were produced to bring back into the circle of the old confederation the erring and rebellious Attica. So, too, what shall we find in the memories of the Revolution, or in the eloquence with which we have been taught to revere them, that will not urge us all, by every duty to the past, to the present, and to the future, to do what we can, whenever a duty is reposed in us, to sustain the Government in its rightful assertion of authority and in the maintenance of its power? Let me ask your attention to what has been said by the genius of Webster on so great a theme as the memory of Washington, bearing directly on all these questions of union, of glory, of hope, and of duty, which are involved in this inquiry. See whether, from the views thus invoked, there will not follow the same influence as from the chorus of the Electra, for the preservation, the protection, the restoration of every portion of what once was, and now is, and, let us hope, ever shall be, our common country.

On the occasion of the centennial anniversary of the birthday of Washington, at the national Capital, in 1832, Mr. Webster, by the invitation of men in public station as well as of the citizens of the place, delivered an oration, about which I believe the common judgment of his countrymen does not differ from what is known to have been his own idea, that it was the best presentation of his views and feelings which, in the long career of his rhetorical triumphs, he had had the opportunity to make.

No man ever thought or spoke of the character of Washington, and of the great part in human affairs which he played, without knowing and feeling that the crowning glory of all his labors in the field and in the council, and the perpetual monument to his fame, if his fame shall be perpetual, would be found in the establishment of the American Union under the American Constitution. All the prowess of the war, all the spirit of the Revolution, all the fortitude of the effort, all the self-denial of the sacrifice of that period, were for nothing, and worse than nothing, if the result and consummation of the whole were to be but a Government that contained within itself the seeds of its own destruction, and existed only at the caprice and whim of whatever part of the people should choose to deny its rightfulness or seek to overthrow its authority. In pressing that view, Mr. Webster thus attracts the attention of his countrymen to the great achievement in human affairs which the establishment of this Government has proved to be, and thus illustrates the character of Washington:

"It was the extraordinary fortune of Washington that, having been intrusted, in revolutionary times, with the supreme military command, and having fulfilled that trust with equal renown for wisdom and for valor, he should be placed at the head of the first Government in which an attempt was to be made, on a large scale, to rear the fabric of social order on the basis of a written Constitution and of a pure representative principle. A Government was to be established, without a throne, without an aristocracy, without castes, orders, or privileges; and this Government, instead of being a democracy, existing and acting within the walls of a single city, was to be extended over a vast country, of different climates, interests and habits, and of various communions of our common Christian faith. The experiment certainly was entirely new. A popular Government of this extent, it was evident, could be framed only by carrying into full effect the principle of representation or of delegated power; and the world was to see whether society could, by the strength of this principle, maintain its own peace and good government, carry forward its own great interests, and conduct itself to political renown and glory. * * * * *

"* * * * I remarked, gentlemen, that the whole world was and is interested in the result of this experiment. And is it not so? Do we deceive ourselves, or is it true that at this moment the career which this Government is running is among the most attractive objects to the civilized world? Do we deceive ourselves, or is it true that at this moment that love of liberty and that understanding of its true principles, which are flying over the whole earth, as on the wings of all the winds, are really and truly of American origin? * * * * *

"* * * Gentlemen, the spirit of human liberty and of free Government, nurtured and grown into strength and beauty in America, has stretched its course into the midst of the nations. Like an emanation from Heaven, it has gone forth, and it will not return void. It must change, it is fast changing, the face of the earth. Our great, our high duty, is to show, in our own example, that this spirit is a spirit of health as well as a spirit of power; that its longevity is as great as its strength; that its efficiency to secure individual rights, social relations, and moral order, is equal to the irresistible force with which it prostrates principalities and powers. The world at this moment is regarding us with a willing, but something of a fearful, admiration. Its deep and awful anxiety is to learn whether free States may be stable as well as free; whether popular power may be trusted, as well as feared; in short, whether wise, regular, and virtuous self-government is a vision for the contemplation of theorists, or a truth established, illustrated, and brought into practice in the country of Washington.

"Gentlemen, for the earth which we inhabit, and the whole circle of the sun, for all the unborn races of mankind, we seem to hold in our hands, for their weal or woe, the fate of this experiment. If we fail, who shall venture the repetition? If our example shall prove to be one, not of encouragement, but of terror, not fit to be imitated, but fit only to be shunned, where else shall the world look for free models? If this great *Western Sun* be struck out of the firmament, at what other fountain shall the lamp of liberty hereafter be lighted? What other orb shall emit a ray to glimmer, even, on the darkness of the world? * * * * *

"* * * * The political prosperity which this country has attained and which it now enjoys, has been acquired mainly through the instrumentality of the present Government. While this agent continues, the capacity of attaining to still higher degrees of prosperity exists also. We have, while this lasts, a political life capable of beneficial exertion, with power to resist or overcome misfortunes, to sustain us against the ordinary accidents of human affairs, and to promote, by active efforts, every public interest. But dismemberment strikes at the very being which preserves these faculties. It would lay its rude and ruthless hand on this great agent itself. It would sweep away, not only what we possess, but all power of regaining lost, or acquiring new, possessions. It would leave the country, not only bereft of its prosperity and happiness, but without limbs, or organs, or faculties, by which to exert itself hereafter in the pursuit of that prosperity and happiness.

"Other misfortunes may be borne, or their effects overcome. If disastrous war should sweep our commerce from the ocean, another generation may renew it; if it exhaust our treasury, future industry may replenish it; if it desolate and lay waste our fields, still, under a new cultivation, they will grow green again, and ripen to future harvests. It were but a trifle even if the walls of yonder Capitol were to crumble, if its lofty pillars should fall, and its gorgeous decorations be all covered by the dust of the valley. All these might be rebuilt. But who shall reconstruct the fabric of demolished Government? Who shall rear again the well-proportioned columns of constitutional liberty? Who shall frame together the skilful architecture which unites national sovereignty with State rights, individual security, and public prosperity? No, if these columns fall, they will be raised not again. Like the Coliseum and the Parthenon, they will be destined to a mournful, a melancholy immortality. Bitterer tears, however, will flow over them, than were ever shed over the monuments of Roman or Grecian art; for they will be the remnants of a more glorious edifice than Greece or Rome ever saw—the edifice of constitutional American Liberty. * * * * *

"* * * * A hundred years hence other disciples of Washington will celebrate his birth, with no less of sincere admiration than we now commemorate it. When they shall meet, as we now meet, to do themselves and him that honor, so surely as they shall see the blue summits of his native mountains rise in the horizon, so surely as they shall behold the river on whose banks he lived, and on whose banks he rests, still flowing on toward the sea, so surely may they see, as we now see, the flag of the Union floating on the top of the Capitol; and then, as now, may the sun in his course visit no land more free, more happy, more lovely, than this our own country!"

If, gentlemen, the eloquence of Mr. Webster, which thus enshrines the memory and the great life of Washington, calls us back to the glorious recollections of the Revolution and the establishment of our Government, does it not urge every man everywhere that his share in this great trust is to be performed now or never, and wherever his fidelity and his devotion to his country, its Government and its spirit, shall place the responsibility upon him? It is not the fault of the Government, of the learned District Attorney, or of me, his humble associate, that this, your verdict, has been removed, by the course of this argument and by the course of this eloquence on the part of the prisoners, from the simple issue of the guilt or innocence of these men under the statute. It is not the action or the choice of the Government, or of its counsel, that you have been drawn into higher considerations. It is not our fault that you have been invoked to give, on the undisputed facts of the case, a verdict which shall be a recognition of the power, the authority, and the right of the rebel Government to infringe our laws, or partake in the infringement of them, to some form and extent. And now, here is your duty, here your post of fidelity—not against law, not against the least right under the law, but to sustain, by whatever sacrifice there may be of sentiment or of feeling, the law and the Constitution. I need not say to you, gentlemen, that if, on a state of facts which admits no diversity of opinion, with these opposite forces arrayed, as they now are, before you—the Constitution of the United States, the laws of the United States, the commission of this learned Court, derived from the Government of the United States, the venire and the empanneling of this Jury, made under the laws and by the authority of the United States, on our side—met, on their side, by nothing, on behalf of the prisoners, but the commission, the power, the right, the authority of the rebel Government, proceeding from Jefferson Davis—you are asked, by the law, or under the law, or against the law, in some form, to recognize this power, and thus to say that the folly and the weakness of a free Government find here their last extravagant demonstration, then you are asked to say that the vigor, the judgment, the sense, and the duty of a Jury, to confine themselves to their responsibility on the facts of the case, are worthless and yielding before impressions of a discursive and loose and general nature. Be sure of it, gentlemen, that, on what I suppose to be the facts concerning this particular transaction, a verdict of acquittal is nothing but a determination that our Government and its authority, in the premises of this trial, for the purposes of your verdict, are met and overthrown by the protection thrown around the prisoners by the Government of the Confederate States of America, actual or incipient. Let us hope that you will do what falls to your share in the post of protection in which you are placed, for the liberties of this nation and the hopes of mankind; for, in surrendering them, you will be forming a part of the record on the common grave of the fabric of this Government, and of the hopes of the human race, where our flag shall droop, with every stripe polluted and every star erased, and the glorious legend of "Liberty and Union, now and forever, one and inseparable," replaced by this mournful confession, "Unworthy of freedom, our baseness has surrendered the liberties which we had neither the courage nor the virtue to love or defend."

CHARGE OF JUDGE NELSON.

Judge Nelson then proceeded to deliver the Charge of the Court, in which *Judge Shipman*, his associate, concurred:

The first question presented in this case is, whether or not the Court has jurisdiction of the offence? This depends upon a clause of the 14th section of the Act of Congress of 1825, as follows: "And the trial of all offences which shall be committed upon the high seas or elsewhere, out of the limits of any State or District, shall be in the District where the offender is apprehended, or into which he may be first brought." The prisoners, who were captured by an armed vessel of the United States, off Charleston, South Carolina, were ordered by the commander of the fleet to New York for trial; but the Minnesota, on board of which they were placed, was destined for Hampton Roads, and it became necessary, therefore, that they should be there transferred to another vessel. They were thus transferred to the Harriet Lane, and, after some two days' delay, consumed in the preparation, they were sent on to this port, where they were soon after arrested by the civil authorities. It is insisted, on behalf of the prisoners, that inasmuch as Hampton Roads, to which place the prisoners were taken and transferred to the Harriet Lane, was within the Eastern District of the State of Virginia, the jurisdiction attached in that District, as that was the first District into which the prisoners were brought. The Court is inclined to think that the circumstances under which the Minnesota was taken to Hampton Roads, in connection with the original order by the commander that the prisoners should be sent to this District for trial, do not make out a bringing into that District within the meaning of the statute. But we are not disposed to place the decision on this ground. The Court is of opinion that the clause conferring jurisdiction is in the alternative, and that jurisdiction may be exercised either in the District in which the prisoners were first brought, or in that in which they were apprehended under lawful authority for the trial of the offence. This brings us to the merits of the case.

The indictment under which the prisoners are tried contains ten counts. The first five are framed upon the third section of the Act of Congress of 1820, which is as follows: "That, if any person shall, upon the high seas, commit the crime of robbery, in or upon any ship or vessel, or upon any of the ship's company of any ship or vessel, or the lading thereof, such person shall be adjudged to be a pirate," and, upon conviction, shall suffer death. The five several counts charge, in substance, that the prisoners did, upon the high seas, enter in and upon the brig Joseph, the same being an American vessel, and upon the ship's company, naming them; and did, then and there, piratically, feloniously, and violently make an assault upon them, and put them in personal fear and danger of their lives; and did, then and there, the brig Joseph, her tackle and apparel, her lading (describing it), which were in the custody and possession of the master and crew, from the said master and crew and from their possession, and in their presence, and against their will, violently, piratically and feloniously seize, rob, steal, take and carry away, against the form of the statute, &c. There are some variances in the different counts, but it will not be material to notice them. It will be observed that this provision of the Act of Congress prescribing the offence applies to all persons, whether citizens or foreigners, making no distinction between them, and is equally applicable, therefore, to all the prisoners at the bar. The remaining five counts are framed under the 9th section of the Act of Congress of 1790, which is as follows: "That if any citizen shall commit any piracy or robbery aforesaid, or any act of hostility against the United States, or any citizen thereof, upon the high sea, under color of any commission from any foreign Prince or State, or on pretence of authority from any person, such offender shall, notwithstanding the pretence of any such authority, be deemed, adjudged, and taken to be a pirate, felon, and robber," and, on conviction, shall suffer death. These five counts charge that the prisoners are all citizens of the United States, and that they committed the acts set forth in the previous five counts, on pretence of authority from one Jefferson Davis.

As the provision of the Act of Congress upon which these counts are framed is applicable only to citizens and not to foreigners, but four of the prisoners can be brought within it, as the other eight are admitted to be foreigners. The four are Baker, Howard, Passalaigue, and Harleston. The distinction between the provisions of the third section of the Act of 1820 and the ninth section of 1790, and the counts in the indictment founded upon them, arises out of a familiar principle of international law, and which is, that in a state of war existing between two nations, either may commission private armed vessels to carry on war against the enemy on the high seas, and the commission will afford protection, even in the judicial tribunals of the enemy, against a charge of the crime of robbery or piracy. Such a commission would be a good defence against an indictment under the third section of 1820, by force of the above rule of international law. The ninth section of the Act of 1790 changes the rule as it respects citizens of the United States who may take service under the commission of the private armed vessels of the enemy of their country. It declares, as it respects them, the commission shall not be admitted as a defence; and, as this legislation relates only to our own citizens, and prescribes a rule of action for them, and not as it respects the citizens or subjects of other countries, we do not perceive that any exception can be taken to the Act as unconstitutional or otherwise. But, upon the view the Court has taken of the case, it will not be necessary to trouble you with any remarks as it respects this ninth section, nor in respect to the several counts framed under it, but we shall confine our observations to a consideration of the third section of the Act of 1820. There can be no injustice to the prisoners in thus restricting the examination, as any authority for the perpetration of the acts charged in the indictment, founded upon the Act of 1820, will be equally available to them. Nor can there be any injustice to the prosecution, for unless the crime of robbery, as prescribed in the Act of 1820, is established against the four prisoners, none could be under the ninth section of the Act of 1790. The crime in the two Acts is the same for all the purposes of this trial. The only difference is the exclusion of a particular defence under the latter. Now, the crime charged is robbery upon an American vessel on the high seas, and hence it is necessary that we should turn our attention to the inquiry, what constitutes this offence? It has already been determined by the highest authority—the Supreme Court of the United States—that we must look to the common law for a definition of the term robbery, as it is to be presumed it was used by Congress in the Act in that sense, and, taking this rule as our guide, it will be found the crime consists in this: the felonious taking of goods or property of any value from the person of another, or in his presence, against his will, by violence, or putting him in fear. The taking must be felonious—that is, taking with a wrongful intent to appropriate the goods of another. It need not be a taking which, if upon the high seas, would amount to piracy, according to the law of nations, or what, in some of the books, is called general piracy or robbery. This is defined to be a forcible depredation upon property upon the high seas without lawful authority, done *animo furandi*—that is, as defined in this connection, in a spirit and intention of universal hostility.

A pirate is said to be one who roves the sea in an armed vessel, without any commission from any sovereign State, on his own authority, and for the purpose of seizing by force and appropriating to himself, without discrimination, every vessel he may meet. For this reason, pirates, according to the law of nations, have always been compared to robbers—the only difference being that the sea is the theatre of the operations of one and the land of the other. And, as general robbers and pirates upon the high seas are deemed enemies of the human race—making war upon all mankind indiscriminately—the crime being one against the universal laws of society— the vessels of every nation have a right to pursue, seize, and punish them. Now, if it were necessary, on the part of the Government, to bring the crime charged in the present case against the prisoners within this definition of robbery and piracy, as known to the common law of nations, there would be great difficulty in so doing either upon the evidence, or perhaps upon the counts, as charged in the indictment—certainly upon the evidence. For that shows, if anything, an intent to depredate upon the vessels and property of one nation only—the United States—which falls far short of the spirit and intent, as we have seen, that are said to constitute essential elements of the crime. But the robbery charged in this case is that which the Act of Congress prescribes as a crime, and may be denominated a statute offence as contra-distinguished from that known to the law of nations. The Act, as you have seen, declares the person a pirate, punishable by death, who commits the crime of robbery upon the high seas against any ship or vessel, or upon any ship's company of any ship or vessel, &c.; and the interpretation given to these words applies the crime to the case of depredation upon an American vessel or property on the high seas, under circumstances that would constitute robbery, if the offence was committed on land, and which is, according to the language of Blackstone, the felonious and forcible taking from the person of another of goods or money, to any value, by violence or putting him in fear. The felonious intent which describes the state of mind as an element of the offence, is what is called in technical language *animo furandi*, which means an intent of gaining by another's loss, or to despoil another of his goods *lucri causa*, for the sake of gain. Now, if you are satisfied, upon the evidence, that the prisoners have been guilty of this statute offence of robbery upon the high seas, it is your duty to convict them, though it may fall short of the offence as known to the law of nations. We have stated what constitute the elements of the crime, and it is your province to apply the facts to them, and thus determine, whether or not the crime has been committed. That duty belongs to you, and not to the Court. We have said that, in a state of war between two nations, the commission to private armed vessels from either of the belligerents affords a defence, according to the law of nations, in the Courts of the enemy, against a charge of robbery or piracy on the high seas, of which they might be guilty in the absence of such authority; and under this principle it has been insisted, by the learned counsel for the prisoners, that the commission of the Confederate States, by its President, Davis, to the master and crew of the Savannah, which has been given in evidence, affords such defence.

In support of this position, it is claimed that the Confederate States have thrown off the power and authority of the General Government; have erected a new and independent Government in its place, and have maintained it against the whole military and naval power of the former; that it is a Government, at least *de facto*, and entitled to the rights and privileges that belong to a sovereign and independent nation. The right, also, constitutional or otherwise, has been strongly urged, and the law of nations and the commentaries of eminent publicists have been referred to as justifying the secession or revolt of these Confederate States. Great ability and research have been displayed by the learned counsel for the defence on this branch of the case. But the Court do not deem it pertinent, or material, to enter into this wide field of inquiry. This branch of the defence involves considerations that do not belong to the Courts of the country. It involves the determination of great public, political questions, which belong to departments of our Government that have charge of our foreign relations— the legislative and executive departments; and, when decided by them, the Court follows the decision; and, until these departments have recognized the existence of the new Government, the Courts of the nation cannot. Until this recognition of the new Government, the Courts are obliged to regard the ancient state of things remaining as unchanged. This has been the uniform course of decision and practice of the Courts of the United States. The revolt of the Spanish Colonies of South America, and the new Government erected on separating from the mother country, were acknowledged by an Act of Congress, on the recommendation of the President, in 1822. Prior to this recognition, and during the existence of the civil war between Spain and her Colonies, it was the declared policy of our Government to treat both parties as belligerents, entitled equally to the rights of asylum and hospitality; and to consider them, in respect to the neutral relation and duties of our Government, as equally entitled to the sovereign rights of war as against each other. This was, also, the doctrine of the Courts, which they derived from the policy of the Government, following the political departments of the Government as it respects our relations with new Governments erected on the overthrow of the old. And if this is the rule of the Federal Courts, in the case of a revolt and erection of a new Government, as it respects foreign nations, much more is the rule applicable when the question arises in respect to a revolt and the erection of a new Government within the limits and against the authority of the Government under which we are engaged in administering her laws. And, in this connection, it is proper to say that, as the Confederate States must first be recognized by the political departments of the mother Government, in order to be recognized by the Courts of the country, namely, the legislative and executive departments, we must look to the acts of these departments as evidence of the fact. The act is the act of the nation through her constitutional public authorities. These, gentlemen, are all the observations we deem necessary to submit to you. The case is an interesting one, not only in the principles involved, but to the Government and the prisoners at the bar. It has been argued with a research and ability in proportion to its magnitude, both in behalf of the prisoners and the Government; and we do not doubt, with the aid of these arguments, and the instructions of the Court, you will be enabled to render an intelligent and just verdict in the case.

The Jury retired at twenty minutes after three o'clock.

At six o'clock they came into Court. Their names were called, and the inquiry made by the Clerk whether they had agreed upon their verdict. Their

Foreman said they had not. One of the prisoners having felt unwell, had been removed from the close air of the Court-room, and some little delay occurred until he was brought in. Judge Nelson then said: "We have had a communication from one of the officers in charge of the Jury, from the Jury, as we understood, though it had no name signed to it. I would inquire whether the note was from the Jury?"

The Foreman: It was.

Judge Nelson: We would prefer that the Jurymen, or any of them who may be embarrassed with the difficulties referred to, should himself state the inquiry which he desires to make of the Court.

Mr. Powell, one of the Jurors, said that the question was, "whether, if the Jury believed that civil war existed, and had been so recognized by the act of our Government, or if the Jury believe that the intent to commit a robbery did not exist in the minds of the prisoners at the time, it may influence their verdict."

After consultation with Judge Shipman, Judge Nelson said: As it respects the first inquiry of the Juror—whether the Government has recognized a state of civil war between the Confederate States and itself—the instruction which the Court gave the Jury was, that this Court could not recognize a state of civil war, or a Government of the Confederate States, unless the legislative and executive Departments of the Government had recognized such a state of things, or the President had, or both; and that the act of recognition was a national act, and that we must look to the acts of these Departments of the Government as the evidence and for the evidence of the recognition of this state of things, and the only evidence. As it respects the other question— whether or not, if the Jury were of opinion, on the evidence, that these prisoners did not intend to commit a robbery on the high seas against the property of the United States, they were guilty of the offence charged—that is a mixed question of law and fact. The Court explained to you what constitutes the crime of robbery on the high seas, which was the felonious taking of the property of another upon the high seas by force, by violence, or putting them in fear of bodily injury, which, according to the law, is equivalent to actual force; and that the term felonious, as interpreted by the law and the Courts, was the taking with a wrongful intent to despoil the others of their property. These elements constitute the crime of robbery. Now, it is for you to take up the facts and decide whether the evidence in the case brings the prisoners within that definition. The Court will not encroach upon your province in these respects, but will confine itself to the definition of the law.

Another of the Jury—*George H. Hansell*—rose and said: One of the Jury—not myself—understood your honor to charge that there must be an intent to take the property of another for your own use.

Judge Nelson: No, I did not give that instruction. The Jury may withdraw.

The Jury again retired, and, as there was no probability of an agreement at half-past seven o'clock, the Court adjourned to eleven o'clock Thursday morning.

EIGHTH DAY.

Oct. 31.

The Jury, who had been in deliberation all night, came into Court at twenty minutes past eleven o'clock. The names of the prisoners were called, and, on the Jury taking their seats—

The Clerk said: Gentlemen of the Jury, have you agreed on your verdict?

Foreman: No, sir.

The Court: Is there any prospect of your agreeing?

Foreman: I am sorry to say there is no prospect at all that we can come to an agreement.

After some consultation with Judge Shipman—

Judge Nelson inquired: Is the opinion expressed by the Foreman that of the other Jurymen?

Mr. Powell and *Mr. Cassidy* (Jurors) rose and responded in the affirmative.

Mr. Taylor further remarked: The prospect seems to be that way. So far as we have gone, there does not seem to be any idea of coming together at all. The only idea of coming to a judgment would be that some of the Jurors, we think, do not understand the charge. They think they do, and we think they do not. It is for them to say, or not, whether they understand the charge correctly.

To this implied invitation to the Jurymen to express themselves there was no response.

Judge Nelson: If the Court supposed that there would be any fair or reasonable prospect of your coming to an agreement, we would be inclined to direct you to retire and pursue your consultations further. You have now been together about twenty hours, and unless there is some expression from the Jury that there is a possibility or probability that they may agree, we are inclined not to detain you longer.

Mr. Costello (a Juror): With respect to the Court, I think there is no likelihood of our coming to an agreement.

Foreman: If the Court will allow me, after the instructions we got yesterday evening, at the instance of many of the Jury, we stand just in the same position we stood when we left your presence the first time.

Judge Nelson: The Court, then, will discharge you, gentlemen.

The Court entered an order remanding the prisoners, and, as they were about being removed—

Mr. E. Delafield Smith (District Attorney) said: I desire, if the Court please, to move, in the case of the Savannah privateers, their trial at the earliest day consistent with the engagements of the Court, and of the counsel engaged for the defence; and I would name a week from next Monday, as it will, probably, be necessary to issue an order for a new panel of Jurors.

Judge Nelson: So far as I am concerned, I can only remain until the 20th of November, and the business of the Court is such that the trial cannot take place while I am here, as I must devote the rest of my time to other causes.

Mr. Smith: Then the motion for a new panel will be reserved until we see at what time it will be possible to bring the case on.

Mr. Lord: Before that application shall be seriously entertained by the Court, we would like to be heard upon the subject. I will say nothing now, because it is very evident it cannot be discussed at this time.

Judge Nelson: The counsel may assume that I cannot take up the second trial during the present term. They may act upon that view.

The prisoners were then remanded to the custody of the Deputy Marshals.

APPENDIX.

I.

PRESIDENT'S PROCLAMATION, APRIL 15, 1861. (*Page 109.*)

By the President of the United States.

Whereas, the laws of the United States have been for some time past, and now are, opposed, and the execution thereof obstructed, in the States of South Carolina, Georgia, Alabama, Florida, Mississippi, Louisiana, and Texas, by combinations too powerful to be suppressed by the ordinary course of judicial proceedings, or by the powers vested in the Marshals by law: Now, therefore, I, ABRAHAM LINCOLN, President of the United States, in virtue of the power in me vested by the Constitution and the laws, have thought fit to call forth, and hereby do call forth, the militia of the several States of the Union, to the aggregate number of 75,000, in order to suppress said combinations and to cause the laws to be duly executed.

The details for this object will be immediately communicated to the State authorities through the War Department. I appeal to all loyal citizens to favor, facilitate, and aid this effort to maintain the honor, the integrity, and existence of our national Union, and the perpetuity of popular government, and to redress wrongs already long enough endured. I deem it proper to say that the first service assigned to the forces hereby called forth will probably be to repossess the forts, places, and property which have been seized from the Union; and in every event the utmost care will be observed, consistently with the objects aforesaid, to avoid any devastation, any destruction of, or interference with, property, or any disturbance of peaceful citizens of any part of the country; and I hereby command the persons composing the combinations aforesaid to disperse and retire peaceably to their respective abodes within twenty days from this date.

Deeming that the present condition of public affairs presents an extraordinary occasion, I do hereby, in virtue of the power in me vested by the Constitution, convene both houses of Congress. The Senators and Representatives are, therefore, summoned to assemble at their respective Chambers, at twelve o'clock, noon, on Thursday, the fourth day of July next, then and there to consider and determine such measures as, in their wisdom, the public safety and interest may seem to demand.

In witness whereof, I have hereunto set my hand, and caused the seal of the United States to be affixed.

Done at the City of Washington, this fifteenth day of April, in the year of our Lord one thousand eight hundred and sixty-one, and of the independence of the United States the eighty-fifth.

ABRAHAM LINCOLN.

By the President.

WILLIAM H. SEWARD, Secretary of State.

II.

PROCLAMATION OF THE PRESIDENT, DECLARING A BLOCKADE. (*Page 109.*)

By the President of the United States of America.

Whereas, an insurrection against the Government of the United States has broken out in the States of South Carolina, Georgia, Alabama, Florida, Mississippi, Louisiana, and Texas, and the laws of the United States for the collection of the revenue cannot be efficiently executed therein conformably to that provision of the Constitution which requires duties to be uniform throughout the United States:

And whereas a combination of persons engaged in such insurrection have threatened to grant pretended letters of marque, to authorize the bearers thereof to commit assaults on the lives, vessels, and property of good citizens of the country lawfully engaged in commerce on the high seas, and in waters of the United States:

And whereas an Executive Proclamation has been already issued, requiring the persons engaged in these disorderly proceedings to desist therefrom, calling out a militia force for the purpose of repressing the same, and convening Congress in extraordinary session to deliberate and determine thereon:

Now, therefore, I, ABRAHAM LINCOLN, President of the United States, with a view to the same purposes before mentioned, and to the protection of the public peace and the lives and property of quiet and orderly citizens pursuing their lawful occupations, until Congress shall have assembled and deliberated on the said unlawful proceedings, or until the same shall have ceased, have further deemed it advisable to set on foot a blockade of the ports within the States aforesaid, in pursuance of the laws of the United States and of the laws of nations in such cases provided. For this purpose a competent force will be posted so as to prevent entrance and exit of vessels from the ports aforesaid. If, therefore, with a view to violate such blockade, a vessel shall approach, or shall attempt to leave any of the said ports, she will be duly warned by the Commander of one of the blockading vessels, who will indorse on her register the fact and date of such warning; and if the same vessel shall again attempt to enter or leave the blockaded port, she will be captured, and sent to the nearest convenient port for such proceedings against her and her cargo, as prize, as may be deemed advisable.

And I hereby proclaim and declare, that if any person, under the pretended authority of said States, or under any other pretence, shall molest a vessel of the United States, or the persons or cargo on board of her, such person will be held amenable to the laws of the United States for the prevention and punishment of piracy.

ABRAHAM LINCOLN.

By the President.

WILLIAM H. SEWARD, Secretary of State.

Washington, April 19, 1861.

III.

CORRESPONDENCE BETWEEN GOV. PICKENS, OF SOUTH CAROLINA, AND MAJOR ANDERSON, COMMANDING AT FORT SUMTER, IN RELATION TO THE FIRING ON THE STAR OF THE WEST. (*Page 110.*)

To his Excellency the Governor of South Carolina:

SIR: Two of your batteries fired this morning on an unarmed vessel bearing the flag of my Government. As I have not been notified that war has been declared by South Carolina against the United States, I cannot but think this a hostile act, committed without your sanction or authority. Under that hope, I refrain from opening a fire on your batteries. I have the honor, therefore, respectfully to ask whether the above-mentioned act—one which I believe without parallel in the history of our country or any other civilized Government—was committed in obedience to your instructions? and notify you, if it is not disclaimed, that I regard it as an act of war, and I shall not, after reasonable time for the return of my messenger, permit any vessel to pass within the range of the guns of my fort. In order to save, as far as it is in my power, the shedding of blood, I beg you will take due notification of my decision for the good of all concerned. Hoping, however, your answer may justify a further continuance of forbearance on my part,

I remain, respectfully,

ROBERT ANDERSON.

GOV. PICKENS' REPLY.

Gov. Pickens, after stating the position of South Carolina towards the United States, says that any attempt to send United States troops into Charleston harbor, to reinforce the forts, would be regarded as an act of hostility; and in conclusion adds, that any attempt to reinforce the troops at Fort Sumter, or to retake and resume possession of the forts within the waters of South Carolina, which Major Anderson abandoned, after spiking the cannon and doing other damage, cannot but be regarded by the authorities of the State as indicative of any other purpose than the coercion of the State by the armed force of the Government; special agents, therefore, have been off the bar to warn approaching vessels, armed and unarmed, having troops to reinforce Fort Sumter aboard, not to enter the harbor. Special orders have been given the Commanders at the forts not to fire on such vessels until a shot across their bows should warn them of the prohibition of the State. Under these circumstances the Star of the West, it is understood, this morning attempted to enter the harbor with troops, after having been notified she could not enter, and consequently she was fired into. This act is perfectly justified by me.

In regard to your threat about vessels in the harbor, it is only necessary for me to say, you must be the judge of your responsibility. Your position in the harbor has been tolerated by the authorities of the State, and while the act of which you complain is in perfect consistency with the rights and duties of the State, it is not perceived how far the conduct you propose to adopt can find a parallel in the history of any country, or be reconciled with any other purpose than that of your Government imposing on the State the condition of a conquered province.

F. W. PICKENS.

SECOND COMMUNICATION FROM MAJOR ANDERSON.

To his Excellency Governor Pickens:

SIR: I have the honor to acknowledge the receipt of your communication, and say that, under the circumstances, I have deemed it proper to refer the whole matter to my Government, and intend deferring the course I indicated in my note this morning until the arrival from Washington of such instructions as I may receive.

I have the honor also to express the hope that no obstructions will be placed in the way, and that you will do me the favor of giving every facility for the departure and return of the bearer, Lieut. T. TALBOT, who is directed to make the journey.

ROBERT ANDERSON.

IV

EXTRACTS FROM PRESIDENT LINCOLN'S INAUGURAL, MARCH 4, 1861. *(Page 110.)*

The power confided to me will be used to hold, occupy, and possess the property and places belonging to the Government, and collect the duties on imports; but, beyond what may be necessary for these objects, there will be no invasion, no using of force against or among the people anywhere. Where hostility to the United States shall be so great and so universal as to prevent competent resident citizens from holding the federal offices, there will be no attempt to force obnoxious strangers among the people with that object. While the strict legal right may exist of the Government to enforce the exercise of these offices, the attempt to do so would be so irritating, and so nearly impracticable withal, that I deem it better to forego for the time the use of such offices. * * * * *

I do not forget the position assumed by some that constitutional questions are to be decided by the Supreme Court, nor do I deny that such decision must be binding in any case upon the parties to a suit, while they are also entitled to very high respect and consideration in all parallel cases by all other departments of the Government; and while it is obviously possible that such decision may be erroneous in any given case, still the evil effect following it, being limited to that particular case, with the chances that it may be overruled and never become a precedent for other cases, can better be borne than could the evils of a different practice. At the same time, the candid citizen must confess that, if the policy of the Government upon the vital questions affecting the whole people is to be irrevocably fixed by the decisions of the Supreme Court, the instant they are made in ordinary litigations between parties in personal actions, the people will have ceased to be their own masters,—having, to that extent, practically resigned their Government into the hands of that eminent tribunal. Nor is there, in this view, any assault upon the Court or the Judges. It is a duty from which they may not shrink, to decide cases properly brought before them; and it is no fault of theirs if others seek to turn their decisions to political purposes.

V.

THE PRESIDENT'S SPEECH TO THE VIRGINIA COMMISSIONERS. *(Page 110.)*

To Honorable Messrs. Preston, Stuart, and Randolph:

GENTLEMEN: As a Committee of the Virginia Convention, now in session, you present me a preamble and resolution in these words:

"Whereas, in the opinion of this Convention, the uncertainty which prevails in the public mind as to the policy which the Federal Executive intends to pursue towards the seceded States is extremely injurious to the industrious and commercial interests of the country; tends to keep up an excitement which is unfavorable to the adjustment of the pending difficulties; and threatens a disturbance of the public peace; therefore—

"*Resolved*, That a committee of three delegates be appointed to wait on the President of the United States, present to him this preamble, and respectfully ask him to communicate to this Convention the policy which the Federal Executive intends to pursue in regard to the Confederate States."

In answer, I have to say, that having, at the beginning of my official term, expressed my intended policy as plainly as I was able, it is with deep regret and mortification I now learn there is great and injurious uncertainty in the public mind as to what that policy is, and what course I intend to pursue. Not having as yet seen occasion to change, it is now my purpose to pursue the course marked out in the inaugural address. I commend a careful consideration of the whole document as the best expression I can give to my purposes. As I then and therein said, I now repeat—"The power confided in me will be used to hold, occupy, and possess property and places belonging to the Government, and to collect the duties and imposts; but beyond what is necessary for these objects, there will be no invasion, no using of force against or among the people anywhere." By the words "property and places belonging to the Government," I chiefly allude to the military posts and property which were in possession of the Government when it came into my hands. But if, as now appears to be true, in pursuit of a purpose to drive the United States authority from these places, an unprovoked assault has been made upon Fort Sumter, I shall hold myself at liberty to repossess, if I can, like places which had been seized before the Government was devolved upon me; and in any event I shall, to the best of my ability, repel force by force. In case it proves true that Fort Sumter has been assaulted, as is reported, I shall, perhaps, cause the United States mails to be withdrawn from all the States which claim to have seceded, believing that the commencement of actual war against the Government justifies and possibly demands it. I scarcely need to say, that I consider the military posts and property situated within the States which claim to have seceded as yet belonging to the Government of the United States as much as they did before the supposed secession. Whatever else I may do for the purpose, I shall not attempt to collect the duties and imposts by any armed invasion of any part of the country; not meaning by this, however, that I may not land a force deemed necessary to relieve a fort upon the border of the country. From the fact that I have quoted a part of the inaugural address, it must not be inferred that I repudiate any other part,—the whole of which I re-affirm, except so far as what I now say of the mails may be regarded as a modification.

VI.

EXTRACTS FROM PRESIDENT LINCOLN'S MESSAGE TO CONGRESS, JULY 4, 1861.

At the beginning of the present presidential term, four months ago, the functions of the Federal Government were found to be generally suspended within the several States of South Carolina, Georgia, Alabama, Mississippi, Louisiana, and Florida, excepting only of the post-office department. Within these States all the forts, arsenals, dockyards, custom-houses and the like, including the movable and stationary property in and about them, had been seized and were held in open hostility to this Government, excepting only Forts Pickens, Taylor, and Jefferson, on and near the Florida coast, and Fort Sumter, in Charleston harbor, South Carolina.

In accordance with this purpose, an ordinance had been adopted in each of these States, declaring the States respectively to be separated from the National Union. A formula for instituting a combined Government of those States had been promulgated, and this illegal organization, in the character of the "Confederate States," was already invoking recognition, aid, and intervention from foreign powers.

Finding this condition of things, and believing it to be an imperative duty upon the incoming Executive to prevent, if possible, the consummation of such attempt to destroy the Federal Union, a choice of means to that end became indispensable. This choice was made, and was declared in the inaugural address.

[After reciting the measures previously taken, he continues]:

Other calls were made for volunteers to serve three years, unless sooner discharged, and also for large additions to the regular army and navy. These measures, whether strictly legal or not, were ventured upon under what appeared to be a popular demand and a public necessity,—trusting then, as now, that Congress would readily ratify them.

It is believed that nothing has been done beyond the constitutional competency of Congress. Soon after the first call for militia, it was considered a duty to authorize the Commanding General, in proper cases, according to his discretion, to suspend the privilege of the writ of habeas corpus, or, in other words, to arrest and detain, without resort to the ordinary process and forms of law, such individuals as he might deem dangerous to the public safety.

This authority has purposely been exercised but very sparingly. Nevertheless, the legality and propriety of what has been done under it are questioned, and the attention of the country has been called to the proposition that one who is sworn to take care that the laws are faithfully executed should not himself violate them.

VII.

EXTRACTS FROM PRESIDENT BUCHANAN'S MESSAGE TO CONGRESS, DECEMBER 4, 1860.

The Fugitive-Slave Law has been carried into execution in every contested case since the commencement of the present administration, though often, it is to be regretted, with great loss and inconvenience to the master, and with considerable expense to the Government. Let us trust that the State Legislatures will repeal their unconstitutional and obnoxious enactments. Unless this shall be done without unnecessary delay, it is impossible for any human power to save the Union.

The Southern States, standing on the basis of the Constitution, have a right to demand this act of justice from the States of the North. Should it be refused, then the Constitution, to which all the States are parties, will have been willfully violated, in one portion of them, in a provision essential to the domestic security and happiness of the remainder. In that event, the injured States, after having first used all constitutional and peaceful means to obtain redress, would be justified in revolutionary resistance to the Government of the Union.

What, in the meantime, is the responsibility and true position of the Executive? He is bound by a solemn oath before God and the country "to take care that the laws are faithfully executed;" and from this obligation he cannot be absolved by any human power. But what if the performance of this duty, in whole or in part, has been rendered impracticable by events over which he could have exercised no control? Such, at the present moment, is the case throughout the State of South Carolina, so far as the laws of the United States, to secure the administration of justice by means of the federal judiciary, are concerned. All the federal officers within its limits, through whose agency alone these laws can be carried into execution, have already resigned. We no longer have a District Judge, a District Attorney, or a Marshal, in South Carolina. In fact, the whole machinery of the Federal Government, necessary for the distribution of remedial justice among the people, has been demolished, and it would be difficult, if not impossible, to replace it.

The only Acts of Congress upon the Statute Book bearing on this subject are those of the 28th February, 1795, and 3d March, 1807. These authorize the President, after he shall have ascertained that the Marshal, with his posse comitatus, is unable to execute civil or criminal process in any particular case, to call forth the militia, and employ the army and navy to aid him in performing this service—having first, by proclamation, commanded the insurgents to disperse and retire peaceably to their respective homes within a limited time. This duty can not by possibility be performed in a State where no judicial authority exists to issue process, and where there is no Marshal to execute it, and where, even if there were such an officer, the entire population would constitute one sole combination to resist him.

The bare enumeration of these provisions proves how inadequate they are, without further legislation, to overcome a united opposition in a single State, not to speak of other States who may place themselves in a similar attitude. Congress alone has power to decide whether the present laws can or can not be amended, so as to carry out more effectually the objects of the Constitution.

The course of events is so rapidly hastening forward, that the emergency may soon arise when you may be called upon to decide the momentous question, whether you possess the power, by force of arms, to compel a State to remain in the Union. I should feel myself recreant to my duty were I not to express an opinion upon this important subject.

The question, fairly stated, is: Has the Constitution delegated to *Congress* the power to coerce a State into submission which is attempting to withdraw, or has virtually withdrawn, from the Confederacy? If answered in the affirmative, it must be on the principle that the power has been conferred upon Congress to declare and to make war against a State. After much serious reflection, I have arrived at the conclusion that no such power has been delegated to Congress, or to any other department of the Federal Government. It is manifest, upon an inspection of the Constitution, that this is not among the specific and enumerated powers granted to Congress; and it is equally apparent that its exercise is not "necessary and proper for carrying into execution" any one of these powers. So far from this power having been delegated to Congress, it was expressly refused by the Convention which framed the Constitution.

It appears, from the proceedings of that body, that on the 31st May, 1787, the clause authorizing the exertion of the force of the whole against a delinquent State came up for consideration. Mr. Madison opposed it in a brief but powerful speech, from which I shall extract but a single sentence. He observed: "The use of force against a State would look more like a declaration of war than an infliction of punishment, and would probably be considered by the party attacked as a dissolution of all previous compacts by which it might be bound." Upon his motion, the clause was unanimously postponed, and was never, I believe, again presented. Soon afterwards, on the 8th June, 1787, when incidentally adverting to the subject, he said: "Any Government for the United States, founded upon the supposed practicability of using force against the unconstitutional proceedings of the States, would prove as visionary and fallacious as the Government of Congress"— evidently meaning the then existing Congress of the old Confederation.

Without descending to particulars, it may be safely asserted that the power to make war against a State is at variance with the whole spirit and intent of the Constitution.

VIII.

PROCLAMATION OF AUGUST 16, 1861, PURSUANT TO ACT OF CONGRESS OF JULY 13, 1861.

Whereas, on the 15th day of April, the President of the United States, in view of an insurrection against the laws and Constitution and Government of the United States, which had broken out within the States of South Carolina, Georgia, Alabama, Florida, Mississippi, Louisiana, and Texas, and in pursuance of the provisions of the Act entitled "An Act to provide for calling forth the militia to execute the laws of the Union, to suppress insurrection and repel invasion, and to repeal the Act now in force for that purpose," approved February 18th, 1795, did call forth the militia to suppress said insurrection and cause the laws of the Union to be duly executed, and the insurgents having failed to disperse by the time directed by the President, and—

Whereas such insurrection has since broken out and yet exists within the States of Virginia and North Carolina, Tennessee and Arkansas, and—

Whereas the insurgents in all of the said States claim to act under authority thereof, and such claim is not disclaimed or repudiated by the person exercising the functions of Government in each State or States, or in the part or parts thereof in which combinations exist, nor has such insurrection been suppressed by said States—

Now, therefore, I, ABRAHAM LINCOLN, President of the United States, in pursuance of an Act of Congress passed July 13th, 1861, do hereby declare that the inhabitants of the said States of Georgia, South Carolina, Virginia, North Carolina, Tennessee, Alabama, Louisiana, Texas, Arkansas, Mississippi, and Florida, except the inhabitants of that part of the State of Virginia lying west of the Alleghany Mountains, and of such other parts of that State and the other States hereinbefore named as may maintain a loyal adhesion to the Union and the Constitution, or may be, from time to time, occupied and controlled by the forces engaged in the dispersion of said insurgents, are in a state of insurrection against the United States, and that all commercial intercourse between the same and the inhabitants thereof, with the exception aforesaid, and the citizens of other States, and other parts of the United States, is unlawful, and will remain unlawful until such insurrection shall cease or has been suppressed; that all goods and chattels, wares and merchandize, coming from any of the said States, with the exceptions aforesaid, into other parts of the United States, without a special license and permission of the President, through the Secretary of the Treasury, or proceeding to any of the said States, with the exceptions aforesaid, by land or water, together with the vessel or vehicle conveying the same, or conveying persons to or from States, with the said exceptions, will be forfeited to the United States; and that, from and after fifteen days from the issue of this proclamation, all ships and vessels belonging in whole or in part to any citizen or inhabitant of any State, with the said exceptions, found at sea, or in any port of the United States, will be forfeited to the United States; and I hereby enjoin on all District Attorneys, Marshals, and officers of the revenue and of the military and naval forces of the United States, to be vigilant in the execution of said Act, and in the enforcement of the penalties and forfeitures imposed or declared by it, leaving any party who may think himself aggrieved thereby the right to make application to the Secretary of the Treasury for the remission of any penalty or forfeiture, which the said Secretary is authorized by law to grant, if, in his judgment, the special circumstances of any case shall require such remission.

In witness whereof, I have hereunto set my hand, and caused the seal of the United States to be affixed. Done in the City of Washington, this 16th day of August, in the year of our Lord 1861, and of the independence of the United States the eighty-sixth.

ABRAHAM LINCOLN.

WM. H. SEWARD, *Secretary of State.*

FOOTNOTES

[1]_At the request of the United States District Attorney, the publishers state that the Indictment was mainly the work of Mr. JOHN SEDGWICK, of the New York bar.

[2]_The second trial of Gordon, resulting in a conviction, took place before a full Court, Mr. Justice NELSON sitting with Judge SHIPMAN.

[3]_"Gone along, caught along, hanged along."

[4]_An interesting fact, not published previously, I believe, has been communicated to the public recently by Mr. Dawson, of New York, a historical student and writer of great research and culture. He has found an original minute in the records of the General Court of Massachusetts, whereby, as early as May 1st, 1776, the sovereignty and independence of that *Colony* was declared formally.

[5]_See pages 105, 106, and 107.